Backgammon

Backgammon

PAUL MAGRIEL

Quadrangle/The New York Times Book Co.

Library of Congress Cataloging in Publication Data

Magriel, Paul.
  Backgammon.

  1. Backgammon. I. Title.
GV1469.B2M34   795'.1   75-36253
ISBN 0-8129-0615-2

For L.F.H.

Acknowledgments

I gratefully acknowledge the advice and help given me by many friends in preparing this work for publication. My deepest thanks go to Renee Magriel, who worked with me at every stage.

Contents

Section IV. Endgame

Section V. Advanced Positional Play

Introduction

BACKGAMMON IS an ancient and fascinating game, a gambling game which requires both luck and skill. With a single roll of the dice a winning position can crumble or a seemingly hopeless position can be salvaged. Luck keeps the game interesting, but skillful play will always be rewarded. Backgammon is an easy game to learn and for this reason is deceptively simple. It is actually a game of great strategic richness and subtlety which must be studied to be fully appreciated. *The Complete Book of Backgammon* is unique in that for the first time it breaks down all the elements of strategy into recognizable components.

If you are a new player, begin with Section I, **Basics.** Read quickly through Chapters 1, 2 and 3. After these chapters are understood you may immediately begin to play along with the four games that follow. Chapters 4, 6, 8 and 9 each illustrates a different game plan and is followed by a summary of the basic ideas which have been presented. These summaries contain much valuable information which should be studied carefully.

As you practice, begin incorporating the strategies you have learned into your own play. In order to learn from the sample games, study each position. Decide on your *own* move (don't worry if it's right or wrong) before looking at the correct move and reading the explanation. New terms are introduced and defined throughout the text — if you are unfamiliar with a term, check the glossary.

Chapters 10 and 11 deal with more technical aspects of the game. Don't get bogged down or turned off if the numbers and counting are distasteful. Backgammon is emphatically *not* a game of mathematical calculations; it is primarily a game of position and strategy — a game of recognizing and anticipating visual patterns. Every player can study and easily understand the remaining sections of this book without spending too much time on the pip count and basic odds.

If you have more experience with the game, you may wish to skip Section I completely and go directly to Section II, but Chapter 2 (Notation) should be read in any case. Even experienced players are advised to review the idea-summaries after each of the games in Section I and to look at Chapters 10 and 11, which discuss odds and pip count.

Sections II through V assume some familiarity with the game. These four sections, however, are not arranged in order of difficulty or technicality. In fact you may read through them, omitting more difficult sections which you can go back to as you become more familiar with the game.

Section II, **Using Men Effectively,** explains the tactics of checker movement, making points and leaving shots. It is designed to help you create a more flexible and dynamic position.

Section III, **Middle Game Strategy,** is the heart of the book in terms of more advanced strategy and tactics. It is probably the most important of the sections.

Section IV, **Endgame,** is the most technical of the sections, since it deals with cases where the bear-off has already begun.

Section V, **Advanced Positional Play,** introduces some of the deeper and more subtle structures underlying backgammon. These chapters will serve to give insight into an expert's thought.

No matter how well you play, I am sure that you will find backgammon extremely enjoyable — both to study and to play.

Section I

Basics

CHAPTER 1.
RULES

Object of the Game

Backgammon is a dice-and-board game for two players. Each player begins the game with fifteen checkers of a different color from his opponent, a pair of dice, a dice cup, and a doubling cube. Players move their checkers around the board according to the roll of the dice. The first player to get all of his checkers, or men, around and finally off the board is the winner.

In this book, you will be referred to as "X" and your opponent as "O."

Position 1
Starting Position

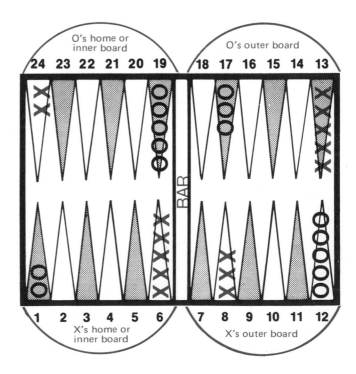

The Board

As Positions 1 and 2 indicate, the playing board has twenty-four triangles called **points,** divided into four quadrants. Each quadrant contains six points. The quadrants are referred to as your (X's) **home** or **inner board,** your (X's) **outer board**, your opponent's (O's) **home** or **inner board,** and your opponent's (O's) **outer board.** The home and outer boards are separated by the **bar.**

Starting the Game

The checkers are initially placed as shown in Position 1. (Alternately, the mirror image of this starting position can also be used, as shown in Position 2.) In this book the starting position for each game will always be Position 1. A new player, however, should be familiar with both positions.

Play begins with each player rolling one die. The player having the higher number moves first. For his first move, he *must* use the two numbers already cast by him and his opponent. Ties are re-rolled but may affect the scoring (see **automatic doubles** at the end of this chapter). After the first throw, each player uses two dice on each turn. Players alternate after each throw.

Position 2
Mirror Image of
Starting Position

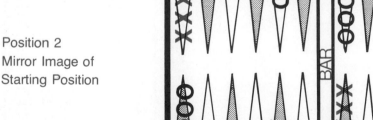

Moving the Checkers

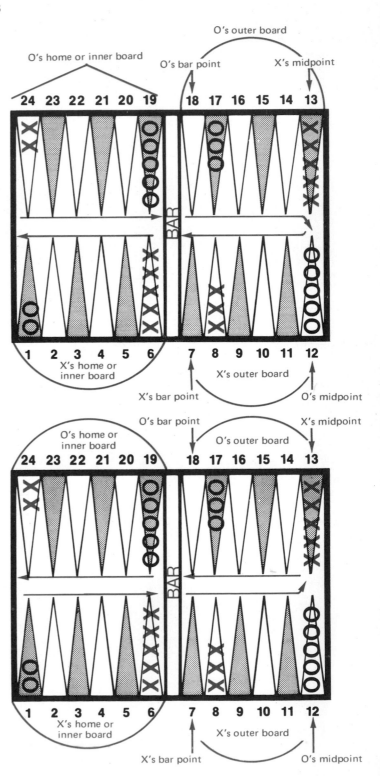

Position 3
Movement of X's
Checkers

Position 4
Movement of O's
Checkers

Imagine the board as a U-shaped playing track. Any checker at any point on the board can be advanced around the U, but only by moving it "forward."

The movement of X's checkers is shown in Position 3. For X, "forward" is the line of movement from O's home board, over the bar to O's outer board, around the closed end of the U into X's outer board, and finally back over the bar into X's inner board. In other words, X's checkers move from the twenty-four point to the one point. The bar does not count as a point.

The movement of X's checkers is shown in Position 3. For X, "forward" is the line of movement from the twenty-four point to the one point. In other words, X moves from O's home board, over the bar to O's outer board, around the closed end of the U into X's outer board, and finally back over the bar into X's home board. The bar does not count as a point.

The movement of O's checkers is shown in Position 4. Your opponent moves his checkers around the same U-shaped track, *but in exactly the opposite direction as you*. In other words, O moves his checkers from the one point to the twenty-four point. No checker can ever move backward.

The throw of the dice determines the number of **points** or **pips** that checkers may be advanced. The two numbers thrown are considered as two separate moves (though both moves may be made by the same checker) rather than a total. Thus, a throw of 3–5 does not represent one move of 8, but rather two moves: one of 3 and one of 5. A player who rolls 3–5 may advance one checker 3 pips and then advance that same checker another 5 pips (he may play the 5 first and the 3 second); or he may move one checker 3 pips and a different checker 5 pips.

As an example, let us return to the opening position. If X rolls 3–5, three possible moves from the starting position are:

1. X advances a checker 3 pips from the twenty-four point to the twenty-one point, and then advances the same checker 5 pips from the twenty-one point to the sixteen point (as shown in Position 5).

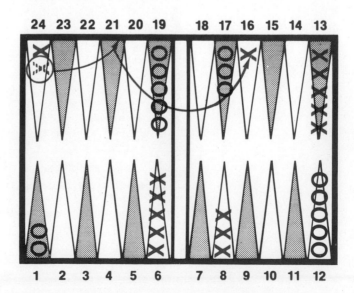

Position 5

2. X moves one checker down from the thirteen point to the ten point, and moves a second checker down from the thirteen point to the eight point (Position 6).

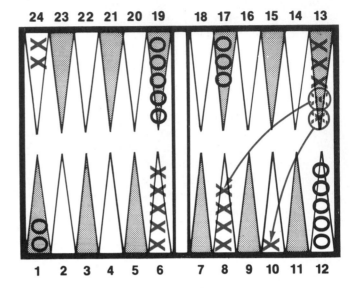

Position 6

3. X moves one checker from the eight point to the three point, and moves another checker from the six point to the three point (Position 7).

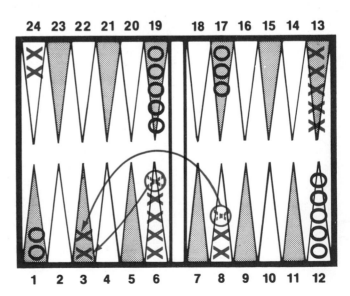

Position 7

Throwing Doubles

Whenever doubles (1–1, 2–2, 3–3, 4–4, 5–5, 6–6) are thrown, a player moves *twice* the number shown on the face of the dice. A throw of 5–5, for

example, means that the player has four 5's to move. These moves may be made in any of the following combinations:
1. Move one checker four 5's.
2. Move one checker three 5's and another checker one 5.
3. Move two checkers two 5's each.
4. Move one checker two 5's and two other checkers one 5 each.
5. Move four checkers one 5 each.

Where Checkers May Land

A checker may land on any vacant point. It may also land on any point occupied by a player's own checkers (there is no limit to the number of any one player's checkers that may occupy a single point); or on any point occupied by only *one* of his opponent's checkers. All the points on which a checker may land are called **open points.**

A checker may *not* land on a point that is occupied by *two or more* opposing checkers. You may not even stop at such a point "in passing" when moving a single checker (remember that the two numbers on the dice are considered separate moves). You can, however, pass over points occupied by your opponent.

For example, if X rolls 3–5 when the nineteen and twenty-one points are each occupied by two or more of O's checkers, X cannot move either of his back checkers from the twenty-four point, even though the sixteen point is empty (Position 8).

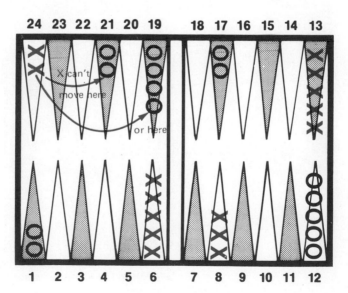

Position 8

If, in Position 8, X were to roll 6–3, he could play his 6 first and then his 3, passing over the blocked twenty-one and nineteen points to land on the empty fifteen point.

A player is not permitted to pass his turn. Both numbers on the dice must be played, if legally possible. Since the entire roll is considered an entity, it is *not* legal to play one number in such a way as to make the other number impossible to play. If only one number can be played, then the *higher* number must be played, if possible. Numbers that cannot be played are forfeited.

Hitting and Re-entering

Two or more checkers of the same color on a point are said to **own** that point. A lone checker is called a **blot.** Should a player's checker land on an opponent's blot, that blot has then been **hit** and is placed **on the bar,** where it is temporarily out of play. (Note that players are not obliged to hit a blot every time they are presented with an opportunity to do so.)

If a player has one or more checkers on the bar, he cannot move any other checker until *all* of his checkers on the bar have been re-entered. A checker on the bar must re-enter the game in the opposing player's home board. This can be done only when the player rolls a number corresponding to an **open point** in his opponent's home board.

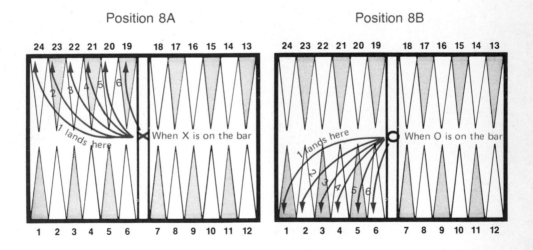

| Position 8A | Position 8B |

If X rolls a 1 on either die, he may land on the first point (the twenty-four point) in O's home board *if* that point does not contain two or more of O's checkers.

Similarly, if X rolls a 2 he may land on the twenty-three point; a 3, the twenty-two point; 4, twenty-one point; 5, twenty point; 6, nineteen point.

If O has a checker on the bar, a 1 on a die corresponds to the one point in X's inner board. Similarly, if O rolls a 2 he can land on the two point; 3, three point; 4, four point; 5, five point; 6, six point.

The specific number needed to re-enter must come up on at least one die. The *sum* of the two dice is not used to re-enter.

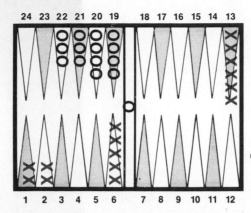

Position 8C
O Rolls 2–1

O rolls 2–1;
O cannot re-enter
X's home board

For example, in Position 8C the one, two, and six points are owned by X. O is on the bar. If O rolls 2–1 he *cannot* land on the open three point; he must roll a specific 3 on one die to land on that point.

Points occupied by two or more opposing checkers are called **closed points,** and the opponent's checkers cannot land on them. If both numbers on a player's dice correspond to closed points, the player cannot re-enter his checker on that roll. He must wait and try again on his next turn. In the meantime, since he cannot move any of his other checkers either, his opponent continues to move.

In Position 9, O has closed the nineteen, twenty, and twenty-three points. X has one checker on the bar. If X rolls 5–3, he must, before doing anything else, use the 3 to bring his checker on the bar back into play in his opponent's home board. The 5 cannot be used to re-enter because the fifth point in O's inner board, the twenty point, is closed. X must re-enter on the twenty-two point, the third point in O's inner board. After X has re-entered his checker, he may play any legal 5.

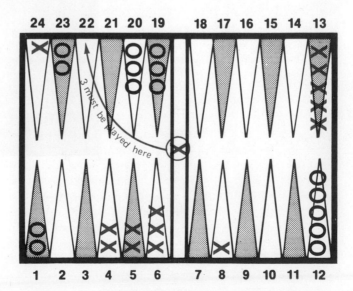

Position 9
X Rolls 5–3

If X rolls 5–2 in Position 9, he would have to give up his turn. Neither the 5 nor the 2 re-enter because both the fifth point (the twenty point) and the second point (the twenty-three point) are closed in O's inner board. The checker on the bar cannot move directly to the eighteen point because the sum of the dice may not be used.

Position 10

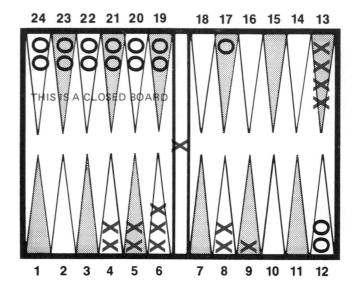

O has all of his home-board points closed and X has a checker on the bar in Position 10. X must wait until one of O's home-board points is opened before he can re-enter his checker from the bar and then continue moving his other checkers.

When you or your opponent closes all six home-board points, this is known as a **closed board.** In Position 10, O would continue to roll until he opened one of his home-board points. Then it would be X's turn to roll.

Bearing Off

Once you have brought *all* your checkers into your home-board, you can begin to remove them. This is called **bearing off.** A checker that has been borne off the board is not re-entered for the rest of the game. If a checker is hit by your opponent during the bearing-off process, no more checkers can be borne off until that checker has re-entered your opponent's inner board and has been brought back to your inner board. The first player to bear off all of his checkers wins the game.

Procedure in Bearing Off: In bearing off, you are, in effect, bringing your checkers just past the first point in your home board.

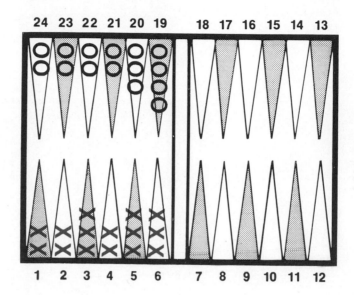

Position 11
X Rolls 6–4

If X rolls 6–4 in Position 11, where he has two or more checkers covering each point in his home board, the 6 must be used to bear one checker off the board from the six point. The 4 may be used to bear off a checker from the four point (as seen in Position 11A).

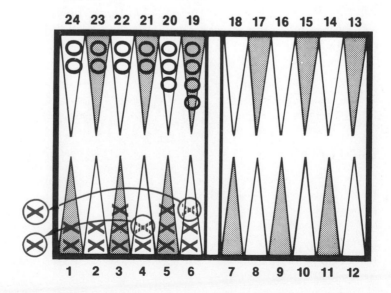

Position 11A

The 4 in 6–4 may also be used to advance a checker from the six point to the two point (Position 11B),

Position 11B

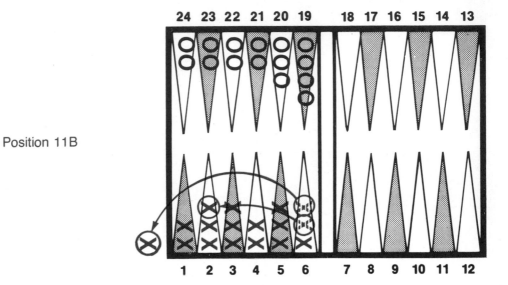

or to advance a checker from the five point to the one point (Position 11C).

Position 11C

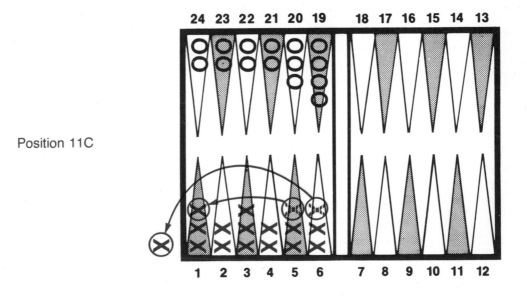

A 2–1 could be used to bear two checkers off: one from the one point and one from the two point; or to bear one checker off the three point by first moving it to the one or two point and then using the remaining number to bear it off.

If a player rolls a number higher than any point on which a checker rests, the checker on the next highest point is taken off instead.

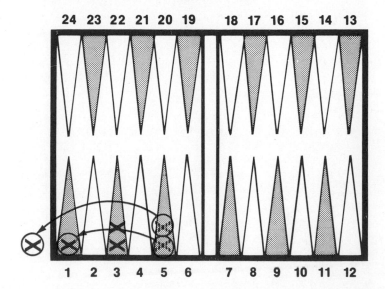

Position 12

In Position 12, X has two checkers on the five point and two checkers on the three point. If he rolls 6–4, the 6 must be played by bearing off one checker from the five point. X cannot now use the 4 to bear a checker off the three point because he still has a checker on the five point and the *full* number must be used whenever possible. Therefore, the 4 *must* be used to move a checker from the five point to the one point.

Similarly, when O is bearing off checkers, a 6 on the dice can be used to bear a man off the nineteen point; a 5 off the twenty point; a 4 off the twenty-one point; a 3 off the twenty-two point; a 2 off the twenty-three point; a 1 off the twenty-four point.

Scoring

The game begins with a value of one point, or unit. This is won by the first player to bear off all his checkers. The **doubling cube,** with the numbers 2, 4, 8, 16, 32, and 64 on its faces, is used for keeping track of the increase in units or points, for which the game is being played.

At the beginning of the game, the doubling cube is placed halfway between the two players with 64 facing up. This indicates that the game is being played for one point. If one player feels he has gained an advantage in the course of play, he may **double** the stakes by turning the cube to 2 and offering it to his opponent. This is done *before* he rolls the dice for his turn. Note that when a player is closed out, he does *not* forfeit his right to double.

His opponent then has a choice: He can refuse the double (or **pass**), thus conceding the game and losing one point; or he can accept the double (**take**), take possession of the doubling cube, and continue playing the game for two points. A player who accepts a double **owns the cube** and is then the only person in a position to re-double the stakes.

The game can be doubled and re-doubled any number of times subject to the following conditions:

1. Initially, the cube is in the middle and either player may double. Subsequently, only the player who owns the cube may re-double. The same player cannot double twice consecutively.

2. A player can only double *prior* to his roll. If the double is accepted by his opponent, the player then proceeds to roll the dice and take his move.

Gammons, Backgammons, and Variations

The player who wins the game scores the number of points indicated on the doubling cube, unless there is a **gammon** or **backgammon**. A **gammon** (or double game) occurs when the winner bears off all of his checkers before his opponent bears off *any* checkers at all. In this case, the winner receives *double* the amount shown on the doubling cube.

A **backgammon** occurs when the winner bears off all his checkers before his opponent bears off any, *and* while his opponent has one or more checkers in the winner's home board. In this event, the winner receives *triple* the points shown on the doubling cube. (Outside the United States, a backgammon is only scored as a double game.)

Here are two variations that players may adopt by agreement *prior* to beginning play:

1. **Automatic Doubles:** If each player rolls the same number on the first roll of the game, the doubling cube remains in the middle, but is turned to 2. Players usually agree to limit the number of automatic doubles to one per game. The players then throw the dice again to see who goes first.

2. **The Jacoby Rule:** If neither player has doubled during the course of a game, gammons and backgammons do not count. They are scored as single games.

Chouette

Chouettes provide an opportunity for three or more people to play in the same backgammon game. To begin a chouette, each person rolls one die. The individual with the highest number becomes the **man in the box** and plays against the remaining people, who act as a team.

The second-highest roller becomes the team **captain.** He actually moves the checkers against the man in the box while his teammates advise. Should disagreements arise among the team players, the captain's decisions are final. The first throw of the dice also establishes the order in which each team member assumes the position of captain in subsequent games.

If the team loses the first game, the captain is replaced by the next player, and becomes last in the team's order of rotation. The man in the box remains in the box. If the team wins, the captain becomes the man in the box, the next team member assumes the captain's position, and the former man in the box becomes the last in the team's order.

The team acts in concert when doubling the player in the box. Should the box double, however, *each* individual team member has the option of accepting or declining. Those declining each lose to the player in the box and drop out of that particular game.

Those accepting the double continue to play as a team for the increased number of points. If they win, they each gain the number of points indicated on the doubling cube from the player in the box. If they lose, they each give up the number on the cube to the man in the box.

Procedure and Courtesy of Play

1. A player must roll his dice in the board to his *right*.

2. A roll is invalid and must be re-rolled if a die lands out of the right-hand board, if it lands cocked, or if it lands on a checker.

3. A player's move is not final until he has picked up his dice.

4. A player may not roll his dice until his opponent has completed his move and picked up his dice. This rule, however, is not strictly adhered to in bear-off situations where no further contact is possible, or when a player's move is forced.

5. Illegal moves may be corrected by either player, but the correction must be made *before* the next player rolls. Any errors not corrected in time remain as played.

CHAPTER 2.
NOTATION

IN THE DIAGRAMS and text to follow we have developed a simple numerical notation to indicate the numbers rolled on the dice and the movement of the checkers.

Dice Rolls

Numbers rolled on the dice are separated by a dash (–).

Position 1
X to Play 3–3

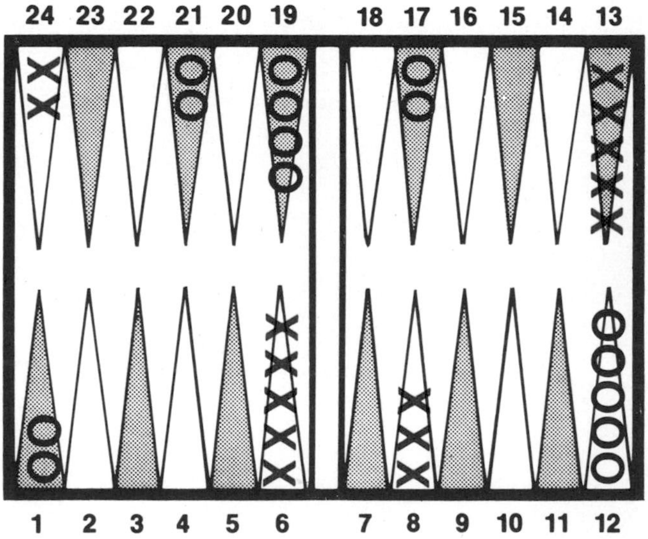

In Position 1, the notation X to Play 3–3 indicates that X has double 3's to play.

Occasionally, in demonstrating a particular position, only half a roll (one number on the dice) may be indicated: X to Play 3.

Checker Moves

Typically, as in Position 1, a diagram shows the position *before* the indicated dice roll has been played, in order to enable you to guess beforehand what the move might be.

In many positions — and particularly during the course of describing a game — we also indicate how a man has already moved. Thus when the move (in parentheses) is indicated on the diagram, it has already occurred. The numbers showing a move are separated by a slash (/). The first number indicates the starting point; the second, the landing point. 4/2, for example, indicates that one checker was taken from the four point and moved to the two point.

24 23 22 21 20 19   18 17 16 15 14 13

Position 2
(X 3–3 6/3[2], 8/5[2])

1 2 3 4 5 6   7 8 9 10 11 12

In Position 2, X has rolled 3–3. He has played four 3's. The notation indicates that he moved two men from the six point to the three point 6/3(2) and two men from the eight point to the five point 8/5(2).

When a move, or part of a move, cannot be played legally, the symbol ø is used. 6/1, ø indicates that the player moved one checker from the six point to the one point, but was unable to use the remaining number on the dice. X ø indicates that X was unable to play any part of his roll legally.

Numbering the Points

In this book, points are described (counted) from *X's point of view.* They are numbered one through twenty-four beginning in X's inner board to X's outer board, to O's outer board, to O's inner board.

From O's point of view, however, X's twenty point is the same as O's five point. Occasionally we refer to O's making *his* four point; on the diagram this will appear as the twenty-one point. Also, in general discussions of the value of certain points, we may refer, for example, to a player's five point without further specification. For X, this would refer to the point labeled "five"; for O, the point labeled "twenty."

Hitting

When an opposing checker has been hit, the indicated move is followed by an asterisk (*). In Position 2, let's assume that O rolls 6–1. He plays it by moving one man off the one point to the seven point and then continuing it to the eight point, hitting a blot. The resulting position is shown in Position 3. The move taken is indicated by (1/8*). To repeat, when a move is indicated on a diagram in parentheses, *it has already occurred.*

Position 3
(O 6–1 1/8*)

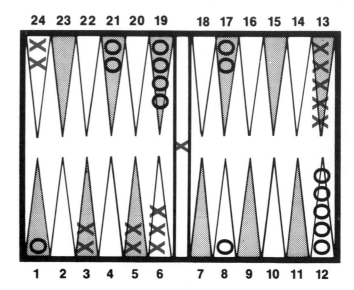

Re-entering from the Bar

When a checker re-enters the game from the bar, the move is indicated by the word *bar* followed by a slash (/), followed by the number of the point the checker landed on. (Bar/22) indicates that a checker from the bar re-entered the game and moved to the twenty-two point.

Bearing Off

When a checker is borne off the board in the latter stages of the game, the move is indicated by the number of the point the checker was moved from, followed by a slash (/), followed by the word "off." 6/off means that a checker on the six point was borne off the board. Checkers already borne off the board are indicated by the X's and O's to the left of the playing surface.

The Cube

The position of the doubling cube in a diagram indicates which player may double next. If neither player has doubled, the cube is in the middle. When the cube is owned by O, it is at the top right of the diagram; when owned by X, at bottom right.

When the cube is not pertinent to a particular position, it is not shown.

Bar Point, Midpoint

Bar always refers to the raised area between the inner and outer boards where a checker rests after being hit.

Bar point refers to the seven point of the player moving the checkers (the eighteen point for O, the seven point for X).

Midpoint refers to the thirteen point of the player moving the checkers (the twelve point for O, the thirteen point for X).

CHAPTER 3.
BASIC CHECKER
PLAY

IF YOU HAVE never played a single game of backgammon, the hardest aspect involved initially may be counting pips, or figuring out exactly where a checker goes on a particular move. Although this is a cumbersome task at first, you should carefully count out one point at a time until you become more accustomed to moving the checkers. Don't worry if your first few games seem to be moving slowly — even the best players in the world began by counting one by one.

You will probably discover within a relatively short time that you are moving the checkers more rapidly. When you become less concerned with the mechanics of counting, you will be better able to appreciate the strategy of the game. In any case, the best way to learn backgammon is to play it. Even if you are not always making the theoretically correct play, you will be acquiring valuable experience which will improve your judgment and help you get the feel of the game.

To help the novice player, we begin by giving some exercises in hitting and making closed points. The next chapter illustrates the first sample game. Let us emphasize again the importance of getting out a board yourself, setting up the indicated positions, and making the moves.

Position 1
X on Roll. What Does X
Need to Hit?

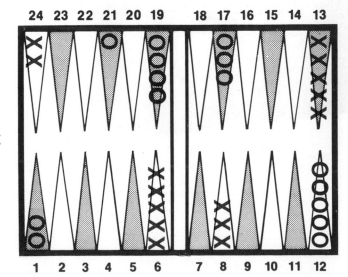

Hitting

X is on roll in Position 1. O has a blot on the twenty-one point. What number does X need to hit this man and send him to the bar?

X needs a 3 to hit. If the number on either die comes up 3, or if the sum of the numbers on the dice enables X to move exactly 3 pips forward, then X may land on the twenty-one point and hit O. In this position, 6–3, 5–3, 4–3, 3–3, 2–3, and 1–3 all hit, as well as 2–1 and 1–1 (because of the doubles rule: X has four 1's to play). A 4 does not hit the blot; it merely passes over it.

In this position, the opportunity which X has to hit O is called a **direct shot.** We define a direct shot as a blot which is 6 pips or less away from an opposing checker. The number needed to hit the blot can show on *either* die, or as a combination of both dice.

When the number needed to hit a blot is 7 or more pips away, we call that a **combination** or **indirect shot.** In that case only a specific combination requiring *both* dice can give the needed number.

A direct shot is much more likely to be hit than an indirect shot. (For specific odds, see Chapter 11.)

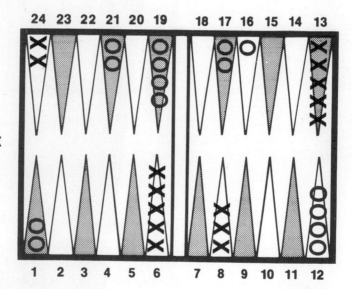

Position 2
X on Roll. What Does X
Need to Hit?

In Position 2, O's blot is 8 pips in front of X's man on the twenty-four point. X therefore needs an 8 to hit. This is an indirect shot. Only a combination of both dice can produce the needed number: 6–2 and 4–4. 5–3 does not hit in this instance because neither the 5 nor the 3 may be played legally from the twenty-four point. Because of the special nature of doubles, 2–2 also hits.

X's men on the thirteen point do not threaten to hit because they cannot move backward.

Note that you do *not* have to hit whenever you have the opportunity to do so; if you do not wish to hit, you may take your move elsewhere.

With more experience in counting, you will know just by looking at the board what numbers hit your opponent and what numbers you yourself are exposed to should you leave a blot. Two hints a new player may find useful in the mechanics of counting are:

1. A man to be moved an *even* total remains on the *same color* point. A man to be moved an *odd* total will *switch colors*. This observation of the color of points facilitates counting and acts as a quick check.

2. Notice that each quadrant is six points long. If you move from one quadrant to the corresponding point in the next quadrant, the move will always be exactly 6 pips away.

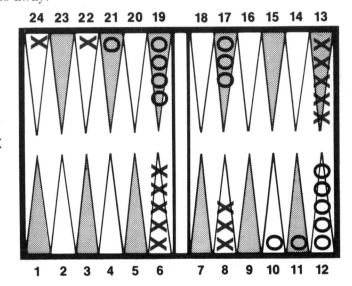

Position 3
X on Roll. What Does X
Need to Hit?

O has two blots in Position 3. Since they are both less than 6 pips in front of X's men on the thirteen point, they are both directly exposed. This is called a **double direct shot** (or **double shot**). Any simple 2 or 3 will hit. A 2–1 hits *both* men, which is particularly dangerous for O. (This would be called a double hit.) 1–1 does not hit because the twelve point is owned by O.

The two blots are also 11 and 12 pips away from X's man on the twenty-two point. 6–5 and 6–6 hit from the twenty-two point, as well as 4–4 (moving three of the four 4's). This shot alone would be a **double indirect shot.**

Remember to keep both your and your opponent's direction in mind!

In Position 4, the blot on the one point is exposed to 5's (a direct shot), and also to 7's and 12's (combination shots). Position 4 is our first example of a case where hitting may be possible but not desirable. To see why, let's briefly examine the reasons for hitting.

As a rule, you try to hit your opponent when possible. By hitting a blot you send it to the bar from which it must re-enter in your inner board — the very beginning of its journey around the board. Since backgammon is basically a race, every time you hit one of your opponent's checkers, you put him further behind in the race. The closer a checker is to home, the more pips are lost when it is hit. Hitting a blot in your opponent's inner board (as in Position 1) is particularly good since that checker will lose many pips in making the journey around again. On the other hand, hitting a blot in *your* inner board is of limited value since that checker is already about as far back as it can be; a blot hit in your inner board doesn't lose much ground so far as the race is concerned.

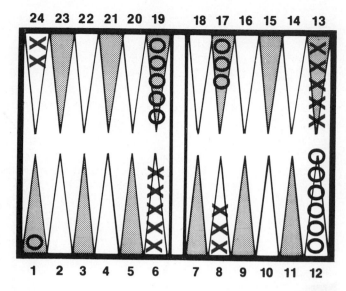

Position 4
X on Roll. What Does X
Need to Hit?

Conversely, you generally try to avoid being hit yourself. The closer a checker is to home, the more serious the loss of pips if hit. You lose a lot of ground if you are hit in your own inner board, whereas being hit in your opponent's inner board has little significance so far as the race is concerned.

You can never play completely safe even if you try to; leaving blots is inevitable and, as we shall see later, often desirable. Blots, however, must never be left needlessly. When you are forced to leave a blot, consider placing it where it is least likely to be hit and/or where the hit will cost you the least number of pips. You must be aware not only of what number you need to hit your opponent, but also to what numbers you, yourself, are exposed.

In Position 5 we see that X could hit on the one point with a 5. If X hit, however, his checker would then be in danger of being hit back by O as O re-enters from the bar. If X were hit, he would have to re-enter himself in O's

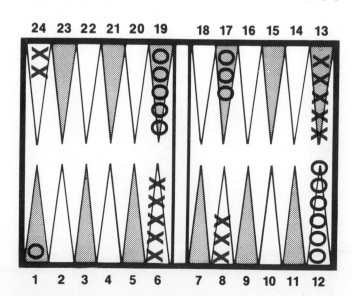

Position 5
X to Play 5–1

inner board. Because of this **return shot** (a shot which your opponent has back at you after you have hit him), X has little to gain but much to lose by such a hit. If X plays 13/8, 24/23, he leaves two men exposed in O's inner board. However, O has little to gain by hitting these blots.

Making Points

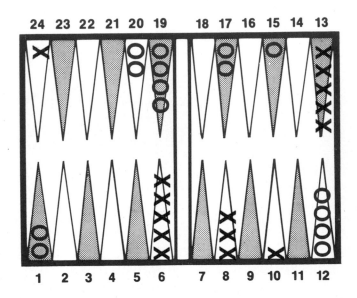

Position 6
X to Play 6–2

In order to avoid leaving blots, it is often necessary to bring two men together to **close** or **make points**. In Position 6, X can bring his blot to safety by playing 10/8, but then has no way to play his 6 without leaving a direct shot.

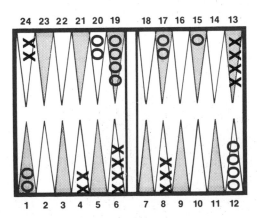

Position 6A
(X 6–2 10/4, 6/4)

The correct play is 10/4, 6/4 as seen in Position 6A. This play makes the four point. Before analyzing the benefits of making points, let's examine how to find plays that do make points.

In Position 6, the two men that came together to make the four point started out 4 pips apart on the six point and the ten point. A 6–2 was the number rolled; the difference between 6 and 2 is 4. Therefore, if we can find two checkers which are 4 pips apart they will end up on the same point, making that point. We move the man furthest away from the point to be made 6 pips, and the closer man 2 pips.

Let's look at another example:

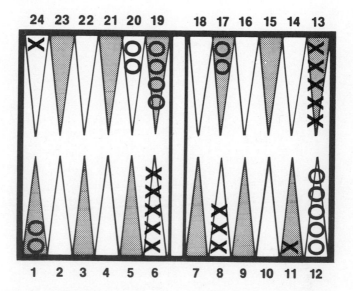

Position 7
X to Play 6–3

In Position 7, X has 6–3 to play. 6 minus 3 = 3; therefore, we look for two checkers which are 3 pips apart. We see that the men on the eight and eleven points are 3 pips apart so that they will come together on the five point. The correct move is 11/5, 8/5 as shown in Position 7A.

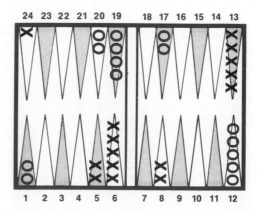

Position 7A
(X 6–3 11/5, 8/5)

Let's look at Position 7 again. Assume that X has instead a 6–4 to play. 6 minus 4 = 2; therefore, two checkers which are 2 pips apart will end up on the same point. The men on the eight and six points are 2 pips apart. Thus we move 8/2, 6/2, making the two points as shown in Position 7B.

In Position 7, the men on the thirteen and eleven points are also 2 pips apart. If, with our roll of 6–4, we move 13/7, 11/7, as shown in Position 7C, we can make the **bar point**.

Position 7B
(X 6–4 8/2, 6/2)

Position 7C
(X 6–4 13/7, 11/7)

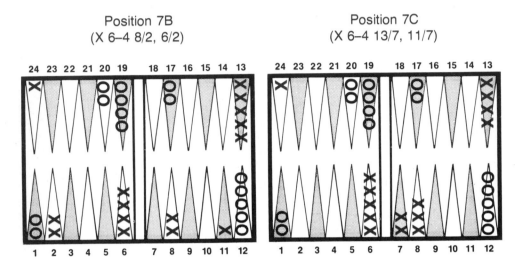

In Position 7, then, we have a choice of which point to make with a roll of 6–4. The relative value of each point will be discussed shortly.

Notice that while this "difference method" is the easiest way to search for ways in which to make new points with a particular roll, it does not automatically *create* new points.

Position 8
X to Play 3–1

Position 9
X to Play 3–1

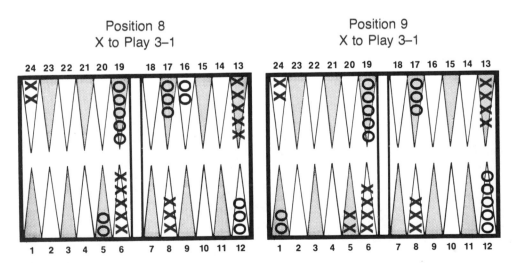

In Positions 8 and 9, X has 3–1 to play and in both cases there are men 2 pips apart on the six and eight points.

In the case of 8, you cannot create a *new* point since O already owns the five point. If O had a single man on the five point, X could make a point *on O's head* by hitting O and sending him to the bar.

In 9, X cannot create a new point since he already owns the five point.

Why do you want to make points?

In Position 6, you want to make your blots safe by making them into points. Already established points may also act as landing places to safely park your spare men. If you are short of points, you may be forced to expose men which you don't want hit. In Position 9, for example, X could play 6–2 safely by playing 13/5 and resting on the five point.

Another fundamental reason for creating points is to hinder your opponent's movement. Since your opponent cannot land on your points, every point you make restricts his choice of moves. Controlling three or more points in a row forms a blockade and makes it more difficult for your opponent to get past you.

These ideas will be illustrated and explained in later chapters. We advise you *first* to get out a backgammon set and follow along during the sample games. The best way to play with the book is to look at the dice roll and then try to make the moves yourself before looking at the answer. Better yet, get a friend to make all the moves for O while you play all the moves for X.

Summary

On every roll you will be faced with many possible legal plays. If you are a beginner, concentrate on the following *three primary goals* in considering your move. When you become more familiar with basic checker play, you will be in a good position to look at the strategic aspects of the game.

1. *Hit your opponent advantageously.* Sometimes a hit may not be advantageous — see Position 5.

2. *Play safely to avoid being hit.* Never leave men exposed to your opponent needlessly. When you do leave men exposed, leave the fewest possible direct shots. Avoid double or triple shots and leave indirect shots (7 pips or more away) in preference to direct shots.

3. *Make points.*

CHAPTER 4.
GAME I: RUNNING GAME

EVERY GAME OF backgammon is essentially a race: the first person to success-fully move his men around the board and bear them off is the winner. However, if the game were just a race, then there would be little skill involved — the player rolling the higher numbers would win. This is not the case in backgammon. Because your opponent can block you by making points and you are always in danger of being hit, the game may be better thought of as an obstacle course.

Game I illustrates the basic strategy of safely navigating the obstacles and winning the race. It is called a **running game** because your primary strategy is to enter directly into a favorable race. Game I, as well as Game II, will be completely concerned with the play of the men, and thus the doubling cube will not be used.

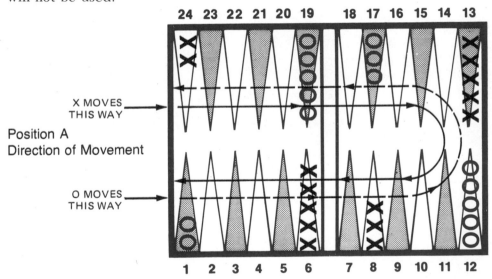

First, set up your checkers in the opening position (Position A). Remember that the direction of movement is indicated by the arrows in the diagram. Thus X moves from the twenty-four point around to the twelve point and over to the one point, while O moves in the opposite direction: from the one point to the thirteen point and then over to the twenty-four point.

On the opening roll, as stated in the rules, each player rolls one die. The player having the higher number moves first and must use for his first move the two numbers which have just been rolled.

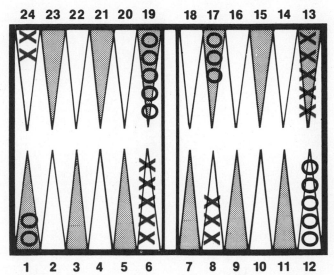

Roll 1
X 6, O 5, X to Play 6–5

The notation on the diagram above indicates that X has rolled a 6 and O, a 5. Therefore X takes the first move, 6–5. What are the possibilities for X? Try to make the move yourself before reading on.

The correct play is 24/13. This is indicated in the diagram below, O's Roll 2, where X 6–5 24/13 in parentheses indicates that X has already played his number. By moving one checker from the twenty-four point to the thirteen point, X begins to move the checkers that have the furthest to go in the circuit around the board. This is an important part of the opening strategy of the game. 6–5 is considered a good opening roll because it enables one **back man** to flee to complete safety.

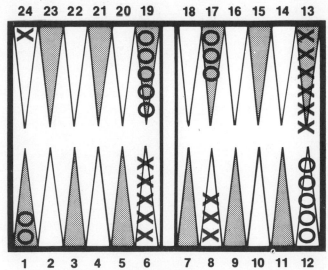

Roll 2 for O
O to Play 6–1
(X 6–5 24/13)

After the opening roll, players alternately roll both their dice to determine the move they will make. It is now O's turn. The diagram above indicates that, following X's opening move, O has rolled 6–1. How would you play this roll? Remember that O moves in the opposite direction from X.

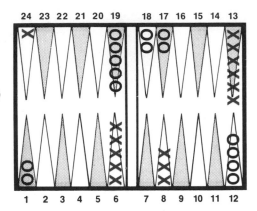

Correct Play: Roll 2 for O
(O 6–1 12/18, 17/18)

The correct play is 12/18, 17/18. The new point that O has made, the eighteen point, is called O's **bar point.** (Similarly, X's bar point would be the seven point.) The bar point is one of the most important points you can make at the beginning of the game. (Remembering our discussion in the previous chapter on the "difference method" of spotting rolls that make a point, we can see that 6–1 forms a point since 6 minus 1 = 5, and since the men on the twelve and seventeen points start 5 pips apart and thus go to the same place.)

Let's examine some alternate plays for O's roll of 6–1.

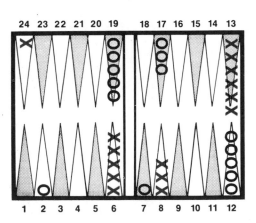

Alternate Move 1:
Roll 2 for O
(O 6–1 1/7, 1/2)

O can move 1/7, 1/2, as shown above to the left. Although O, following the logic of X's first move, would also like to begin to get his back men home, this move would leave the man on X's bar point exposed to a double direct shot.

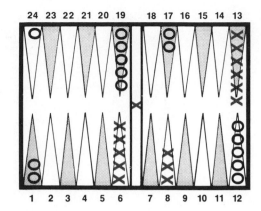

Alternate Move 2:
Roll 2 for O
(O 6–1 17/24*)

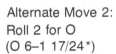

In the second alternate move, O can hit X by playing 17/24*. But, as pointed out in Chapter 3, O has little to gain by hitting on the twenty-four point since this move would expose O to a return shot by X's checker on the bar. If X re-enters on the one point hitting O, O will lose considerable ground in the race.

Let's return to the position after the correct move for O has been made.

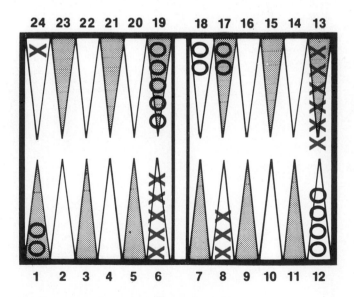

Roll 2 for X
X to Play 3–1
(O 6–1 12/18, 17/18)

X now has 3–1 to play. How would you play this move?

The correct play is 8/5, 6/5. (Again, by taking the difference of the numbers on the dice you can see that two men that start 2 pips apart will end up together on the same point.) The five point which we have made is also one of the most valuable points in the game. At the beginning of the game, you not only want to "escape" your back runners, but you also want to contain your opponent's back runners by making points in *front* of him.

Roll 3 for O
O to Play 5–4
(X 3–1 8/5, 6/5)

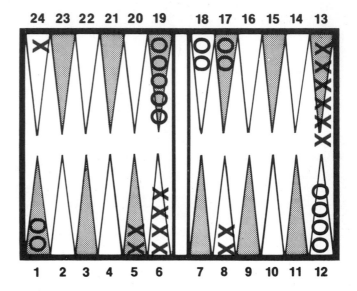

O's correct play of 5–4 in Roll 3 is 12/17, 12/16, shown below.

Correct Play: Roll 3 for O
(O 5–4 12/17, 12/16)

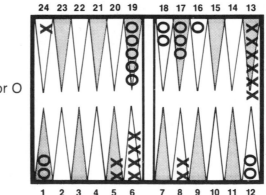

There is no "perfect play" for every roll in backgammon; you must often choose the best of several possible moves, or one which does nothing spectacular but isn't as harmful as another. Although this play exposes a man to an indirect shot (an 8), any other play would leave a *direct* shot (6 pips or less away), which is far more likely to be hit. (Remember that X's men on the thirteen point do not threaten your blot, since they cannot move backward.)

Let's look at some alternate plays.

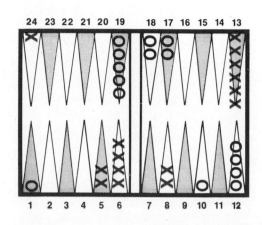

Alternate Move 1:
Roll 3 for O
(O 5–4 1/10)

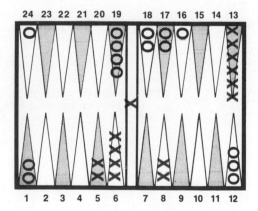

Alternate Move 2:
Roll 3 for O
(O 5–4 19/24*, 12/16)

The first alternate move, 1/10, is not legal. Remember that the numbers on the dice have to be taken *separately;* you cannot simply hop to the point corresponding to the sum of the two numbers. Since X has covered both the six and five points, neither the 4 nor 5 on the dice may be legally moved from the one point.

The second alternate move is 19/24*, 12/16. This hit exposes O to a return shot and thus a considerable loss of pips.

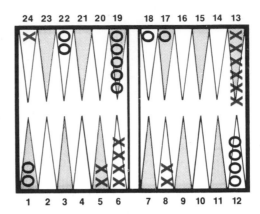

Alternate Move 3:
Roll 3 for O
(O 5–4 17/22, 18/22)

The third alternate move is 17/22, 18/22. You may have noticed that, since the difference in the two numbers on the dice is 1 (5 minus 4=1), a new point can be made by moving one checker from the seventeen and one from the eighteen points which are 1 pip apart. However, there are two drawbacks to creating the twenty-two point: First of all, you are making one new point at the expense of giving up two other points (the seventeen and eighteen), which are more valuable. Secondly, by making the twenty-two point you expose yourself to a direct shot, 6, and an indirect shot, 7. If either of these men are hit, they will have to start back again in X's inner board. It is important to be aware of the hitting possibilities that your opponent will have as a result of your own play.

Let's go back to the position after the correct move for O has been played.

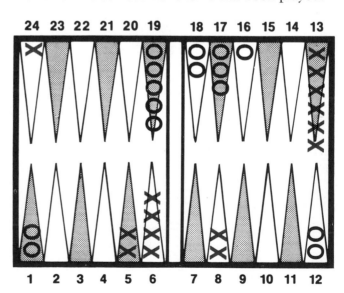

Roll 3 for X
X to Play 5–5
(O 5–4 12/17, 12/16)

X has now rolled double 5's and has four 5's to play.

The correct move is 13/3 (2). Since X's back man cannot escape with a 5, X makes another point in front of O to block O's back men.

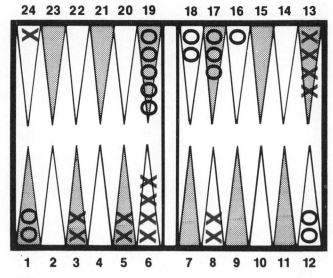

Roll 4 for O
O to Play 5–2
(X 5–5 13/3[2])

By correctly moving 16/21, 19/21, O can make a valuable point, the twenty-one point. O also **safeties** his man who was on the sixteen point; by **safety** we mean bringing a blot to a position where it cannot be hit. Another advantage of this move is that by making the twenty-one point, O is now beginning to seriously impede X's escape from the twenty-four point.

Remember, the difference method may help you find ways to make new points. If we look at O's last roll, 5–2, we can see that 5 minus 2 = 3. Therefore, in order for two checkers to make a point in this position, they must initially start 3 pips apart.

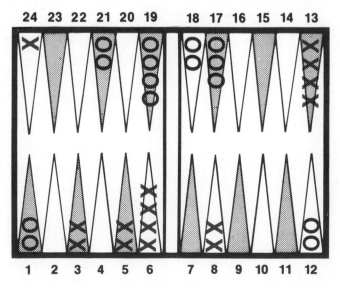

Roll 4 for X
X to Play 6–2
(O 5–2 16/21, 19/21)

The correct play is 24/16. X is beginning to feel trapped and seizes this opportunity to make a run for it. This is a calculated risk since the back man is exposed to a direct 4-shot.

A possible alternate move would be to play it safe by moving 13/5. This play is sound; however, in this case, the advantage of escaping a second back man is worth the risk of even a direct shot that would send the escapee back 8 pips.

Roll 5 for O
O to Play 4–2
(X 6–2 24/16)

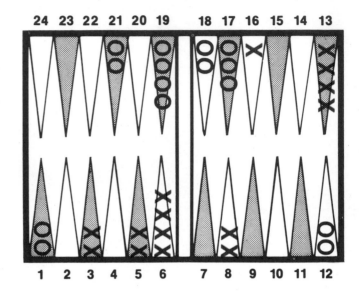

The correct play is to bring two men down from the twelve point: 12/16* (hitting the blot), 12/14. It is fortunate for O that he hit X since otherwise X might have been able to complete his escape.

Correct Play: Roll 5 for O
(O 4–2 12/16*, 12/14)

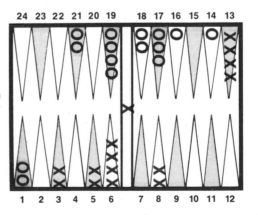

An alternate play would be to move 12/16*/18.

Alternate Move:
Roll 5 for O
(O 4–2 12/16*/18)

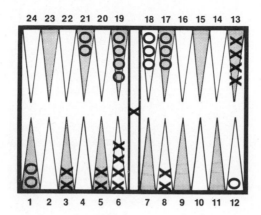

Although this move might appear safer than the correct play since it leaves only one blot on the twelve point (instead of two blots — on the fourteen and sixteen points), that one blot would be exposed to a direct 1-shot from the men on the thirteen point. By correctly playing 12/16*, 12/14, O is not exposed to any direct shots since the men on the thirteen point cannot move backward. Even several indirect shots are often less likely to be hit than a single direct shot.

Roll 5 for X
X to Play 4–3
(O 4–2 12/16*, 12/14)

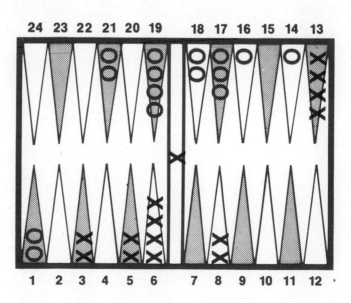

Before we discuss this play, remember that according to the rules a player may not move *any* men until all his checkers on the bar have been re-entered in his opponent's home board. You must re-enter with a number that corresponds to an open point in your opponent's home board. Here a 1 on the dice corresponds to the first point in O's home board, the twenty-four point; 2 to the twenty-three point; 3, the twenty-two point, etc.

In this position, the twenty-four, twenty-three, twenty-two, and twenty points are open; the twenty-one and nineteen points are closed. If X rolls 6–4 in this position he would be unable to re-enter and would forfeit his turn.

X's correct play for 4–3 is bar/22, 13/9. X *must* come in on the twenty-two point with the 3 since the twenty-one point is closed (corresponding to the 4 on the dice). Playing 13/9 leaves an indirect shot, but it is the safest move possible in this position. Taking any other 4, such as 8/4 or 6/2, would leave a direct shot.

Roll 6 for O
O to Play 4–1
(X 4–3 bar/22, 13/9)

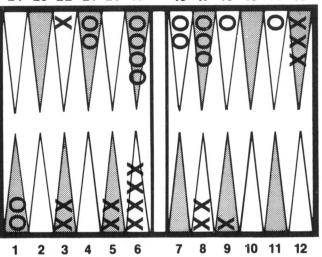

The correct play is 16/20, 19/20, making the twenty point. You now have several points in a row forming a blockade in front of X's back man. It is very hard for X to escape from behind five points in a row. X needs at least a specific 6 on the dice to escape.

An alternate move for O would be 16/17, 14/18.

Alternate Move:
Roll 6 for O
(O 4–1 14/18, 16/17)

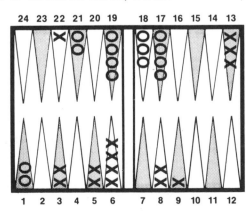

This play leaves no man exposed but fails to make the twenty point. The correct play leaves one man exposed to an indirect shot, an 8. The only number which could possibly hit in this case is 6–2, so the risk is minimal.

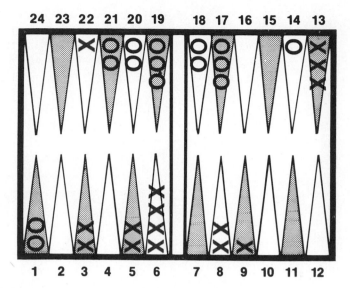

Roll 6 for X
X to Play 6–4
(O 4–1 16/20, 19/20)

The correct play is 22/12.

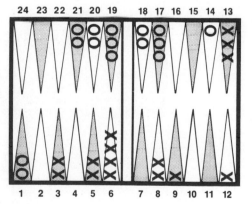

Correct Play: Roll 6 for X
(X 6–4 22/12)

X rolls the vital 6 and escapes.
    An alternate play is 8/2, 6/2.

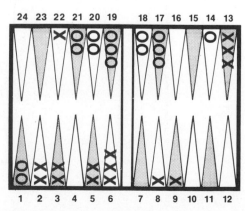

Alternate Move 1:
Roll 6 for X
(X 6–4 8/2, 6/2)

This move makes the two point in front of O's back men. It is more important, however, to escape from O's inner board.

Another alternate play is 22/16, 13/9.

Alternate Move 2:
Roll 6 for X
(X 6–4 22/16, 13/9)

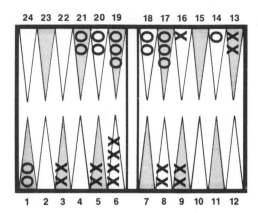

This play leaves you exposed to one direct 2-shot. The correct play leaves you exposed to two indirect shots, 8 and 11, but this single shot is twice as likely to be hit as both indirect shots, so we reject this play.

Let's stop for a moment and assess the position: Despite O's efforts, X has escaped both back men and is well ahead in the race because of the 5–5 which X rolled earlier. Both of O's back men are still in X's inner board. X, therefore, has a significant advantage at this time.

Roll 7 for O
O to Play 6–6
(X 6–4 22/12)

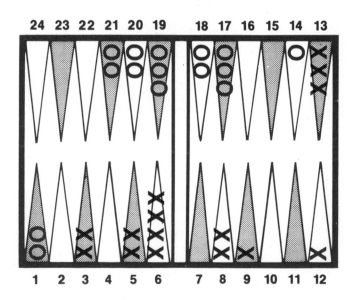

To return to the game, O is on roll and rolls 6–6.

The correct play is 1/7(2), 17/23(2). O seizes the opportunity to bring both his back men out safely to X's bar point (the seven point). The second part of the move, 17/23(2), establishes a new point in O's inner board. O doesn't worry about the blots he leaves on the seventeen and fourteen points since these men are not exposed to any of X's checkers.

O's strategy at this time is to hope to hit X as X comes home. A hit is necessary for O since he is still behind in the race. The more closed points O has in his inner board, the harder it will be for X to re-enter if he is hit. If X is hit now, only two numbers, 1 and 3, will allow him to re-enter.

If O were able to close *all* his inner-board points, he would have a **closed board.** If X were then hit, he would be unable to re-enter and would forfeit all his turns, remaining on the bar, until O opened one of his inner-board points. Therefore, one basic strategy in backgammon is to close as many inner-board points as possible to make the position dangerous for your opponent if he is hit.

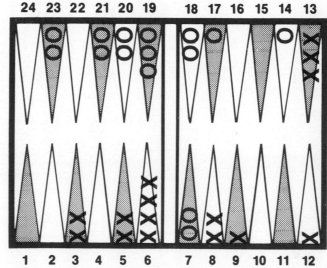

Roll 7 for X
X to Play 5–3
(O 6–6 1/7 [2], 17/23 [2])

X correctly moves 13/8, 12/9. With a single number, 3, X safeties both his blots and avoids the danger of being hit.

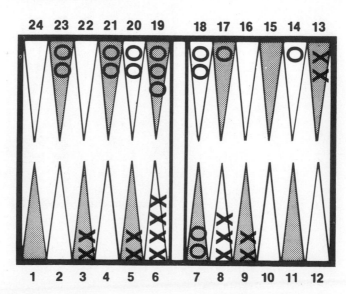

Roll 8 for O
O to Play 5–4
(X 5–3 13/8, 12/9)

The correct play is 17/22, 18/22. O closes another inner-board point. He cannot bring his two back men on the seven point closer to home without exposing himself to a double or triple shot.

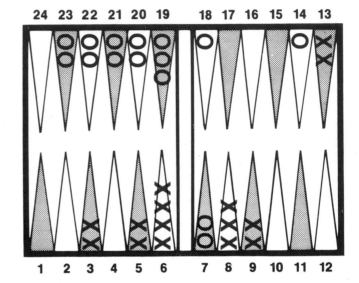

Roll 8 for X
X to Play 4–4
(O 5–4 17/22, 18/22)

The correct play is 13/5(2). X moves his men closer to home. He is still ahead in the race.

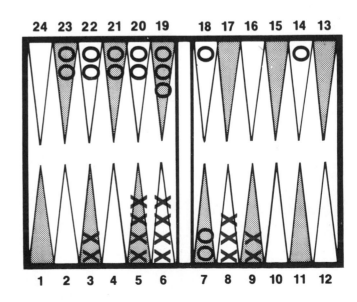

Roll 9 for O
O to Play 3–1
(X 4–4 13/5 [2])

The correct play is 14/17, 18/19. The object of the game is to bring all your men around the board and into your inner board in preparation for the bear-off. Remember, the bear-off process may not begin until you have *all* your men in your inner board. This is why O brings one man in and another closer to his inner board.

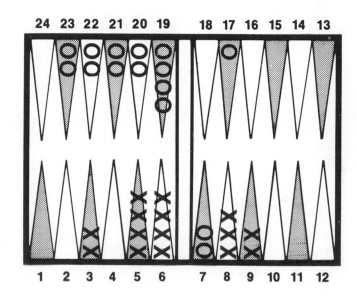

Roll 9 for X
X to Play 5–4
(O 3–1 14/17, 18/19)

The correct play is 9/4, 9/5. X brings two men into his inner board. He does not make his one point since, in this position, little contact is likely, and the game is basically a race. The player who rolls the higher numbers and gets off the board first will win.

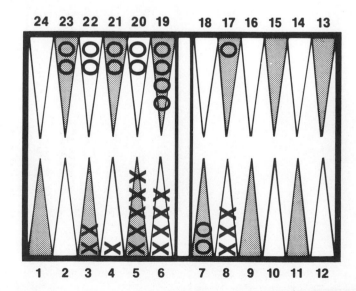

Roll 10 for O
O to Play 6–4
(X 5–4 9/4, 9/5)

The correct play is 7/13, 7/11. O brings his two rearmost men closer to home. Even though he is behind in the race, there is no reason to remain on X's bar point since there is no longer any real prospect of hitting X.

Roll 10 for X
X to Play 5–4
(O 6–4 7/13, 7/11)

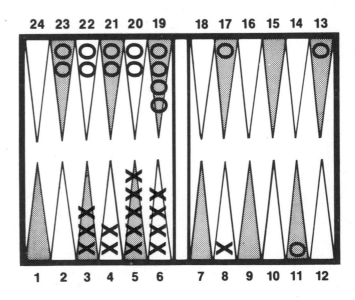

The correct play is 8/3, 8/4. X continues bringing his men into his inner board as quickly as possible. Since the game is now completely a race and no further contact is possible, the players do not have to worry about exposed checkers.

Roll 11 for O
O to Play 4–3
(X 5–4 8/3. 8/4)

The correct play is 11/15, 17/20. O moves closer to home.

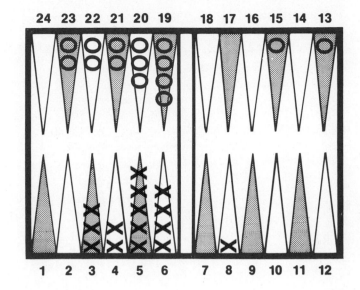

Roll 11 for X
X to Play 4–1
(O 4–3 11/15, 17/20)

The correct play is 8/4, 3/2. X brings one checker into his inner board and moves another on to an empty point in preparation for bearing off.

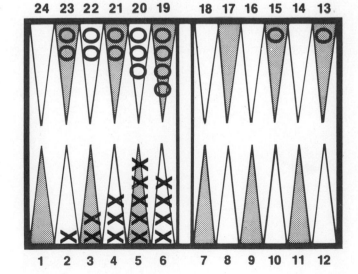

Roll 12 for O
O to Play 5–3
(X 4–1 8/4, 3/2)

O moves 15/20, 13/16 closer to his home board.

It is now X's roll. On his last move he completed bringing all his men into his inner board. He may now begin the bear-off process. The ultimate objective of the game is to bear all your men off the board before your opponent does so. Remember that each number rolled may be used to bear off a man from the corresponding point. Thus, the most economical way to bear off is to use one number on the dice for each bear-off — 3, for example, to take a man off the third point in your inner board. You can also move your checkers to unoccupied points within your inner board. 2–1 (when there are no checkers on either the two or one point) can be used to move a checker from the three point to either the two or one point, and thence off the board.

Roll 12 for X
X to Play 5–4
(O 5–3 15/20, 13/16)

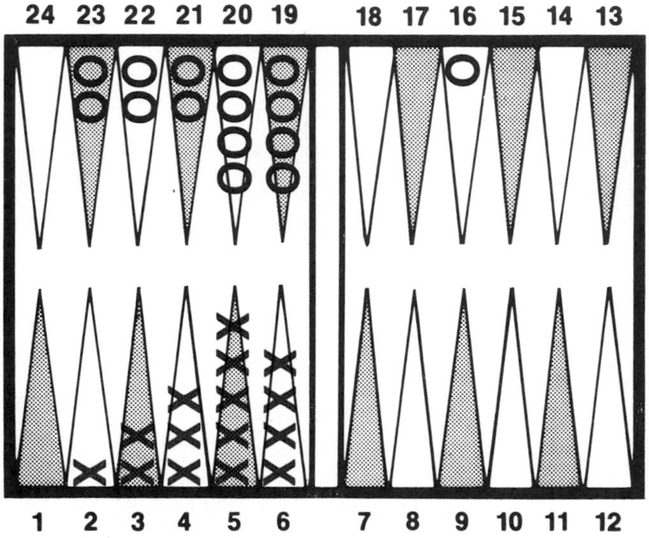

X uses his 5 to take a man off the five point and the 4 to take a man off the four point: 5/off, 4/off. You want to take off as many men as possible on each roll. These men go off the board and remain permanently out of the game.

Roll 13 for O
O to Play 6–2
(X 5–4 5/off, 4/off)

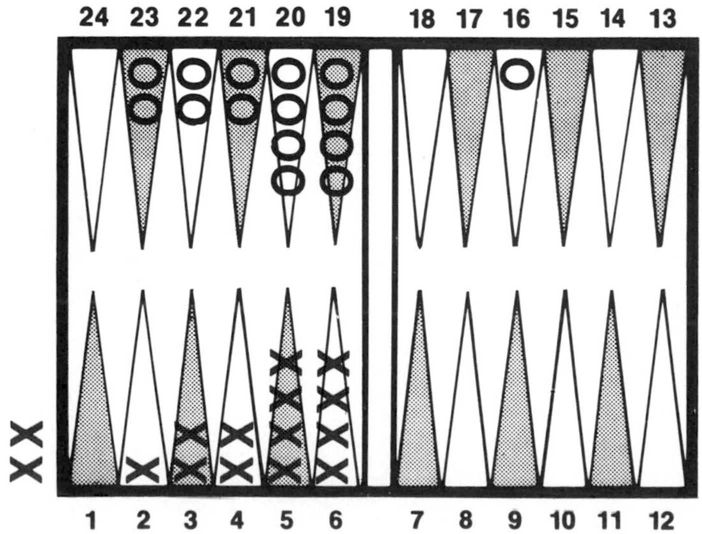

O brings the last man in and begins bearing off by moving 16/22, 23/off.

Roll 13 for X
X to Play 5–5
(O 6–2 16/22, 23/off)

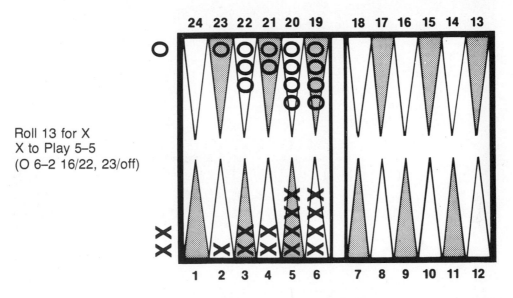

Doubles can be especially effective in the bear-off process. X correctly takes his four 5's off the five point: 5/off (4).

Roll 14 for O
O to Play 6–5
(X 5–5 5/off [4])

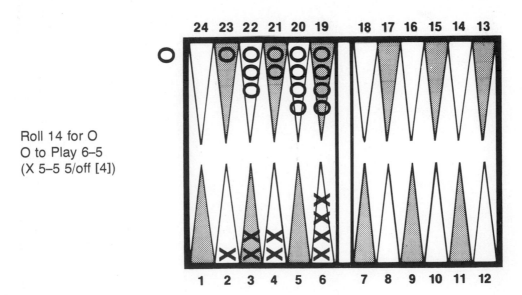

O moves 19/off, 20/off.

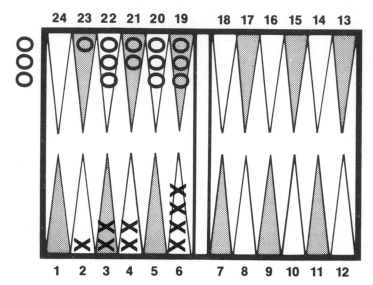

Roll 14 for X
X to Play 6–1
(O 6–5 19/off, 20/off)

X correctly plays 6/off, 6/5. Since X cannot take any men off with the 1, he moves a checker to an empty point so as to increase the possible number of bear-offs on the next roll. When you cannot take a checker off, try to fill up gaps.

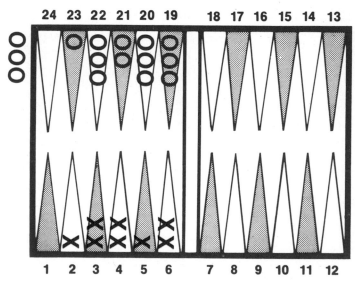

Roll 15 for O
O to Play 3–3
(X 6–1 6/off, 6/5)

O plays 22/off(3), 19/22. After taking three men off the twenty–two point, the fourth 3 is played to fill the empty point, or gap.

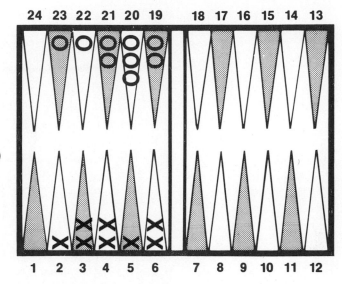

Roll 15 for X
X to Play 4–3
(O 3–3 22/off [3], 19/22)

X plays 4/off, 3/off.

In the next five moves, each player bears off as many men as possible. Diagrams are omitted until Roll 18 for X.

Roll 16 for O: O rolls 5–4. O plays 20/off, 21/off.
Roll 16 for X: X rolls 6–3. X plays 6/off, 3/off.
Roll 17 for O: O rolls 5–2. O plays 20/off, 23/off.
Roll 17 for X: X rolls 6–2. X plays 6/off., 2/off.
Roll 18 for O: O rolls 5–4. O plays 20/off, 21/off.

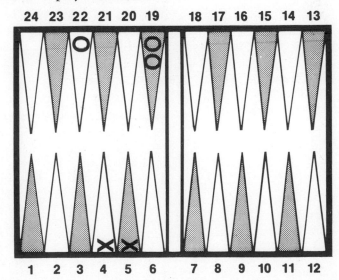

Roll 18 for X
X to Play 6–1
(O 5–4 20/off, 21/off)

Remember that if a player rolls a number higher than the furthest point from "off" on which a checker rests, the checker on the *next-highest* point must be taken off instead.

X plays 5/off, 4/3. By moving the last checker to the three point, he insures getting off on his next turn since any roll will be sufficient to do so.

In order for O to win now, he must bear off all three of his men on this roll. This can only be done with 6–6.

Roll 19 for O
O to Play 5–4
(X 6–1 5/off, 4/3)

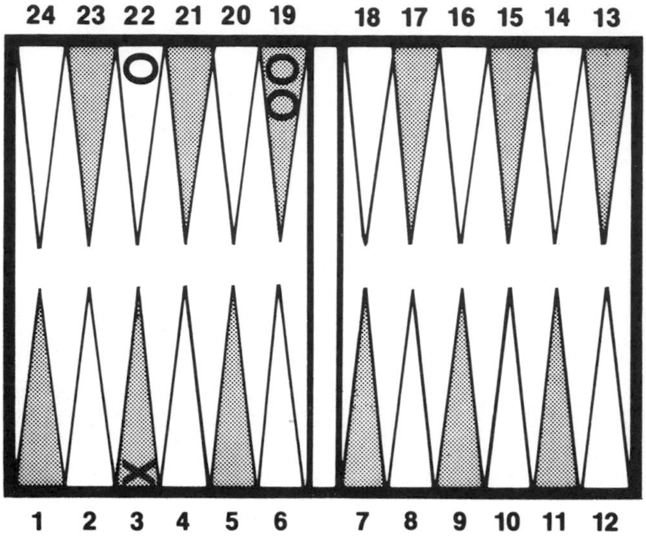

Unfortunately, O does not roll the needed 6–6. Having failed to do so, he would actually concede the game now. However, we shall play out the move to make the bear-off rules clear.

O moves 19/24, 19/23. O may not use either the 5 or the 4 to bear the man off the twenty-two point, despite the fact that the twenty and twenty-one points are empty. In backgammon you must take the *full* number whenever possible. Only if there is no man on a higher-numbered point than the number rolled can you take a man off the next-lowest point than the number rolled. Here the 5 and 4 *must* be played from the nineteen point.

If O, on the other hand, had men only on the twenty-two point, then the 5–4 could be used to bear two men off.

Roll 19 for X
X to Play Anything
(O 5–4 19/24, 19/23)

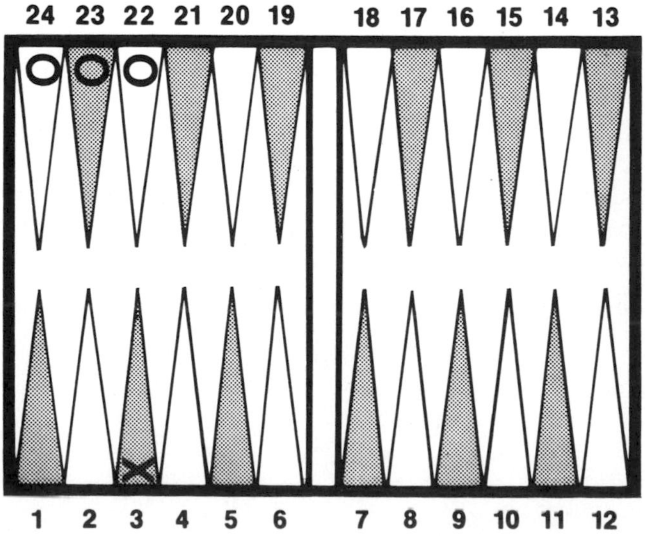

Any roll wins for X. He automatically bears off his last man and wins the game.

Game I — Summary of Ideas

Initial Strategy

A. Start to move your back men because they have the furthest to go.

B. Try to contain your opponent's back men.

Middle Game

A. Avoid being hit. Since backgammon is a race, men should never be exposed needlessly — any man hit loses ground in the race. The closer a man is to your home board, the more ground he has to lose, and the more careful you should be about leaving him exposed.

B. Try to hit your opponent. However, be aware of possible **return shots.** In particular, hitting in your home board and leaving a blot risks losing ground in the race if that blot is subsequently hit.

C. Direct vs. indirect shots: When leaving men exposed, try to leave them 7 or more pips away (an indirect shot) rather than 6 or less pips away (direct shot) from your opponent. In that way you considerably minimize your chances of being hit.

D. Taking strategic risks: The safest possible play is not always the most strategic play. For example, in Roll 4, X left his back man exposed to a direct shot in order to escape from O's inner board; in Roll 6, O left a man indirectly exposed so that he could make a vital point to block X in his inner board.

E. Making points: This is one of the chief objectives of the game (see Basic Checker Play, page 24, for hints on how to recognize when it is possible to make new points). By making points: 1. You bring men together, removing blots and making safe places for future men to land; 2. You block your opponent and hinder his movement — especially if you form several points in a row to form a blockade; 3. You hinder his re-entry in your inner board should he be hit. The more inner-board points you are able to close, the harder it will be for your opponent to re-enter.

Bearing Off

Try to bear off as many men as possible as soon as possible. If you cannot take a checker off, move to fill up gaps so that future rolls offer more opportunities to bear men off.

CHAPTER 5.
OPENING ROLLS

A KNOWLEDGE OF the standard opening moves and the reasons for making them is essential to mastering backgammon. If you are a new player, spend some time studying the opening moves. They should become second nature after several games.

For the more experienced player, alternate opening moves are possible and may be adapted according to the particular position. These alternate openings will be discussed at the beginning of Section III. The plays indicated here, however, may be used with confidence since they are in no way inferior to the alternates discussed later.

For convenience we will divide the opening rolls into groups.

Closing Strategic Points

The beginning of the game is essentially a two-fold struggle: extricating your back checkers and, by closing points on your side, trapping O's checkers. The order in which you close points to contain O is important. The most valuable points to close first are your *five* point, *bar* point (seven point), and *four* point in that order. The best opening rolls are those that enable you to make these points immediately: 3–1, 6–1, 4–2.

Position 1
(X 3–1 8/5, 6/5)

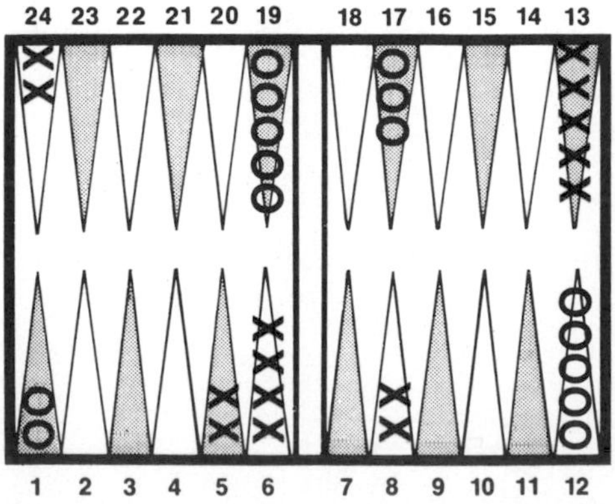

Position 2
(X 6–1 13/7, 8/7)

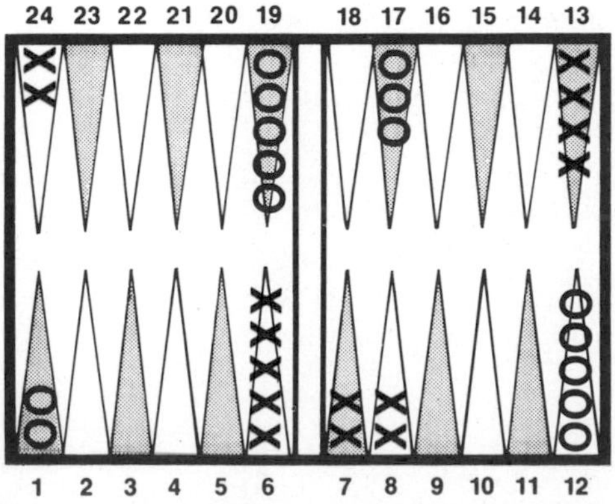

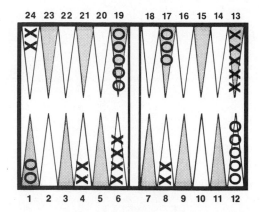

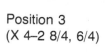
Position 3
(X 4–2 8/4, 6/4)

Bringing Checkers from the Midpoint as Builders

In order to increase the chance of forming these key points (five, bar, four), it is necessary to have spare men or **builders** to bear upon these points. Points do not form automatically; you have to work to make them. For this reason, the concept of builders is extremely important (Chapter 12 discusses this key concept in detail). The following group of moves enables you to bring checkers down from the midpoint (thirteen point of player moving the checkers) into the outer board as builders: 5–4, 4–3, 5–2, 5–3, 3–2.

Position 4
(X 5–4 13/8, 13/9)

Position 5
(X 4–3 13/9, 13/10)

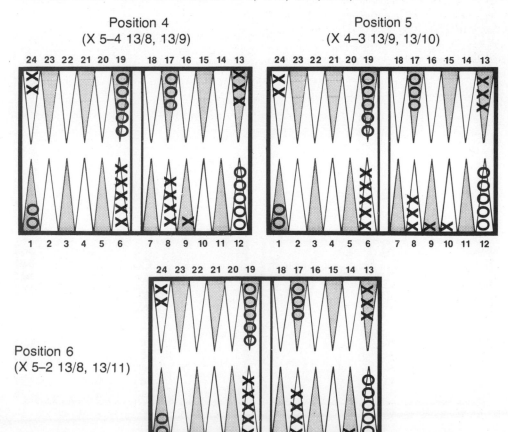

Position 6
(X 5–2 13/8, 13/11)

Position 7
(X 5–3 13/8, 13/10)

Position 8
(X 3–2 13/10, 13/11)

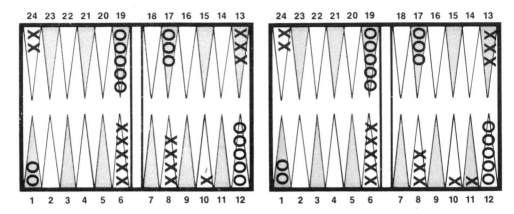

Note that 4–3, 5–3, 5–2, 3–2 could be played safely without leaving any blots. However, the value of the builders created by the indicated plays more than offsets the danger of being hit by certain indirect shots.

5–3 could also be used to make the three point. However, despite the importance of making points in your home board, deep points — namely the three, two, and especially the one — are not effective in blocking opposing checkers unless the intervening four and five points have already been made. Closing these deep points takes checkers out of play that may be used more constructively elsewhere.

Running with One Back Man

The third group of rolls does not enable you to safely make useful points or create builders, use them to begin to extricate your own back men: 6–5, 6–4, 6–2, 6–3.

Position 9
(X 6–5 24/13)

Position 10
(X 6–4 24/14)

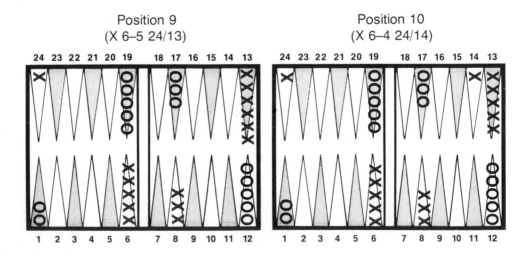

Position 11
(X 6–2 24/16)

Position 12
(X 6–3 24/15)

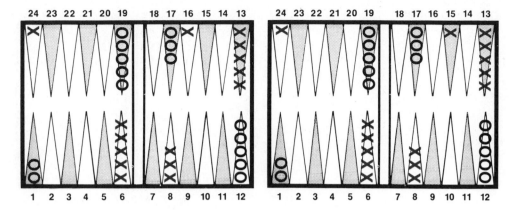

With each of these moves you run a back checker to O's outer board. The 6–5 move goes to the midpoint. There is no safe way to play the other numbers, but, if the checker escapes being hit, you will have only one checker remaining in O's home board.

Although 6–4 could make the two point, this is definitely inadvisable since the two point is too far advanced to have much blocking potential.

Creating a Builder and Splitting Your Back Men

In this last group you play the higher number from the midpoint into your outer board and split the back checkers by moving one of them to the twenty-two point. Splitting the back checkers facilitates their escape at small risk since O gains little by hitting on a point deep in his inner board: 4–1, 2–1, 5–1.

Position 13
(X 4–1 13/9, 24/23)

Position 14
(X 2–1 13/11, 24/23)

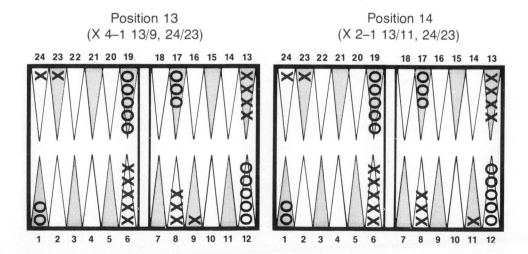

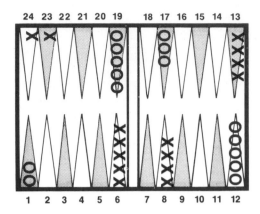

Position 15
(X 5–1 13/8, 24/23)

Rolling Doubles

Since play begins with each player rolling one die, and ties are re-thrown, doubles can never be the opening roll of the game. The standard first moves for double rolls are listed below. Bear in mind that variations may have to be used, depending upon your opponent's opening move.

6–6: Close your opponent's bar point and your own bar point.

5–5: Move two checkers from your midpoint to the three point.

Position 16
(X 6–6 24/18 [2], 13/7 [2])   Position 17
(X 5–5 13/3 [2])

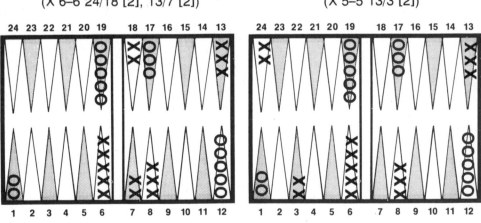

4–4: Close the twenty point and the nine point.

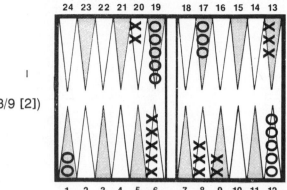

Position 18
(X 4–4 24/20 [2], 13/9 [2])

The twenty point (O's five point) has tremendous defensive value for you. It is probably the single most important point in the game. Controlling this point gives you a measure of security throughout the game by providing you with a direct shot at any blot in your opponent's outer board, by making it difficult for your opponent to block these checkers behind a prime, and by providing you with a secure entry point should you be hit.

3–3: Close the twenty-one point and the five point. The twenty-one point has a strategic value similar to the twenty point.

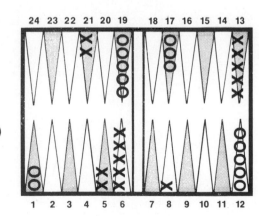

Position 19

(X 3–3 24/21 [2], 8/5 [2])

2–2: Close the twenty point. Another strong play would be to close the eleven and four points.

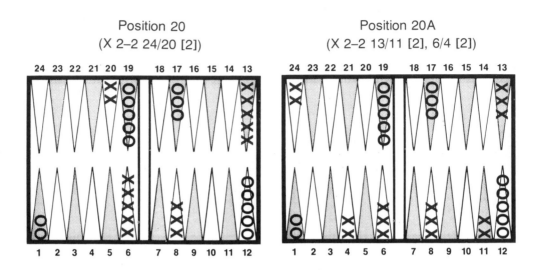

Position 20
(X 2–2 24/20 [2])

Position 20A
(X 2–2 13/11 [2], 6/4 [2])

1–1: Close your bar point (seven point) and five point.

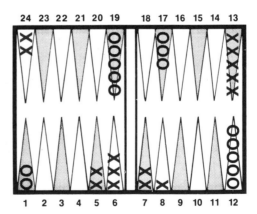

Position 21
(X 1–1 8/7 [2], 6/5 [2])

CHAPTER 6.
GAME II: HOLDING GAME

GAME II IS an example of a different type of game from a running game — a **holding game.** A holding game is characterized by holding a point or points in your opponent's inner and/or outer boards, hoping to hit him as he comes home. Unlike the running game, in a holding game a player can be way behind in the race and still win.

Roll 1
X 6, O 4, X to Play 6–4

X has won the first roll and has a 6–4 to play. What is your move?

X moves 24/14 as seen in Roll 2 for O, escaping with one of his back men but leaving that man exposed to a direct 2-shot.

Roll 2 for O
O to Play 3–1
(X 6–4 24/14)

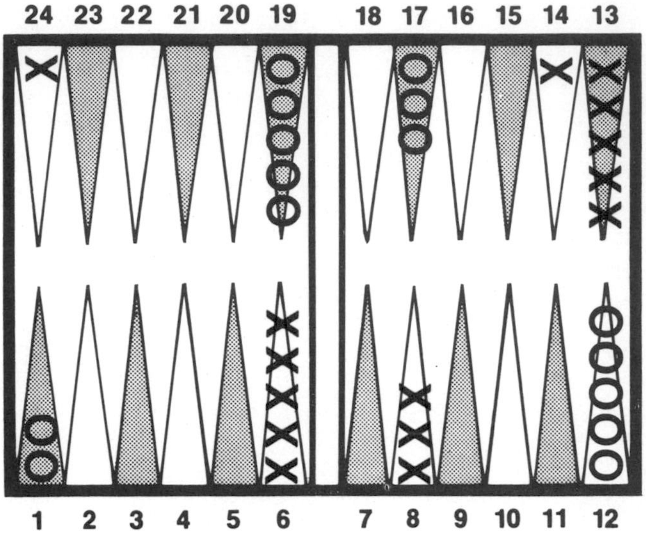

It is now O's turn. O chooses to make the key twenty point (O's five point) 19/20, 17/20. He would have liked to hit X but is unable to.

Roll 2 for X
X to Play 6–2
(O 3–1 19/20, 17/20)

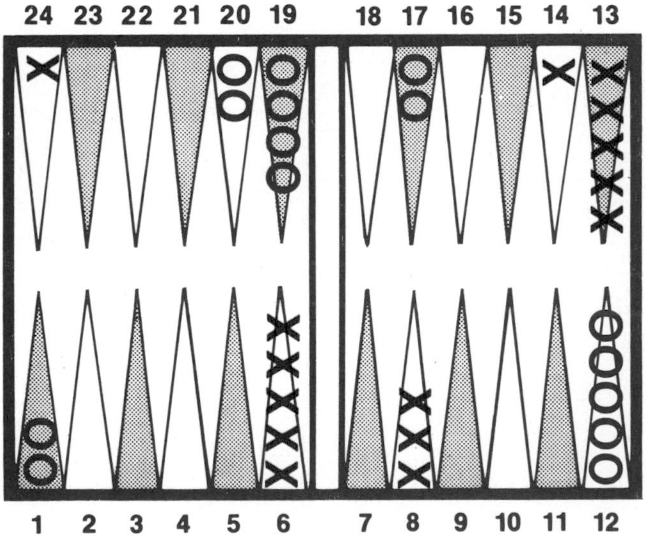

X moves 14/8, bringing his blot to safety, and 24/22 to begin moving the remaining back man out of O's inner board. Another good alternate move would be 14/8, 13/11, safetying the blot and bringing a builder down from his midpoint. This builder greatly increases X's chance of making the five or bar point.

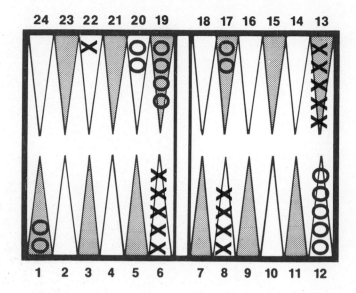

Roll 3 for O
O to Play 6–3
(X 6–2 14/8, 24/22)

O moves 1/10, trying to run. Hitting X on the twenty-two point is not advisable since X would then have a return shot which would send the O checker all the way back to X's inner board.

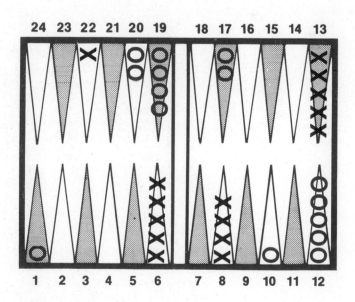

Roll 3 for X
X to Play 5–3
(O 6–3 1/10)

X moves 13/10*, hitting O's blot, and 13/8 bringing a man down safely from the midpoint.

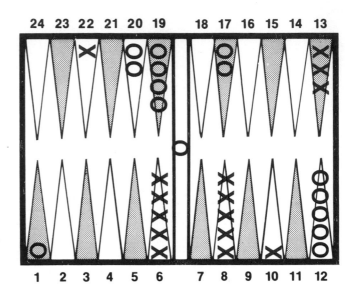

Roll 4 for O
O to Play 4–3
(X 5–3 13/10*, 13/8)

O moves bar/4, 1/4. This move brings in the checker from the bar, safeties both blots, and brings them closer to home. O has established a point in X's inner board called an **anchor**.

Whenever a player makes his opponent's four or five point, this is called making an **advanced anchor.** Holding such an advanced anchor is an extremely important strategic objective since it affords a great amount of protection and security. The importance of such a point is underscored by the fact that it is preferable even to the player's own four or five point. (Throughout Section III, particularly Chapter 20, we discuss the strategic importance of the advanced anchor.)

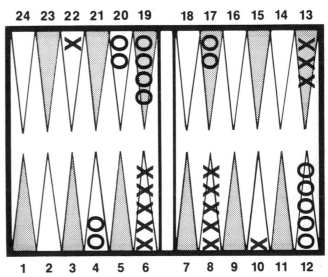

Roll 4 for X
X to Play 6–6
(O 4–3 bar/4, 1/4)

X moves 22/10, 8/2(2).

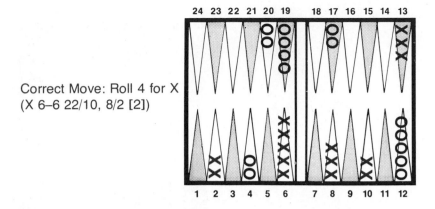

Correct Move: Roll 4 for X
(X 6–6 22/10, 8/2 [2])

X escapes completely from O's inner board and makes a new point in his own inner board. By making the ten point, you make it harder for O to escape his back men from the four point. As a general rule, if your opponent has a point in your inner board, the single most effective blocking point is the one which is 6 (or sometimes 5) pips in front of the opponent-held point.

Alternate Move #1 — 22/10, 13/1 — is also safe but does not make an inner-board point.

Alternate Move #2 — 22/10, 13/7(2) — makes the valuable bar point, which will serve as an effective landing spot to bring X's remaining checker home safely. The drawback in making this play is that it leaves X exposed to a direct 1-shot.

Alternate Move 1: Roll 4 for X   Alternate Move 2: Roll 4 for X
(X 6–6 22/10, 13/1)   (X 6–6 22/10, 13/7 [2])

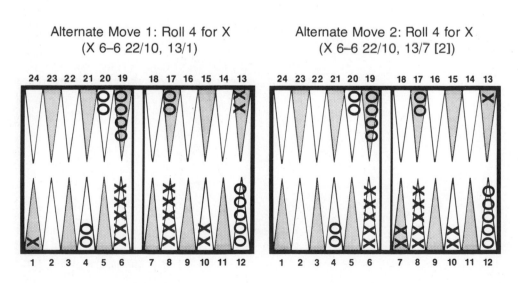

Before continuing Game II, let's assess the position. X has escaped both his back men and is ahead in the race because of the 6–6 he rolled. If X can come the rest of the way home safely, he will win the game. O's only chance is to hold X's four point and hope that X will have to leave a blot for O to hit.

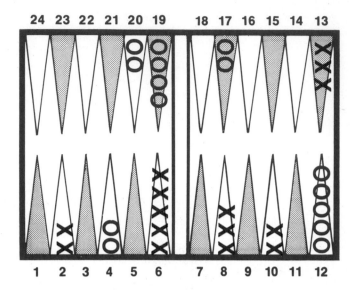

Roll 5 for O
O to Play 4–2
(X 6–6 22/10, 8/2 [2])

O moves 17/21, 19/21, making the valuable twenty-one point. According to the game plan outlined above, O hopes to get the chance to hit a shot. In preparation for this, he wants to rapidly close as many points in his own inner board as possible.

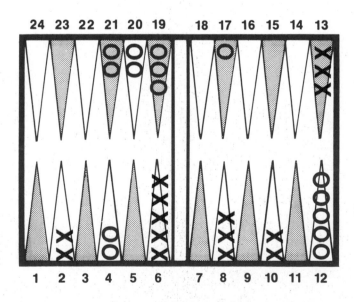

Roll 5 for X
X to Play 6–5
(O 4–2 17/21, 19/21)

X moves one checker 13/2. He does not want to leave any shots for O. X brings a man down from the thirteen point in preparation for **clearing** (removing all the checkers from) this point.

An alternate move for X is 8/2, 6/1. This is also safe but leaves an extra man on the thirteen point.

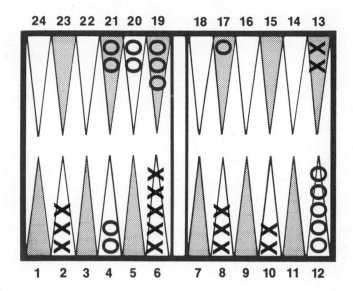

Roll 6 for O
O to Play 6–2
(X 6–5 13/2)

O moves 12/18, 12/14, bringing two builders down in preparation for making the bar point or another **inside point** (a point in his inner board). Note that despite O's three blots there is no danger involved in this move since X is not in a position to hit any of these blots.

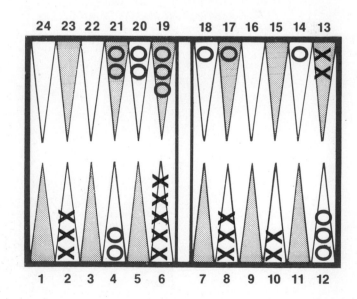

Roll 6 for X
X to Play 5–1
(O 6–2 12/18, 12/14)

X correctly moves 6/1, 2/1. X would like to make the five point with 10/5, 6/5, but this would leave him exposed to a direct shot. Similarly, bringing a man down from the midpoint with 13/8 would leave the remaining man on the midpoint exposed.

66   *Basics*

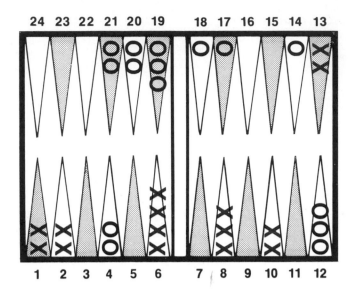

Roll 7 for O
O to Play 6–5
(X 5–1 6/1, 2/1)

O moves 17/23, 18/23, making another inner-board point and still hoping to hit X. Every new point closed in his inner board makes the position more perilous for his opponent since re-entry from the bar becomes more difficult. Remember that O's basic strategy at this time is to prevent X from getting home safely since O is behind in the race.

By remaining on the four point and twelve point (O's midpoint), O makes it hard for X to avoid leaving a shot as he comes home. For this reason O is playing a "holding game."

O has no guarantee that his holding game will be effective. X may be able to get home without leaving any shots, or X may leave a shot which O might miss. In some cases a well-played holding game will be an overwhelming favorite to win. In the present game O should not be considered a favorite, but nevertheless he pursues his most rational method of winning. It is important to play correctly in poor positions, giving yourself every possible opportunity to win.

An alternate move for O would be 12/18, 12/17.
This move would give O five consecutive points, a strong position. However,

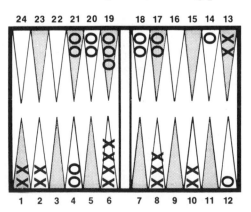

Alternate Move:
Roll 7 for O
(O 6–5 12/18, 12/17)

O would be giving up his midpoint and leaving a checker exposed to a direct shot in the process.

The midpoint has strategic value in itself which is often overlooked. In this holding game O's midpoint helps restrain the men on X's midpoint. If X wishes to move his last two men off the midpoint, he must wait until he rolls a number that enables him to bring *both* men down simultaneously; a single man left on the midpoint would be exposed to a direct 1-shot.

On the other hand, if O did not own his own midpoint, X would be able to clear his midpoint one checker at a time, leaving himself exposed to only an indirect 9-shot from O's checkers on the four point. O's midpoint has much more holding power than would appear since the majority of rolls do not permit X to safely bring both his men down simultaneously.

Roll 7 for X
X to Play 2–2
(O 6–5 17/23, 18/23)

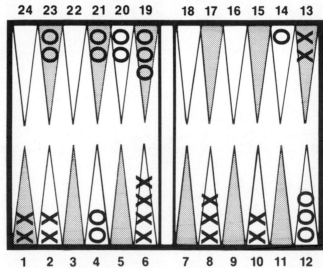

X moves 13/9(2), clearing his midpoint and further blocking O's back men. Owning the nine and ten points most effectively blocks the men on the four point.

An alternate move would be 13/11(2), 10/8(2).

Alternate Move:
Roll 7 for X
(X 2–2 13/11 [2], 10/8 [2])

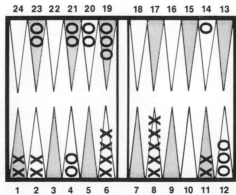

This play also clears the midpoint but does not effectively block O's men. However, in this position, with X ahead in the race, X is more concerned with bringing his men home safely than blocking O. For this reason the alternate move would be superior in an actual game; we use the inferior roll here simply to illustrate holding-game tactics.

Roll 8 for O
O to Play 4–3
(X 2–2 13/9 [2])

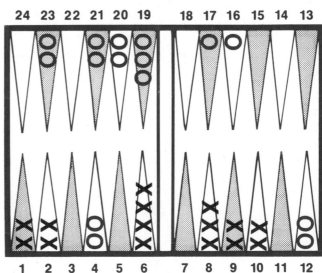

O moves 12/16, 14/17. O next wants to make the twenty-two point, so he brings two new builders to bear upon this point.

Roll 8 for X
X to Play 6–2
(O 4–3 12/16, 14/17)

X moves 10/2. This is an unfortunate roll for X because there is no way he can avoid leaving a direct shot. When merely trying to get home safely, you should clear your points starting with the outermost ones first and working down to avoid leaving gaps. Since X has to leave a shot anyway, he takes this opportunity to begin to clear the ten point.

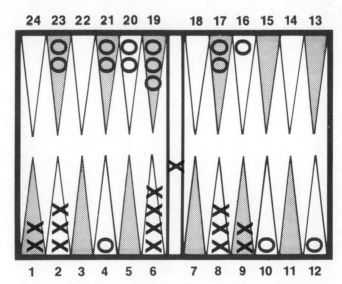

Roll 9 for O
O to Play 6–5
(X 6–2 10/2)

O jubilantly moves 4/10*, hitting X's blot, and 12/17, covering the seventeen point.

Despite the fact that enormous skill and complex decisions are involved in backgammon, many positions come down to the luck of hitting or missing a single shot. Thus the greatest players may be subject to unfortunate rolls, while the new player can defeat a more experienced player if he rolls the right numbers. This is one reason that backgammon is such a fascinating game; unexpected changes of fortune can affect the best players, although careful play can reduce the possibilities for disaster.

Roll 9 for X
X to Play 5–2
(O 6–5 4/10*, 12/17)

The symbol ø means that X can't move. Both the twenty-three and twenty points are covered so that X cannot re-enter with his roll of 5–2. X's checker remains on the bar, and X forfeits his turn since he is not permitted to make any other move until he has re-entered all his men.

In addition to being lucky in hitting X, O's last few moves have paid off. He had carefully built up his inner board in preparation for such a possibility.

Roll 10 for O
O to Play 3–3
(X 5–2 φ)

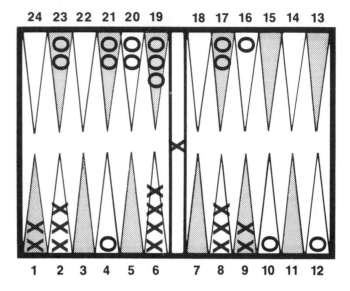

O moves 16/22, 19/22, covering the twenty-two point, and 17/20 bringing a builder in to bear upon the last open point (the twenty-four point). X now must roll a 1 to re-enter.

Again we point out how rapidly the game has changed. Two rolls ago, X was far ahead in the race, with matters seemingly well in hand. Now X is in a desperate position on the bar against a 5-point board, and even if he does re-enter he will be behind a 5-point prime.

Backgammon is much more than a simple racing game: It is a game of position and strategy. As we study Games III and IV, we shall see other game plans for winning besides merely getting ahead and staying ahead in the race.

Roll 10 for X
X to Play 3–1
(O 3–3 16/22,
19/22, 17/20)

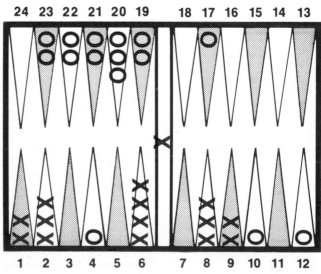

X moves bar/24, 6/3. The 1 enables him to re-enter, and he plays the 3 safely behind O.

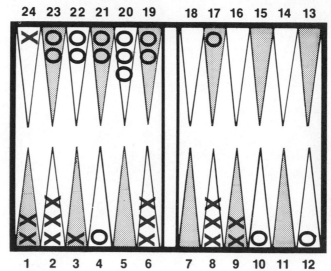

Roll 11 for O
O to Play 4–2
(X 3–1 bar/24, 6/3)

O moves 20/24*, 17/19. Here O takes a calculated risk in hitting X. It is true that X may re-enter with a 1 on the twenty-four point, sending O's blot all the way back to X's inner board. However, the odds are that X will not roll a 1, and O will then be able to close the sixth point in the inner board, completely shutting X out. This move also denies X the chance of rolling a 6, escaping from behind the prime and getting back into a winning race.

When examining the risks involved in being hit, you should not only consider the danger of losing ground in the race but also the danger of possibly failing to re-enter. In this case, X has only 3 points closed (O has 5), so O can be much more confident about re-entering should he be hit. Moving 17/19 brings another builder to bear directly on the twenty-four point; if X fails to re-enter, O can cover the point with a direct 5.

Since the nineteen point is closed, X fails to re-enter.

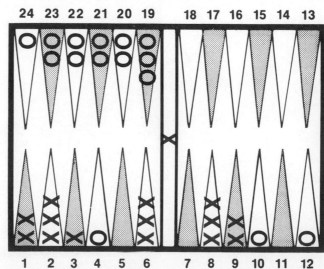

Roll 11 for X
X to Play 6–6
(O 4–2 20/24*, 17/19)

Roll 12 for O
O to Play 5–1
(X 6–6 Ø)

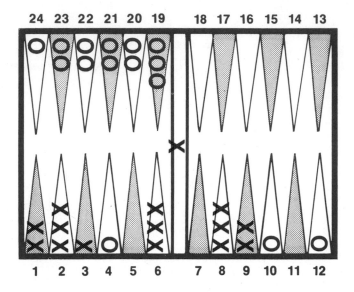

O moves 19/24, closing his board, and 4/5, bringing his last back man closer to freedom. At this point O continues rolling since there is no possible way for X to re-enter as long as all 6 inner-board points are closed. When O breaks one of these points, X may roll.

Roll 13 for O
O to Play 2–1
(O 5–1 19/24, 4/5)

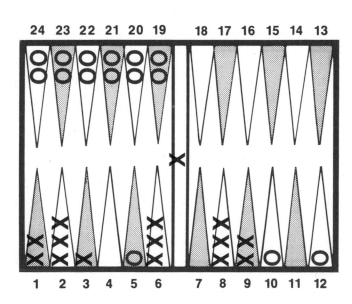

O moves 5/7, 12/13 bringing his men closer to home.

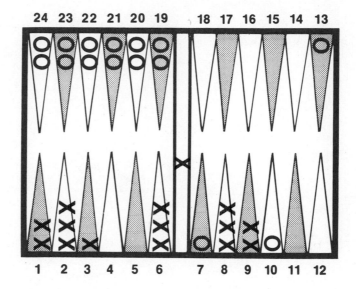

Roll 14 for O
O to Play 6–6
(O 2–1 5/7, 12/13)

O moves 7/19, 13/19, 10/16.

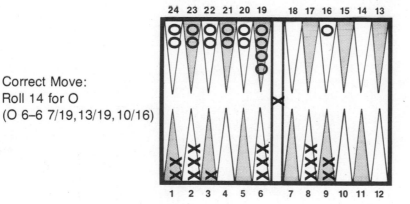

Correct Move:
Roll 14 for O
(O 6–6 7/19, 13/19, 10/16)

Let's stop for a moment to discuss the fundamental principles of bearing in and off *against opposition*, that is, when your opponent still has a man deep in your inner board or on the bar. In Game I we discussed the bear-off in a simple race, where the object was to bear off as *quickly* as possible; here we wish to bear off as *safely* as possible. Clearly, when your opponent is in a position to hit you, you do not bear a man off at every opportunity — especially if you must leave a blot to do so.

Here are some principles to follow:

1. Avoid leaving yourself vulnerable to "freak" doubles — doubles which force you to leave a shot. In the present position, if O rolls another 6–6, O will be forced to leave a shot after taking one man into his inner board and bearing three men off the nineteen point. There was nothing O could have done to avoid this on his previous roll. In many cases, however, a little extra precaution will keep your men safe from danger even if you roll high doubles.

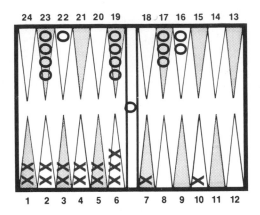

Position A
X to Play 1

In Position A, for example, if X has a 1 to play he should not play 7/6 or 10/9, either of which will force him to leave a man exposed to 6–6 on the next roll. The correct play is 6/5. Now 6–6 and all other rolls play safely. 6–6 followed by being hit may seem like a remote possibility, but there is no reason to risk it since playing safely costs nothing.

2. When bearing into your inner board, avoid going in "deep"; in other words, to the one, two, or perhaps three point.

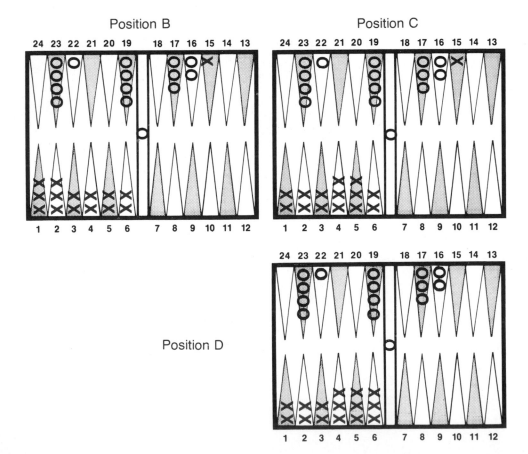

Position B

Position C

Position D

In Position B, X has brought two spare men deep to his one and two points. Although this position looks perfectly safe, it is much more dangerous than Position C, where X's two spare men are not deep.

By bringing men deep, you eliminate spare men. This hurts your flexibility and increases the chance for leaving a later shot. Position D is ideal, with spare men spread out on the high points.

3. When you bear off, clear your points in order beginning with points furthest from home. Don't leave gaps.

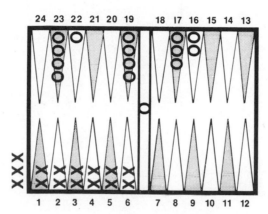

Position E
X to Play 5–3

In Position E the correct play is 6/1, 6/3.

4. Avoid leaving an isolated checker on your furthermost points. One way of doing this is to make sure that you have an *even* number of checkers on the highest points.

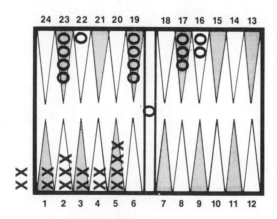

Position F
X to Play 5–2

In Position F you must not bear two men off 5/off, 2/off. This would leave a single spare checker on the five point and two high numbers on your next roll would force you to leave a shot.

The correct play is 5/off, 5/3. Remember that the object is to get off as safely as possible — not as quickly as possible.

Let's return now to the game.

Roll 15 for O
O to Play 6–4
(O 6–6 7/19,
13/19, 10/16)

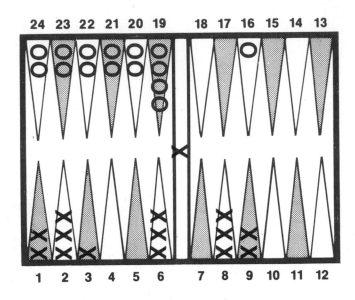

O moves 16/20, 19/off. This move allows him to safely play all future numbers and avoids going deep into his inner board. The alternate play 16/22, 19/23 would leave him with an isolated checker on the nineteen point.

Roll 16 for O
O to Play 6–3
(O 6–4 16/20, 19/off)

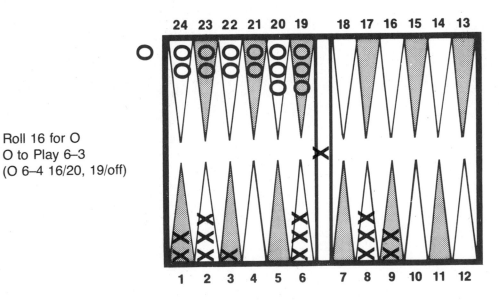

O correctly moves 19/off, 20/23. Remember that just because you may legally bear two men off in this position you are not obligated to do so if you can take another legal move. If O moved 19/off, 22/off, he would leave a blot on the twenty-two point.

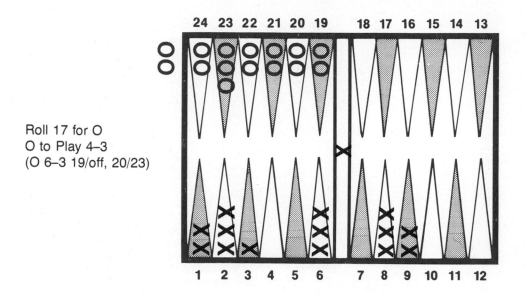

Roll 17 for O
O to Play 4–3
(O 6–3 19/off, 20/23)

O moves 19/23, 19/22. Again he wisely refrains from taking any men off and instead clears his points in order. He starts with the point furthest away from home — the nineteen point. Since this point is now open, X may finally take a roll.

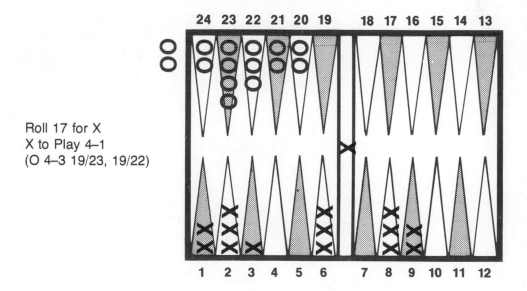

Roll 17 for X
X to Play 4–1
(O 4–3 19/23, 19/22)

X ø. Unfortunately, both the twenty-one and twenty-four points are closed and X cannot re-enter.

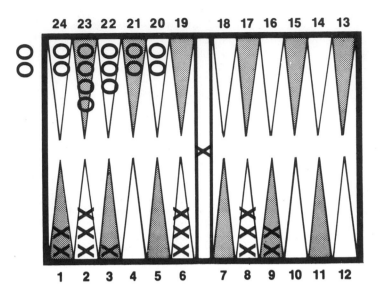

Roll 18 for O
O to Play 6–2
(X 4–1 Ø)

O moves 20/off, 20/22. This roll leaves him in an extremely safe position since he has an even number of checkers on the points furthest from home.

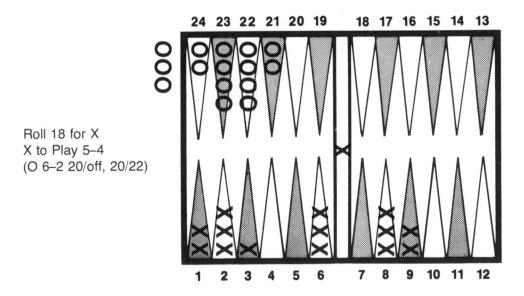

Roll 18 for X
X to Play 5–4
(O 6–2 20/off, 20/22)

X moves bar/16, successfully re-entering on the twenty point with the 5 and moving on to the sixteen point with the 4 in the race to get home.

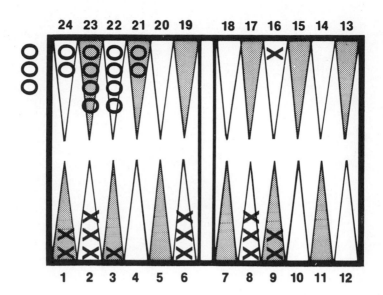

Roll 19 for O
O to Play 2–2
(X 5–4 bar/16)

O moves 23/off(4). Since the last opposing man has come in and is on the way home, O can begin bearing off expeditiously. This technique — bearing off without opposition — was described in Game I. O wants to bear off as many men as possible on each roll.

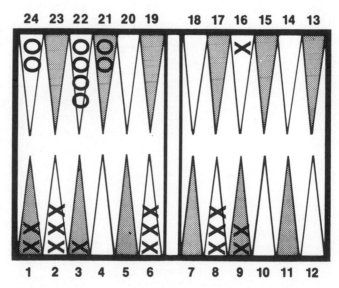

Roll 19 for X
X to Play 4–3
(O 2–2 23/off [4])

X moves 16/12, 9/6. X is clearly hopelessly behind in the race and has no chance to win. The game continues, however, to see whether or not X will lose a **gammon,** or double game. A gammon, you remember, occurs when a player bears off all his men before his opponent bears off any.

X cannot begin his bear-off until *all* his men are in his inner board. In order to avoid being gammoned, he must get his men home as quickly and as efficiently as possible. X should therefore use all his pips economically, taking them outside his home board and avoiding wasting them in his home board. He is trying to basically pile all his men up on his six point. If X played his 4 by moving 9/5 (or worse yet, 8/4), he would be using a pip or two inside his inner board that should be used outside.

Roll 20 for O
O to Play 3–1
(X 4–3 16/12, 9/6)

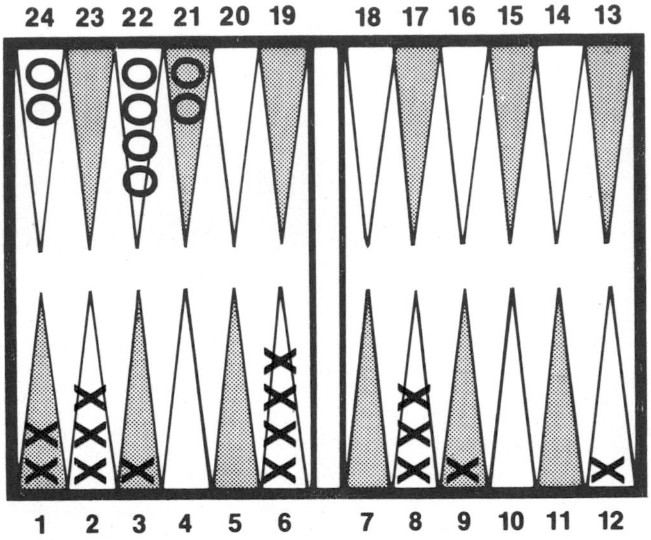

O moves 22/off, 24/off.

Roll 20 for X
X to Play 5–2
(O 3–1 22/off, 24/off)

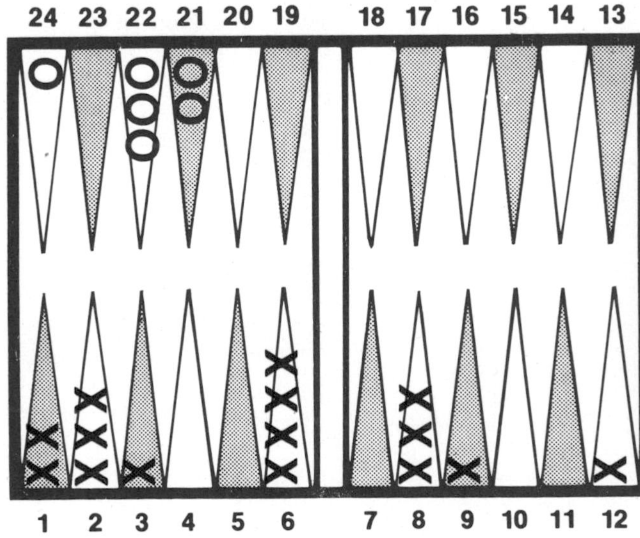

X moves 12/7, 8/6.

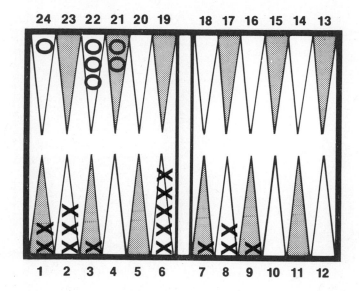

Roll 21 for O
O to Play 5–3
(X 5–2 12/7, 8/6)

O moves 21/off, 22/off.

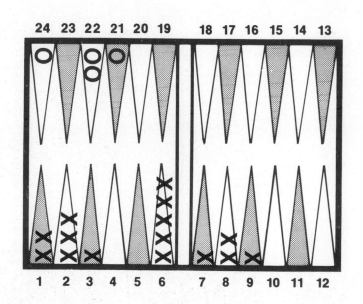

Roll 21 for X
X to Play 6–3
(O 5–3 21/off, 22/off)

X moves 9/3, 8/5. The race to save the gammon promises to be close.

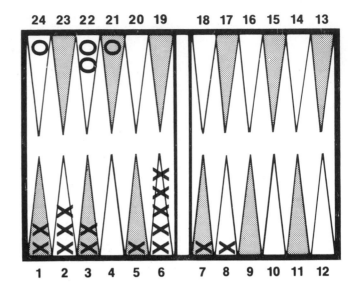

Roll 22 for O
O to Play 3–1
(X 6–3 9/3, 8/5)

O moves 22/off, 24/off.

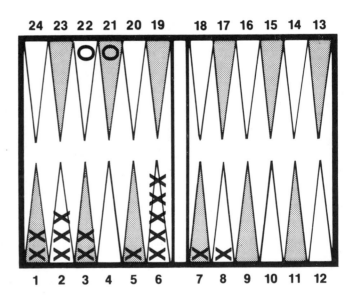

Roll 22 for X
X to Play 2–1
(O 3–1 22/off, 24/off)

X moves 7/4. This is a strategic play that may save X the gammon. By making the "normal" play of bringing both men in (8/6, 7/6 as seen below), X looks as if he is guaranteed to get a man off next roll, but a closer inspection reveals that 4–4 fails to take any men off.

By moving correctly 7/4, X will be able to remove a man on his next turn no matter what he rolls. That is, if he is given the opportunity to roll. O may be able to bear his two remaining men off immediately (the chances are almost even).

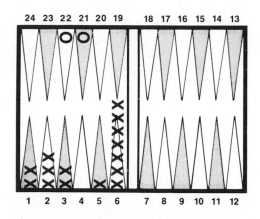

Alternate Move:
Roll 22 for X
(X 2–1 8/6, 7/6)

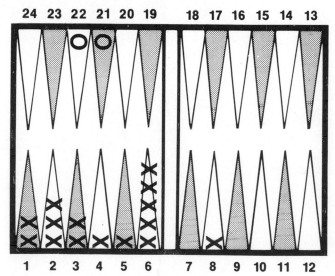

Roll 23 for O
O to Play 2–2
(X 2–1 7/4)

O moves 21/off, 22/off, winning the game and gammoning X!

Summary for Game II and Opening Moves

1. The best points on your side to own are, in order of importance, your five point, bar point, and four point. (When given the choice of making the bar point or five point, the five point is usually preferable.)

Although inner-board points are a threat to your opponent, it is usually not advisable to make the deep points (one, two, and sometimes three) too early in the game.

Points have more blocking value if they are made together, avoiding large gaps.

2. In order to make points quickly, it is essential to create builders to bear on the points you wish to make. Small risks (such as a few indirect shots) may be necessary to create builders.

3. It is of great value to establish an **advanced anchor** (your opponent's four or five point). Such a point is more important than any point you can make on your side of the board.

Beginners often make their opponent's two point. Although this gives you an anchor on which to re-enter, it is more difficult to escape from than the one point. Many games are lost by making the two point and never being able to leave it.

4. If your opponent has a point in your inner board, the single most effective blocking point is the one 6 pips in front of him. (This is another reason why it is wrong to make your opponent's two point. Since your opponent begins the game holding the eight point, you place yourself directly in front of the point that most effectively blocks you.)

5. Your midpoint has strategic value whenever you have men in your opponent's inner board, or on his bar point. If you are behind in the race, the midpoint may aid your holding game by making it harder for your opponent to extricate his back men and clear *his* midpoint. If you want to escape your own back men, the midpoint usually serves as the only safe landing space in the outer boards.

6. When bearing off against opposition (that is, when your opponent holds a deep point in your inner board, or is on the bar), you want to bear off as *safely* as possible. There are four principles to follow:

A. Avoid bringing your spare builders *deep* into your inner board. Leave them spread out on points further from home.

B. Begin by clearing your points in order, starting from the point furthest from home. By doing this you can avoid leaving gaps.

C. Avoid situations where two high numbers will force you to leave a blot. Do not leave a single spare checker on your furthermost points. This can be done by leaving an even number of checkers on the furthermost points.

D. Plan ahead, if possible, so that large doubles (usually 5–5 or 6–6) will play safely.

The bear-off will be discussed in more detail in Section IV.

7. There are two basic cases when you bear in without opposition: when you want to save the gammon, or when the game is a simple race.

A. Saving the gammon is the simplest case of bearing in because you try to bring your men in as quickly and efficiently as possible. You should not waste any pips in your inner board, but move them all in the outer boards. (Exception: Sometimes when only one roll remains, moving a pip in the inner board gives you a better chance to bear off on the next roll.)

B. In a race, although you are trying to bring your men in as quickly as possible in order to bear off, it is unwise to pile them all up on the six point. It is better to "waste" a few pips when bearing in in order to make sure that the four and five points have enough spare checkers. In this way, even if you lose a roll bearing your first man off, you will usually get your last man off quicker. A detailed discussion can be found in Section IV.

C. When bearing in, with or without opposition, you should try to maximize the number of **cross-overs.** A cross-over means moving a checker from one quadrant to another. Do this as efficiently as possible, moving 1 or 2 pips into the next quadrant, not 5 or 6.

CHAPTER 7.
BASIC DOUBLING STRATEGY

DOUBLING IS ONE of the most important and exacting aspects of backgammon. Good doubling decisions will often make the difference between winning and losing a series of games.

Let us review the rules:

The doubling cube starts out "in the middle." That is, either player may double whenever he feels he has a significant advantage. In doubling, he offers to double the stakes of the game by turning the cube to 2 and passing it to his opponent. The double must be made when the player is on roll, but *before* he has rolled the dice.

His opponent then has two options:

1. He may refuse (**pass**) the double and lose the original one unit, thus ending the game.

2. He may accept (**take**) the double, in which case the game continues with a value of two units — double the original stake.

The player who has been doubled is said to **own the cube,** which gives him the exclusive right to re-double should he feel at any time that *he* is the favorite. If he re-doubles, his opponent may pass, giving up the present stake of the game — two units; or he can take, playing on at the re-doubled stake of four units.

Re-doubling can, in theory, continue on forever, keeping in mind that only the player who owns the cube (the last player to have been doubled) may offer a re-double. Experienced players seldom re-double a game beyond the four or eight level.

Offering Doubles

The question of when you possess a sufficient advantage to warrant doubling is unanswerable in easy terms. The player owning the cube has a built-in advantage in that he alone may decide whether to make the next double. You should therefore avoid doubling with a trifling advantage, for this gives your opponent ownership of the cube (which can be a powerful weapon against you) too cheaply. On the other hand, you must have the courage to double when you have a solid lead.

The double may have two effects: First, it may force your opponent to pass, thus ensuring a definite win. Failure to double allows your opponent to play on "for free" and possibly get a lucky sequence of rolls to reverse the position and win the game. In such a case you have only yourself, not the dice, to blame.

Secondly, if your opponent takes, he is now faced with a loss of twice as much. Failure to double allows him to escape with a lesser penalty than he deserves. In backgammon there is no reward for such humane treatment — your opponent cannot be expected to extend the same courtesy to you.

Taking Doubles

Assume that you have been doubled. Unless your opponent has made a serious miscalculation, he is the favorite. Why, then, should you consider taking at all and playing on at a higher stake?

The answer is that by passing you give up a sure point, whereas by taking you may hope to turn the tide of the game and win two points yourself. Thus, if you have a reasonable chance to win, you are better off taking than resigning yourself to a sure loss.

What constitutes reasonable? One criterion often used is whether you have better than a 25% chance to win the game (Chapter 22 explains where this number comes from). However, except in a few well-defined endgame situations, there is no practical way of evaluating what the true odds of winning actually are.

Every position is different, so there is no easy formula for deciding what your practical chances are in a given position. In fact, many of the world's best players often disagree strongly about the merits of accepting certain doubles.

Gammon Possibilities

Sometimes your position will rapidly become so overwhelmingly strong that you have virtually no chance of losing and have an excellent chance of gammoning your opponent. In such a case, doubling would be a great error — because your game is *too* good. If you double, your opponent will quickly pass, giving you half what you would gain if you played the game out and gammoned him.

Gammon possibilities may also strongly influence your decision about whether to *accept* a double. Consider the case where you have a reasonable chance to win, but sense that you will be gammoned if you lose. In such a case, you must be far more careful in accepting, for you are risking losing not twice as much, but four times as much. (This is one reason why the 25% rule mentioned earlier for taking doubles is not always an adequate criterion.)

Conversely, when considering whether to double, if you have a significant chance to gammon your opponent but run little risk of being gammoned yourself, you may consider doubling earlier than usual. The ability to judge when a position involves a possible gammon comes with experience.

In sum, good doubling strategy goes hand in hand with a knowledge of the game — the ability to correctly assess positions and predict the game's resolution. As you play more and read further in this book, you will acquire an understanding of the underlying concepts of the game, which in turn will better enable you to assess your overall chances. We will resume the subject of doubling in more detail in Chapter 22.

Note: The question of when to double and when to take in a racing position is discussed in Chapter 10.

CHAPTER 8.
GAME III: PRIMING GAME

BACKGAMMON IS NOT just a game of running and hitting, but also very much a game of position. Game III illustrates the importance of blocking your opponent's back men.

The best way to block your opponent is to form several points in a row. Such a sequence of consecutive points is called a **prime.** Game III illustrates how blockading or priming your opponent can be an effective winning strategy. In particular, we emphasize the strength of a 6-point or full prime (6 points together in sequence).

As we saw in Game II, the player who takes an early lead in the race is not necessarily the winner. In fact, his lead may prove ultimately to be his undoing! For this reason, Game III also illustrates the strategic concept of *timing*. As you become more experienced, you will learn to evaluate not only the immediate position, but also the game's long-range evolution.

In Game III we introduce the doubling cube. You should begin playing with the cube in practice games. At first you may be unsure about when to double or take; however, as you gain experience and are better able to evaluate positions, you will gradually obtain a better understanding of when you possess a sufficient advantage to double, and, if doubled, whether you should accept or refuse the cube.

In the diagrams, the doubling cube is shown at first in the middle. This means that either player may, before he rolls the dice, offer the first double.

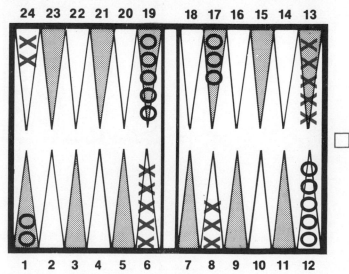

Roll 1
X 3, O 2, X to Play 3–2

X has won the first roll. The correct play is 13/10, 13/11, bringing two builders down from his midpoint.

Roll 2 for O
O to Play 6–1
(X 3–2 13/10, 13/11)

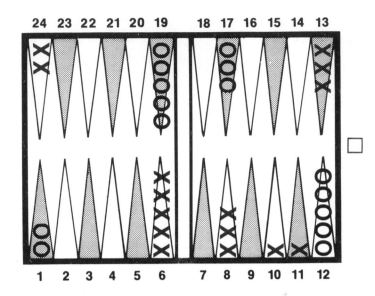

O moves 12/18, 17/18, making his bar point.

Roll 2 for X
X to Play 5–1
(O 6–1 12/18, 17/18)

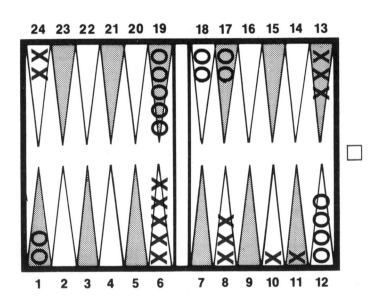

X moves 10/5, 6/5, making the five point. The five point is X's most valuable point on his side of the board. It is generally more valuable than the bar point. If X had rolled 6–1, with a choice of making either the five or bar point, the correct move would be to make the five point.

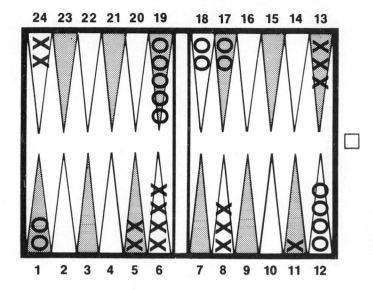

Roll 3 for O
O to Play 5–3
(X 5–1 10/5, 6/5)

O moves 12/17, 12/15, bringing two builders down to bear upon the twenty and twenty-one points (or O's four and five points). This move is preferable to making the twenty-two point (O's three point).

The alternate move 1/9 is too risky since this man would be exposed to a double shot.

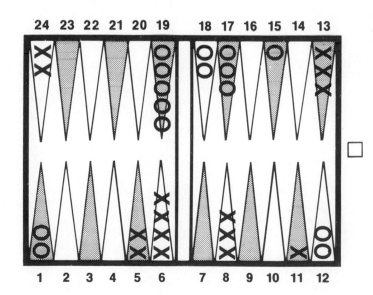

Roll 3 for X
X to Play 6–4
(O 5–3 12/17, 12/15)

This is another good roll. X moves 13/7, 11/7, making a point. Now X has four points in a row and is well on his way to effectively blocking and trapping O's back men.

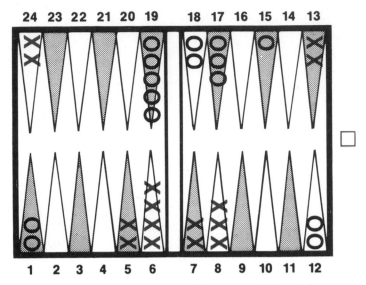

Roll 4 for O
O to Play 6–5
(X 6–4 13/7, 11/7)

O moves 12/18, 12/17. Ordinarily, on an opening roll, O would be able to move one of his back runners to safety on his midpoint 1/12, but X's blockade prevents this. The indicated play is the only way to move without exposing himself to a direct shot.

Backgammon is a game of position where big numbers in themselves are often not favorable. Here, O is forced to relinquish his midpoint, the twelve point. As a general principle, one should try to maintain this point — especially if there are still men trapped back in the opposing inner board. By giving up this point, the back runners become stranded from the other checkers and have no safe landing place in the outfield.

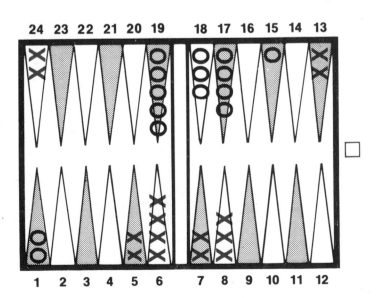

Roll 4 for X
X to Play 4–2
(O 6–5 12/18, 12/17)

X moves 8/4, 6/4, making the four point and constructing a 5-point prime.

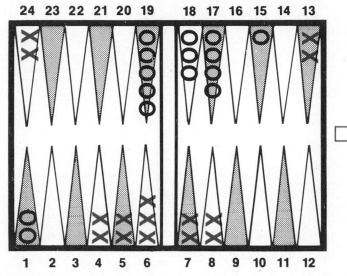

Roll 5 for O
O to Play 4–4
(X 4–2 8/4, 6/4)

O moves 17/21(2), 19/23(2), making 2 points in his inner board. The two point is not very desirable but is the best available. Once again, the value of large numbers per se is misleading; O must extricate his two back runners before racing numbers have any value.

X *doubles*; O *accepts the double*. While both X and O have the same number of points, X has a far superior position because he has 5 points together to form a solid prime. For reasons that will be clear in two or three moves, X has reason to believe that O's position will deteriorate.

The fact that X has doubled will be indicated on the diagrams by the cube's position on O's side of the board. After this initial double, O alone has the option of re-doubling.

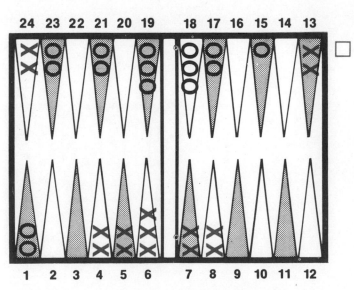

Roll 5 for X
X to Play 5–3
(O 4–4 17/21 [2],
19/23 [2])

X moves 6/3, 8/3 maintaining the 5-point prime while advancing further into his inner board. This further restricts O and also threatens to allow X to achieve a full 6-point prime by rolling a 5. The opportunity to construct a full prime is well worth the risk of being hit by a specific 6–1 (a 17-to-1 shot).

Roll 6 for O
O to Play 5–2
(X 5–3 6/3, 8/3)

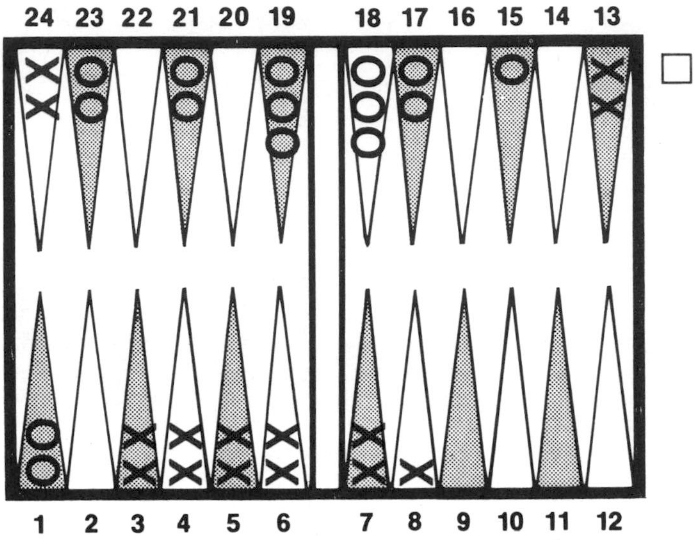

O moves 15/20, 18/20. This is an excellent roll giving O a 5-point prime.

Let us stop now and assess the position. Both sides have 5-point primes, so superficially the positions seem similar. Both X and O have back men seemingly trapped. Does this mean that the game will be a stand-off with neither player able to escape?

No! Both players must keep moving forward whether they like it or not until eventually their primes collapse. Who, then, will be able to maintain his prime longest?

The answer is that X will since he has two spare men on his midpoint to play with, whereas O is rapidly running out of moves. The men on X's midpoint give him *time* (timing often is the crucial factor in advanced play).

As you become more sophisticated in backgammon, you will learn to view

Roll 6 for X
X to Play 4–1
(O 5–2 15/20, 18/20)

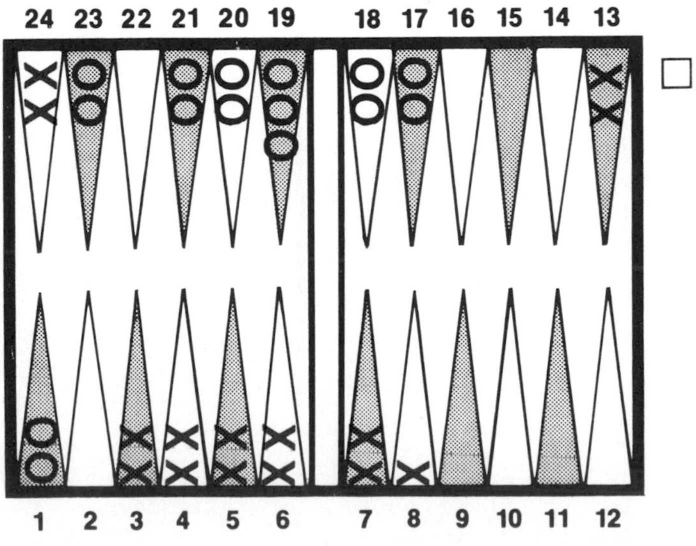

each position not as a static entity but part of a pattern that continually changes. When X doubled, he anticipated that time was on his side. O is ahead if the position is viewed as a race. However, it is precisely because O is ahead in the race that he has less time to maintain his prime. In such a position, *large* numbers on the dice are disadvantageous.

X moves 13/8 forming a full 6-point prime. Forming a 6-point prime is always your ultimate objective when trying to trap your opponent. As long as the prime remains intact, there is no possible way for O to bypass it, regardless of what he rolls. The only way to ever get past a 6-point prime is to wait until your opponent breaks it up.

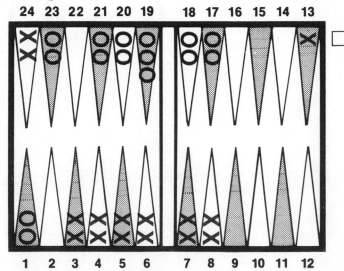

Roll 7 for O
O to Play 4–3
(X 4–1 13/8)

O moves 17/21, 17/20. The disintegration of his prime begins. O would, of course, rather not move at all, but the rules require every move to be played if legally possible.

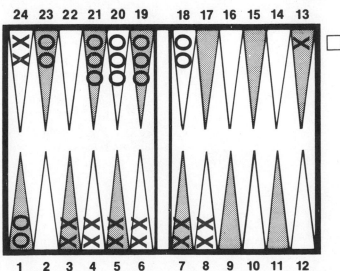

Roll 7 for X
X to Play 4–2
(O 4–3 17/21, 17/20)

X moves 13/9, 24/22. At first glance, this move may appear extremely reckless. O has countless ways to point on X's two blots. Why, then, does X take this chance?

The answer is that X has a full 6-point prime. X does not care whether he is pointed on or not. O can never escape his back runners, so he must continue moving his remaining men, even if it leads to his own self-destruction.

Roll 8 for O
O to Play 6–3
(X 4–2 24/22, 13/9)

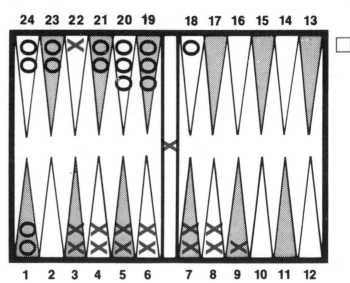

O moves 18/24*, 21/24 pointing on X.

Roll 8 for X
X to Play 5–2
(O 6–3 18/24*, 21/24)

X ∅; X fails to re-enter.

On Roll 9, O moves 18/22*, 20/22, pointing on a second blot. At this time, O has completely closed X out with two men on the bar. Ordinarily, closing one's opponent out allows for an almost certain win, as in Game II. Here, however, the close-out merely underscores the strength of X's 6-point prime and the futility of O's position.

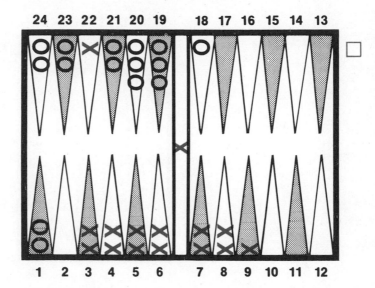

Roll 9 for O
O to Play 4–2
(X 5–2 Ø)

If you examine the position carefully, you will see that no conceivable set of rolls will allow O to escape his back runners. Since X is closed out, he cannot play and need not even bother rolling the dice. No matter what O rolls in the meantime, he will eventually be forced to open points in his inner board and allow X to come in. Remember that the rules do not allow O to bear any men off until *all* his men are in his own inner board.

O continues to roll.

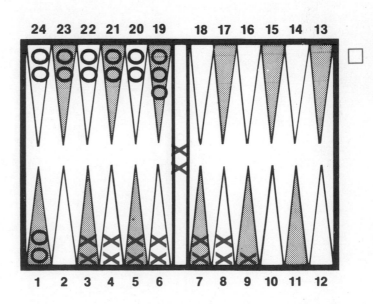

Roll 10 for O
O to Play 5–1
(O 4–2 18/22*, 20/22)

O moves 19/24, 1/2. O realizes his position is lost and begins to clear the point furthest from home first to avoid possibly exposing a man in his inner board. Allowing a third man to be sent back would increase the chance that he would be gammoned.

Roll 11 for O
O to Play 4–3
(O 5–1 19/24, 1/2)

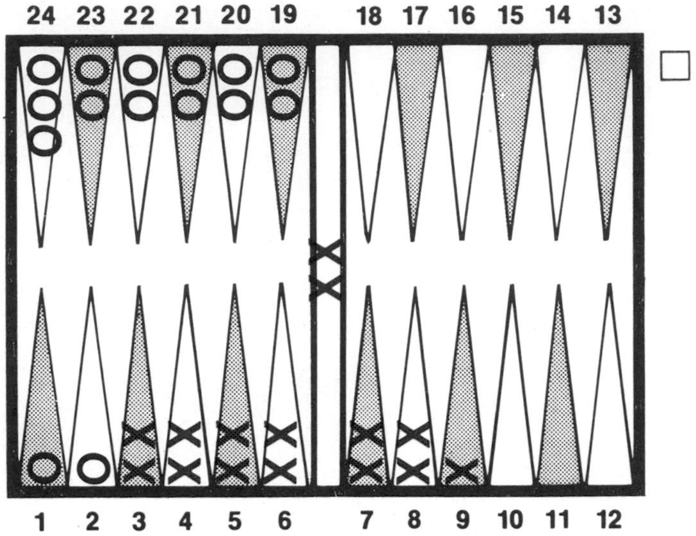

O moves 19/22, 19/23. He is forced to break a point in his inner board. This move illustrates a position that is commonly misplayed. When establishing points in the inner board, you try to make the points furthest away from home first. Nevertheless, when you are forced to break up your board, it is important to give up the points *in order* starting with those *furthest* away from home. In this position, O has the choice of clearing either the nineteen or twenty point; he correctly chooses to clear the nineteen point first.

X can now roll.

Roll 11 for X
X to Play 6–1
(O 4–3 19/22, 19/23)

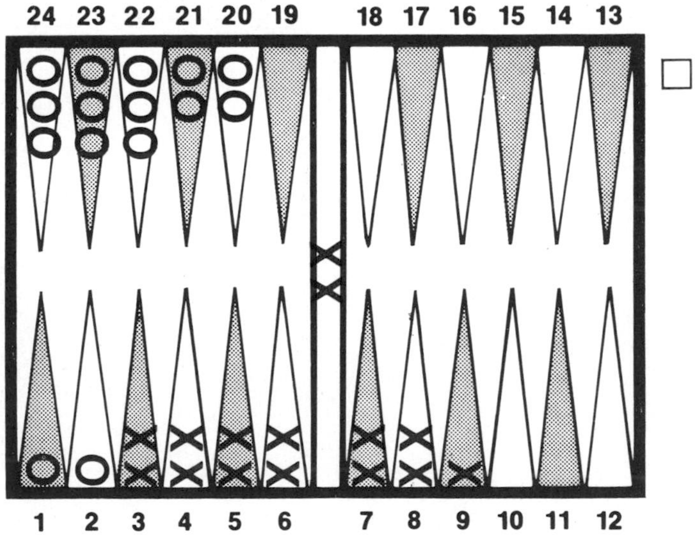

X moves bar/19, ø. He is forced to bring a man in on the nineteen point with the 6. X is unable to re-enter the second man with the 1, and he cannot legally take the 1 elsewhere.

Roll 12 for O
O to Play 6–4
(X 6–1 bar/19, Ø)

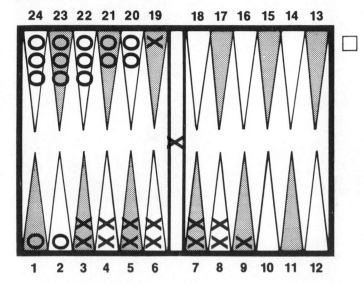

O moves 20/24, ø. The 4 is forced; there is no legal 6.

Roll 12 for X
X to Play 6–3
(O 6–4 20/24, Ø)

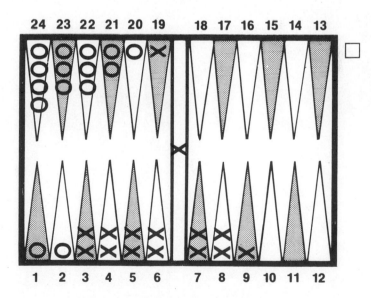

X moves bar/19, 9/6. X had hoped to roll a 5 hitting O's blot. X moves 9/6 to bring his spare checker into range to attack O's back runners.

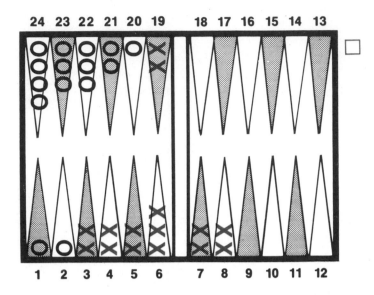

Roll 13 for O
O to Play 4–1
(X 6–3 bar/19, 9/6)

O moves 20/24, 1/2. Although he has little chance of winning the game, it is imperative that he bring his back men together for safety. If O leaves his back men exposed, he may be closed out — this would give X a definite chance to win a gammon. By maintaining the two point, O should avoid being gammoned.

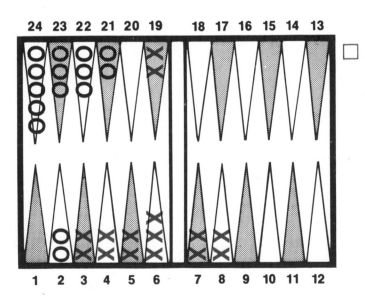

Roll 13 for X
X to Play 6–6
(O 4–1 1/2, 20/24)

X moves 19/7(2). These big doubles are not really advantageous since X is free to move his men around the board at his leisure. X's play is certainly sound and should lead to an easy win.

The more experienced and/or greedy player may wish to experiment with another play: 19/13(2), 7/1(2)!

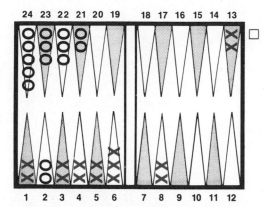

Alternate Move:
Roll 13 for X
(X 6–6 19/13 [2], 7/1 [2])

This trap play may appear foolish since X breaks his prime before he has to and gives O the chance to escape with a 5. Actually, X is setting a cunning trap: He *hopes* that O will come out with one 5. (Note that if O rolled one 5 he would have no choice but to emerge from the two point since he has no legal 5's elsewhere.)

Since O has destroyed part of his board, and since X now has a 5-point board, X hopes to lure O out and then pounce on his two defenseless blots. If X succeeds in picking up the two blots and closing O out, X will have greatly enhanced his chance for winning a gammon (four points, since the game has been doubled once).

Of course, this alternate strategy is not without some risk. O might come out with 5–5 and win the resulting race easily, or X might have trouble hitting and closing O out after a single 5. In either case, X may be jeopardizing a potentially won game for the added chance for a gammon. The expert would evaluate the net gain as worth the risk, but we shall pursue the game along the safer indicated path.

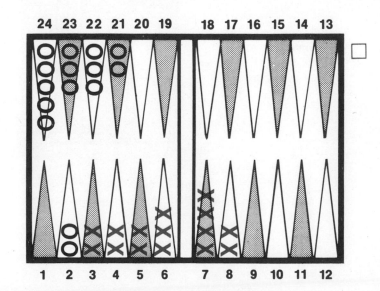

Roll 14 for O
O to Play 6–3
(X 6–6 19/7 [2])

O moves 21/24, ø.

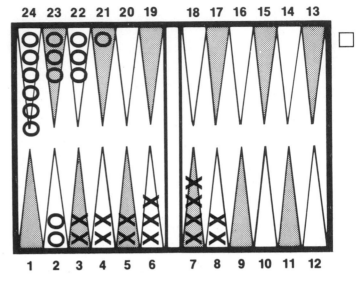

Roll 14 for X
X to Play 5–4
(O 6–3 21/24, ∅)

X moves 8/3, 8/4. X wishes to come home safely. The principles for bearing in safely when your opponent holds a point in your inner board are basically the same as those in bearing off:

1. Clear your points in order from the point furthest away from home, hoping to avoid leaving gaps.

2. Avoid, if possible, bearing your extra men in deep.

3. Avoid, if possible, bearing a single spare checker in on the point furthest away from home.

An alternate move would be 6/1, 7/3, which would maintain X's full prime one additional roll.

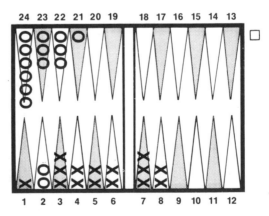

Alternate Move:
Roll 14 for X
(X 5–4 6/1, 7/3)

This move would leave a potentially dangerous position. Putting spare checkers deep on the three point and leaving a spare checker on the seven point is a possible source of trouble; 6–1, 6–3, 6–4, and 6–5, for example, would all force you to leave an exposed man. Even at this late stage in the game, care must be taken to bear in correctly and avoid accidents.

Roll 15 for O
O to Play 5–2
(X 5–4 8/3, 8/4)

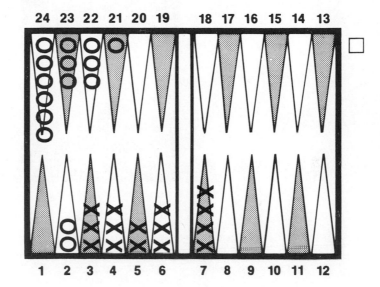

O moves 21/23, ∅.

Roll 15 for X
X to Play 6–4
(O 5–2 21/23, ∅)

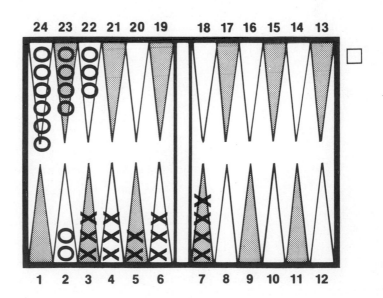

X moves 7/1, 7/3.

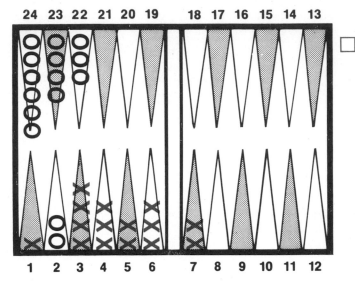

Roll 16 for O
O to Play 6–2
(X 6–4 7/1, 7/3)

O moves one checker 2/10, escaping from behind X's prime. Even if O escapes his second back man, he will find he has fallen far behind in the race.

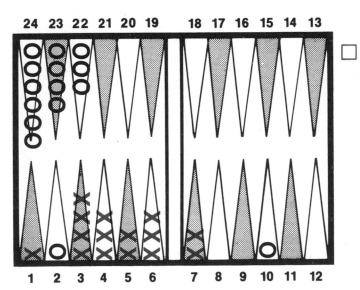

Roll 16 for X
X to Play 2–1
(O 6–2 2/10)

X moves 4/2*, 3/2. This is another play where care must be exercised. Let's look at the alternate moves.

First, X could have played 7/5, 7/6, as seen in Alternate Move #1.

This move, in preparation for bearing off, would give X a substantial lead (although a lucky 6–6 for O would bring O far ahead).

A second alternate move would be 4/2*/1, hitting and covering the one point without leaving a blot.

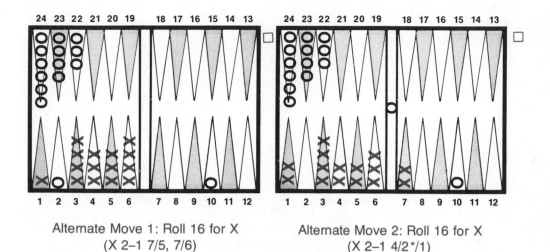

Alternate Move 1: Roll 16 for X
(X 2–1 7/5, 7/6)

Alternate Move 2: Roll 16 for X
(X 2–1 4/2*/1)

Playing 4/2*, 3/2 is recommended above these two alternatives. It gives O the least chance for a lucky win despite the blot on the one point. X has again reconstructed a full 6-point prime (from the two point through the seven point) and therefore need not fear being hit on the one point.

The key idea here is that even if O re-enters on the one point, his man can never escape and so X is in no danger. In fact, it is probably to X's advantage to have O re-enter on the one point so that X has a chance to come around again and possibly hit the blot now on the ten point. Such a series of events would give X good gammon prospects.

Roll 17 for O
O to Play 5–5
(X 2–1 4/2*, 3/2)

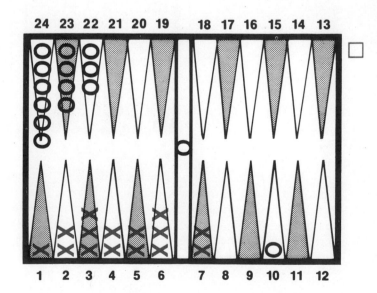

O ø.

Roll 17 for X
X to Play 6–2
(O 5–5 Ø)

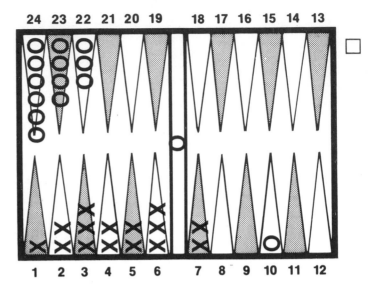

X moves 7/1, 7/5. O is closed out, and X continues to roll.

Roll 18 for X
X to Play 6–1
(X 6–2 7/1, 7/5)

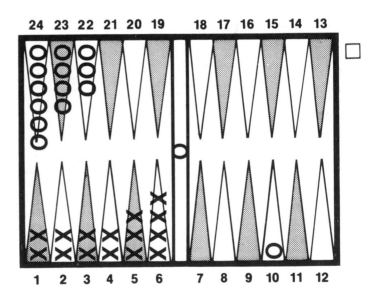

X moves 6/off, 5/4. Remember that when you bear off against opposition (opposition here being the O blot lurking on the bar), you do not remove your men as quickly as possible, but as safely as possible. X's play leaves him in a position where no roll can force him to leave a shot.

If X had carelessly played 6/off, 3/2, he would be left with a spare checker near the right-hand side of his board.

This move could potentially lead to trouble; a subsequent 5–5 or 6–6 would leave a shot.

Alternate Move:
Roll 18 for X
(X 6–1 6/off, 3/2)

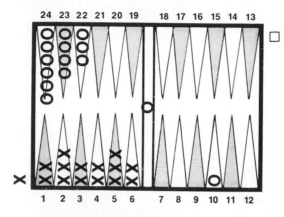

Roll 19 for X
X to Play 5–5
(X 6–1 6/off, 5/4)

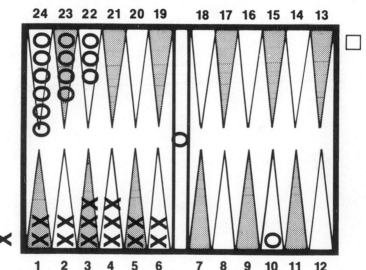

X moves 6/1(2), 5/off(2). Because he played his last move with care, X is able to safely play 5–5. Little sympathy should be extended to a player who played the alternate move on Roll 18 and was subsequently hit after leaving a blot on Roll 19. Such a player might bemoan his fate and declare how unlucky he is, but we can see that his pitfall can be prevented at no cost.

Occasionally, even with the best bear-off technique, you will lose a game because of an unfortunate sequence of rolls which forces you to leave a shot which is hit. It is, in fact, the potential for disaster in seemingly won positions that makes backgammon exciting. If you follow the rules for bearing off, however, you will have fewer tales of woe to tell.

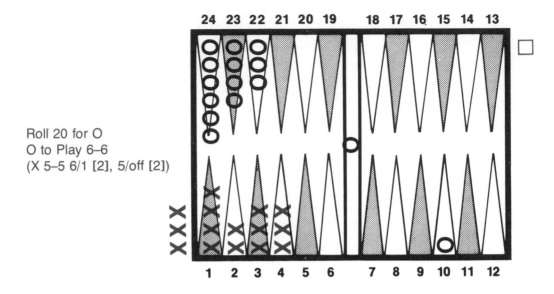

Roll 20 for O
O to Play 6–6
(X 5–5 6/1 [2], 5/off [2])

    O moves bar/18, 10/16. With this roll, any chance of O's being gammoned is eliminated. We leave the game now since the rest is a simple bear-off, which X should be able to win quite easily. Since X doubled the game earlier, X should win two points.

Game III Summary

    1. One of the basic objectives in backgammon is to block your opponent's forward progress and especially to trap his back men. This is usually done by forming points in a row, called a **prime**. The more points you own in a row, the more difficult it becomes for your opponent to bypass the blockade. A 5-point prime is extremely difficult to bypass, especially if your opponent is not directly in front of it (at the edge of the prime). Ideally, you wish to form a 6-point prime, a full prime. This is then impossible to bypass — any checker trapped behind a full prime must wait until the player possessing the prime dissolves it himself.

    The value of the full prime is underscored by the fact that the player owning it can afford to have some of his remaining men hit, and even closed out, without jeopardizing his game. (If you are unsure of the reason for this, review Game III to understand this important idea.)

    2. Often the only way to defeat a prime which you are trapped behind is to form your own prime to trap your opponent. The idea is to force him to break *his* prime first.

    3. When you have closed your inner board but are unfortunately forced to break it up, it is best to break the points furthest away from home first.

    4. When you have a commanding lead in the race and wish merely to come home safely, care must still be taken to bear in and off safely. You must exercise vigilance even in "won" positions to avoid unpleasant "accidents."

The principles for successful bearing in are basically the same as for bearing off:

  A. Clear your points in order beginning with the point furthest away from home in order to avoid leaving gaps.

  B. Avoid, if possible, bearing your extra men in deep.

  C. Avoid, if possible, leaving an isolated spare man on your point furthest away from home. Try to leave an even number of men there.

 5. Even when the game is hopeless, take care not to compound the loss by being needlessly gammoned. Conversely, even in positions where you are an almost certain winner, you should examine ways to increase your win with a gammon.

CHAPTER 9.
GAME IV:
ATTACKING GAME

THE FINAL SAMPLE game in Section I demonstrates another winning game plan: the **attack.** Some games of backgammon are long, protracted positional struggles, while others — such as this one — may be decided quickly by a series of sharp blows.

After finishing this game, you should review the basic winning methods in all four games (running, holding, priming, and attacking). It is never correct strategy to have one preconceived game plan; rather, you must be flexible and choose the best one as the position evolves. Familiarity with all four of these basic strategies will come with experience. Sections II and III will consider the criteria for selecting the proper game plan and the tactical means of carrying it out in more detail.

This game illustrates special advanced tactical plays which demonstrate that even in seemingly routine positions you must be careful to make the best play. It is not important to memorize all these plays at this time — later in the appropriate chapter the principles involved in each play will be more fully explained.

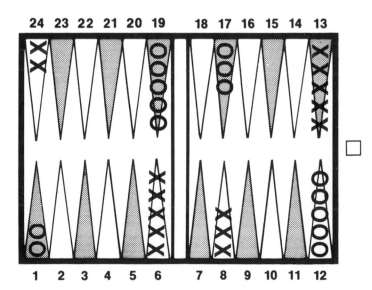

Roll 1
O 5, X 2, O to Play 5–2

O moves 12/17, 12/14.

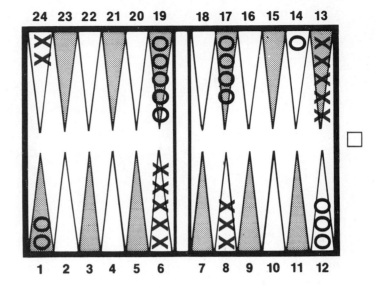

Roll 2 for X
X to Play 4–4
(O 5–2 12/17, 12/14)

X moves 24/20(2), 13/9(2). 4–4 allows you to make what is considered to be the strongest opening move: establishing your opponent's five point (the twenty point here). This is the single most important point for you to control in the middle game.

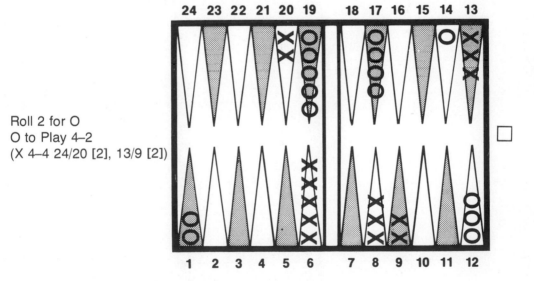

Roll 2 for O
O to Play 4–2
(X 4–4 24/20 [2], 13/9 [2])

O moves 1/5, 12/14. When your opponent holds a point in your inner board, the most effective blocking point is the one which is 6 pips in front of him (5 pips in front is also excellent). Since X has succeeded in making the twenty point, O rightly makes the fourteen point 12/14. Similarly, if X had made the twenty-two point, O would then make the sixteen point to block effectively.

Since X has made the valuable twenty point, O would like to equalize the position by making the five point. O therefore splits to the five point, 1/5, hoping to cover it on a subsequent roll. It is usually risky to come up to your opponent's four or five point when he has extra builders bearing on these points.

Roll 3 for X
X to Play 3–1
(O 4–2 12/14, 1/5)

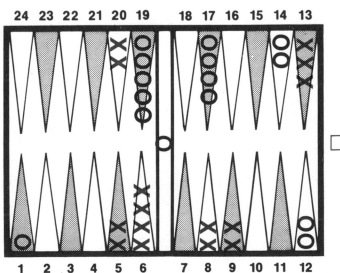

X moves 8/5*, 6/5. This excellent roll makes the important five point and also hits O's blot. X now controls both his five point and O's five point, and X has the beginnings of a good blocking position since he controls the five, six, eight, and nine points.

Roll 3 for O
O to Play 4–2
(X 3–1 8/5*, 6/5)

O moves bar/4, 19/21. Again O chooses the somewhat more dangerous line of play by re-entering on the four point rather than the two point. O realizes that the game has not been going very well for him, and his move bar/4 is a gamble to improve his standing. He hopes to make the four point on a subsequent roll and establish an advanced anchor in X's board.

O simultaneously slots a man on the twenty-one point 19/21. He wants to build up his inner board quickly in order to threaten X.

X, however, has no intention of letting O equalize the game. He decides to take advantage of his present superiority.

X *doubles!* This double demonstrates the tremendous variability of the game. Many games last a large number of moves — even going as far as the end of the bear-off — before one player possesses a sufficient advantage to double; in other games, as here, one side is able to double after only three moves.

O *accepts.* Although it is certainly understandable that O is reluctant to decline the double (and lose one point) in a game only three moves old, an experienced player would see that the position is very dangerous. O is exposed to a powerful attack and, if the attack is successful, will probably be gammoned. By accepting the double, then, O ultimately risks losing not one extra point, but three since if he is gammoned he will lose four points.

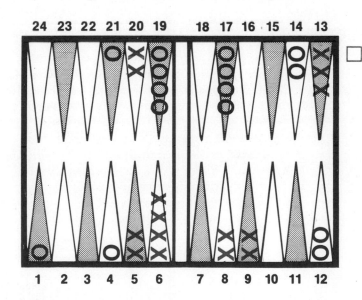

Roll 4 for X
X to Play 3–2
(O 4–2 bar/4, 19/21)

X moves 6/4*/1*. X launches his attack! Ordinarily, X would be reluctant to hit in his inner board with a blot since he would lose ground in the race by being hit back. Here, however (as in most cases in advanced play), the loss or gain of pips is not the most important consideration.

X can afford to be hit back since he has a secure anchor on the twenty point. Holding this **golden point** gives him enormous security, so much so that even after a most unfavorable sequence of rolls, X is almost certain to have a playable and probably still favorable game.

The reason for X's double early in the game (and why O should have passed) is becoming increasingly clear. If X is successful with his attack, he stands to gammon O. And even if X's attack is not an immediate success, merely owning the golden point assures X of at least an equal position. O is certainly tempting the fates by accepting the double: First he must survive the attack and the possibility of being gammoned, and then he must try to win a game in which he will never be a clear-cut favorite in the foreseeable future.

Let's return again to X's play 6/4*/1*. X would have preferred to point on O's blot on the four point; however, since he is unable to do so, he hits two men. As a rule, hitting two opposing men is a strong play even when it requires leaving a blot in your inner board. Such a play always keeps your opponent off balance since his entire roll is then required to re-enter (unless he rolls doubles). Furthermore, O is not a favorite to re-enter with *both* men even though there are only two points closed in X's inner board. X hits two men to capitalize on the early positional advantage he has gained. By keeping the momentum of the attack going, he hopes that O will never have a chance to consolidate his own position.

There are several conditions which indicate the advisability of making an aggressive play:

1. You hold an advanced anchor in your opponent's inner board. Here X holds O's five point. We cannot stress the importance of this point too highly.

2. You have closed more points in your inner board than your opponent. Here X holds two inner-board points, O one. Whenever embarking on a variation where an exchange of hits is possible or likely, the relative number of inner-board points is an important consideration. The player with more points closed will always be at an advantage since his opponent will be more likely to have difficulty re-entering. Even staying out once may be fatal, especially without the protection of an advanced anchor.

3. Blots in your opponent's inner board tend to make attacking more desirable because of the possibility of return shots. Here O has a blot on the twenty-one point. Since O has two men on the bar, there is no possible roll (except doubles) on which O can both re-enter and simultaneously cover his blot. Therefore, even if O re-enters on the one point hitting X, X will have a direct return shot at O's twenty-one-point blot.

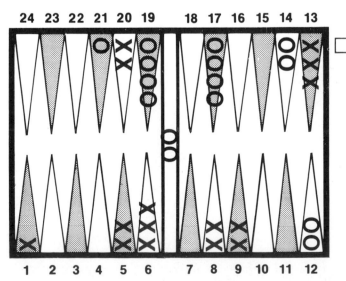

Roll 4 for O
O to Play 6–3
(X 3–2 6/4*/1*)

O moves bar/3, ø.

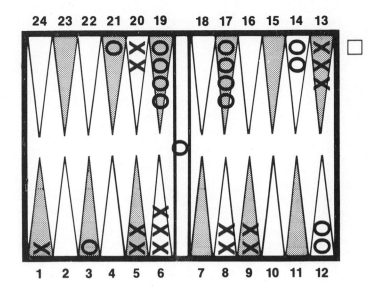

Roll 5 for X
X to Play 6–5
(O 6–3 bar/3, Ø)

X moves 9/3*, 8/3, pointing on O's head and continuing the attack. By making your points in order (beginning with the points furthest from home), you assure yourself of a superior position even if your opponent survives the attack and makes an anchor. Should O manage to make the one point in this position, he will still have great difficulty getting past X's blockade.

Let's consider what might happen if X foolishly decides to cover the one point and hit the blot 9/3*, 6/1. Now O is forced to re-enter on the two, three, or four point. If he succeeds in making one of these points — particularly the three or four point — X will be in a weaker position. The men on the one point are out of play.

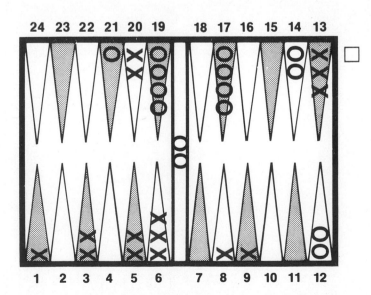

Roll 5 for O
O to Play 4–3
(X 6–5 4/3*, 8/3)

O moves bar/4, ø. This move is forced. O is faced with a grim struggle for survival and hopes to establish a foothold somewhere in X's board to avoid being closed out completely. Every additional point that X closes makes O more desperate. The outcome of the game will depend on the next few critical rolls.

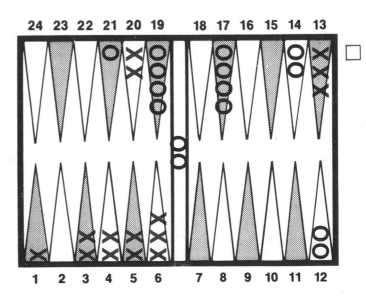

Roll 6 for X
X to Play 5–4
(O 4–3 bar/4, Ø)

X moves 9/4*, 8/4, pointing on O again and putting a second man on the bar. X closes the four point rather than the one point in order to make his points in order. Owning the three, four, five, and six points will make X a favorite in the game even if O manages to survive the blitz.

Roll 6 for O
O to Play 4–1
(X 5–4 9/4*, 8/4)

O moves bar/1*, ø, finally hitting the blot on the one point. Notice, however, that since X doubled he has kept pounding O constantly and left him no opportunity to move any men other than his back runners: O's other checkers haven't moved since the third roll of the game! Since O has been too busy to cover the blot on the twenty-one point, X now has a direct 4-shot at it.

Roll 7 for X
X to Play 6–1
(O 4–1 bar/1*, Ø)

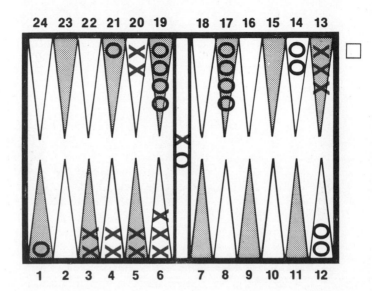

X moves bar/24, 13/7. X brings more ammunition into the battle by moving a new builder to his bar point. X's primary strategy is to continue his attack — he can afford to wait until later to bring his back men out. By playing to the bar point 13/7, X threatens to establish a powerful 5-point prime from the three point to the seven point. Even if O rolls a 1 and establishes an anchor on the one point, he will still be hopelessly trapped. In any case, X should win the game easily.

Roll 7 for O
O to Play 3–3
(X 6–1 bar/24, 13/7)

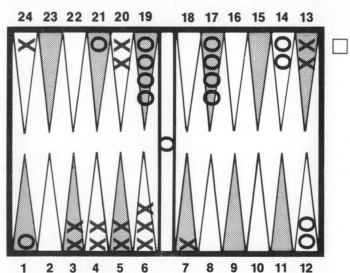

O ø.

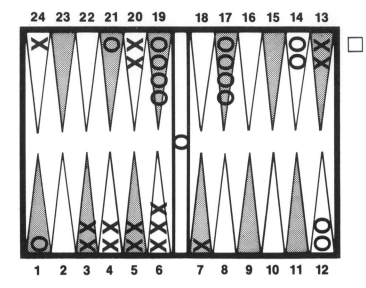

Roll 8 for X
X to Play 4–4
(O 3–3 Ø)

X moves 13/1*, 13/9. Once again X presses his attack. X could have hit O's second man without leaving a blot by **switching points,** that is, by moving both men off the five point and making the one point 5/1(2). Switching points can be an effective strategy in some cases, especially when rolling small doubles.

Here, however, it would be extremely unwise to play 5/1(2). We have seen that even if O is fortunate enough to survive the attack, X's 4- or 5-point prime will still assure X of an almost certain win. Should X make the structurally unsound play of breaking his prime by relinquishing the five point for the one point, then O might win if he survives the blitz. There is no reason not to play soundly in case O, for example, should come in with a double. X need not worry about being hit on the one point; O has only a 1-point board with a blot and X still maintains his advanced anchor.

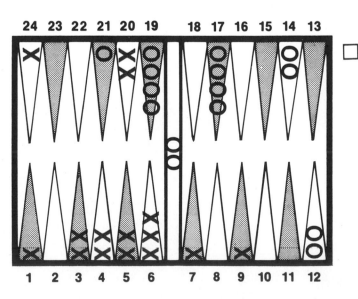

Roll 8 for O
O to Play 3–2
(X 4–4 13/1*, 13/9)

O moves bar/2, ø.

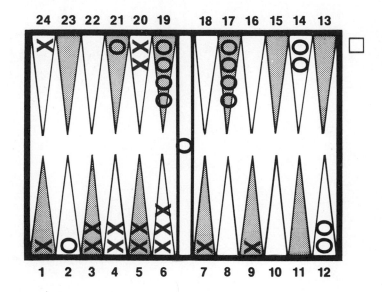

Roll 9 for X
X to Play 4–1
(O 3–2 bar/2, Ø)

   X moves 6/2*/1. With one checker X simultaneously hits another man and covers his own blot, creating a 5-point board. O is now in his death throes — he is no longer favored to come in with even one man, much less two. Only a miraculous roll 2–2 will enable him to survive.

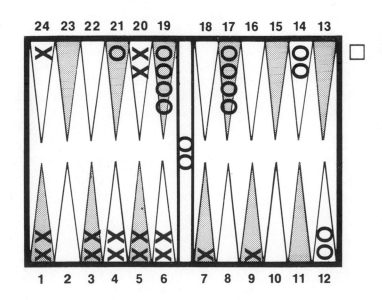

Roll 9 for O
O to Play 6–5
(X 4–1 6/2*/1)

   O ø.

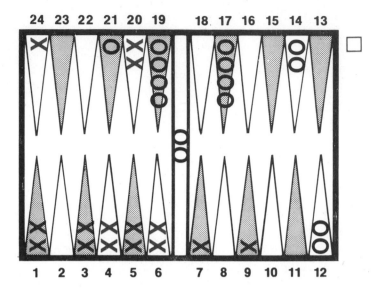

Roll 10 for X
X to Play 3–2
(O 6–5 Ø)

X moves 9/6, 20/18. X has passed up the opportunity to hit O again and to cover his bar point, 24/21*, 9/7, which would make a 5-point prime. He has also given up the twenty point. Has X gone mad??

No. X is no longer interested in a 5-point prime; his main concern is to complete the close-out. X wants to be able to hit O on the two point should he re-enter. By using the 3 to bring a man into the six point 9/6, X creates a second builder bearing directly on the two point. The idea here is to either make the two point directly on one roll, or to hit O on the two point if he re-enters and then cover the point if he fails to come in.

What about 24/21*? It is not really necessary for X to hit the blot on the twenty-one point; if X completes the close-out, he will easily be in a position to gammon O since O has not advanced far from the starting position with most of his men. If X wishes, he can probably hit this blot later at his leisure.

However, for technical reasons to be discussed later, if X closes O out and begins to bear off, it is probably safer for him with only two men on the bar rather than three. Hitting the third man may actually be a liability.

X can now afford to give up the twenty point because he is not in immediate danger. With two men on the bar against a 5-point board, O no longer presents a threat.

As a general rule, whenever your opponent has two or more men on the bar (whether you have a 5-point board or not), you should not be concerned about blots outside your inner board. Remember that even if your opponent rolls a good number, he must use the full roll to bring both his men in (with the exception of doubles, which would enable him to move elsewhere as well). He therefore has no numbers left to hit you with. When your opponent has two men on the bar, then, take advantage of this opportunity to deploy your men well and diversify your builders.

The indicated play 9/6, 20/18 is also superior to an alternate play 9/6, 24/22 for a technical reason. Let's compare the positions which result from both plays.

Correct Play: Roll 10 for X
(X 3–2 9/6, 20/18)

Alternate Move: Roll 10 for X
(X 3–2 9/6, 24/22)

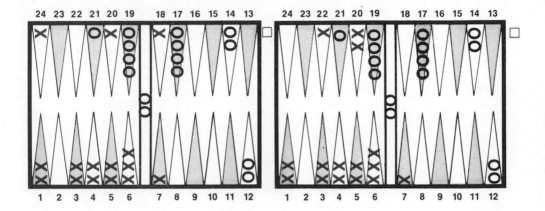

What would happen if your next roll was 3–3?

If you had played 9/6, 24/22, your three back men would be unable to move. You would be forced to take the entire roll with your remaining men. In order to maintain a 5-point board, you would have to switch points 5/2(2) and play 7/1, **killing a checker** (that is, taking it permanently out of play).

By correctly moving 9/6, 20/18, you can see that 3–3 subsequently plays without having to give up the five point or kill a man.

It is important to be aware of freak rolls which could destroy your position on the next move.

Roll 10 for O
O to Play 6–5
(X 3–2 9/6, 20/18)

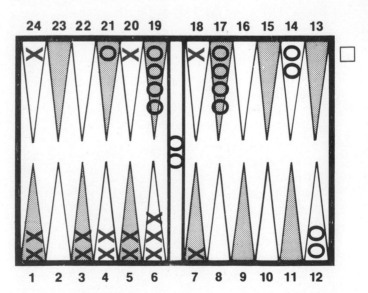

O ø.

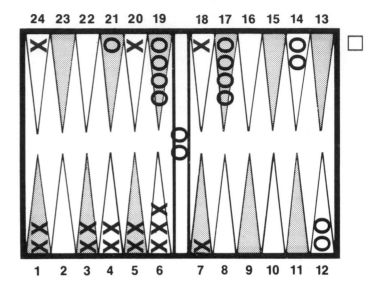

Roll 11 for X
X to Play 5–5
(O 6–5 Ø)

X moves 18/8, 20/10, bearing on the two point with a third builder. A player impatient for the close-out might slot a man 7/2 hoping to cover on the next roll if O stays out. It is seldom correct to slot with two men on the bar. The proper procedure is to wait until your opponent comes in and *then* hit him with a blot if necessary. (See Chapter 17 for a full discussion of the slotting procedure.)

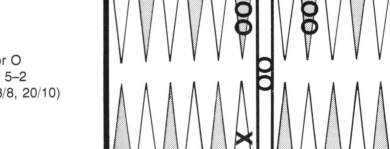

Roll 11 for O
O to Play 5–2
(X 5–5 18/8, 20/10)

O moves bar/2, ø.

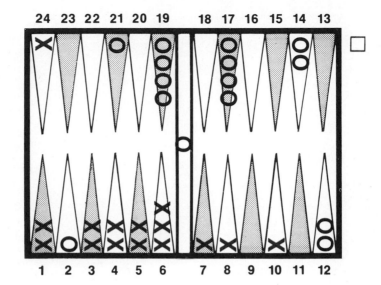

Roll 12 for X
X to Play 3–1
(O 5–2 bar/2, Ø)

X moves 6/2*. X hits the blot, trying to close O out. This is more important than hitting the blot on the twenty-one point (see discussion after Roll 10). The best — and in the long run safest — strategy is to complete the close-out and deny O an anchor to fight from.

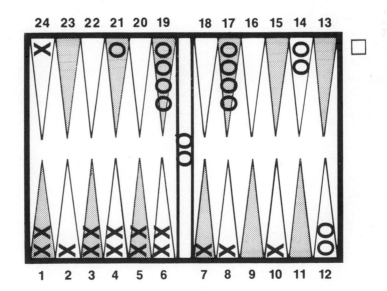

Roll 12 for O
O to Play 5–1
(X 3–1 6/2*)

O ø.

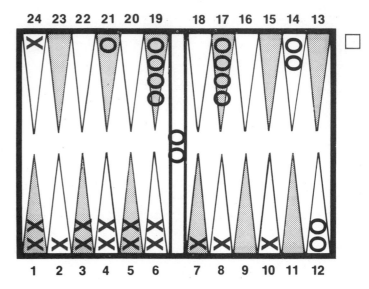

Roll 13 for X
X to Play 6–4
(O 5–1 Ø)

X moves 8/2, 24/20. X completes the close-out and now starts to extricate his back man. X is not interested in waiting to pick up O's blot. By bringing his last man home and bearing off carefully, X should easily win a gammon.

You should review the rules for a successful bear-off against opposition given after Game II and then roll the rest of the game out yourself to practice the bear-off technique. Barring an unlikely accident, O should be gammoned. He will lose four points instead of the one point he would have lost had he passed the double.

Game IV Summary

1. The single most important point to control in the middle game is the opponent's five point (called the **golden point**). This advanced anchor usually gives a strong measure of security throughout the game. With this security, you may be able to make plays that are otherwise too dangerous. A common error of the average player is to fail to make this point, or to relinquish it prematurely (see Section III, especially Chapter 20).

2. The following are some important factors which motivate aggressive plays:

    A. You hold an advanced anchor.

    B. You have more points closed in your inner board than your opponent.

    C. There are enemy blots lying around the board which may be hit before your opponent recovers from your attack and can safety them. Opposing blots in your opponent's home board offer prospects for return shots if you are hit.

3. If there is a chance of being gammoned, be especially cautious about accepting doubles.

4. It is risky to move up in your opponent's inner board when he has extra builders in his outer and/or inner boards.

5. Hitting two men in your inner board is a strong play even when you must leave a blot to do so. It keeps your opponent off balance and allows you to move freely elsewhere.

6. When launching an all-out attack, it is sometimes correct to make deep points — especially if this leaves your opponent on the bar against a strong inner board. However, if you have a choice, making the higher point in your inner board is preferable. Making points in the proper order may guarantee a strong game should your attack fail.

7. When your opponent has two or more men on the bar, concentrate primarily on bringing builders to bear on your inner board — not on safetying blots outside your inner board.

8. Technical close-out procedures:

A. The best technical procedure for closing out an opponent is usually *not* to slot if he has two or more men on the bar (see Chapter 17).

B. Move carefully when your opponent is closed out and you wish to bring your remaining men into your inner board. Try not to expose yourself to those doubles that will leave your outside men blocked, thus forcing you to break your inner board prematurely.

C. When your opponent is closed out and the gammon seems a certainty, avoid hitting extra men since this will increase the possibility of trouble in the bear-off.

CHAPTER 10.
PIP COUNT

♦

SINCE BACKGAMMON IS essentially a race to move all your men around and off the board before your opponent, being able to determine your relative position in this race is often essential. Although you can make an approximate determination by eye, sometimes this is not accurate enough.

A more precise method is to count pips. This counting, though annoying and tedious at times, is essential to determine your standing in the race — especially where the position is at all complicated.

Three methods for making the count follow.

Pip Count Methods

Direct Method

A player bringing his checkers home in a race wants to do so in the most economical way. The **pip count** represents the difference between the total number of points each player must roll in order to take all his checkers off the board, assuming that no pips are wasted. By *wasted*, we mean that no number higher than necessary is used to bear a man off.

The number of pips represented by *each checker* is simply the number point the checker is on, *counting 1 as the first point in each player's home board.* For X, a checker on the five point is 5 pips, two on the ten point are 20 pips, one on the sixteen point is 16 pips, and so on. (Since the twenty-four point counts as 1 for O, an O checker on the twenty point is 5 pips, two on the fifteen point are 20 pips, one on the nine point is 16 pips.)

To compute your total number of pips (*not* the same as the pip count), you add up the pips of all your checkers. Then you add up the pips of your opponent's checkers. The difference between these two sums indicates whether you are *ahead* or *behind* in pips, and by how much. This is called the **pip count**. By *ahead*, we mean the player who has the *lower* number of pips, and thus is closer to home; by *behind*, we mean the player who has the *higher* number of pips, and thus is further from home.

A full example of the direct method of pip counting is given below:

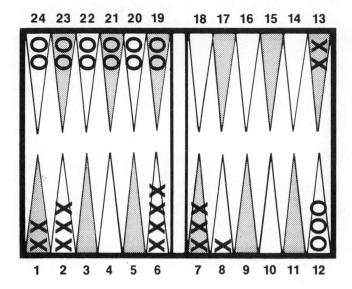

Position 1

X's Count
Two men on the one point = 2 × 1 = 2
Three men on the two point = 3 × 2 = 6
Four men on the six point = 4 × 6 = 24
Three men on the seven point = 3 × 7 = 21
One man on the eight point = 1 × 8 = 8
Two men on the thirteen point = 2 × 13 = 26

X's total is 87 pips. X needs 87 points rolled on the dice to bear his men off, assuming that no numbers are wasted.

O's Count
Remember that for O we count the twenty-four point as 1, twenty-three as 2, etc.
Two men on O's one point = 2 × 1 = 2
Two men on O's two point = 2 × 2 = 4
Two men on O's three point = 2 × 3 = 6
Two men on O's four point = 2 × 4 = 8
Two men on O's five point = 2 × 5 = 10
Two men on O's six point = 2 × 6 = 12
Three men on O's thirteen point = 3 × 13 = 39

O's total is 81 pips. X's total is 87 pips. X is 6 pips further from bringing his men off the board than O. X is 6 pips *behind* O.

Saving Time
To count quickly, it is useful to memorize the positions of the points which represent 10, 13, and 20 pips for each player. Also, keep in mind that a closed board with two men on each inner board point equals 42 pips.

Various mental exercises also make the calculations go faster. Here is a symmetry trick: If point A and point B have the same number of men *and* are separated by an odd number of points, the total number of pips on A + B would equal the total number of pips on the central point, C, if all the men were there. For example, if you have three men on the nine point and three men on the eleven point, you have a total of $(3 \times 9) + (3 \times 11) = 60$ pips. This is equal to six men on the ten point $(6 \times 10) = 60$ pips.

Another trick is to omit counting the number of men on a point if your opponent has the same number of men on the corresponding point. In Position 1, both X and O have two men on their respective one points. If we omit counting either point, the 2 pips lost by each player will cancel out and the final pip count will be the same.

Comparison Method

This method of finding the pip count gives us the same result as the direct method. It provides a running total of the pip count. The comparison method is preferable to the direct method because it eliminates the need to figure out and then compare two separately totaled sums.

Using the comparison method, you compare the number of checkers that you and your opponent have on corresponding points. You subtract the number of men your opponent has from the number of men you have. Then you multiply this difference by the number of the point you are comparing. You now have a pip count for a particular point. If you have more checkers on the point than your opponent, you will end up with a plus pip count; if you have less, you will end up with a minus pip count for that particular point.

As you compare each pair of points in turn, you keep a running total of the pip counts for each point, subtracting a pip count when you have less pips than your opponent, and adding when you have more. When you have finished comparing the sets of points, the final running total will indicate the complete pip count for the entire position. If it is plus, you are behind; if it is minus, you are ahead.

Let's use the comparison method to determine the pip count in Position 1.

Point #	# of X men on point	# of O men on point	#X men minus #O men	col. 4 x col. 1	X's running total of pip count
one	2	2	$2 - 2 = 0$	$0 \times 1 = 0$	0 (even)
two	3	2	$3 - 2 = +1$	$1 \times 2 = +2$	+2
three	0	2	$0 - 2 = -2$	$-2 \times 3 = -6$	$+2 - 6 = -4$
four	0	2	$0 - 2 = -2$	$-2 \times 4 = -8$	$-4 - 8 = -12$
five	0	2	$0 - 2 = -2$	$-2 \times 5 = -10$	$-12 - 10 = -22$
six	4	2	$4 - 2 = +2$	$2 \times 6 = +12$	$-22 + 12 = -10$
seven	3	0	$3 - 0 = +3$	$3 \times 7 = +21$	$-10 + 21 = +11$
eight	1	0	$1 - 0 = +1$	$1 \times 8 = +8$	$+11 + 8 = +19$
thirteen	2	3	$2 - 3 = -1$	$-1 \times 13 = -13$	$+19 - 13 = +6$

The final total indicates that X is +6, or 6 pips *behind* in the race against O.

Experience has shown that the comparison method is usually quicker and more reliable than the direct method — especially when the positions of the two players are similar.

Mental Shift Method

This method is a modification of the comparison method. In this case you mentally move men of one player to make a position identical with the other player. Then you count the number of pips you had to move each checker to make the positions identical. If you have to move your men toward your home board, you add the number of pips; if you have to move your men away from your home board, you subtract the number of pips moved.

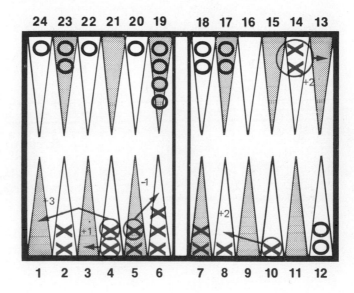

Position 2
2 + 2 − 1 + 3 + 1 = 7

In Position 2, we have indicated how a few of X's men may be rearranged to yield identical positions with O. In order to make the positions identical, we must move X's men a net total of 7 pips forward, so therefore X is 7 pips *behind* in the race.

The advantage of this method is obvious — with practically no work or calculation, you get the total pip count in a matter of seconds. For those who hate having to remember and total long strings of numbers, as the author does, this is a real blessing.

The disadvantage is that there is no set way of determining which checkers to move to make the positions identical. Furthermore, there may be many different ways to shift the men to arrive at identical positions.

To determine when to use this method, study various positions and find the one where the fewest checkers need be moved to make X's and O's positions identical. When the two positions are entirely dissimilar, the number of men to be shifted may well make this method more trouble than it is worth. With practice, however, it is often surprising how few checkers have to be moved to equate the positions.

(Note: It is permissible to mentally rearrange your opponent's checkers. If you move his forward, you subtract the number of pips; if you move them backward, away from his home board, you add the number of pips.)

You can facilitate counting even in very dissimilar positions by mentally moving a few men so that opposing men will cancel out, and, keeping track of the pips you moved, do the rest of the counting by one of the other methods.

The next four positions can be used to practice the mental shift method.

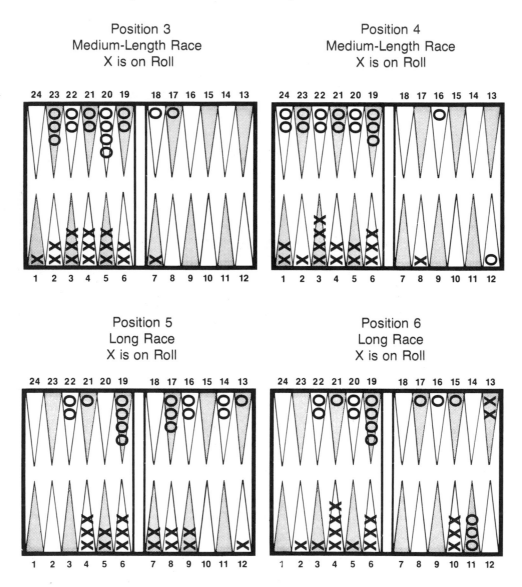

Position 3
Medium-Length Race
X is on Roll

Position 4
Medium-Length Race
X is on Roll

Position 5
Long Race
X is on Roll

Position 6
Long Race
X is on Roll

Positions 3A, 4A, 5A, and 6A each illustrate one possible rearrangement to quickly find the total pip count.

Position 3A
7 − 1 + 1 = 7

Position 4A
10 + 1 − 1 = 10

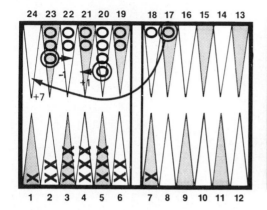

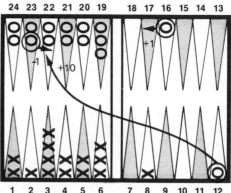

Position 5A
− 2 − 1 + 1 + 12 = 10

Position 6A
1 + 1 + 2 + 4 − 1 + 4 + 2 = 13

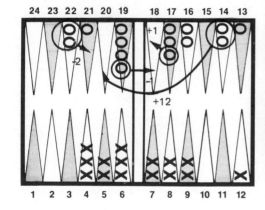

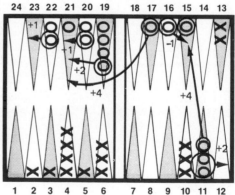

Keeping Track of the Count

Once you enter into a race, there may be several occasions when it is necessary to know what the exact pip count is. Rather than recalculating it every time, it is usually easier to keep a running total. After the pip count has been made, you may readjust it after each roll by the number of pips actually rolled on the dice.

Begin with the pip count figure. Remember that if it is minus you are ahead, and if plus, behind. If you are 8 pips ahead and you roll 3–2 (or 5 pips), you are now 13 pips ahead. Your opponent then rolls 5–4 (9 pips), so you are now 13 minus 9 = 4 pips ahead. You roll 2–2 (8 pips) and are now 12 pips ahead. He rolls 4–4 (16 pips), so now you are 4 pips behind, etc.

Evaluating the Race

In backgammon, the average number of pips thrown on a roll of the dice is $8^1/_6$; it isn't 7, as one might expect, because of the special rule for playing doubles. If you wish to see how many *rolls* ahead or behind you are, simply take the total pip count and divide by 8 (dividing by 8 is not only easier than $8^1/_6$, but actually gives you a better indication). If, for example, you are 20 pips ahead in the race, $^{20}/_8 = 2^1/_2$ tells you that you are $2^1/_2$ rolls ahead in the race.

If you are on roll, what pip count would constitute an even race?

If the pip count were exactly even, the player on roll would have the advantage.

It is sometimes wrongly maintained that being on roll compensates for being 8 pips behind. Assume, however, that you get an average roll. The pip count will now be even. Now your opponent has the advantage because he is on roll with an even count.

The correct answer is that if you are 4 pips behind *and* on roll the position is even. If you then roll an average 8 pips, your opponent comes on roll, like you, 4 pips behind.

Offering and Accepting Doubles

How many pips ahead should you be to double? And how many behind to accept?

Many authorities disagree on the exact number of pips needed. Rather than give an exact mathematical formula (which most players would probably never bother to use), we offer a simple rule of thumb, along with a discussion of its limitations and exceptions.

Number of pips you have	Minimum pips ahead to double	Maximum allowable pips behind to accept
Medium-length race (about 60)	7	10
Long race (about 100)	10	13

In most races you will never have exactly 60 or 100 pips, so modifications must be made. The longer the race, the more pips needed to double and the more pips behind you can be to take. In a 90-pip race, for example, slightly less than 10 pips ahead are needed to double, and slightly less than 13 behind allow you to take. Some races are even longer than 100 pips, in which case higher numbers would be used.

Although this rule may seem imprecise, it is the one actually used by the author and several other knowledgeable players. The exact number of pips remaining in the game is not emphasized because it is often easier to find the total pip count using the comparison or shift method. Unlike the direct method, however, the other methods do not give the actual number of pips remaining on both sides — only the difference in the two pip totals. When using the comparison method, then, a rough evaluation of the race will usually suffice. Misevaluating the *length* of the race even by as much as 10 or 15 pips is unlikely to change your doubling decision significantly. Since the doubling rules given are approximations anyway, the actual equity lost in the game will be negligible.

In contrast, miscounting the total pip count by even a small amount may contribute to a significant misassessment. In a long race, for example, a mistake of 5 pips in the pip count could drastically alter your decision to double: If you thought you were ahead only 9 pips, you would not double, whereas if you were ahead 14 pips, you would not only double, but your opponent might pass!

The doubling criteria were given in terms of a "medium-length race" and a "long race," by which we meant races with about 60 and 100 pips remaining. The exact length of the race is not important, so we shall give some rough criteria which will enable you to look at a position to approximately determine its length.

A medium-length race may be thought of as one in which almost all the men are relatively smoothly distributed in the inner board and the bear-off is about to begin. Since there are fifteen men, the "average" checker will be on the four point in a medium-length race.

A long race may be thought of as one in which there are usually three or four rolls left until the bear-off can begin. Or a long race would be one in which the men are evenly distributed about the bar, that is, there are about the same number of pips needed to reach the bar from the men in the outer boards as there would be from the men in the inner boards.

To give you an idea of what medium- and long-length races look like, look back at Positions 3, 4, 5, and 6. In Positions 3 and 4, X has exactly 60 pips, and in Positions 5 and 6, X has 100 pips.

In order to apply the rules for accepting and refusing doubles, you must know the exact pip count. You may wish to practice the pip count in these four positions to determine what the correct doubling strategy is. Any method for counting may be used; the mental shift method is the one illustrated in Positions 3A, 4A, 5A, and 6A.

In Position 3, X is 7 pips ahead. He should double and O should accept. This constitutes the minimum lead with which X should double here.

In Position 4, X is 10 pips ahead. X should double and O should still take. However, this is a borderline take for O; if he were any further behind, he would refuse.

In Position 5, X is 10 pips ahead and should double; O takes. If X had any smaller lead, he should probably wait to double.

In Position 6, X is 13 pips ahead and doubles; O has a borderline take.

In races such as those in Positions 3, 4, 5, and 6, the pip count is a highly reliable indicator of the standing in the race. There are positions, however, where the pip count alone may be somewhat misleading and appropriate modifications must be made. Consider the following situations:

1. In applying our doubling rule based on the pip count, a distinction must be made between a first double and a re-double. You should be slightly freer about doubling when the cube is in the middle, and slightly more conservative if you own the cube.

Owning the cube and being, therefore, the only person able to double, gives you an increased equity in the game. By re-doubling you give up this equity, whereas if the cube is in the middle you have less to lose since you are not the sole owner. This is discussed further in Chapter 22.

2. The way your men are distributed has a bearing on the race. When there are gaps in your inner board, you are more likely to miss taking men off (thus wasting pips). You should especially avoid leaving gaps on your four or five point (see Chapter 23 for a complete discussion). If you are unable to avoid bearing in with a stripped four or five point, your position will probably be somewhat worse than the pip count indicates.

3. Your bear-off will also be adversely affected if you have too many men piled on points deep in your inner board. If (taking an extreme case) you had four men on your one point while your opponent had only one man on his six point, obviously your 2-pip lead in the race would mean nothing. What matters is the *number of rolls left to complete the bear-off*.

Whenever a bear-off has begun in a short race, and each side has several men off, it is easiest to evaluate the position by estimating the probable number of *rolls* each side has left.

Position 7

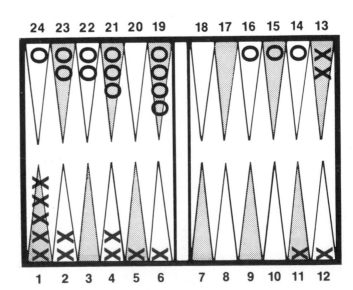

In a medium-length or long race, having men piled on your one and two points will also adversely affect your chances. The reason for this is that eventually large numbers will probably be used to remove men from the one and two points and pips will be wasted. The pip count will be misleading when many pips are wasted, or when there are gaps in the inner board.

In Position 7, the pip count is exactly even, but O's men are better distributed. O has a gap on the five point which could potentially cause trouble, but fortunately he has a few rolls to rectify this before the bear-off begins. O should therefore make every attempt to bear into the five point and not to the six point to avoid leaving this gap.

X, on the other hand, already has men piled on his one point, and there is nothing he can do about this. Inevitably this will cause pips to be wasted in the bear-off. If you wish numerically to compensate for this in terms of the pip count, imagine that three of the surplus men on the one point are on the three point instead. This gives a more realistic count of 83 for X.

Pip Count Applications

Holding Positions

The pip count is primarily applied in racing positions where no further contact is possible. There is, therefore, little point in keeping track of the pip count in typical middle-game positions where there is little chance of the game's evolving directly into a pure race. Occasionally, however, a holding position may arise in which there is a significant chance of the game's being completed with no further contact. In such positions, the prospects for winning the race may determine the correct play.

In this position, the only possible remaining contact involves the men on the ten and fifteen points.

Problem A: O rolls 2–2. How would you play this number?

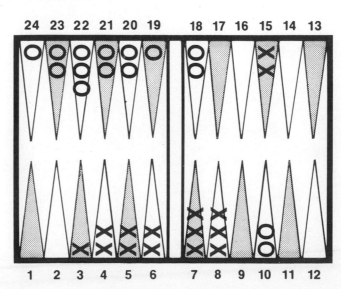

Position 8
(A) O to Play 2–2
(B) X to Play 2–2

W̄ithout bothering with an exact pip count, O realizes he is far ahead. Therefore, the correct play is 10/14(2) effectively eliminating further contact and leaving O a clear winner.

Problem B: X rolls 2–2. How would you play this number?

X has almost no chance in a straight race and his only hope is that O will have trouble clearing the ten point. Therefore, X plays 7/3, 8/4 and keeps his two men back on the fifteen point. These two men serve to *hold* O's men on the ten point. Eventually O must move these men. If O does not roll a double which would enable him to move them together, he will eventually have to move one of them, leaving X a direct shot.

Since X is behind in the race, he tries to hold O. Since O is ahead, however, he has no desire to hold X but merely wants to come home safely. In order to know who's holding whom, you must know the leader in the race. In Position 8, a simple inspection can determine who is ahead.

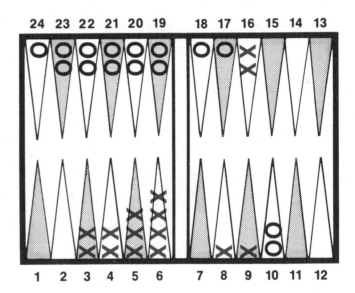

Position 9
X to Play 3–3

In Position 9, the relative standing in the race after X takes the 3–3 is sufficiently close to warrant a pip count. Fortunately, X's and O's positions may easily be compared by mentally rearranging the men as shown in Position 9A to show that X is 16 pips behind as the position stands *before* the roll.

Therefore, *after* X's move, O will be 16 minus 12 = 4 pips ahead and on roll — a clear-cut favorite in the race.

Since X is behind, he wishes to hold O as effectively as possible and so chooses to stay on the sixteen point, 6 pips in front of O's two men on the ten point. Since O is ahead, he does not want to hold X — he just wants to get home safely and will run at the first opportunity with a double (except 6–6).

What will happen if O remains ahead in the race and neither player rolls a double? Eventually, one of the players (probably O since he is ahead) will be forced to break the point in the outfield, leaving a man exposed. This will happen when a player is unable to legally play his move in his inner board, in

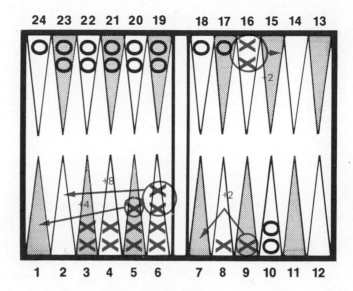

Position 9A
2 + 2 + 8 + 4 = 16

particular when he has no other 6's to play except with his outside point. For this reason, both players must attempt to conserve as many 6's as possible. Each player here has two spare 6's; the third 6 rolled by either side will force a shot.

Returning to Position 9, we see that X should not move forward off the sixteen point and should not bring the men on the eight and nine points into the inner board. The exact play with the remaining men is not critically important, but the best play is probably 4/1(2), 6/3, 5/2.

A subtler version of the same ideas (who's holding whom) is shown in Position 10.

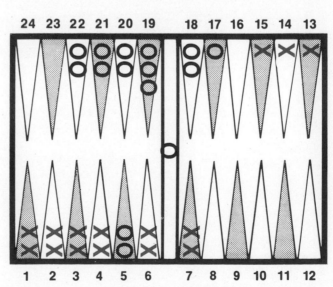

Position 10
X to Play 3–2

Even many experienced players make their eleven point, 14/11, 13/11. This is a serious mistake; the correct play is 15/12, 14/12.

In this position, X is clearly far ahead in the race so he wants to get home safely and doesn't want to hold O back. In Game IV we emphasized that the best single point to hold when you want to block your opponent is the point 6 pips in front of him. However, X has no desire to restrain O's men on the five point and, therefore, no reason to make his eleven point. In fact, if X makes the eleven point and O re-enters, O will be holding X because the eleven point is difficult to clear without leaving a direct shot. Rather than being an asset for X, the eleven point will be an enormous liability.

The correct play, 15/12, 14/12, presents no such problems. Even when O re-enters, clearing the twelve point will at worst involve only leaving an indirect 7-shot.

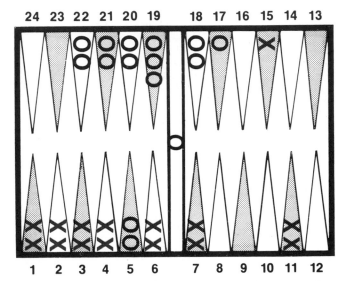

Position 11
X to Play 3–2

In Position 11, X has a 3–2 to play. Moving 15/10 so you are only exposed to 5–5 is a common error. While this is the safest immediate play, the real problem in this position is to clear the eleven point safely. Maintaining the eleven point can be fatal on the next roll if O re-enters. It will then be hard to clear without leaving a direct shot.

The correct play is 11/6. Since O is on the bar, X seizes this opportunity to clear the eleven point immediately. The risk of being hit with a 6–5 is more than compensated by the fact that you are clearing a potentially dangerous point.

Another common variant of the same theme is illustrated in Position 12.

The pip count reveals that after X plays 2–1 he will still be 4 pips behind despite the fact that O still has two men back. Because X is behind in the race, he wishes to make it as difficult as possible for O to escape and plays 6/3, maintaining 4 points in front of O.

Let's look at a different problem using the same position. How would O play 2–1?

Playing 18/20, 19/20, making the twenty point would be a dangerous mistake. O wants to leave X's five point with *both* men to maintain his lead in the race — leaving with a single man would be very dangerous. If he plays 18/20, he will be forced to run with one man if he rolls a 6 (except 6–6, 6–5), leaving

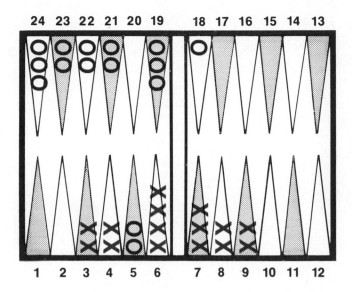

Position 12
(A) X to Play 2–1
(B) O to Play 2–1

the remaining man to X's tender mercies. If, on the other hand, O correctly takes his whole roll within his inner board 19/22; he will be able to move the man on the eighteen point if he rolls a bad 6 and will not be forced to run from the five point prematurely.

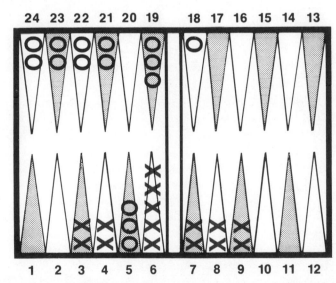

Position 13
(A) X to Play 2–1
(B) O to Play 2–1

In contrast, X will have a 16-pip lead after his roll in Position 13. With a clearly favorable race, X need not worry about containing O — his chief concern is bearing his men in as safely as possible. Towards this end, X plays 9/8, 9/7, following the principles outlined in Game II for safe bear-in: Clear the points furthest from home and avoid leaving gaps. In Position 13, if O rolled 2–1 the correct play would be 19/20, 18/20, giving O a closed board. O has no reason to save 6's because he has a third man on the five point to run with a 6.

CHAPTER 11.
BASIC ODDS

LET US EXAMINE the structure of a single roll of two dice. There are 36 possible combinations of the dice, as listed in Table 1.

Table 1. Combinations of the Dice

Dice Roll	Number of Combinations	Dice Roll	Number of Combinations
1–1	1	2–3, or 3–2	2
2–2	1	2–4, or 4–2	2
3–3	1	2–5, or 5–2	2
4–4	1	2–6, or 6–2	2
5–5	1	3–4, or 4–3	2
6–6	1	3–5, or 5–3	2
1–2, or 2–1	2	3–6, or 6–3	2
1–3, or 3–1	2	4–5, or 5–4	2
1–4, or 4–1	2	4–6, or 6–4	2
1–5, or 5–1	2	5–6, or 6–5	2
1–6, or 6–1	2	Total Combinations	36

A given double, on the average, occurs only 1 time out of 36 possible rolls (odds are 35-to-1 against), whereas a non-double such as 2–1 occurs 2 times out of 36 possible rolls (odds 17-to-1 against). Non-doubles can occur in 2 different ways: 2–1, for example, can occur as 2 on the first die and 1 on the second, or 1 on the first die and 2 on the second. In actual games the two dice may be indistinguishable; this doesn't alter the fact, however, that non-doubles occur in 2 different ways.

Odds are calculated with the 36 possible dice rolls as the frame of reference. When we speak of 21 *ways* or 21 *combinations*, for example, we always mean 21 out of the possible 36 dice combinations, or 21/36.

In order to count the number of shots that hit a blot or blots, you don't have to learn elaborate tables of odds to cover different situations. With a little practice, anyone can learn to count quickly and accurately — no mathematical wizardry is required.

Counting shots is a much overrated skill. It is far more important to understand the underlying structure of the game than to be able to count shots rapidly. Even in positions where you don't want to be hit, there are almost always other considerations besides simply minimizing the number of shots you are exposed to (see Chapter 14).

Direct Shots

A **direct shot** is one in which a blot is 6 pips or less away from an opposing checker. There are several types of direct shots.

Single Shots

A blot exposed to one particular number is called a **single shot**.

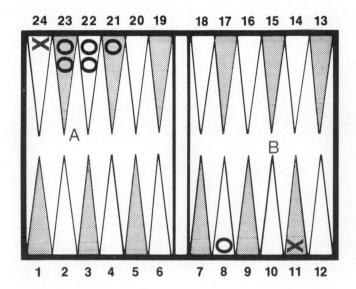

Position 1A–1B

In Positions 1A and 1B, O is exposed to a direct 3-shot. Let's compare the number of ways that X has to hit in both positions.

In Position 1A, X has a **simple direct shot,** that is, the blot may be hit by only a single specific number (a 3) showing up on either die.

By going through Table 1 and adding up all the combinations containing a specific 3 on either die, we find there are 11 combinations. *There are always 11 ways out of 36 to roll any one specific number.* This means that a simple direct shot will be hit just slightly less than 1/3 of the time ($^{11}/_{36}$).

In Position 1B, X has another single direct 3-shot. Here, however, X can hit not only with a *specific* 3, but also with combinations 2–1 and 1–1. This is not just a simple direct shot. To compute the total number of ways to hit, you begin by taking the base number 11 (the number of ways in which to hit a simple direct shot), and add on all the combinations that hit *without* a specific 3. In this case there are 3 extra ways to hit: 2–1 (2 ways) and 1–1 (1 way). This gives us a total of 14 ways.

Table 2 summarizes the chances of hitting a single direct shot (or of throwing a given number of 6 or less).

Table 2. Chances of Hitting a Single Direct Shot (or throwing a number 6 or less)

Number or Distance to Blot	Simple Direct Shot	Extra Possible Combinations	Total number of Ways to Hit	Probability of Hitting
1	11	0	11	$^{11}/_{36}$ or 31%
2	11	1	12	$^{12}/_{36}$ or 33%
3	11	3	14	$^{14}/_{36}$ or 39%
4	11	4	15	$^{15}/_{36}$ or 42%
5	11	4	15	$^{15}/_{36}$ or 42%
6	11	6	17	$^{17}/_{36}$ or 47%

When leaving a direct shot, the further away, the more likely to be hit. The 1-shot is hardest of all to hit since there are no extra possible combinations, while the 6-shot is easiest to hit, with 6 extra combinations. The chances of hitting a single direct shot vary from 11 ways (about ⅓ of the time) to 17 ways (almost even chance).

Double Shots

A **double shot** occurs when you have two direct numbers which hit (either two blots exposed to one opposing checker, or one blot exposed to two opposing checkers).

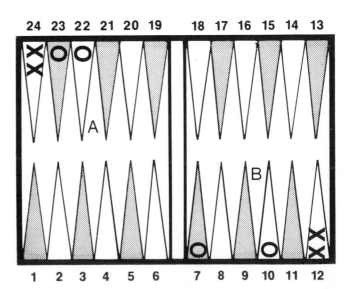

Position 2A–2B

In Position 2A, X has a **simple double shot**, i.e., a shot with no extra combinations. He may only hit O with a specific 1 or a specific 2 which must appear on at least one die.

There are 20 ways out of a possible 36 rolls to hit a simple double shot. Intuitively, then, the basic double shot will be hit slightly more than ½ the time (if you add up all the possible combinations in Table 1 which contain a 2 or a 1, without counting any twice, you will obtain the same result: 20).

In Position 2B, X also has a double shot in his outer board: 2's and 5's. Here, however, X can hit not only with a specific 2 or specific 5, but also with combinations 1–1 and 4–1. This is not just a simple double shot. To compute the total number of ways to hit, you begin by taking the base number 20 (the number of ways in which to hit a simple double shot) and add on all the extra combinations that hit *without* a specific 2 or specific 5. In this case there are 3 extra ways to hit: 1–1 (1 way) and 4–1 (2 ways). 2–3 is not counted as an extra combination since it contains a specific 2 and thus has been already included in the basic 20 combinations. The total number of ways to hit is 23.

You may wish to practice your shot-counting by figuring the number of shots in the next slightly more complicated position.

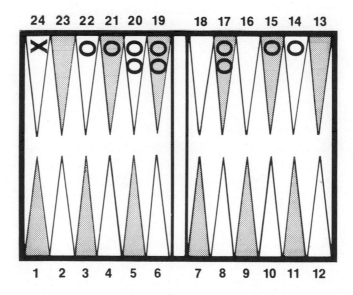

Position 3

If we analyze this position, we see that it is basically a double shot (2's and 3's), with some extra combinations. To compute the total number of ways to hit, you begin by taking the base number 20 (the number of ways to hit a simple double shot) and add on the extra combinations which hit and do not contain either a specific 2 or 3.

1–1 hits (1 way) and 6–4 also hits (2 ways) to give us a total of 20+1+2 or 23 ways to hit. 2–1, 6–3, and 3–3 are not counted because they are included in the total of simple double shots, and 5–4, and 5–5 are not counted because they are blocked. Note that the number of shots would be the same even if O did not have a blot on the fifteen point.

Triple Shots

A **simple triple shot** (when you have 3 specific numbers to hit, without combinations) occurs in 27 ways, or exactly ¾ of the time. When there are also extra combinations that hit, which do not include any of the 3 specific numbers, they must be added to 27 to give you a final total.

Other Multiple Direct Shots

A **quadruple shot** (with 4 specific numbers to hit) occurs in 32 ways, not counting extra combinations. With 5 different specific numbers to hit (a **quintuple shot**), there are 35 ways, and if all 6 numbers hit, there are, of course, 36 ways out of 36 possible rolls — in other words, any roll will hit.

Summary for Counting Direct Shots

If the shot is **direct** (6 pips away or less), whether single or multiple, begin with the base figure: $^{11}/_{36}$ (for a single shot), $^{20}/_{36}$ (double), or $^{27}/_{36}$ (triple). That base number will be the probability of hitting unless there are also additional combinations that hit. If so, add them to the base figure *without* including those which contain the specific number (or numbers) needed to hit. Also do not count combinations that are blocked.

Indirect Shots

An **indirect shot** is one in which a blot is 7 or more pips away from an opposing checker. Since there are no single numbers on one die which are 7 or more, you simply add up all the combinations on both dice which hit to compute the total number of shots.

To calculate the number of ways to hit a 9-shot, for example, you enumerate the possible combinations which add up to 9: 5–4 (2 ways), 6–3 (2 ways), and 3–3 (1 way) for a total of 5 ways. When you have a multiple indirect shot, you simply add up all the combinations of the number which hit, being careful not to count the same combination twice.

Table 3 shows the chances of hitting a single blot which is 7 or more pips away from an opposing checker. This table assumes that all possible combinations are playable; that is, that they are not blocked by opposing points. When certain combinations are blocked, you do not count them (or, if using Table 3, subtract them from the totals given). Note that the further away the indirect shot, the *less* likely it is to be hit (with the exception of a 12-shot).

Applications to Re-entering

When you are on the bar with a man against a 5-point board, you need 1 specific number to re-enter. Thus, the odds on re-entering are the same as hitting a simple (single) direct shot: $^{11}/_{36}$.

Table 3. Chances of Hitting a Single Indirect Shot
(or Throwing a Number 7 or more)

Number or Distance to Blot	All Possible Ways to Hit	Probability of Hitting
7	6	$6/36$ or 17%
8	6	$6/36$ or 17%
9	5	$5/36$ or 14%
10	3	$3/36$ or 9%
11	2	$2/36$ or 6%
12	3	$3/36$ or 9%
15	1	$1/36$ or 3%
16	1	$1/36$ or 3%
18	1	$1/36$ or 3%
20	1	$1/36$ or 3%
24	1	$1/36$ or 3%

Table 4. Probability of
Entering Opponent's Home Board
from the Bar

Number of Open Points in Opponent's Home Board	Number of Closed Points	Number of Ways to Enter	Percent of Successful Rolls
0	6	0	0%
1	5	$11/36$	31%
2	4	$20/36$	56%
3	3	$27/36$	75%
4	2	$32/36$	89%
5	1	$35/36$	97%
6	0	$36/36$	100%

Similarly, with 4 points closed and 2 points open, the odds of re-entering are $20/36$, the same as a double shot. This means that you stand to re-enter against a 4-point board slightly more than ½ of the time.

When 3 points are closed, you have the same chances of entering as hitting a triple shot: $27/36$. On the average, you will re-enter a 3-point board exactly ¾ of the time.

Many players are surprised by this last figure; they feel that they stay out of a 3-point board more than the indicated ¼ of the time. This feeling may be due to the psychological tendency to remember all the unlucky rolls you've gotten, while forgetting all the times that you easily came in against a 3-point board.

The chances of coming in against a 2- or 1-point board are $^{32}/_{36}$ and $^{35}/_{36}$ respectively. These odds correspond to the probability of hitting the rare quadruple and quintuple shots.

Summary

Once again we emphasize that it is not essential to memorize the exact totals and percentages in the tables of this chapter. If the basic concepts in this summary are fully grasped, you will be well equipped to deal with any situation where the odds are relevant.

The only numbers that need be remembered (and for which you should acquire an intuitive grasp) are the chances of hitting a simple single, double, or triple shot: $^{11}/_{36}$, $^{20}/_{36}$, $^{27}/_{36}$ respectively. These also represent the chances of re-entering with a single man against a 5-, 4-, or 3-point board. (Intuitively it may help to think of these probabilities as slightly less than $^1/_3$, slightly more than $^1/_2$, and exactly $^3/_4$.)

Any other probabilities of hitting may be derived from these three figures using the basic method of counting — that is, take the basic simple-direct-shot figure and then add to it extra combinations that hit. Indirect shots consist entirely of these extra combinations.

When leaving a single shot, you need not memorize Tables 2 and 3, or calculate the exact odds every time. The following basic observations will be sufficient to guide you to the correct play:

1. An indirect shot is much more unlikely to be hit than any direct shot. Indirect shots will occur frequently and are usually not the key consideration for a play. Because direct shots are much more likely to be hit, they should be avoided unless there is a good reason for leaving them.

2. When leaving a direct shot, the further away, the more likely to be hit. The 1-shot is hardest of all to hit since there are no extra combinations, while the 6-shot is easiest to hit with 6 extra combinations. The chances of hitting a single direct shot vary from 11 ways (about $^1/_3$ of the time) to 17 ways (almost even chance).

3. Unlike the direct shots, the further away the indirect shot, the *less* likely it is of being hit (with the exception of a 12-shot).

Section II
Using Men Effectively

Section II begins a more advanced discussion of the principles involved in evaluating positions. We assume in this section, and those to follow, that your familiarity with the game has increased. Although the remainder of the book delves more deeply into the underlying structure of backgammon, the overall organization is not strictly linear in terms of difficulty; comparatively simple but important ideas occur later on.

In studying the book, don't get bogged down in the more technical parts (especially Chapter 13). Feel free to return to any chapters which trouble you at a later time. It is much more important to read through the material to get an idea of what is involved, analyzing each position yourself and deciding on a move *before* you read the explanation which follows. Making your own moves is a valuable learning tool which will give you experience in recognizing patterns which occur in backgammon. A firm grasp of the hierarchy of the strategic principles can only come with continued play.

Note: the doubling cube is shown only where it is directly relevant to the material being discussed.

CHAPTER 12.
BUILDERS AND FLEXIBILITY

BACKGAMMON, UNLIKE CHESS, is a game with a large element of chance. A player cannot decide upon a particular course of action without taking future possible dice rolls into account; he must consider both the immediate and future effects of his play. He must utilize his checkers to give himself the maximum opportunities for improving his game at each stage by creating positions which will increase the number of possible good rolls that occur. At the same time, he must try to limit the number of options his opponent will have by creating positions where the least number of dice rolls are good for his opponent.

Many weaker players complain about the large number of useless rolls they get, rolls which are not overtly constructive or which play awkwardly. They fail to notice or understand why good players' games so frequently fall into place naturally.

As we shall see in this chapter, the useful numbers that a good player rolls do not appear magically, and the checkers which make the needed points and hit the blots are not there by accident. An experienced player not only tries to play each move for maximum immediate effect, but also takes into consideration future moves — and the dice rolls these moves will require — for both him and his opponent. He tries to make his own position as fluid as possible by effectively utilizing his checkers so as to increase the number of dice combinations which will be good for him. At the same time, he tries to limit the number of rolls which will be good for his opponent.

Builders

In order to create new points for both defensive and offensive purposes, you should not wait passively hoping for a lucky number. Instead, you must use your men actively as building blocks, positioning them to **bear** on points you wish to make so that the greatest number of dice rolls will be useful. (By **bearing** on a point, we mean positioning a checker so that it is 6 pips or less away from the point you wish to make, so that one number on one die can bring the builder to the point.) Your checkers are all potential builders and thus must be thought of as positive assets, rather than liabilities merely to be brought around the board.

Clearly, the *number* of builders you have bearing on a particular point affects the chance you have of making that point. Just how much difference a single extra builder can make in increasing your chances for making points is usually not fully appreciated. Having three builders instead of two bearing on a point, for example, is not a fine technical difference; your chance of making that point at least *doubles!* Similarly (the *exact* chances depending upon the particular position), having four builders instead of three doubles, again, your chances of making that point.

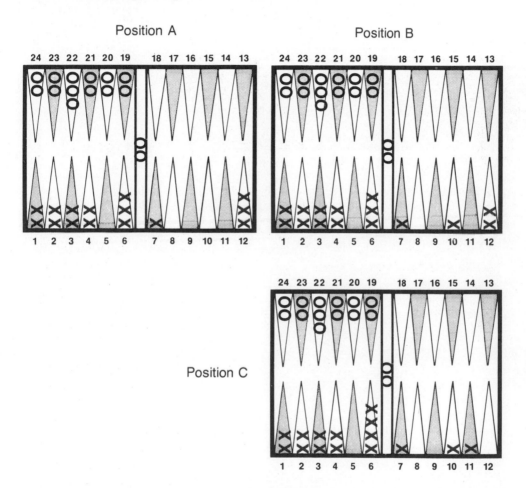

Position A

Position B

Position C

For example, in Position A, X has two builders bearing on the five point and has only 3 chances out of 36 to make this point on the subsequent roll. In Position B with three builders your chances are more than doubled to 7/36, and in Position C with four builders your chances again double to 14/36.

For a complete table of the number of ways to make a given point depending upon the number of builders bearing on it, see Table 6, p. 404.

Creating Extra Builders

One key to winning at backgammon lies not in dramatic or exotic plays but in carefully creating builders at every opportunity. If you consistently deploy your men to maximum advantage, you will be rewarded by a game which will fall more rapidly and naturally into place.

Many times an extra builder can be created with little or no extra risk.

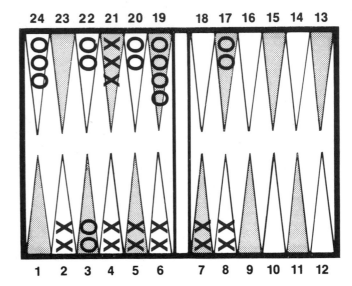

Position 1
X to Play 1–1

In Position 1, O has two checkers back behind a 5-point prime and a blockade of his own which will deteriorate on his next roll if he doesn't escape at least one of his back men. Thus, O will probably run with one of these checkers if he can. Assuming that he does leave, it is very important for X to have the most men possible bearing on the remaining blot.

Most players incorrectly move 8/7, 8/5 as shown in Position 1A, or 8/6(2) as in Position 1B.

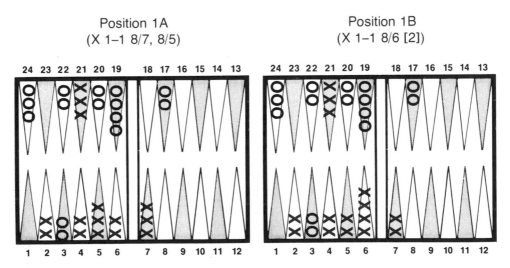

Position 1A
(X 1–1 8/7, 8/5)

Position 1B
(X 1–1 8/6 [2])

Either of these plays will leave you with only two effective builders bearing on the three point: in Position 1A, builders on the five and seven points; in Position 1B, builders on the six and seven points. (The checkers on already established points in X's home board do not count as builders, since X would not break one of these points to hit a blot on his three point.)

The proper play is 7/6, 7/4 (Position 1C).

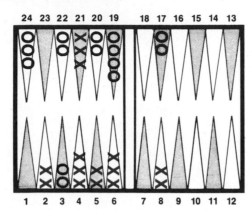

Position 1C
(X 1–1 7/6, 7/4)

You now have three builders on the four, six, and eight points — giving you *twice* as many ways to point on a blot on your three point. The one extra builder you create doesn't increase the chance of making the point by merely 10% or 20%, but by over 100%!

In addition, while the incorrect plays give you a double shot (two numbers) to hit the blot, the correct play gives you three numbers (1's, 3's, and 5's) — or a triple shot — to hit him. Since the entire game depends largely on what happens on the next roll, it is clear how important it really is to play carefully to create an *extra* builder.

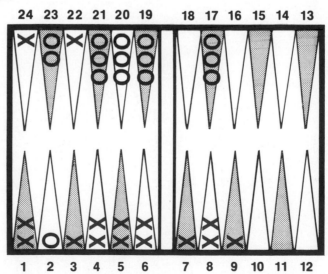

Position 2
X to Play 6–5

Because of the extreme danger and vulnerability of your position here, your best hope lies in hitting your opponent on the two point. You would then attempt to close your entire inner board.

There are several possible ways to try doing this, but only one correct play: 8/2*, 7/2.

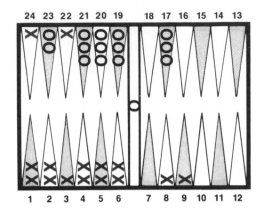

Position 2A
(X 6–5 8/2*, 7/2*)

This leaves you with two builders on the eight and nine points to cover the blot on your three point. Any other play gives you only one builder to cover the resulting blot in your inner board.

What Is an Active Builder?

In Position 3, X wishes to contain the opposing checker on the one point. To do this, X would like to strengthen his blockade by making the four or five point.

If you play 13/8, 13/12 (Position 3A), it might appear that you have three builders on the six, seven, and eight points bearing on the two key points. However, since you would not break the seven point — leaving a blot and giving O a direct 6-shot — to make the four or five point, you really have only two *active* builders on the six and eight points. The man on the seven, or bar point, cannot be an *active builder.* An **active builder,** then, is a checker which you are willing to use to hit a blot or make a point — as opposed to a checker which simply bears on a point, but which you are not willing to move.

Position 3
X to Play 5–1

Position 3A
(X 5–1 13/8, 13/12)

Position 3B
(X 5–1 13/7)

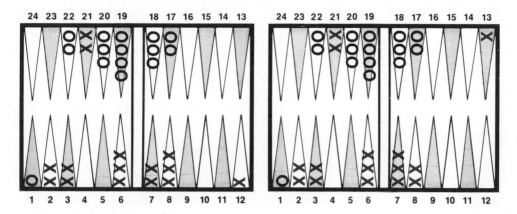

The correct play is 13/7 (Position 3B). You now have *three* active builders since you are willing to break the eight point, leaving a blot, but giving O no *direct* shots. By creating this extra active builder, you greatly increase your chance of making either the four or five point.

By playing correctly 13/7, the alert reader may notice that you expose yourself to being hit by 4–4. The additional active builder created by making the correct play is well worth the risk of this 35-to-1 shot. (Actually the danger of 4–4 should be disregarded in any case because this roll will be disastrous whether or not you have a blot on your midpoint.)

Position 3C

Position 3D

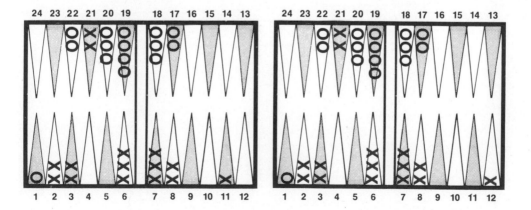

If you were offered a choice between Positions 3C and 3D, you would be wise to choose Position 3C despite being exposed to 6–4. An experienced player recognizes that the enormously increased chances for making the five point outweigh the danger of being hit by a 17-to-1 shot.

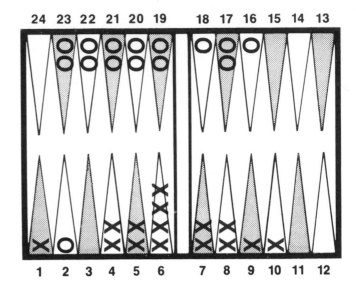

Position 4
X to Play 2–1

In Position 4, most players instinctively play 10/9, 6/4 to form a full 6-point prime as in Position 4A.

Position 4A
(X 2–1 10/9, 6/4)

But let's analyze the original position. We see that X is an enormous favorite: He has escaped all his back men while O still has a checker in X's inner board. At this point, all X has to do is come home safely. He would like to make his three point so that he can bring his men in without leaving O any shots. Making the nine point is unnecessary for two reasons: X already blockades him quite well since only a specific 1–6 will allow O to escape. Furthermore, X will have to break the nine point on his next roll anyway as he brings his checkers in.

Now let's see what happens if X does move 10/9, 6/4 to make the full 6-point prime. In this case, X has three active builders — on the four, six, and nine points — bearing on the three point. The men on the seven and eight points are not *active* builders because to break these points would leave a blot a direct 5- or 6-shot away.

The correct play is 10/8, 6/5.

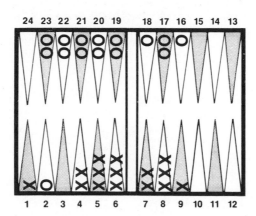

Position 4B
(X 2–1 10/8, 6/5)

This gives you four active builders on the nine, eight, six, and five points. You greatly increase your chances of making the three point with four active builders, and then coming home in an orderly manner. The danger of O's escaping and hitting the blot on the nine point with 1–6 is more than outweighed by the excellent opportunity you will have to make the three point and bear in safely.

The failure to differentiate between active and inactive builders can often lead to the wrong play.

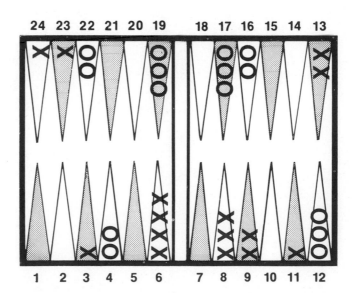

Position 5
X to Play 2

There are no very constructive plays in this position. 3/1 only takes a checker out of play. 13/11 leaves a direct shot and accomplishes nothing. 23/21 is too dangerous because O has three men on the nineteen, seventeen, and sixteen points bearing on the twenty-one point. In general, splitting to your opponent's four or five point (twenty, twenty-one) when he has three or more builders bearing on you is inadvisable. (The reasons for this rule are discussed in detail in Chapter 21.)

The correct play is 11/9.

Position 5A
(X 2 11/9)

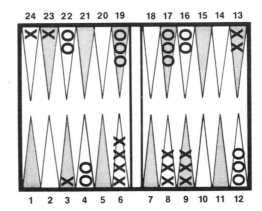

This move safeties the checker on the eleven point and maintains the number of active builders (three) bearing on the five and bar points. While moving 11/9 appears to take away a builder from the eleven point, it actually leaves the same number of active builders as before the move is taken. In the original position, the men on the nine point are not active builders because you would not break the nine point (leaving a blot a direct 5-shot away from O) in order to make the five or bar points. The immediate visual impression that 11/9 decreases the number of active builders is thus an illusion.

Position 6
X to Play 1

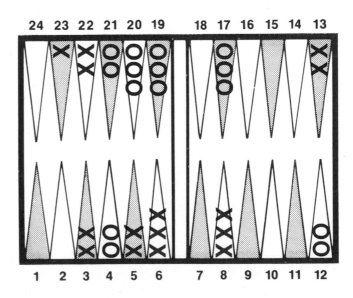

In this position, it appears that X should stay back on the twenty-three point in order to have an extra number (5) to escape with. However, this is an illusion. It is unlikely that X will escape with one man from the twenty-two point with a 4 or 6 because the remaining blot would be exposed to a direct 2-, 3-, or 5-shot. Thus, if X remains on the twenty-three point, he actually only has 5's to escape with.

The correct play is 23/22, moving up to the twenty-two point. By seemingly limiting your escape options you actually increase them, for now you have more ways to escape (i.e., a 4 or 6).

Naturally, you not only try to increase your own flexibility and mobility by correctly positioning the checkers; you also try to limit your opponent's mobility. Chapter 13 discusses how to limit the specific number of good rolls your opponent can have.

The following position shows how to restrict your opponent's number of active builders.

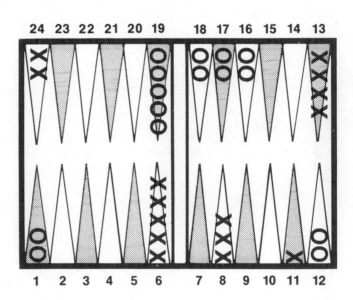

Position 7
X to Play 2

In this position, O would like to move checkers from the seventeen or sixteen point to build more important points (twenty-one, twenty) in his inner board. By playing a 2 to the twenty-two point (24/22), you effectively "freeze" the seventeen- and sixteen-point builders since he can no longer break the points without leaving a direct 5- or 6-shot. You thus limit his chances of improving his position by changing active builders into inactive builders.

The danger, in return, of O's pointing on you after you move a checker up is not as great as it appears. O holds only one inner-board point, which makes you a favorite to re-enter immediately. Furthermore, he does not wish to make either the twenty-two or twenty-four points, which are deep in his inner board.

Additional Risks for Builders

Position 8
X to Play 3–1

If X plays 9/5 in Position 8, safetying his blots, he will have two active builders bearing on his inner board from the six and eight points (Position 8A).

Position 8A (X 3–1 9/5)	**Position 8B** (X 3–1 8/5, 6/5)

But if he plays 8/5, 6/5 (Position 8B), he will have three and one-half active builders: one each on the five, six, and nine points, and one-half on the eight point. A builder is called **semi-active** when there is a question as to whether a player is willing to use it. In this position, X would break the eight point, leaving a blot, in order to make a point directly on one of O's checkers. Since half of O's roll would have to be used for re-entry, X thus would leave only an indirect shot.

Although the first play, 9/5, is completely safe, the more experienced player will realize that the suggested play (8/5, 6/5) is superior. This is true despite the fact that it immediately leaves O two indirect shots to hit the blot on the nine point.

As this example shows, you must sometimes take additional risks to create new builders. The player who plays supersafe and piles all his men on already established points (a style of playing referred to as "making candlesticks") will usually find himself with a static game which is ultimately more dangerous than fluid play.

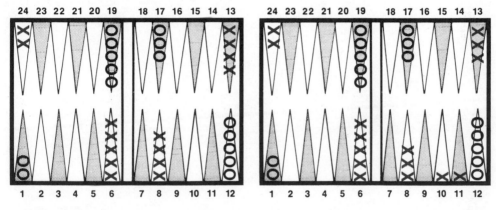

Position 9A
(X 3–2 13/8)

Position 9B
(X 3–2 13/11, 13/10)

A glaring example of overly timid and nonconstructive play is to move 13/8 with a 3–2 on the opening roll, as illustrated in Position 9A.

The correct play is to bring two builders down from the midpoint 13/11, 13/10 to bear on the key four, five, and bar points (Position 9B). The risk of being hit by an indirect shot is outweighed many times by the possible gain of making one of these points. You must not wait passively for a good position or a lucky roll to make needed points. Instead, you must actively mobilize your resources and create positions where good rolls can occur.

The first three examples (Positions 1, 2, and 3) of this section showed positions where careful play allowed for the creation of extra builders with no extra risk. However, in practice, a general conflict often arises: In order to give yourself maximum deployment and builders, you must often leave blots which increase the danger of your being hit. Therefore, you must always weigh the constructive potential of a checker as an extra builder against the loss of safety of the checker as a blot. Many of the following chapters, particularly Chapter 16, deal with just such questions of when extra risks are justified.

The last example indicates that near the beginning of the game, gaining an extra builder more than offsets the risk of being hit by an indirect shot. Sometimes even leaving direct shots in order to increase your builder power is advisable.

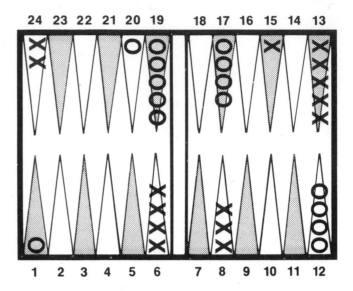

Position 10
X to Play 4–2

This is a frequently misplayed position. The correct play is 24/20*, 13/11 despite the fact that this leaves a direct 3-shot on both the fifteen point and twenty point in return.

(The reader who is familiar with the next chapter will notice that the importance of this 3-shot is somewhat lessened by duplication.) This play gives you three builders in the outfield instead of one (if you safety the man on the fifteen point) and thus gives you the chance to gain a significant lead in development early in the game. This early lead in development is enough to justify a direct shot.

When You Can Create Builders Safely

We shall now examine some special types of situations in which extra builders *can* be created at little or no additional risk. Despite their special nature, these situations occur frequently and should be thoroughly mastered.

When Opponent Is Harmless

First, let us examine a position where your opponent *isn't* completely harmless.

In Position 11A, an unwarranted risk is involved in creating an extra builder. X begins by pointing on O, 6/5*(2). X would like to split a man to his bar point (8/7) with the rest of his roll in order to create an extra builder, but the risk is unnecessarily great. X would be foolish to give O ten winning numbers to come in and hit (2–5, 2–6, 3–4, 3–5, 3–6) when he basically already has the game won. Since no extra builder can be created safely, the correct play is 6/5*(2), 11/9.

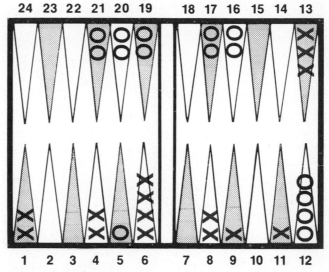

Position 11A
X to Play 1–1

Let's contrast this position with Position 11B.

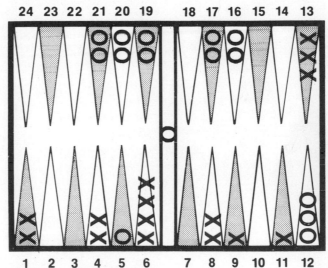

Position 11B
X to Play 1–1

O already has one man on the bar. The correct play for X is 6/5*(2), 8/7, 11/10. By making your five point, you put a second man on the bar and create a situation where you can freely leave blots since O now must use *both* halves of his next roll for re-entry; he has no free numbers to hit blots anywhere else. By breaking your eight point and moving to the bar point, you increase your firepower bearing on your inner board.

The principle is that whenever your opponent has *two* men on the bar, you should always concentrate on creating new builders in the outer boards. You should move your men constructively without concentrating on safetying them. When your opponent has two men on the bar, his entire roll (except if he rolls doubles) will be needed to re-enter. Thus, he will have nothing left over to hit you with — in fact, he will be fortunate if he even brings both men in on one roll.

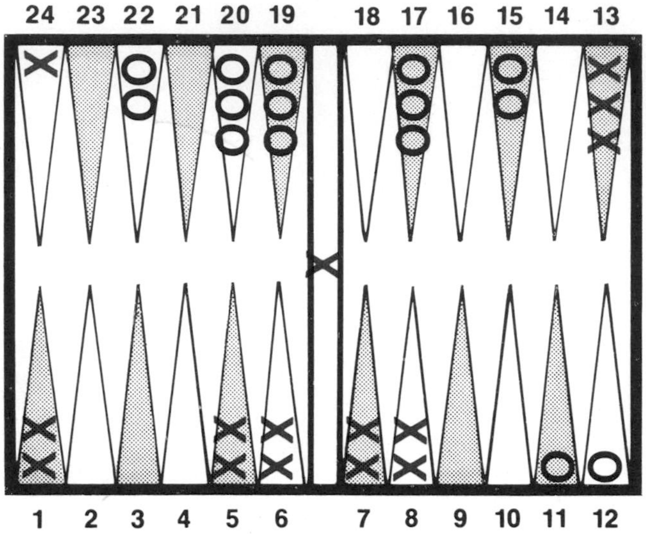

Position 12
X to Play 1–1

Similarly, in Position 12 the correct play is bar/24, 13/12*/11*, 7/6. Once again, by puttng two of your opponent's men on the bar you have made him harmless. In this case, instead of keeping points in your outer board, it is better to break them up to create extra builders to pounce on opposing checkers should they re-enter your inner board. Note that playing the fourth 1 7/6 is superior to 11/10 because this creates an extra builder for all three open points (two, three, four) in your inner board. Moving a man to the ten point would create an extra builder only for the four point.

The same principle of spreading your men to maximum advantage also applies when your opponent has three or more men on the bar.

Another example where your opponent is harmless and so you can spread your checkers for maximum diversification without danger is shown in Position 13.

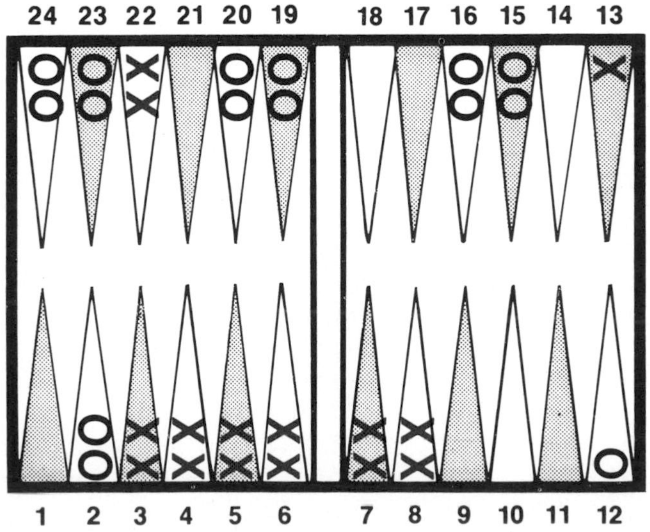

Position 13
X to Play 4

The correct play is 22/18. Here, O is trapped behind a full 6-point prime. X cannot lose the game by being hit and staying out, not even by being closed out, since O's two back men can never escape unless X breaks his prime. To avoid the possibility of rolling a number that might force him to break his prime (such as 3–3 or 6–6), X comes out to his opponent's bar point. Spreading your men not only insures your winning the game but also increases your chances of hitting another man and winning a gammon.

An even more obvious example of your opponent being defenseless is shown in Position 14, where you have a full closed board.

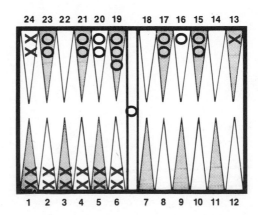

Position 14
X to Play 3–2

Here the correct play is 13/10, 24/22. By splitting your back men, you bring a builder to bear on O's exposed man and make it easier to escape.

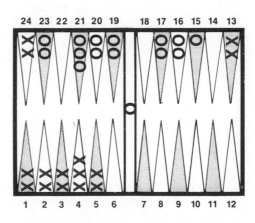

Position 15
X to Play 6

In Position 15, O has one checker on the bar which must re-enter in X's 5-point inner board. O is not a favorite to come in. Although O is not completely harmless, X must now start to extricate his back men and begin coming home. Thus the correct move is 24/18. If O re-enters immediately, X may be in very serious trouble; however, waiting back on the twenty-four point leaves you with very dim prospects. You should take the opportunity to move your men advantageously while O is occupied with re-entering his checker.

Creating Builders When Opponent Has Inner-Board Blots
Another special opportunity to create builders sometimes arises when your opponent has a blot or blots in his inner board.

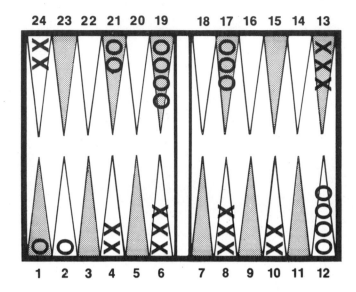

Position 16A
X to Play 1

In this position, O has *no* blots in his inner board. Here, X would like to split 10/9 to create an extra builder to make the critical five point or bar point. The risk, however, is too high. Despite the fact that X leaves no direct shots for O's blots on the one and two points, there are, in fact, sixteen indirect shots. Sixteen indirect shots offer O a greater opportunity to hit than a single simple direct shot would.

A constructive play without this risk is 24/23. This move allows an additional checker to bear indirectly on O's outer board in much the same way as O's blots bear indirectly on X's outer board.

Position 16B is almost identical to the previous position with the exception of O's blot on the twenty point. This difference, however, is critical to the move X will make.

Again, X wishes to split the ten point, 10/9, to bear upon the five and bar points, but again the threat of being hit by 16 numbers may act as a deterrent. It shouldn't! As in the previous example, your opponent can only hit you with an indirect or combination shot which will take up his entire roll, so he will not be able to both hit you *and* cover his twenty-point blot (unless he rolls 4–4). If he does hit you, you will have a double direct shot (4's from the twenty-four point, and 5's from the bar) to hit his inner-board blot.

The principle illustrated in comparing Positions 16A and 16B is that you can always be freer about leaving combination shots — whether to create builders or for some other purpose — when your opponent has a blot or blots in in his inner board.

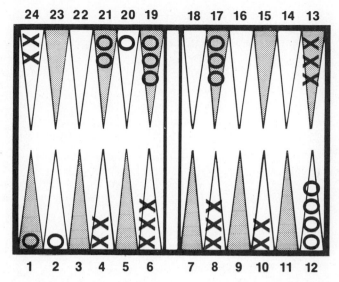

Position 16B
X to Play 1

So far we have been mainly concerned with utilizing your men effectively by creating builders. Let us now examine more generally how to place your checkers to give them the best chance to be used constructively.

Flexibility

Instead of viewing men as liabilities to be gotten around the board, it is more useful to consider them as positive assets to be used constructively.

To illustrate this important principle, consider the following proposition: Your opponent offers to begin the game with two extra men — one on his midpoint and one on his six point. Purely in terms of the race, you now have the advantage since he has 19 pips more than you. However, if you played the position several times, you would discover that in fact he would be a considerable favorite.

The reason for this is that his two extra men may enable him simultaneously to hold critical points in your inner board, to close points in his own inner board, and most importantly, to try to prime you. Remember that the reason a full 6-point prime is difficult to achieve is that it requires twelve out of your fifteen men, leaving you only three spares. Think how much easier it would be to construct a prime if you had two extra men.

Consider a complementary proposition, where your opponent begins with his full number of men but you begin with only thirteen. Although again you will be ahead in the race, you will find it more difficult to win since you lack the material to make key points. In advanced play, few games evolve immediately into a race. Most games involve considerable contact and depend on who can best block and hold his opponent. With only thirteen men, you would thus be at a considerable disadvantage.

Keeping Men in Play

Generally, your strategic objectives include holding key points in your opponent's inner board, holding points in the outer boards, priming your opponent, and closing as many points as possible in your inner board. Since you have only a limited number of men to work with, it is important to keep them all working for you, deployed to maximum advantage. This explains the reluctance of experienced players to make their one point. Once the one point has been made, these checkers are permanently out of play; they are no longer builders, nor can they form part of a prime. They have nowhere to go except off the board. Their only function is to keep the one point closed, possibly making it harder for your opponent to re-enter when he is hit. After you make this point, then, you really only have thirteen active men left to play with.

Even worse, positionally, is having a third man on the one point. Such a checker serves absolutely no useful function other than being closest to home in a bear-off situation. Such a checker is called a **dead checker**, and putting it completely out of play is referred to as **killing** it.

Whenever you take men deep into your inner board, you run the risk of taking them out of active play. For this reason, making the two point early in the game is usually undesirable. Similarly, having builders which bear only on points deep in your inner board (sometimes called **dilly builders**) is wasteful.

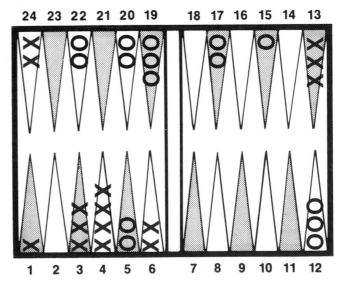

Position 17
X is on Roll

For example, in Position 17, X's three builders on the three and four points may eventually enable X to close the one and two points and create a 5-point board. X, however, would be in a better position if some of these dilly builders were further back on his six point or thirteen point where they would be more likely to enter directly into the struggle against O's men.

Playing Off Heavy Points, or Don't Pile Up

You should generally avoid placing too many additional men on already established points. Leaving five or six men on one point effectively takes men out of play.

Partially for this reason, some players are willing to risk a direct hit by taking a man off their overloaded six point and slotting (usually on the five point, sometimes on the four) early in the game. In the opening position, a player begins with too many men piled on the six point with nowhere to go except into his inner board; the point is top-heavy with extra men. By slotting off his point, he will hopefully be able to use the spare men to create a new point. Even if he is hit, he has at least some consolation in the fact that this man, in coming around the entire board, has now become an active part of the game. In fact, in certain advanced positions, and backgames, players will go to elaborate lengths to keep all their checkers actively circulating and in play.

Whenever two plays seem of approximately equal merit, the underlying distribution of the checkers may give the key to the better play. In other words, other factors being equal, try to play off the heavy points.

Don't Strip Points

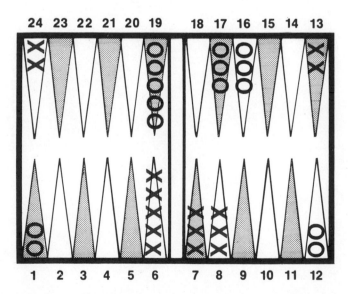

Position 18
X to Play 3–2

In this position, most players automatically make their five point by playing 7/5, 8/5. The correct play, however, is to make the four point 6/4, 7/4. This does not mean that the four point is more valuable than the five point — if the rest of the position were equal, the five point would be superior. However, the resulting distribution of checkers after the play is made is a strong enough factor to make the four point correct in this case.

Let's compare the distribution of the spare men, or builders, after each possible play is made:

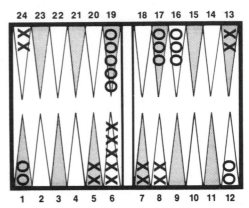

Position 18A
(X 3–2 8/5, 7/5)

If you make the five point 8/5, 7/5, the resulting distribution of builders on the five, six, seven, and eight points is respectively 0, 3, 0, and 0. This is the worst possible distribution. Not only do you have too many men on the six point, you have *no* builders on the other three points. This illustrates another important distributional concept: You should not only avoid having too many men on a point, you should also beware of having too few. Having no extra builders on an established point is referred to as being **stripped**. Since all your potential builders are on the six point, it will probably be several rolls before you can make an additional point naturally.

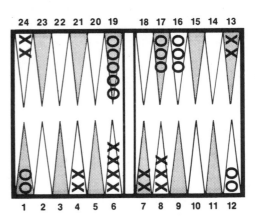

Position 18B
(X 3–2 7/4, 6/4)

If you make the four point 7/4, 6/4 instead of the five point, the resulting distribution of builders on the four, six, seven, and eight points is respectively 0, 2, 0, and 1. This is much better than the previous resulting distribution. You now have two active builders (on the six and eight points) and are not as overstacked and top-heavy on the six point. Thus, you have· better prospects for creating new points, and you also exert more pressure on your opponent's checkers in your inner board.

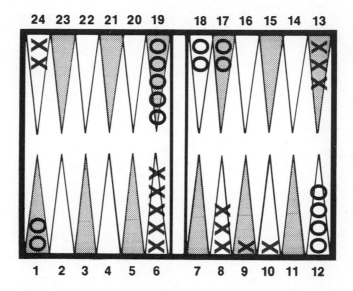

Position 19
X to Play 3–2

Similarly, in Position 19, X has the opportunity to make the bar point 10/7, 9/7. The resulting position, however, leaves him with builders on only the six and eight points with little prospect of immediately making additional good points. Although the bar point is an excellent point to own, a more dynamic and overall superior play is 13/10, 24/22.

The ten point, by itself, is not as valuable as the bar point. By making the indicated play, however, you have builders on the six, eight, nine, and ten points. These checkers put more pressure on O to keep him from advancing in your inner board or escaping. Furthermore, you have an excellent chance of following up by making a key point (the four, five, or bar point) on the next roll.

The second part of the roll, 24/22, brings a checker to the twenty-two point. Splitting a checker to the twenty-two point restricts the flexibility of O's position in two ways: First, it transforms the second checker on the seventeen point from a more or less active builder to a relatively inactive builder since you now have a checker bearing on that point; secondly, you make it much more dangerous for O to bring builders into his own outer board to create new points since your own checker is bearing on his outer board.

As we saw in the discussion of Position 18, it is not only important to avoid having too many men piled up, but also to avoid being **stripped** of men. You should always try to create a fluid, flexible position, with spare men to play with. A failure to have spare men to move often results in awkward and even potentially fatal numbers.

This failure can result from killing checkers, and it can also result from trying to hold too many points without an adequate supply of spare men. Whether the supply of spare men is adequate often depends on more advanced considerations which will be discussed later. However, we shall illustrate one such example now despite its more difficult nature.

Position 20
X to Play 6–2

In this position, X would ordinarily want to keep his ten point, which, being 5 pips away, best contains O's back men. The correct move, however, is 10/8, 10/4. This play leaves X with a spare man on the eight point and allows him to handle big numbers more easily.

If X had played 8/6, 8/2, he would seemingly have a stronger position. However, he is actually more vulnerable since he is now stripped of useful builders and will have trouble holding his position.

The next chapter discusses the question of how to place your men to give you the best opportunity to achieve both your own strategic objectives and to limit your opponent's objectives.

CHAPTER 13.
DUPLICATION
AND DIVERSIFICATION

THIS CHAPTER DISCUSSES how to either increase the number of favorable rolls you have (**diversification**) or to restrict the number of good rolls your opponent has (**duplication**).

This chapter is long and sometimes technical. If you are unfamiliar with these ideas, it is recommended that you study only the first two positions and proceed directly to other fundamental aspects of strategy and play. The succeeding chapters may be profitably read without reference to the duplication and diversification principles. You can return to this chapter later for deeper study.

Let's begin by looking at the defensive half of these two complementary principles: the duplication principle.

Duplication

Duplicating the Numbers Your Opponent Needs to Hit

In Position 1, you are forced to leave two blots at different points of the board. If you move one man as far as possible 18/11 (Position 1A), you leave both men exposed: one to a 4-shot, the other to a 5-shot.

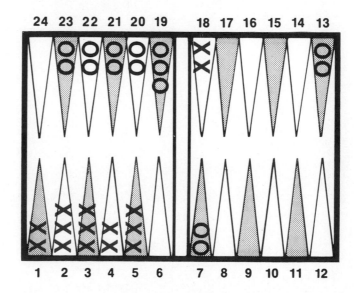

Position 1
X to Play 6–1

Position 1A
(X 6–1 18/11)

Position 1B
(X 6–1 18/12, 5/4)

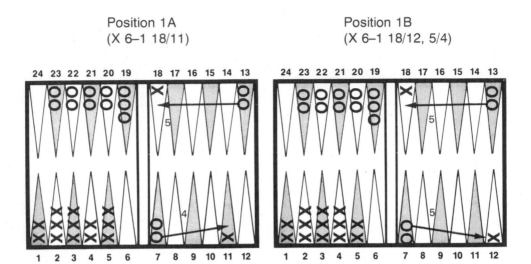

Now consider the correct play: 18/12, 5/4.

Again you have two exposed blots, but your opponent needs specifically 5 to hit in each case. Thus, despite your double exposure, your opponent has on the dice only a *single* direct shot, a 5 (in addition to 1–4, 2–3). You have *duplicated* the number he needs to hit — a 5 in each case — and thus considerably reduced his chances of hitting.

Similarly, consider Position 2.

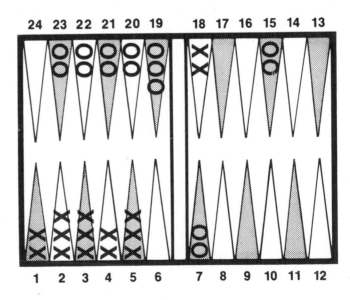

Position 2
X to Play 6–2

Here, the correct play is to continue one man all the way 18/10 (Position 2A).

This play leaves two blots, but each blot is directly exposed only to a 3. You have duplicated your opponent's good number — a 3 — and reduced his chances of hitting. Any other play would leave two *different* numbers for him to hit with, in other words, a double direct shot. (Note that duplication not only reduces the chance of *either* man's being hit, but also makes it extremely difficult for *both* men to be hit. In Position 2A only 3–3 specifically hits both men.)

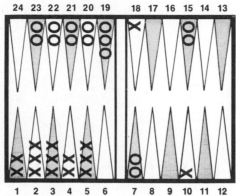

Position 2A
(X 6–2 18/10)

The principle is that *if you must leave more than one man exposed, try to leave them exposed to the same number, thus minimizing the number of ways to be hit.*

Notice that in both these examples, we could have found the safest possible play by counting the exact number of shots in each case. The duplication principle, however, makes tiresome counting unnecessary. A play *with* duplication is sure to give you less shots than a corresponding play *without* duplication. This is one reason that expert players seldom bother counting shots exactly — usually duplication does the work for them.

In Position 3, X must re-enter with the 4 and now consider his 3. If he plays his back checker out to his opponent's bar point (bar/21/18), this gives a triple direct shot to hit his checkers: 4's, 6's, and 1's. Clearly this is not correct.

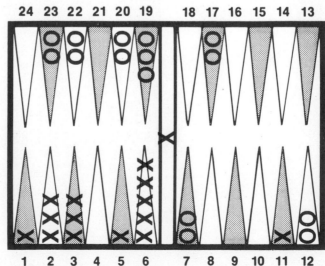

Position 3
X to Play 4–3

If you play the man in your own outer board closer to home (bar/21, 11/8), you again leave a triple direct shot. Your opponent will be able to hit this man with a 1 and the man in his inner board with 2's and 4's (which he will not hesitate to do because of your weak position).

The correct play is bar/21, 6/3. Here you leave only 2's and 4's — a considerable improvement since you have duplicated the 4's.

Position 4
· X to Play 4–3

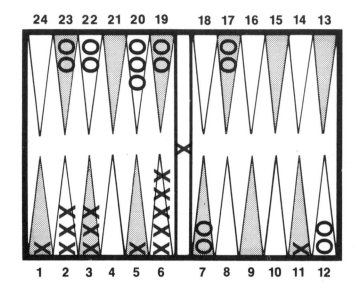

Position 4 is almost identical to Position 3. After re-entering, X sees that the 4's are duplicated if he leaves his outside men as they are bar/21, 6/3. The 1's will be duplicated if he plays bar/21, 11/8. Either way, his opponent will have 4's and 1's to hit with, so as far as the duplication principle is concerned, the two plays are equal and leave the same number of shots.

The slightly preferable play is bar/21, 11/8 to lessen the chance of a second man's being picked up, and to bring this man closer to safety should your opponent miss.

Positions 3 and 4 illustrate one reason why backgammon is a tough and interesting game. Minute changes of position on one side of the board affect how you play a given number in another sector of the board.

The duplication principle may not always help you determine the correct move. Overemphasis on duplication, or looking for it unnecessarily, can be misleading, as in Position 5.

By playing bar/21, 6/3, X can duplicate the 2's that O has to hit with. But this is not the correct play.

The correct play is bar/21, 9/6 safetying the checker on the nine point. There is no need to leave a shot on the nine point just because you duplicate 2's.

The principle is that when you are *forced* to leave men exposed in different

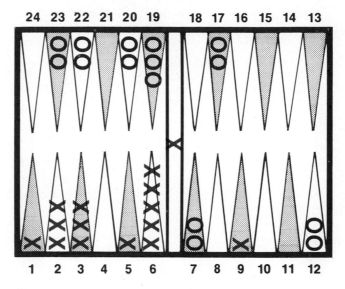

Position 5
X to Play 4–3

parts of the board, you should try to duplicate the numbers that will hit. You should not purposely leave extra blots just to create a duplication.

Sometimes more than one number may be duplicated. Also, you may even triple or quadruple your opponent's hitting numbers.

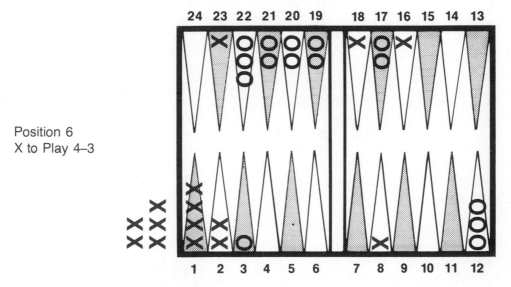

Position 6
X to Play 4–3

Position 6 illustrates both these possibilities. By playing 16/13, 8/4, you have 1's and 6's all over. Although the 1's are left in four different places, they are only one number on the dice. Your prospects are still pretty dim, but any other play would leave at least a triple direct shot and almost guarantee being hit on the next roll.

Try to study and solve for yourself the following examples of duplicating your opponent's numbers which hit: Positions 7A, 7B, 7C, 7D.

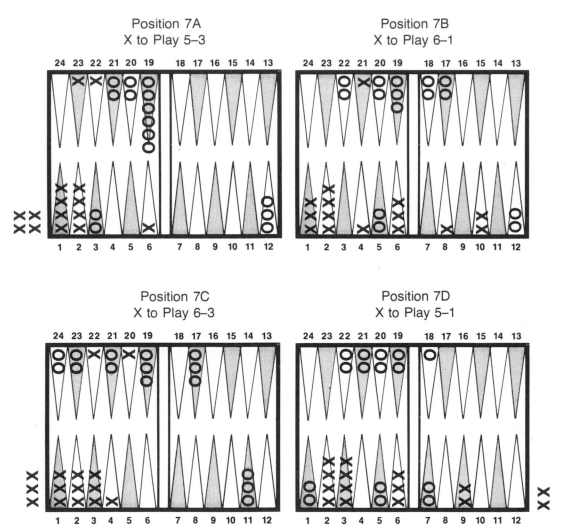

In Position 7A, X can play 23/15. This effectively reduces O to a single direct shot, 3's, which is the only number that hits. Notice that if you make the alternate play, 22/14, your three men are now exposed not to one number, 3's, but to three *different* numbers: 2's, 3's, and 4's — in other words, a triple shot.

A common criticism of the duplication principle is the question: What happens if your opponent rolls a double — the double of the number you are duplicating? You will not only be hit once, but hit twice. In Position 7, in fact, 3–3 would be a disaster for X. It would point on X inside O's home board, and hit two men outside.

The answer is that such numbers cannot be avoided — a specific double occurs 1 out of 36 times (remember that a regular non-double number such as

3–4 occurs 2 out of 36 times), and when it occurs it is your misfortune. There is no way to protect against every number — rather, the purpose of duplication is to lessen the chances of your opponent's rolling a good number.

In Position 7B, X again can escape O's inner board and leave only 3's by playing 21/15, 4/3.

In Position 7C, X should play 20/14, 4/1, leaving 3's (duplicated) and 5's.

In Position 7D, by playing 9/4, 9/8, X leaves 1's and 3's — only a 20-number shot, whereas if X plays 9/3, he leaves direct 2's and 4's in addition to 1–1, 1–3, 3–5 for a total of 25 numbers. In this particular case, leaving 5 fewer shots is correct despite the extra blot.

Other Forms of Duplication

So far we have discussed limiting your opponent's chances to hit by duplicating the number he needs to hit you in different places. Although this is the most basic, and perhaps the most common form, duplication applies whenever your opponent has any numbers that are good (or necessary) for him at different places on the board.

Come In and Hit

For example, consider the situation when your opponent has a man on the bar.

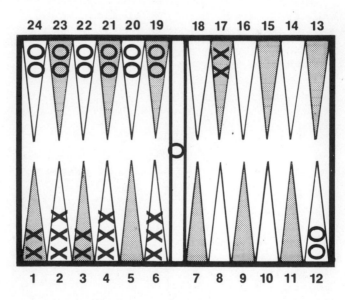

Position 8
X to Play 6–1

We see in Position 8 that O needs a 5 to enter, so if you are forced to leave a shot, you should attempt to leave a 5-shot. By playing 17/10, you leave only a 5-shot and 5–5 is the only number that hits.

If, however, you had carelessly moved both back men 17/16, 17/11, you would leave a 4-shot (from his midpoint) and a 6-shot (assuming he comes in with a 5). This is a net total of 5–4 and 5–6, or 4 hits in all — still small, but four times as many as necessary.

The reduction in O's shots when the numbers to enter and to hit are duplicated can be seen if we compare Positions 9 and 10.

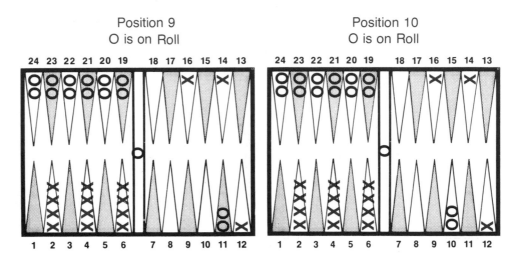

Position 9
O is on Roll

Position 10
O is on Roll

In Position 9, O needs 1's, 3's, or 5's to enter and the *same* numbers to hit. Because of the duplications, only 9 numbers hit.

In Position 10, however, O needs 1's, 3's, and 5's to enter, and different numbers, 2's, 4's, and 6's, to hit. Here there is *no* duplication, and there are 20 numbers that hit — more than twice as many as in Position 9.

Hit and Escape Prime

The duplication principle can be used whenever your opponent needs a number for a specific purpose on one part of the board. By giving him the same good number instead of a new number elsewhere, you have restricted his options.

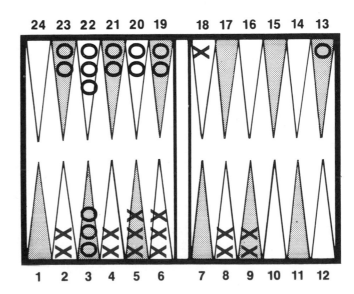

Position 11
X to Play 2–1

For example, in Position 11 the least shots (13) can be given by 18/15. The correct play, however, is 18/17, 6/4. O needs 4's urgently to escape from X's 5-point prime. By duplicating the 4's, you force your opponent (should he roll a 4) to choose between escaping a checker and hitting you. Therefore, since 4's are an essential number for O in one place, it is better to leave a 4-shot than a 2-shot elsewhere.

Up to Edge of Prime and Hit

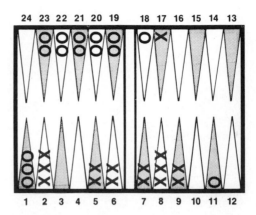

Position 12
X to Play 3–1

In Position 12, depending upon how X plays his 1, he can either leave O a direct 3-shot or 2-shot at his blot. Ordinarily, X would leave a 2-shot which gives O less chances to hit (12, as opposed to 13 for a 3-shot); however, you should first look around and see whether O needs 2's or 3's elsewhere. He clearly needs 3's to come up to the edge of X's prime; therefore, the correct play is 17/14, 8/7. This play duplicates O's only good number, 3's. He needs a 3 to come up to the edge of your prime on the four point, and a 3 to hit you on the fourteen point.

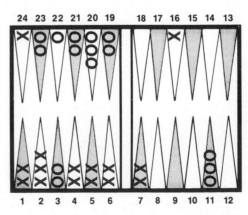

Position 13
X to Play 3–1

In Position 13, O needs a 2 to cover the exposed blot on the twenty-two point. X correctly plays 16/13, 2/1, duplicating 2's. In other words, X leaves O only 2's to cover the blot on the twenty-two point, and 2's to hit X's blot in O's outer board: 2's to cover and 2's to hit.

Position 14
X to Play 6–2
(O 2–1 6/5, 13/11)

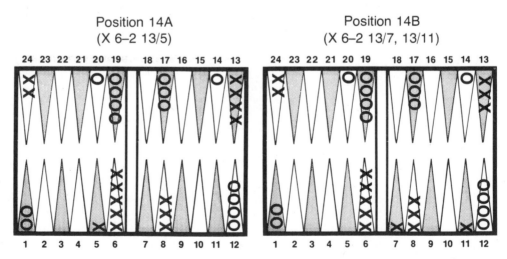

At the beginning of the game, your opponent rolls 2–1. He slots the twenty point 19/20 and brings one man down from his midpoint 12/14. You then roll 6–2. Running a back man all the way 24/16, or to his bar point and down from the midpoint 24/18, 13/11 are unnecessarily risky plays because of the extra shots O has with a builder on the fourteen point.

The way most people play (actually misplay) the move is to slot on their five point 13/5 (Position 14A).

Position 14A
(X 6–2 13/5)

Position 14B
(X 6–2 13/7, 13/11)

This leaves 4's to hit and 1's, 3's, and 6's for your opponent to cover his own twenty-point blot — all different numbers. By leaving several different good numbers, you increase the chance that your opponent will roll at least one of them. You have *diversified* his good numbers. Of course, you want to do just the opposite, that is, *duplicate* his good numbers and thus limit his options.

With this in mind, a slightly better play is to slot the bar point, 13/7, 13/11 (Position 14B).

Instead of presenting him with a new good number, 4's, you duplicate his 6's: 6 to hit and 6 to cover.

What Duplication Accomplishes — And What It Doesn't

A common misconception is that the main point of duplication is to psychologically confound your opponent; if he does roll the number that is duplicated (in Position 14B, a 6), he will be confused about which 6 to take. Although it is true that he may have real choices if he rolls the number which is duplicated, usually these choices are favorable to him and, in any case, the benefits from duplication are a tangible reduction in the number of good shots he has — not an intangible psychological gain.

If, as in Position 14B, your opponent needs the same number for two different purposes at different places on the board, the reduction in his number of good shots comes about in two ways:

By comparing the recommended play 13/7, 13/11 (Position 14B) to the alternate play 13/5 (Position 14A), we can see that you can decrease the chance that he will both hit you and cover himself. By making the recommended play, you also increase the chance he will accomplish *neither* objective.

Although you generally prefer to make the five point rather than your bar point (and thus prefer to slot on the five point as opposed to the bar point), in this case decreasing your opponent's good numbers by duplication makes slotting on the bar point preferable.

In fact, there is even another play, which is recommended only for an advanced player who wishes to move boldly: 13/7, 6/4!

Position 14C
(X 6–2 13/7, 6/4)

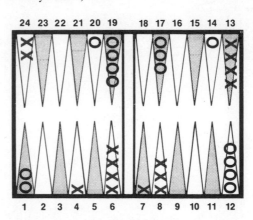

At first glance, this play looks foolish because it is seldom correct to leave such a double shot. However, notice the perfect duplication: 3's and 6's to hit, and 3's and 6's to cover. There are actually extremely few numbers that hit and cover, and only one more number which does so (3–1) than the recommended play. If your opponent hits without covering, you now have a double shot back at his blot on the five point; if he elects to cover, then you can keep pace by rapidly building up your own board.

Once again, we emphasize the importance of considering the game as a whole.

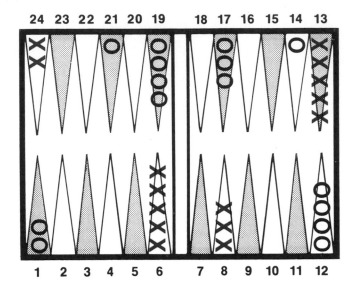

Position 15
X to Play 6–2

In Position 15, we have modified Position 14 by moving O's blot on the twenty point to the twenty-one point. This changes the whole play on your side of the board. Now O needs 2's and 4's to cover. The correct play, then, is to slot on the five point, 13/5, which leaves 4's to hit as well.

Hit and Prime

Still another example of duplication is shown in Position 16.

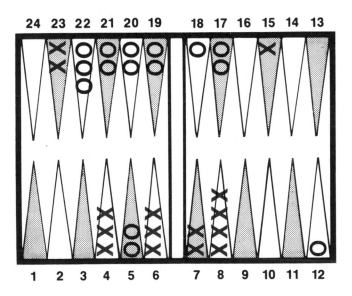

Position 16
X to Play 4–1

O threatens to win the game by rolling a 6, thus creating a full 6-point prime. X cannot safety his blot on the fifteen point with a 4–1 and has a choice of leaving a direct 2-, 3-, 5-, or 6-shot. The correct choice is to duplicate 6's by moving 15/11, 8/7. This leaves O with only one winning number instead of two since the hit is also a likely winner.

Duplicate Indirect Shots

Ordinarily you are only concerned with duplicating your opponent's direct numbers, but occasionally it pays to duplicate indirect shots as well.

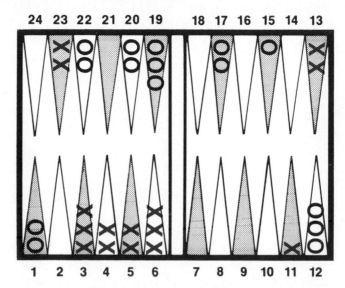

Position 17
X to Play 1

In Position 17, X would usually prefer to keep his builder as far back as possible on the eleven point in case O tries to escape with one man. However, X exposes his checker to a 6–4 as it stands. In this position, 6–3 is a good roll for O since it makes his bar point (eighteen point). The correct play, therefore, is 11/10. This duplicates the 6–3 which hits or points and eliminates 6–4 from O's list of excellent numbers.

Let's compare this example to Position 18.

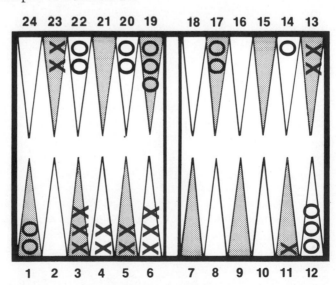

Position 18
X to Play 1

In this position, O's builder is on the fourteen point and O needs a 6–4 to make his bar point (eighteen point). He also needs 6–4 to hit X's blot. The correct play for X would be 6/5, which leaves 6–4 duplicated.

Other Cases

We have seen that whenever a number serves an important function for your opponent the possibility of duplication arises. As we explore strategy and tactics deeper, new possibilities for duplication continue to arise.

One such case is Position 19.

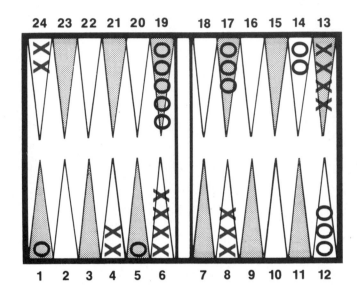

Position 19
X to Play 4

X has a choice of three possible 4's: 24/20, 8/4, and 13/9. The first possibility is inadvisably risky as it involves *coming under the gun*. This concept is explained fully in Chapter 21.

In the last chapter, we saw that 8/4, while harmless, leaves your builders slightly worse off: You have a dilly builder on the four point and are stripped on the eight point. The correct move, 13/9, may only be understood when the enormous value of your opponent's five point is realized. A whole chapter of this book, *Golden Point*, explains the great strategic significance of establishing this point.

With this in mind, the duplication becomes easier to spot. O's best number on his next roll is a 4 to make this prize point, X's five point. Although there is no direct way to stop O from rolling a 4 and making the five point, we can use the fact that O needs a 4 to play 13/9, duplicating 4's: 4's to cover, and 4's to hit.

Let us now consider what may happen in two cases:

Case A: O rolls a 4. O now has a choice, a very difficult and close choice, as to whether to hit or make your five point. We are not pleased with either of his choices, but it is important to realize that 4 is a good number for him whether we have a blot on the nine point or not. We have risked very little, if anything, by being hit because he could always have made the five point instead.

Case B: O doesn't roll a 4. If O doesn't roll a 4, the play we made, 13/9, is much more satisfying than the other two plays and now creates an extra builder; it also puts extra pressure on O's blot on X's five point.

In Position 19 we have not used duplication to directly limit O's number of good shots so much as to enhance our position at little additional risk.

Hit a 6 for Various Reasons

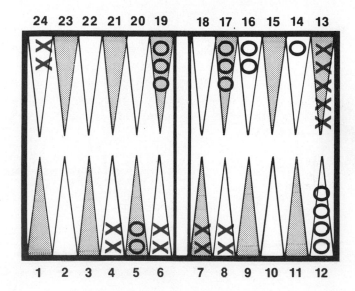

Position 20
X to Play 6–2

In our final example, we again can enhance our position at little additional risk by duplication. At first glance, it is not at all clear how duplication can be of use since O doesn't appear to need one particular number. A close inspection, however, reveals that almost all of O's 6's play extremely well for him for different reasons. 6–1, 6–3, and 6–4 make the twenty point; 6–2, 6–4, and 6–1 make his bar point (eighteen point); and even 6–5 makes the twenty-two point and doesn't play badly.

The correct play for X is 13/7, 13/11, duplicating O's 6's. If O now rolls a 6, we will be no worse off since the 6's play well whether he makes a valuable point or hits. (We have just mentioned the value to O of your five point. In fact, as we shall see later, O would be foolish in this position to hit and give up this point.) If he fails to hit, we then have a chance to roll a 2 and make the eleven point. This is the point which best contains those opposing men on our five point because it is 6 pips away.

Finally, some important words of advice concerning duplication. Duplication can often be extremely difficult to spot and requires much experience and practice. In the vast majority of moves, duplication is of no importance or is overruled by some other idea. A common mistake made by people who have just learned this principle is to overuse it and look for a duplication "behind every tree." Needless to say, we discourage the practice of leaving shots unnecessarily just because a duplication is involved.

The best way to absorb duplication is slowly, through practice. For example, begin by looking for a possible duplication only in cases where you have to leave two or more blots at different points on the board, and wish to avoid being hit on both (*hit-hit*). Another case where it is sometimes worthwhile to look for duplications is when you have two possible similar plays. In order to decide which is better, see if either one duplicates a key number for your opponent. With more experience, you will occasionally recognize other situations where your opponent needs a key number and where duplication may be of value.

Diversification

Diversification and duplication are complementary techniques: Your opponent wants to **duplicate** the favorable numbers you may roll, and you want to **diversify** your good numbers, or avoid having them duplicated. You try to create positions where as many different numbers as possible will be advantageous for you.

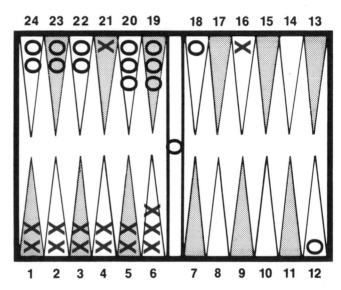

Position 21
X to Play 1

In Position 21, O is on the bar and X has closed his inner board. X has nothing to fear in this position and can freely move his checkers. He would like to hit additional men to increase his chances for a gammon. It would be a mistake to play 16/15, for this would leave X with only 3's to directly hit either of O's blots. In other words, playing 16/15 duplicates your own good numbers. This is your opponent's objective — not yours.

The correct play is 6/5. This gives you both 3's (to hit the eighteen-point blot) and 4's (to hit the twelve-point blot). You have thus left yourself a double direct shot.

In Chapter 12 we saw how to develop your game quickly by creating builders and also by putting men where they will take an active part in the game. Diversification has the same objective: increasing your chances of constructive play. Diversification works by considering the specific numbers that are favorable to you. Whenever you need a specific number to make a constructive play in one part of the board, you should try to arrange your position so that you will need a *different* specific number to make a good play elsewhere. By creating as many different specific good numbers as possible, you are diversifying.

In the first example, you diversified the numbers that you needed to hit with. In Position 22, X again has an opportunity to diversify his favorable numbers.

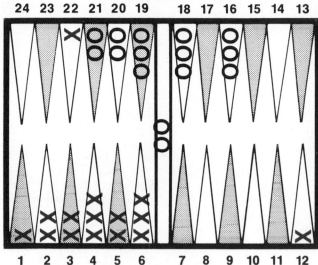

Position 22
X to Play 1

O has two men on the bar and X has closed five points in his own inner board. X has two important objectives: to escape his last back man from O's broken 5-point prime, and to cover his one point and close O out.

As the position stands, X needs 5's to escape and either 5's or 3's to cover his one point. By correctly playing 6/5, X can diversify his own good numbers. Now 3's and 4's are needed to cover, and 5's to escape. There is now a much better chance that X will roll a good number because he has made more numbers helpful for him.

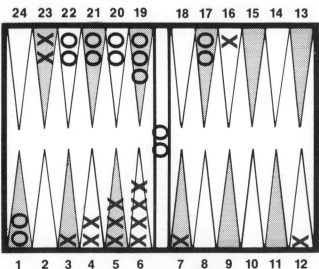

Position 23
X to Play 3–1

Here again, X has two essential goals: to bring out his back men, and to build a prime in front of O. By playing 6/3, 12/11, X diversifies the number he needs to come out with (5) and the number he now needs to make his bar point (4).

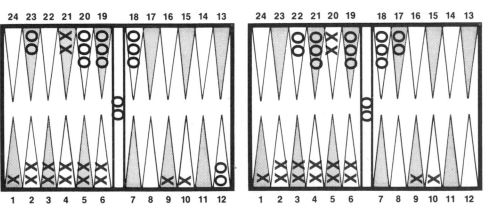

Position 24
X to Play 4–1

The next example, Position 24, is taken from an actual game where an expert player went astray because he failed to realize the possibilities of diversification. The play that he made was bar/21*, 5/4. By making this play, instead of diversifying your good numbers, you duplicate them. Now you need 4's to hit a second man on your nine point, and 4's to cover the blot on your four point.

The correct play is bar/21*, 8/7. Now if your opponent stays out, you have 2's to cover the blot on your five point, and 4's to hit. Thus, you have greatly increased your chances of rolling favorably on the next key roll.

Position 25A
X to Play 6–4

Position 25B
X to Play 6–4

Positions 25A and 25B are examples of the subtlety that diversification may involve. Despite the similarity of the positions, different plays are required. In both positions, X's immediate primary objective is to close out O by completing his one point. X need not worry about escaping from O's inner board on this roll since, after O is closed out, leaping over a 3-point prime should present no problem. In order to make the one point, X should bring both his men from his outer board to his inner board to use as builders. In Position 25A, X should play 10/6, 9/3, whereas in Position 25B, X should play 9/5, 10/4. The reason for this difference becomes apparent when we consider the position if O is fortunate enough to roll a 1 and hit X on the one point.

If O hits X on the next roll, we want to be able to re-enter and hit O back on our one point. To give ourselves the best chance to do this, we must diversify the numbers we need to re-enter and hit. In Position 25A, we play so that 2's and 5's bear on our one point. Now if we are hit, we have 1's, 3's, and 4's to come in with, and 2's and 5's to hit. In Position 25B, we have 1's, 2's, and 5's to re-enter with. Therefore, we play to our four and five points so that 3's and 4's now cover or hit.

Finally, note that duplication concerns the numbers on your opponent's very next roll of the dice. Diversification, on the other hand, looks ahead to two rolls — your opponent's next roll and your next roll. For this reason, clear-cut examples of diversification occur far less frequently than duplication. While it is important to understand the diversification concept, you should not waste time searching actively for such positions.

CHAPTER 14.

WHEN YOU ARE
FORCED TO LEAVE SHOTS

THIS CHAPTER WILL primarily discuss those cases in which a player wishes to avoid being hit but *must* leave his opponent a shot. In making your move, you still wish to construct a position which is as good as possible for you. When you must leave a man exposed, you are not merely interested in minimizing the number of shots (the number of combinations out of 36 that hit). You must also take care to position your men as effectively as possible. Broadly speaking, this is done in two ways: You try to build the most constructive and safest possible resulting positions should you be missed, and make it as inconvenient and dangerous as possible for your opponent should you be hit.

Minimizing the Number of Shots

Since we are concerned here with positions where you wish to avoid being hit, the most obvious answer to the question "How can you best leave a shot?" is to place your men to minimize the number of shots.

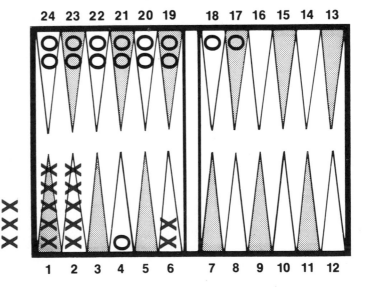

Position 1
X to Play 6–2

For example, in Position 1 the correct play is 6/off, 2/off. This leaves 12 shots, whereas 6/off, 6/4* leaves 13 shots. Since your sole objective is to avoid being hit on the next roll, the play leaving less shots is superior.

However, minimizing the number of shots is *not* usually the paramount consideration. A common misconception held by many players is that the ability to count shots rapidly is a great advantage in playing the game. Many become discouraged because they don't have "mathematical minds," i.e., they aren't good at instant arithmetic. Although this might be heresy in some circles, I feel that the ability to quickly count shots (and also pips) is an overrated skill. In fact, contrary to popular belief, many of the best players in the world rarely count shots at all! I, myself, often play for hours without counting the exact number of shots I am leaving — in most cases, duplication does the work for me.

Backgammon, fortunately, is not just a mechanical game and simply mathematically minimizing the shots will not always give the correct play. You are not only concerned with reducing the immediate danger of your opponent's next roll, but with the overall consequences of the move, including the safety of your checkers and the resulting position. You should never leave extra shots unnecessarily; however, it is rare indeed that a position is so barren that other factors don't come into play.

Most Constructive Resulting Position

You should always try to place your checkers as constructively as possible. Even when extra shots are involved, it is important to consider not only the negative aspect of being hit, but the positive gain if you are missed.

Slotting on a Key Point

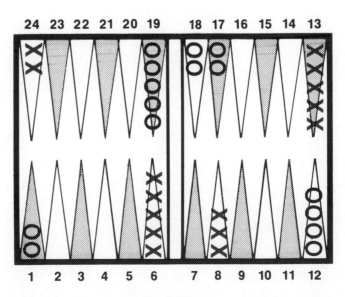

Position 2
X to Play 6–5

In Position 2, your opponent began the game with a 6–1, making his bar point. You roll 6–5. You could leave a minimum number of shots (11) by moving one man all the way off your midpoint 13/2.

A better play, however, is to move two men off the midpoint 13/8, 13/7, leaving one man exposed on your bar point. This gives 17 shots. But if your opponent misses you, you can make the valuable bar point. If you had played safer by leaving a man on the two point, and your opponent missed you, you would gain nothing since the two point has no value at this time.

Creating Builders

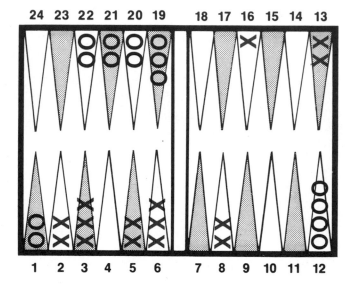

Position 3
X to Play 5–1

In Position 3, X is forced to leave an indirect shot. The minimum shot is obtained by playing 16/11, 3/2, leaving only a 6–4 (2 shots).

The better play, however, is 16/10, creating a new builder for the four point. Although this play exposes you to 6–3 and 3–3 (3 shots), it is safer overall in terms of coming home. Once again, the importance of creating an extra builder outweighs the slightly increased immediate danger of being hit.

Safest Position

Clearing the Hardest Point

When you are trying to get home safely, you must also consider clearing the most difficult point first, even if some extra shots are involved.

In Position 4, X can play 8/2, 8/7, leaving a flat 11 shots. The better play, however, is 11/4, leaving 16 shots but giving excellent prospects of getting home without further trouble. If you make the "safer" play of clearing the eight point, you will likely end up leaving a direct 6-shot (17 numbers) when you try to clear the eleven point later (unless you are lucky and soon roll a small double). This is *in addition* to the immediate 2-shot.

Position 4
X to Play 6–1

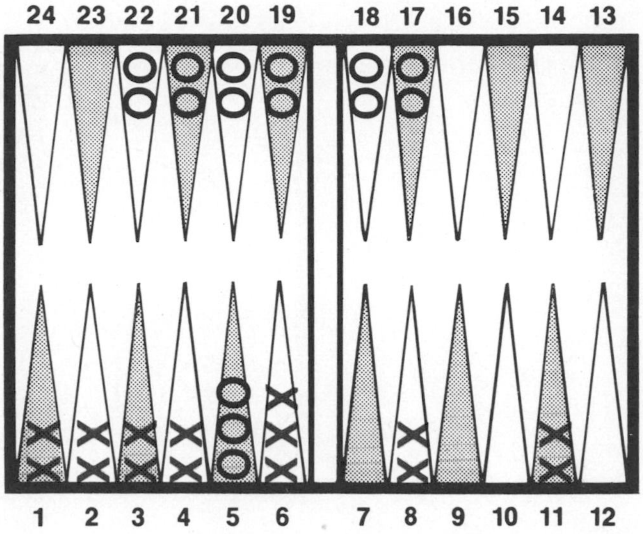

Position 5
X to Play 5–4

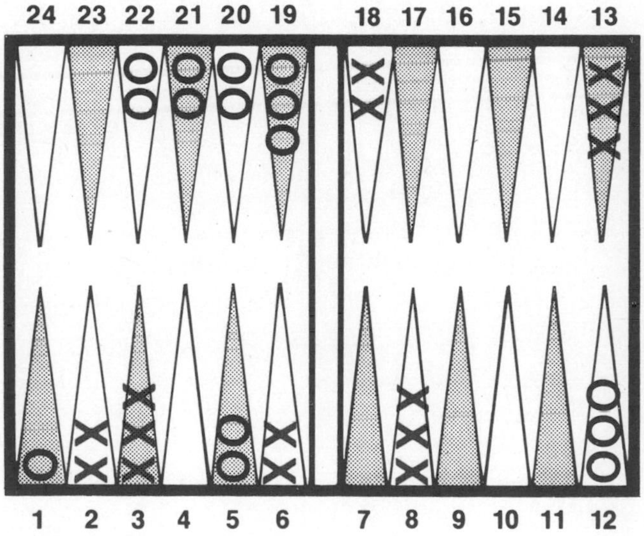

In Position 5, bringing a man 13/4 would leave the minimum direct shot (11 numbers). But the correct play is to clear your opponent's bar point, 18/13, 18/14, leaving a blot on the fourteen point and giving 15 shots. Since you want to get home and must regretfully leave a shot anyway, now is a good time to clear your opponent's bar point.

Ability to Safety Next Roll
Another important consideration in leaving shots is your ability to safety the blot and play your next roll safely should your opponent miss you. In Position 5, above, a strong additional reason to make the indicated play (18/13, 18/14) is that a blot left on the four point would be much harder to safety on the next roll than a blot left on the fourteen point.

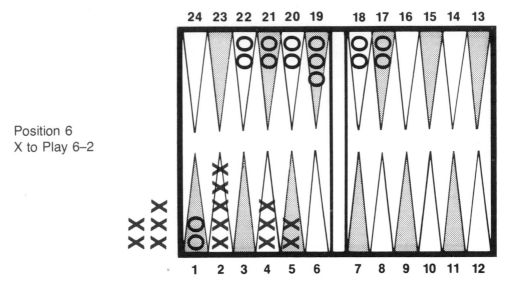

Position 6
X to Play 6–2

Similarly, in Position 6, by bearing a man off and moving to the three point, 5/off, 5/3, you would leave the minimum number of shots (11). However, you would still have the problem of safetying this blot on the next roll. This man will be exposed even *after* the next roll unless you roll certain 1's, 3's, or a large double. Worse yet, you may be forced to leave a double shot if you roll 6–5, 6–4, or 5–4 (6 numbers).

The correct play in this position is to take two men off, 5/off, 2/off. This leaves only 1 extra shot (2–2) in addition to the minimum 11. And should your opponent miss, there will be very few numbers that do not play safely for you on the next roll.

Closer to Home

When you have a single checker left to be brought home safely, you should take into account not only the *immediate* danger (that is, your opponent's next roll), but also the prospects of getting this man home safely from the resulting position.

In Position 7, X rolls a 2–1. If he leaves the outside checker where it stands, O will only have 3 shots which hit it. However, should O miss, X will need a 6–5 or a good double to bring the checker to safety.

Rather than leave his man stranded on the seventeen point, it is better to move it immediately to the fourteen point, 17/14. Although this leaves O 6 shots to hit, it also gives X good prospects of jumping safely into his inner board on the next roll. (Notice, interestingly, that leaving the checker on the fifteen point gains nothing since there are the exact same number of 7's as 8's in backgammon.)

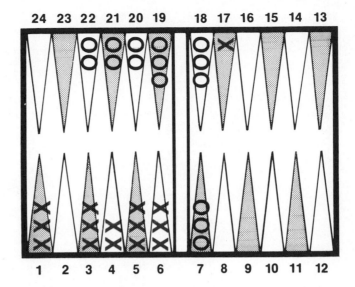

Position 7
X to Play 2–1

Force Him Away

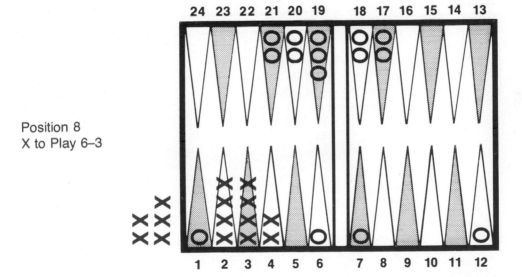

Position 8
X to Play 6–3

In Position 8, X must leave a single simple direct shot no matter how he plays. The correct play is *not* to bear two men off, 4/off, 3/off, but to take one man off and hit on the one point, 4/off, 4/1*. By making this play, you decide the issue once and for all since if O misses you he will probably be forced to come in on the four, five, or six point and be out of your hair forever. Should you bear two men off, there is always the possibility you will have to leave another shot later on. Even if you have more men off, being hit will cost you the gammon. In fact, you may even still lose with as many as thirteen men off if your opponent plays correctly to get a second man. (To see how O can play to get a second man, see Chapter 25.)

Thus far we have considered how to leave yourself in the best position should your opponent miss you. Obviously, you must also weigh the possible resulting positions after being hit.

Leaving the Least Amount of Blots

One consideration when forced to leave a shot is leaving the least amount of blots.

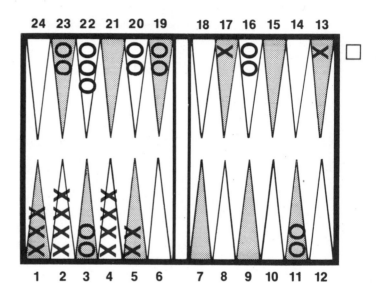

Position 9
X to Play 6–2

For example in Position 9, one can play 17/15, 13/7. By duplication, the number of shots is reduced to 17. However, here is an example where simply duplicating shots will lead you astray.

The correct play is to safety one man completely, 13/5. This gives a double direct shot — 24 numbers. The extra shots given are more than outweighed by the fact that you are now playing with only *one* blot. If you are hit with only one blot, your opponent has not won the game automatically. Since he is still far behind in the race, and since his four point is still open, it will probably be several rolls before he will be in a position to consider re-doubling. In other words, you retain a significant equity in the game after you are hit, provided that you have no other men exposed.

If you are hit after playing 17/15, 13/7, you are in mortal danger. Your opponent threatens to pick up the second exposed man and win easily. Should you stay out, even the threat of picking up a second checker is probably enough for him to double you out of the game.

Regardless of who owns the cube, the possibility of being gammoned is a highly significant consideration. With only one man exposed, there is virtually no chance (in this position) of being gammoned. Whenever there is a good chance of having two men picked up and closed out, however, the gammon is a real possibility.

An additional reason why serious consideration must always be given to minimizing the number of *blots* (rather than the number of *shots*) is that even if your opponent does miss you, the task of scrambling all your men to safety on the next roll is easier with fewer blots.

Return Shots

Even if you leave extra shots, you can often make it dangerous or positionally destructive for your opponent to hit you. A key consideration in any position when leaving shots is the number of return shots (shots back at the opponent) that you will have should you be hit.

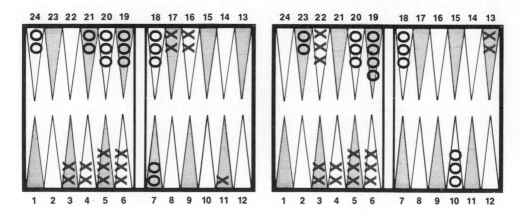

Position 10
X to Play 2–1

Position 11
X to Play 6–1

In Position 10, X would leave the least shots by coming closer to the enemy on the eight point, 11/8. However, should you be hit there, you have no direct return shots back. The correct move is 6/3, leaving a blot on the eleven point. If you are hit there, you will have as many as 10 shots back at the enemy blot on this point — in effect, almost a direct shot back.

In Position 11, X can leave minimum shots by playing 13/12, 13/7. This makes life easy for O, however, since you need the midpoint to stop O from coming home easily.

The correct play is 22/16, 5/4. By going to the fifteen point, 22/15, you leave O 15 numbers to hit with but no possible return shots for you. By making the indicated play, you leave 16 shots, but many of the shots that hit now expose O to dangerous return shots.

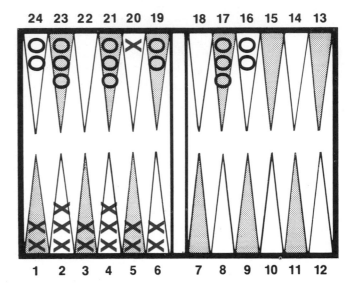

Position 12
X to Play 2

In Position 12, X should stay on the twenty point and move 4/2. Many of the shots that hit will leave X a direct return on the twenty point to win the game and possibly gammon O. If X comes out to O's bar, 20/18, and is then hit, X will probably get few, if any, return shots.

Hit Inside or Outside

Whenever you have a choice of leaving a man exposed in either your opponent's inner board or outer board, you will generally have more return shots by staying in his inner board. The reader should be warned, however, that there are often sound reasons for preferring to be hit in the outer board.

By coming to the opponent's outer board, you make it impossible for him to hit you and close a new point in his inner board. By staying in the inner board, you run the more dangerous risk of allowing your opponent to point on you and simultaneously build his inner board. Furthermore, there is the likelihood that, by remaining in your opponent's inner board, he will hit you with a blot if need be. Having a return shot is then a mixed blessing, for if you miss he may cover the next time and thus build his board more quickly.

In Position 13, for example, O is eager to attack. The correct play for X, therefore, is bar/17. If he hits you outside on the seventeen point, you are not completely lost. However, if he points on you on the twenty-two point or hits you with a blot which he covers next roll, you are in mortal danger. The return shot you may get had you remained on the twenty-two point instead is not worth the additional risk — especially since O can withstand a hit because he owns the five point. Coming out in this position has one further advantage: If O misses you outside, you have likely escaped his clutches, whereas if you stay on the twenty-two point and are missed, your escape is still far from certain.

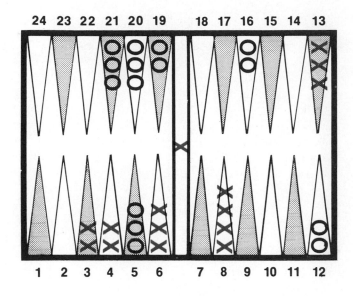

Position 13
X to Play 5–3

Forcing Opponent to Relinquish a Key Point

When leaving a shot, you should also consider whether your opponent can be forced to relinquish a key point in order to hit you.

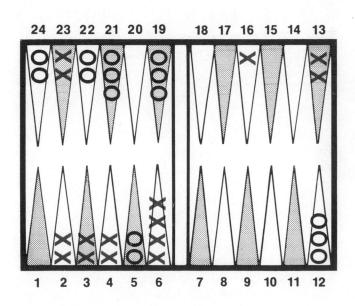

Position 14
X to Play 4–1

For example, in Position 14 the correct play (but not the *safest*) is 16/11. In order for O to hit you, he must abandon the five point. Although your immediate return shots are limited, you have made his overall position much more vulnerable since his advanced anchor on your five point affords him security in a potentially dangerous position.

Duplicating Your Opponent's Key Numbers

Forcing O to give up a key point to hit is an example of one of the central ideas when forced to leave a direct shot: Make O *pay* for hitting. As we have also seen, forcing him to leave as many return shots as possible is yet another way of making him pay to hit.

Often O can only hit at the expense of giving up some other important objective. In Chapter 13 we saw several examples where duplicating the number that hits with the same number needed elsewhere renders the hit less attractive to O. Whenever he has a blot in his inner board, we should consider duplicating the number needed to hit and the number needed to cover this blot. By doing this, we increase our chances for return shots.

Position 15A
X to Play 4

Position 15B
X to Play 4

In Position 15A, we should play 7/3, leaving 5's to hit and 5's to cover. In Position 15B, however, the correct play is 8/4, duplicating 6's. In the last chapter, we also considered several other positions (Positions 11, 12, 16, and 19) where due to duplication we left more than the minimum possible number of shots. Examples included duplicating

(1) the number needed to hit and the number needed to escape from behind a prime (Position 11);

(2) the number needed to hit and the number needed to move up to the edge of a prime (Position 12);

(3) the number needed to hit and the number needed to make another key point (Positions 16 and 19).

Several Options

We have discussed one by one the factors you must weigh when forced to leave a shot. In actual practice, several possible factors may appear simultaneously and be conflicting.

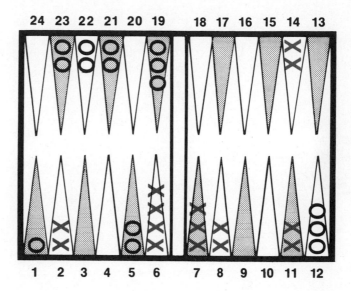

Position 16
X to Play 4–2

For example, in Position 16 several plays each have a valid justification. X may play 14/8 in order to clear the hardest point, or 11/7, 11/9 in order to force O to relinquish the five point.

The preferred play, however, is 7/1* in order to get O off the one point. The reason for this is that O is playing a form of holding game where he hopes to prevent you from playing your numbers and coming home safely. In order for him to play this game successfully, it is critical that he keep a man back on your one point to prevent you from handling difficult numbers by leaving blots in your inner board. By hitting on the one point, you hope to have him come in on the four or five point. If he does this, you can play behind him and build up your board while waiting to clear the fourteen and eleven points.

Section III
Middle Game Strategy

CHAPTER 15.
MODERN
OPENING THEORY

BACKGAMMON HAS NOT always been played in the same way. In the last decade alone, a tremendous change has taken place in the conception of the game.

Originally, backgammon was considered a *race*. You tried to move your men around the board as quickly and effectively as possible, while leaving yourself minimally exposed. In general, the checkers were thought of as liabilities which had to be gotten around the board. For this reason, leaving blots — especially in your inner board — was viewed as an extreme measure since being hit would force you to lose ground in the race.

Although modern backgammon players are still interested in the basic aspects of the race, experts now understand that few games directly evolve into one. As we saw in Chapter 12, greater emphasis is now placed on viewing the men positively and using them constructively. In order to seize a lead in development quickly, it is often correct to create builders and use the checkers actively — even if doing so entails extra risk. The *race* thus holds less interest in modern backgammon theory than other types of games where you hold, block, or attack your opponent.

To develop such games, you need to rapidly mobilize your men and seize key points early in the game. A more dynamic and aggressive style of play is demanded. You are more willing to take chances of being hit — even in your inner board — if this enables you to move your men into an effective position quickly. The old stigma of being hit early inside your inner board has been removed.

Even a significant lead in the race might be worthless if you have made no key points.

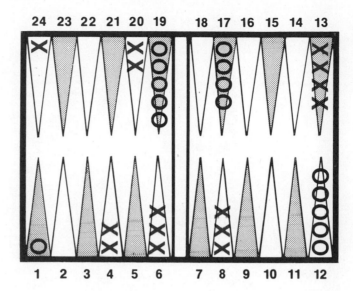

Position 1
O on Roll

In Position 1, O is clearly ahead in the race. He has escaped one of his back men and sent an additional X man back. O, nevertheless, has nothing to be proud of. He has not established a single significant point, whereas X has established two valuable points: the twenty point (his opponent's five point — the **golden point**) *and* the four point. In fact, the modern realization is that O is not only *not* ahead — he is in mortal danger.

In an expert game, X would double on the next roll if O failed to improve his game. O is highly unlikely to escape his back men and then get home safely since he has so few points to land on. He has an extremely inferior game compared to X, who has established key offensive and defensive points.

Position 1 was reached by the following sequence: X 4–1 (13/9, 6/5); O 4–6 (1/5*/11); X 5–4 (bar/20, 24/20); O 5–1 (11/17); X 5–2 (9/4, 6/4). Even though X was hit after slotting on the five point, he reached a superior position. The danger comes not in being hit on the opening roll return when your opponent has no board as yet; the real danger lies in letting your opponent gain a quick lead in development. If you are hit after he has built additional points and improved his position, you may be in trouble.

Another Look at the Opening Moves

Let's see how these ideas and several other important principles of the middle game can be applied to opening moves. Compare the following moves with those given in Chapter 5.

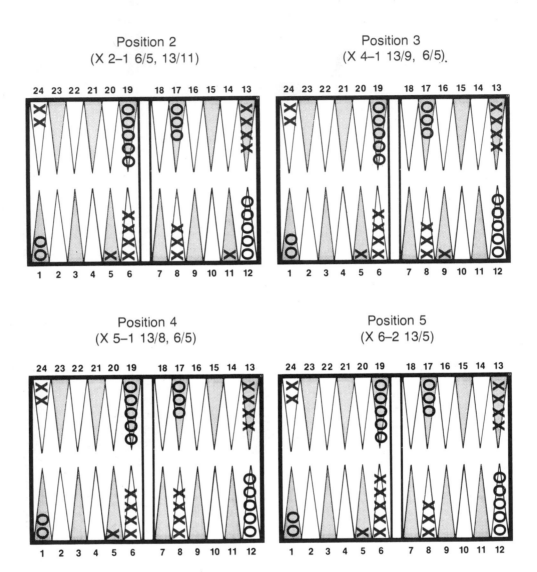

Position 2
(X 2–1 6/5, 13/11)

Position 3
(X 4–1 13/9, 6/5).

Position 4
(X 5–1 13/8, 6/5)

Position 5
(X 6–2 13/5)

Your five point is the most important point on your side of the board. For this reason, the opening roll 3–1 is excellent since it makes the five point 8/5, 6/5.

Because of the importance of the five point, many players use other opening rolls — which do not in themselves make valuable points — to slot a single man on the five point. These are: 2–1 (6/5, 13/11); 4–1 (13/9, 6/5); 5–1 (13/8, 6/5); 6–2 (13/5).

Slotting on the five point is a considerable risk since you may be hit with any 4 (as well as with a combination shot if you have left a second man exposed in your outer board). If you are not hit, however, you are a favorite to cover the five point on the next roll.

The opening plays given in this chapter are variants which lead to dangerous, exciting, but also more difficult games. It should be understood, however, that they are neither necessarily better nor worse than the plays given in Chapter 5; these original plays are perfectly satisfactory and are often made by experts (with the exception of 6–2; few experts would play 24/16). The player just learning the game is advised to gain some experience before using these plays. Once the basics of the game have been mastered, however, you may wish to experiment and get acquainted with this style of play.

Let's look at variant plays for opening rolls 6–2, 6–3, and 6–4.

Position 6
(X 6–2 24/18, 13/11)

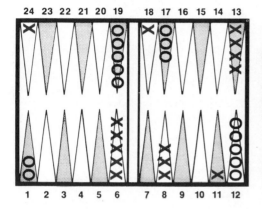

Position 7
(X 6–3 24/18, 13/10)

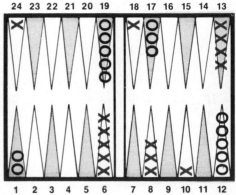

Position 8
(X 6–4 24/18, 13/9)

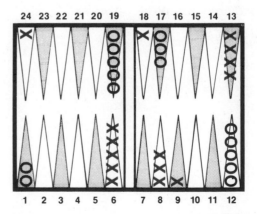

Rather than running (as indicated in Chapter 5), you may move to your opponent's bar point with the 6 and down from your midpoint with the other number. These plays are also more dangerous and aggressive than the plays given earlier. Although you are exposed to a double shot on his bar point (he is a 2-to-1 favorite, with 24 numbers to hit), only 6–1 or 6–6 both *hit* and *cover* the eighteen point. If your opponent hits without covering, you have a 16-number return shot at him.

These plays are more constructive than the moves given in Chapter 5 since you bring a builder into your own outer board. They are also more provocative since the man on O's bar point controls his outer board and the builder you bring down creates added pressure on both your outer and inner boards. This move restricts O's choices and makes it hard for him to develop naturally.

It is hard to say whether these plays are necessarily better or worse than those in Chapter 5. My preferences are as follows: for 6–2 and 6–3, I prefer these plays (the alternate for 6–2, 13/5 is also quite good). For 6–4, I prefer to run 24/14 since this man is exposed only to a direct 2-shot and since it bears on your own outer board.

Let's look at one more group of plays: 3–2 (24/21, 13/11); 5–4 (24/20, 13/8); 4–3 (24/20, 13/10).

Position 9
(X 3–2 24/21, 13/11)

Position 10
(X 5–4 24/20, 13/8)

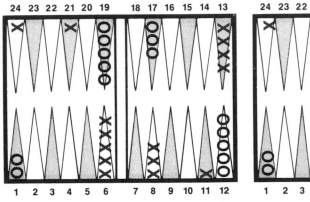

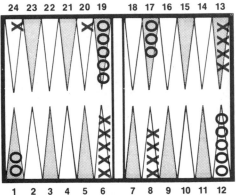

Position 11
(X 4–3 24/20, 13/10)

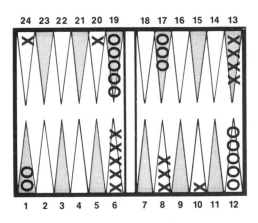

The most important point of all to establish is your twenty point (your opponent's five point). Chapter 20 will elaborate on the many virtues of this golden point.

In order to establish the twenty point, you naturally split a back man to the point, hoping to cover on the next roll. It is wise to do this early — before your position becomes more dangerous. By moving a back man up, you not only try to acquire a valuable point, you also prevent O from bringing builders down to his outer board and developing naturally.

If your opponent has slotted a man on your five point, an expert knows that it is often better to hit on the five point — risking even a double return shot — rather than concede this point to him. Because of the importance of the five points (both yours and his), many expert games begin as vicious "slugging" matches with an exchange of hits to see who can get these points first.

When moving 3–2, 5–4, and 4–3, I have no strong preference between the plays given above and those in Chapter 5. (Note that 5–4 has a third alternative move which is also as good as either of the other plays — simply running 24/15.) The major difference is that these plays are more provocative since your opponent is likely to be forced to hit you immediately. (These plays are especially recommended if you are playing with someone who is afraid to hit immediately in his inner board.)

Although the moves in this chapter are optional on the opening roll, as the game progresses you must make adjustments. Even the immediate response to the opening roll may no longer be optional because the position may already dictate bolder and more provocative plays, or safer and more conservative plays. Chapter 16 deals with the fundamental question of when to play safely and when to play boldly.

CHAPTER 16.
SAFE PLAY VS.
BOLD PLAY

The Problem

Strategically, one of the most fundamental aspects of backgammon is to know when to play safely and when to play boldly. Chapter 14 discussed how to play your men if you basically want to avoid contact but *have* to leave a shot. Here we treat the related questions of whether to play provocatively and force contact, and your willingness to *voluntarily* leave an exposed man in your inner and outer boards and risk being hit by a direct shot.

Chapter 15 examined some reasons for taking chances and leaving blots while hitting your opponent or slotting in your inner board. Later in this section we shall also see many positions where you split your runners dangerously in your opponent's inner board. It is not always correct, however, to play a "wide open" game where you may welcome an exchange of hits. Many times the risk is *not* worth the possible gain. By watching the experts, unfortunately, you may get the impression that this style of play is always right. The true expert not only knows *when* to take these additional risks, but, perhaps more importantly for the non-expert, when *not* to.

The ability to differentiate between when it is reasonable to leave extra shots and when it is folly is a sign of the truly expert player. Many players go from one extreme to the other. When they begin to play, they are timid and avoid leaving shots at all costs. After watching the experts, they swing to the opposite extreme. In the attempt to slavishly employ this more modern style of play, they go "full speed ahead, damn the torpedoes," even though they needlessly risk sinking their ship.

The purpose of this chapter, therefore, is to develop some criteria for when to play *safely* and when to play *boldly*. These decisions (such as whether or not to slot or attack in your own inner board with a blot) do not depend on the exact number of return shots nor on whether you feel lucky and wish to "get away with" a dangerous play. They depend on the exact nature of the position on *both* sides of the board. To become a successful backgammon player, you must learn to survey the whole battlefield and not just the local terrain.

This chapter is important because the principles here will determine your willingness to take risks both at the opening of the game and as it develops.

These same principles will then be applied to specific aspects of strategy involving hitting, slotting, and splitting. In fact, the remainder of Section III is basically a detailed look at the middle game, using the principles outlined in this chapter.

Note: We are still basically concerned with positions where being hit involves at least some loss — in other words, we wish to be able to evaluate and compare both the potential gain and the risk. In several types of advanced positions involving timing, you may actually wish to be hit. We are *not* concerned with these positions in Section III. The principles as stated throughout this section will not *explicitly* exclude these positions, but it should be understood that they may not apply in such cases. In Section IV we will discuss **battle of primes, backgames,** and **advanced holding positions** where timing is the key consideration.

Tactical Criteria

Your Opponent Has Closed Points in His Inner Board

There are a number of criteria which help you determine when it is worthwhile to take extra chances of being hit, and when the position indicates making a relatively safe play. The most obvious consideration involves the immediate tactical dangers you face; clearly, the more points your opponent has closed in his inner board, the greater the danger for you in being hit. It may be correct to take a risk, for example, when your opponent has two points closed, but unacceptable to take the same risk if four or five points are closed.

Position 1
X to Play 1

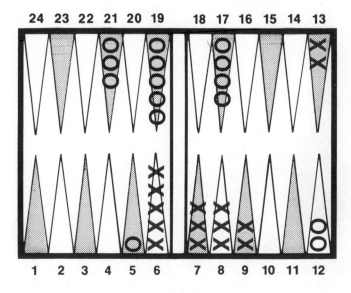

In Position 1, X should hit the blot on his five point. Should O miss the return shot, X will probably have a winning position; should O hit the return shot, X may still have a chance.

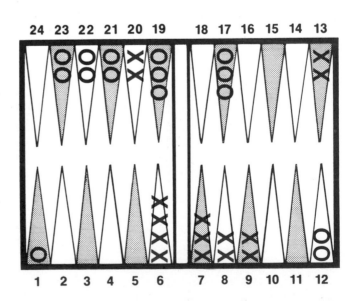

Position 2
X to Play 1

The pip count in Position 2 is the same as Position 1. Because of O's 4-point board, however, X should play safe for a roll, 8/7. O may not escape, and even if he does, X still has a chance in the race. Similarly, you must exercise extra caution if your opponent has formed a prime or a strong blocking position which you will be caught behind if you are hit.

Do You Hold an Anchor in His Board?

Another key criterion is whether you have an **anchor** in your opponent's board. If you do hold a point, you are clearly safer should you be hit since you are assured of eventual re-entry and cannot ever be completely closed out. If your opponent has closed three or four points in his inner board, an anchor will enable you to take risks which you could not afford to take otherwise.

Position 3
X to Play 1

In Position 3, it is reasonable to slot a man on the five point to attempt to create a 5-point prime. Should you be hit, you still retain an anchor which will keep you from being gammoned and still give you a good chance to win the game.

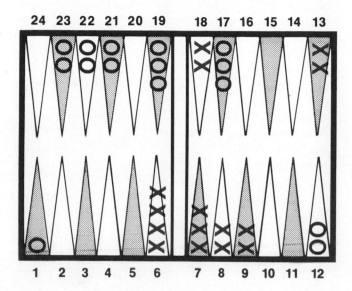

Position 4
X to Play 1

In Position 4, however, it is extremely risky to put a man on the five point. Should you be hit, you may be closed out before you ever get going. If this happens, it is likely that you will be gammoned despite the fact that you have only one man closed out. (A common trap that many players fall into is believing that if they have only one man exposed they are not going to be gammoned. Gammons are very common when you still have a significant number of men in the outer boards and run the risk of not moving again.)

The correct play in Position 4 is not the supersafe play of 7/6. This leaves you with a completely inflexible position and no spare builders. A much better play is 9/8, leaving a more dynamic position with active builders on each point.

In the special case where you have a double anchor in your opponent's inner board, you are obviously prepared to take risks. In this case, other principles as well as advanced concepts in holding and backgames are involved. The quality of the anchor is also very important. If you own your opponent's five point, you are in a position to take many more risks than if you own his one point.

In Section I we mentioned that an **advanced anchor** (your opponent's four or five point) offers a great deal of security. The value and implications of an advanced anchor are examined in more detail in Chapter 20. For now, it is sufficient to remember that this is the most important of all the tactical criteria.

Number of Points You Have Closed

We have discussed the number of points your opponent has closed in his inner board as an important tactical criterion. It is also important to look at the number of points which *you* have closed in *your* inner board. Whenever there is a possibility of both sides hitting each other and being hit back (this may arise, for example, if you hit a blot with a blot on your five point), you should compare the number of points you have closed with the number of points your opponent has closed. The player who has a better closed board count (more inner points closed) is at a considerable advantage in a "slugging contest." The first player to fail to re-enter may be in serious danger of losing the game. Thus, if you have four points closed to your opponent's three, or if you have three points to his two, you are motivated to attack him; whereas if the inner board count is unfavorable, it may be better to hold off.

Blots in Your Opponent's Inner Board

Another consideration in leaving shots is the return shots you will have should you be hit. In particular, if your opponent is reluctant to be hit and he has a blot or blots in his inner board, you can take extra chances because of the possibility of re-entering and hitting the blot.

A variant of this point was discussed in Chapter 12, where we emphasized that one can often afford to leave *indirect* shots in one's outer board if your opponent has a blot or blots in his inner board.

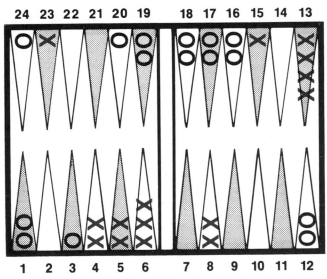

Position 5
X to Play 6–1

In Position 5, an aggressive positional play is called for not only because you have a much stronger inner board than your opponent, but because he has two blots exposed in his inner board. The correct play is to make your bar point, 13/7, 8/7, locking his two men in on the one point and threatening to make a 5-point prime. You can afford to make this play because of the greater strength of your position and the vulnerability of his.

To summarize, we have thus far considered the following four tactical principles approximately in order of importance:

1.   Do you have an advanced anchor?
2.   How strong is your opponent's inner board?
3.   How strong is *your* inner board (especially compared to your opponent's)?
4.   Does your opponent have blots in his inner board?

Strategic Criteria

We shall now consider one or two strategic principles. These are often more important than the immediate tactical criteria because they point up not only the immediate safety of the play but the underlying game plan and what you eventually hope to accomplish. Ignorance of these factors separates the less experienced player from the expert.

Number of Men You Have Back

Basically, the more men you have remaining in your opponent's home board, the freer you can be about taking chances and risking having additional men sent back. To understand why, let's first consider the extreme case where you have no men back while your opponent still has men in your inner board. Presumably, your opponent is behind in the race.

Since you have the game won in terms of the race, your objective is to bring your men home safely. While you might consider taking small risks to increase your opportunity to make points and avoid awkward shots later on, you should be very reluctant to voluntarily leave a direct shot. If you are hit, you will have undone your basic opening objective of freeing your back men. Similarly, if you have only one man back, you should also try to play a relatively old-fashioned conservative game. You are constantly threatening to free the one man back; therefore, having a second man hit is a strategic loss.

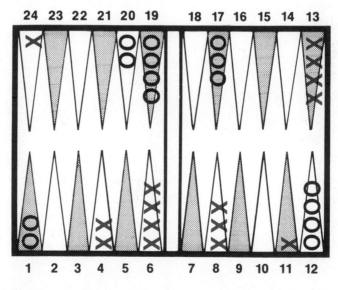

Position 6
X to Play 1

In Position 6, it is unwise for X to slot on the five point. Although X wants to make the five point, the risk is too high. You have a strong game as it is, and having a second man back greatly reduces your chances for an early victory. The more prudent play here is 11/10.

Consider now the case where you have three or more men back in your opponent's inner board. Although you may have nothing to gain by being hit, you have little to lose strategically. Whether you have three or four men back is not of major consequence — as a matter of fact, the extra men back may enable you to establish a double anchor in your opponent's inner board. After all, when you already have three or more men back, you no longer threaten to escape and you are already committed to playing a more positional game.

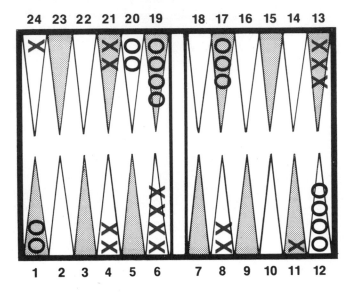

Position 7
X to Play 1

For example, in Position 7, X should slot on the five point. Making the five point will be a considerable gain, while being hit does not particularly hurt you. Note that in this position you also have a solid anchor on the twenty-one point (O's four point).

A word of caution: tactically you must still be careful when you have several men back, especially if your opponent has a good board where you run the risk of staying out a few key rolls.

Positions 6 and 7 dealt with whether you should risk slotting a man in your inner board. Let's examine two related examples where you wish to hit with a blot in your inner board.

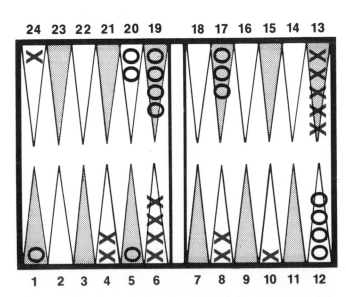

Position 8
X to Play 3

In Position 8, X should play 13/10. Although the temptation to hit on the five point may be strong, O is a favorite to send a second man back.

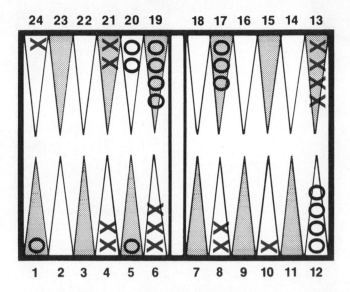

Position 9
X to Play 3

In Position 9, however, X should hit 8/5*. Since X already has three men back, he cannot consider escaping all his back runners immediately and therefore has little to lose by having a fourth man sent back. His anchor on the twenty-one point gives him security, so he attacks. If O fails to hit him back, X can make the five point and develop a very strong game.

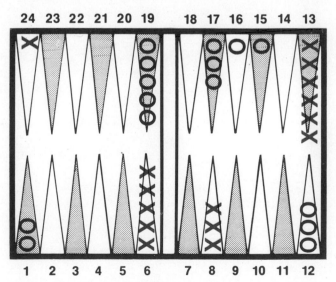

Position 10
X to Play 2–1

Similarly, in Position 10, X has just begun the game with 6–5 escaping one back man 24/13. O played 4–3 12/16, 12/15. Now with 2–1, X conservatively plays 13/10. Although 13/11, 6/5 slotting on the five point would not be a very bad play, X wishes to avoid being hit since this would completely nullify the value of the 6–5.

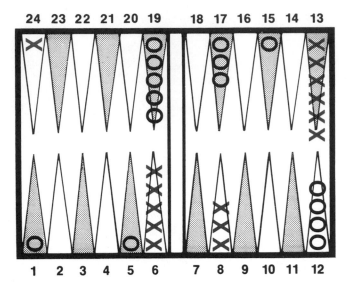

Position 11
X to Play 2–1

Position 11 is a warning not to carry this principle to extremes. Here X could play comparatively safely 24/21 or 24/23, 8/6. The best play, however, is 6/5*, 13/11. The main reason for playing conservatively with only one man back is that you hope to escape the last back man and play a running game. However, if you have not established any new points and, as in Position 11, you have no builders, then escaping the back man is a hollow victory. You are unlikely to get home safely anyway. The basic idea is to play conservatively only if you have the possibility of entering a *successful* running game, not just to escape your back men.

Number of Men Your Opponent Has Back

The other basic consideration is the number of men your opponent has in *your* inner board. Seen from your opponent's point of view, when he has fewer men back he wants to play more safely and you, therefore, tend to play more aggressively. If he has no men back or one man back, you place a high priority on hitting him and keeping him from escaping his last man. These two cases may require special techniques which are the subject matter of Chapters 18 and 19.

Generally speaking, you should compare the number of men you have back to the number of men your opponent has back. If he has less men back than you, you stand to gain by any exchange of hits; whereas if you have less men back he has more to gain than you.

If you are well ahead, you can afford to play to consolidate your gains and avoid complications. If you are losing, you try to complicate the position rather than playing passively, hoping that the complications turn the game around.

Particularly when your opponent has escaped all his back runners (see Chapter 18), you must play more provocatively and "mix it up" in hopes of hitting him or getting a viable holding position. Extra chances may have to be taken to get a playable game when you are no longer negotiating from a position of strength.

When you have more men back than your opponent, you try to force an exchange of hits. For example, if your opponent begins with 6–5 and you then roll 6–2, you must play 24/18, 13/11. This will practically force him to hit you and leave return shots since he has few safe moves. If any exchange of hits occurs, the value of his escaping one man will have been nullified. Whenever your opponent has few men back, you can use his reluctance to attack to your advantage.

Applications

In addition to the four main tactical points already summarized, we have considered the strategic importance of playing aggressively if you have a lot of men back, or if your opponent has only a few. Of course, all these indicators will usually not point the same way, so judgment will have to be exercised. Mechanical rules can never substitute for experience. Looking for these indicators and understanding the basis for them, however, will surely improve one's judgment.

Sometimes all six (four tactical, two strategic) criteria will call for playing aggressively. Bold plays (which might not occur to an average player) no longer appear mysterious or reckless, but become natural.

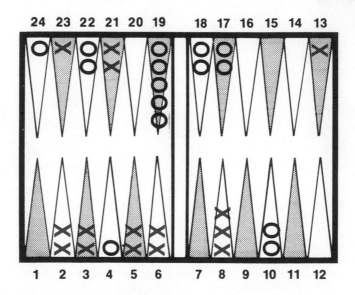

Position 12
X to Play 5–2

In Position 12, for example, virtually all the basic criteria suggest a bold positional play. You have a forward anchor and a strong inner board. O has a weak inner board with blots. O also has only one man in your inner board compared to your having three in his. The correct play is 23/16! Even though this gives O a double return shot, X welcomes the action. The play restricts O's movement, prevents the man on the four point from escaping easily, and challenges O for control of the outfield.

Whenever all the criteria point in favor of a bold play, you should avoid making plays that are awkward or anti-positional.

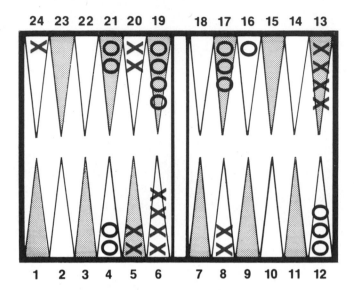

Position 13
X to Play 6–1

In Position 13, playing 13/6 is safe but does nothing constructive and leaves too many men piled up on the six point. (Abandoning the advanced anchor 20/13 would be a terrible blunder.) A better play is 13/7, 6/5. This play brings your spare checkers into a more constructive position. When the criteria all call for a bold play, you should not worry as much about being hit and should concentrate on a more natural positional move.

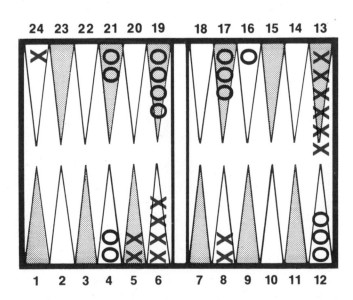

Position 14
X to Play 6–1

In Position 14, X does not want to be hit, so tactical considerations force you to play safe, 13/6.

The ideas and criteria for making safe versus bold plays in this chapter are fundamental to an understanding of the game. Much of the remainder of Section III is an elaboration of these ideas. Before going on, you are strongly advised to review the basic examples in this chapter and make sure you have learned the tactical and strategic criteria illustrated.

Summary

A. Tactical Principles

1. Do you have an advanced anchor? Having an advanced anchor enables you to play boldly.

2. How strong is your opponent's inner board? The stronger your opponent's inner board, the more conservatively you must play.

3. How strong is *your* inner board (especially compared to your opponent's)? If you have more inner board points closed than your opponent, you tend to play boldly; with less points closed, more conservatively.

4. Does your opponent have blots in his inner board? If your opponent has blots in his inner board, you can afford to take more chances because of possible return shots.

B. Strategic Principles

1. How many men do you have back? The more men you have back, the more chances you can take. With no men back or only one man back, you must play conservatively.

2. How many men does your opponent have back? When your opponent has no men back or only one man back, you want to play provocatively to try to force an exchange of hits.

CHAPTER 17.
SLOTTING

BY SLOTTING WE mean to expose a man by placing it on a key point (usually your bar point, or an inner-board point) in order to begin making that point. In general, we will deal with your voluntarily leaving a direct shot by slotting. It is extremely important to know when the risk of slotting is justified and when it is unwise. Winning backgammon does not consist of trying to guess whether you will be hit or not, but in understanding the relevant underlying principles of the position. The six criteria discussed and summarized at the end of Chapter 16 are basic to an understanding of this chapter.

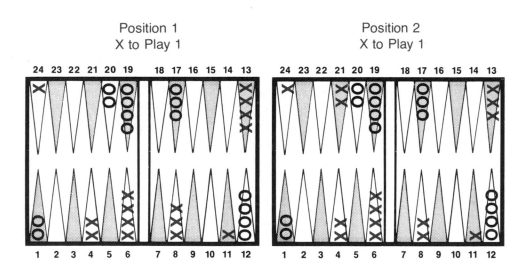

Position 1
X to Play 1

Position 2
X to Play 1

These two positions are the same as Positions 6 and 7 of the previous chapter. You should review the discussion of these positions to understand why Position 2 is a favorable position to slot, while Position 1 is not.

Basic tactical considerations involving duplication may play a large role in deciding not only *when* to slot but also *where*. For example, whenever your opponent needs a certain key number to hit you or to cover a key point, you may consider slotting so as to duplicate the number that hits. Conversely, you should avoid slotting when it would allow him to hit you with a number that would not be good for him anyway — in other words, don't diversify his good numbers. Positions 14, 15, 19, and 20 in Chapter 13 illustrate some of these principles.

When You Shouldn't Slot

Let's begin by looking at some cases where slotting is usually *incorrect*. An obvious case is when the slotted man will be exposed to a *double direct shot*.

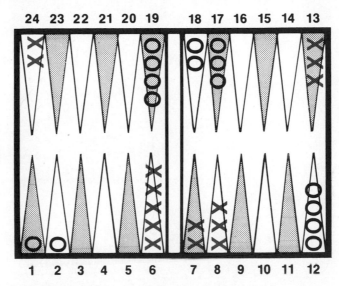

Position 3
X to Play 1

In Position 3, slotting on the five point would leave O a 2-to-1 favorite (24 numbers) to hit — too great a risk. Instead play 24/23.

It is usually wrong to slot while your back men are split or exposed in your opponent's inner board. This is a very important, but commonly misplayed case.

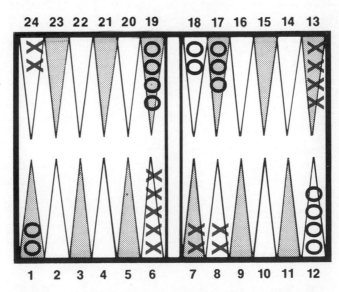

Position 4
X to Play 1

In Position 4, it is reasonable to slot a man on the five point, 6/5; if you escape being hit and make the five point, you will have an excellent 4-point prime.

Position 5
X to Play 1

In Position 5, however, X's back runners are split. Here it is definitely wrong to slot. X should move to the twenty-one point in order to be in a better position to escape or to make that point controlling O's outer board.

One reason it is wrong to slot while split is the danger that your opponent will hit both the slotted blot and a second man. Even if he misses the slotted man, he may attack one or both of the back men which are split. In the ensuing scramble, your opponent may have a good chance of hitting the slotted man before you can cover it. You will have to use the numbers on the dice to come in, and even if you hit your opponent in his inner board, it will only give him another chance to hit the slotted man.

You slot on a point with the expectation that if your opponent misses, you will have a good chance of making the point on your *next* roll. If you slot when your back men are split, you not only risk being hit, but you may be unable to make the point even if the slotted man is missed because you may have to defend your back men.

If you have one man back, you are de facto exposed in your opponent's inner board. One of the strategic criteria of the last chapter tells you to play conservatively when you have only one one man back. If you have several men back, hold an advanced anchor, and are not vulnerable in your opponent's inner board, you may wish to slot even if one of the back men is a blot.

Note that **slotting and splitting** is *not* to be confused with **hitting and splitting**. When you hit and split, you hit an opposing man with a blot in *your* inner board while splitting your back runners. While slotting and splitting is inadvisable, hitting and splitting can be an excellent play.

When to Slot

A prime motivation for slotting is *to make an important point that you would have trouble making otherwise*. Even where it may appear natural to slot, it is incorrect to do so when you have a good chance of making the point *without* slotting.

Consider the following two contrasting examples:

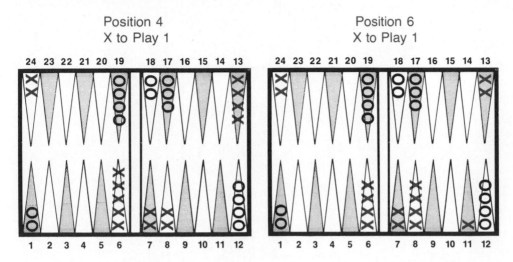

Position 4
X to Play 1

Position 6
X to Play 1

In Position 4, X lacks the material to make the five point naturally. Since the only active builders are on the six, eight, and thirteen points, only 3–1, 1–1, 3–3, or 4–4 would make the five point on one roll. It will probably take several rolls to bring builders down from the thirteen point and then roll the exact combination needed to make the five point. If X slots on the five point in this position and is missed, he can make the point more quickly.

In Position 6, however, X should not slot. He should play 8/7. This gives him a total of four active builders bearing on the five point and a very good chance of making the five or four point without much risk. You should always first consider creating a builder to bear upon a key point without leaving a direct shot, rather than slotting.

If you roll 5–3 on the opening move, you could slot on the five point 13/5, but you expose yourself to *less* risk by bringing two men down, 13/8, 13/10. Now there are many different ways to make the four, five, or bar point without risking a direct shot.

Similarly, on an opening 3–2 there is nothing intrinsically wrong with slotting on the five point and bringing the 2 down (8/5, 13/11). If you bring both men down instead (13/10, 13/11), however, you can create a position with *great* potential at far less risk.

You want to slot to *get men which are otherwise out of play into action*. In Chapter 12 we discussed the importance of having all your men working for you instead of piled up and out of play. In Position 4, we see that X is top-heavy on the six point. These men are not actively in play; this is an excellent reason to begin using them to slot on the five point.

You hope you won't be hit, but even if you are, at least the slotted man actively enters the game and is no longer dead wood. An expert player is always looking for an opportunity to activate as many of his men as possible — even if it sometimes means being hit. Whether hitting in your inner board with blots, or slotting, or making any other play, try to take checkers off points where men are piled up.

Conversely, you must avoid having useful builders hit and, particularly, stripping your points of useful builders.

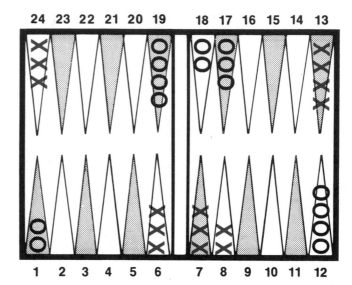

Position 7
X to Play 1

In Position 7, X should split his back men 24/23 because he has three men piled needlessly on the twenty-four point.

Slotting 6/5 is *incorrect* since that play leaves the six point bare. It is rarely correct to slot off the six point when there are only three men there, i.e., when you have only *one* builder on the point. Think twice before slotting your *last* useful builder off a point and leaving it stripped — you may be forced at a later time to give it up when you don't want to. Instead, look for opportunities to slot off "heavy" or "fat" points where you have extra men serving no useful function.

In Position 8, the correct play is 13/11, 8/7 (not 6/5). Leaving an extra builder on the eight point is not nearly as important as leaving an extra builder on the six point. You may wish to give up the eight point later in the game, but it is doubtful that you will ever relinquish the six point. Since O has only one man back and is threatening to escape, your bar point becomes as valuable as the five point in blocking him.

Another reason for slotting is the urgency with which you need a particular point. If you have the time to bring builders to bear on a point to make it naturally, you need not slot it. However, where it is imperative to make a point *quickly*, the fastest way — assuming that you aren't hit — is to slot the point, then cover it.

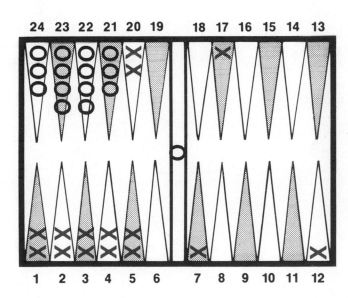

Position 8
X to Play 2–1

Position 9
X to Play 1

In Position 9, the correct play is to immediately slot a man on the six point (7/6). If your opponent misses, you become a strong favorite (actually at least 80%) to cover and win the game before he can re-enter. If you wait, it may take four or five rolls before you can bring enough builders to bear to make the point without slotting. Meanwhile, the accumulated danger of (a) his rolling 6–6, (b) his coming in and hitting, and (c) his coming in and your missing, is greater than the risk of his rolling an immediate 6.

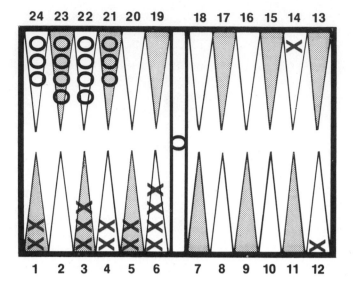

Position 10
X to Play 1

In Position 10, it is wrong to slot on the two point (3/2). If you are hit, you may give O several chances to escape before you can hit him again. Instead, you should bring an extra builder to bear (6/5). If O comes in before you can make the two point, you should hit him and leave the checker on the two point. O is forced to roll two 2's consecutively in order to have any chance at all.

You can afford to have O come in on the two point without jeopardizing your game. In Position 9, you slot because the quicker you make the point, the sooner the danger is over, whereas in Position 10 there is no urgency to make the two point.

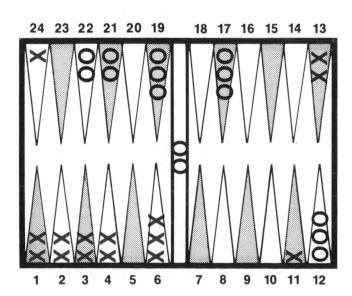

Position 11
X to Play 1

Slotting Against Two Men on the Bar

As a general rule, with few exceptions, *it is wrong to slot when your opponent has two men on the bar*. Even when it is imperative to make the sixth point either to ensure a win or a gammon, the most effective method of closing your opponent out is *not* to slot, but wait until he re-enters with one man and then hit him — even with a blot if necessary.

In Position 11, X is trying to decide whether or not to play 6/5. Let's see what O needs in order to survive if (a) you slot, or (b) you wait until he comes in and then hit him.

In case (a), if he hits you with one 5, you may not be able to hit him back immediately since you are on the bar, and since you have lost a builder. If you fail to hit him back, O needs only one more 5 to establish the five point.

In case (b), you wait for him to re-enter a checker, while bringing more builders to bear on the five point. First he must roll one 5 to come in. Then, after you hit him, he must immediately roll a second 5 to keep from being closed out. This, in turn, must be followed by a third 5 to make the point before you can hit him again. O needs more 5's in rapid succession if you *don't* slot. The same reasoning applies when your opponent has more than two men on the bar: Don't slot — wait until he comes in and then hit him.

An advanced application of this principle is illustrated in Position 12.

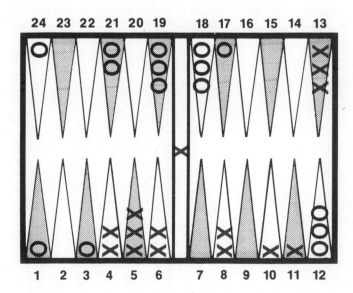

Position 12
X to Play 1–1

With 1–1 to play, X is certainly going to hit O twice and try to close him out. The question is whether to play bar/24*, 5/3*, 8/7 (Position 12A), or bar/24*, 4/3*(2), 8/7 switching points (Position 12B).

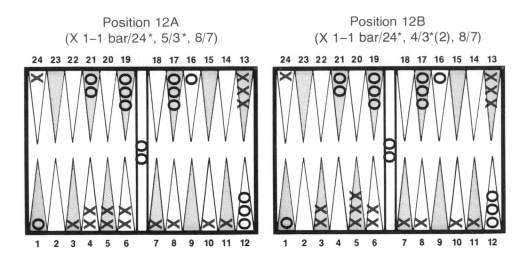

Position 12A
(X 1–1 bar/24*, 5/3*, 8/7)

Position 12B
(X 1–1 bar/24*, 4/3*(2), 8/7)

Although you ordinarily want to keep your points in order, the 12B play is correct. There is not a significant difference between holding the three point or the four point especially since in either case you will go all out to deprive your opponent of the remaining point. 12A is wrong since it is the functional equivalent of slotting with two men on the bar. You can accomplish the same thing (hitting the second man) in Position 12B without leaving a blot. The point is not that leaving a blot is so dangerous, but that O is more likely to establish a good point if you slot. A further advantage of playing 12B is that you have four builders bearing on the four point, whereas you have only two builders bearing on the three point in 12A.

Slotting on Your Bar Point

Let's apply the principles we have been discussing to a common problem: When is it correct to slot on the bar point?

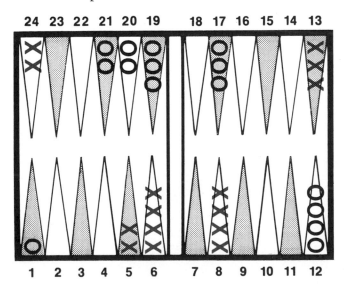

Position 13
X to Play 1

In Position 13, slotting on the bar point 8/7 is dangerous, but correct. You need the bar point to keep your opponent's last checker from escaping.

Why slot? First of all, you lack the builders to make the bar naturally for many rolls. And secondly, you need the bar point immediately. Every roll that you give O increases the danger that he will roll a 6 and leap into your outer board and escape. Rather than continually risk this situation, it is better to take a *bigger* risk on the first roll by slotting a checker on the bar point to cut off the escape route.

There is yet one more vitally important reason for slotting on the bar point: *It is fruitless to avoid numbers which are good for your opponent no matter what you play.* If you look at the position after slotting, you can see it will be good for you if O misses the shot. However, even if he does roll a 6 and hits, does this mean that you have thrown away a possible winning game?

No, probably not. Since most 6's are excellent numbers for O anyway, you have little to lose but a lot to gain by slotting the bar point.

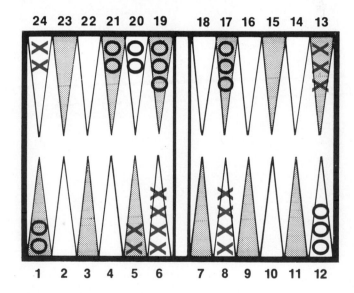

Position 14
X to Play 1

In Position 14, the correct play is to create a new builder by conservatively playing 6/5. The risk of slotting the bar point is too great, for, should you be hit, O becomes a tremendous favorite in the game. In both Positions 13 and 14, making the bar point is excellent for X. However, in 14 the bar point is not needed as urgently as in 13. In 14, if O rolls a 6, he hasn't yet won the game. First, you may get a shot at him in your outer board. More importantly, even if he escapes with one man, he still has a second man stuck back in your inner board. Since 6's are not a clear-cut winning number for O, you have a lot to lose by being hit on the bar point.

Position 14 indicates that you are more prone to take chances and slot the bar point if your opponent has only one man back rather than two. Notice that this conclusion is actually just a special example of the last principle of *Safe Play vs. Bold Play* which states: *The less men your opponent has in your inner board, the more aggressively you should play.*

Exceptions:

You must always consider the *entire* position. The principles stated above are only a guide to the reasoning process which precedes critical plays. Don't be fooled into thinking that it is automatically right to slot a man on the bar point if your opponent has only one man back threatening to escape. Nor is it necessarily wrong to slot the bar point if he has two men back.

Position 15
X to Play 1

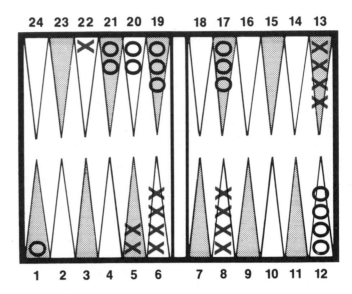

In Position 15, it would be a major mistake to slot, 8/7. First of all, to slot would be a clear-cut violation of the principle discussed in the beginning of this chapter: *It is wrong to slot when you are split or exposed in your opponent's inner board.* Secondly, even though O has only one man back, *you also have only one man back.* Lastly, O's inner board is better than yours, so you should be cautious. The correct move is 6/5.

Position 16A
X to Play 3–1

Position 16B
X to Play 3–1

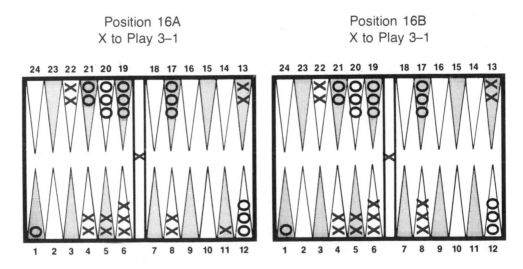

In Position 16A, it is incorrect to slot 8/7, although slotting on the bar point is not entirely unreasonable. The main difference between this position and Position 16B (where you must slot bar/22, 8/7) is the builder on the eleven point. Because of this builder, you have a fair chance of closing the bar point naturally in the next few rolls *without* slotting. Also, making the bar point is not as urgent since all 6's don't win the game for your opponent. Several 6's will leave double or triple return shots if O tries to run. The correct play in Position 16A is bar/22, 6/5. By playing 6/5 instead of 11/10 you maintain better coverage of the outfield.

Slotting Without Opposition

When your opponent has no men back in your inner board, you want to build up the inner board as quickly as possible in preparation for hitting him. An even more important objective, to be sure, is to make certain you get a chance to hit him. Methods for doing this are the subject of Chapter 18.

When you have no opposition from your opponent, and want to build your board rapidly, the basic method is to successively slot and cover. You should not bring builders down and then wait for the precise combinations which make the inner board points.

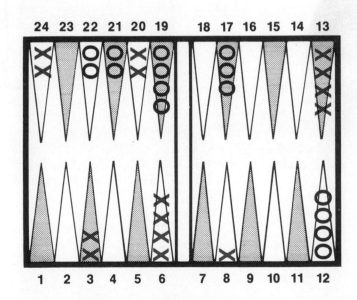

Position 17
(A) X to Play 6–1
(B) X to Play 6–4
(C) X to Play 6–2

In Position 17A, X should play 13/7, 6/5, slotting the five point, which he will cover next time. As a general rule, you should always concentrate on making inner-board points rather than the bar point when your opponent has no men back. Playing 13/7, 8/7 would definitely be a mistake.

You should also try hard to make your points in order. In Position 17B, it would be a mistake to make the two point, 8/2, 6/2. You want to concentrate on making the four or five point, so you should play 13/7, 13/9 (13/7, 8/4 is also acceptable).

In order to make your board rapidly, you must use your men efficiently. Thus, in Position 17C the correct play is 13/7, 6/4 — not 13/5. Even though the five point is slightly more preferable to the four point, slotting on the four point gives you a better distribution of men and more ways to cover the four point and later make the five point.

When there is little or no prospect of getting a shot on the next roll, sometimes the most effective way to build your inner board is to slot two men. It is incorrect to slot when you may get a shot on the next roll and want to avoid any return shots.

Position 18
X to Play 2

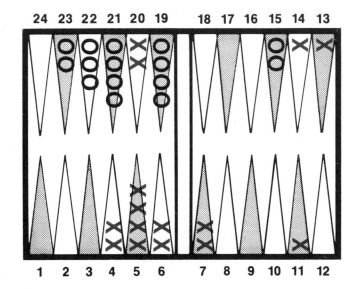

In Position 18, you should not slot 5/3; 11/9 is the correct play.

O may have to leave a shot if he rolls a 6 in Position 18. If this happens, X wants to be able to hit with a 5 without worrying about return shots on the three point. An additional reason why slotting is unnecessarily risky is that if X is able to hit O, he has excellent prospects of winning without making the three point immediately. In fact, if X owns the cube, he will probably be able to re-double O and force him out of the game.

CHAPTER 18.
ACTION PLAY

ASSUME THAT O has escaped both his back runners and you still have two or more men back in his inner board. Because you have more men back and are probably behind in the race, your main chance to win (your *only* chance, in fact) is to hit him. You are willing to take extra chances to get a shot at O and you welcome an exchange of hits. Above all, you don't want to let O consolidate his position by making key points.

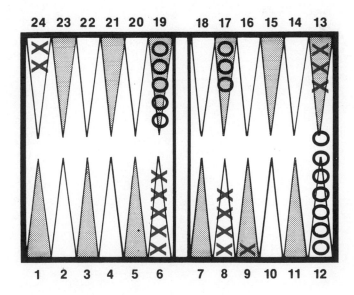

Position 1
X to Play 4–1

O has rolled 6–5 twice and is ahead in the race although he has made no new points. In this position, most players make the five point 9/5, 6/5, hoping to be able to hit later. This is a serious mistake. It is critical to restrain O *now*, before he becomes stronger and consolidates his advantage. The correct play is 24/20, 6/5.

This play leaves O in an awkward position. There are many numbers that force him to leave a direct shot, or that he must play nonconstructively (piling up on already established points) to avoid leaving shots. If you make the five point now, you give O time — a key roll — to either make a good point himself or, more likely, to bring builders down into his outer board. Once he has brought builders into his outer board and/or made additional points, it is much more dangerous for you to move up from the twenty-four point. And every additional builder or point that O makes allows him to play his succeeding numbers more easily and safely. In order to prevent O from coming home, you must restrict his movement *immediately*.

Although you would like to establish your five point before any of the hitting begins, this is a luxury you cannot afford. Each "free" move that you give O makes his task easier and yours more difficult. By moving to the twenty point immediately, you restrict his mobility by exerting pressure on his outer board.

Position 2
X to Play 6–2

O has escaped his back men in Position 2, and X *must* get a shot to win. The correct play is 24/18, 9/7! At first glance, this play looks ridiculous and suicidal — why expose yourself to a quadruple shot? What can you gain? Isn't O a favorite to point on your head? Let's look at the position closely and see first what you have to lose by making this play.

You will almost certainly be hit and lose 7 pips in the race. This in itself, however, is unimportant. You are already far behind in the pip count and trapped behind the enemy's front lines. *The pip count itself* (and thus the 7 lost pips) *means nothing; you will have to establish contact with O and hit him in order to win.*

What about the objection that you provoke O to point on your head?

Actually, by resting on O's bar point you do not increase his chances of making it on the next roll. The exact same number of shots will make the bar point whether you are sitting there or not. The only difference between being there and not being there is that you might be hit and lose 7 pips. You can't prevent him from making the bar point in any case. Remember: *You shouldn't try to avoid numbers that are good for your opponent anyway.*

We have seen that the downside risk is largely illusory; now let's look at what we have to gain by making the action play.

In this position, *we are not trying to avoid being hit, but to get return shots.* By coming to O's bar point, X aims directly at all three of O's exposed men. Because of the blot on the fifteen point, O will have great difficulty in safetying all three of his blots. In fact, if O hits on the bar point, he will have yet another exposed man to deal with. This is why the play is called an **action play.** You expect to be hit, but the possibility of retaliation is to your benefit.

The action play also prevents O from consolidating the advantage he has in the race. As in the previous position, passive play is fatal here. You cannot take the time to build a stronger board before embarking on an action play because in a roll or two O will be more dangerous and less exposed. While you are building up your inner board, he may be making the vital twenty or twenty-one point. If you play passively *now*, you will probably be stuck with the gloomy prospect of sitting on the twenty-four point forever and hoping to find and hit a lucky shot. Assuming that O owns the cube, or that it is still in the middle, he will double you out before you even get a chance to hit a lucky shot.

For O to consolidate his position and bring his men home safely, he must safety his blots and create new points. By making the play we have indicated, you provoke him and distract him from his more important goals. Your blot on the bar point becomes an annoying "fly in the ointment" which must be dealt with before his juggernaut can roll home. On O's next roll it will be hard for him to make new key points — especially inner points such as the twenty-one or twenty point. He has to deal simultaneously with safetying his blots and removing your man from his bar point. He can't let you leave the blot there for, should you roll a 6, you may achieve a viable holding position by owning the bar point.

It is important to keep O from making the twenty-one or twenty point because these points make it easier for him to come home to restrain and endanger your back men. If you make the action play, O will have to forego making an inside point for at least one roll (unless he rolls a double). You prefer that he make the bar point rather than an inside point. Therefore, if you are pointed on, you would rather be hit *outside* than *inside*.

We have now discussed Position 2 at length. If you are still unsure of the reasons for playing 24/18, 8/7, or wish to study the position further, we advise you to examine all the possible 21 distinct rolls for O and compare the resulting positions with and without having made the action play.

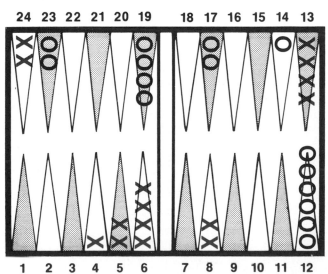

Position 3
X to Play 5

This position is similar to Position 2. The correct play is 23/18. Again, the basic criteria (namely, you have three men back, he has none; you have four inner points made to his two) suggest strongly that a bold and provocative play is called for.

Position 3 is actually much more dangerous for you than Position 2 because of your extra blots and because O has already made the twenty point. Since you have a bad game anyway, you must play aggressively to give yourself a chance to win. If you play passively now, O will probably make additional points in his inner board and attack you.

The action play leaves you open to the danger that O may hit two men. But if he hits a man inside, you will probably get a direct return shot at a time when you have a strong 4-point board. If O hits only one man, you may have return shots from the bar and also several shots which re-enter and make O's bar point.

Position 4
X to Play 4–1

The correct play is 24/20, 6/5. You must not take the time to make the four point, but must act immediately to provoke contact. As a general rule, it is not advisable to move up to your opponent's five point (the twenty point) when he has extra builders bearing on it. However, since a strong play is called for, an exception to this principle must be made. It is hopeless to wait back on the twenty-four point. You must come up to the twenty point now and risk being pointed on or hit twice. There are actually not that many numbers that make the twenty point precisely, and besides, these numbers are good for O anyway. If O hits you with a blot, you will have a large number of return shots and you welcome an exchange of hits. Because the man on the twenty point prevents him from bringing builders down from his midpoint and leaving blots in his outer board, it provokes action.

Position 5
X to Play 5–1

Position 6
X to Play 5–1

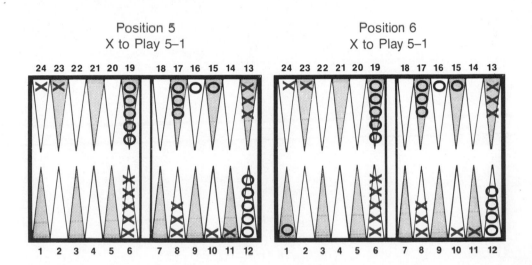

A basic condition for making what we call an **action play** is that your opponent has no men back. The correct play in Position 5 is 23/18, 6/5. This is a typical action-play situation where you slot on O's bar point to prevent him from making a key inner-board point.

Position 6 is similar to Position 5 except that here O has a man back in your inner board. Although you may wish to play boldly, this *cannot* be an action position as we have defined it. Your sole objective is no longer just to get a hit, but also to restrain your opponent's back man. You should therefore make your five point 6/5, 10/5, the normal play.

We will continue our discussion of special techniques used when your opponent has only one man back in the next chapter.

CHAPTER 19.
ONE MAN BACK

WE SHALL NOW look at positions where your opponent has only one man remaining in your inner board and you have at least two men in his inner board. As we have noted, aggressive and provocative play is generally called for. In the particular case where your opponent has only *one* man back, you have two major objectives: (1) You must take extra precautions to prevent your opponent's back man from escaping, and (2) as in Chapter 18, you act provocatively and try to send a second man back.

Containing the Last Back Man

Slotting and Making Your Bar Point

When your opponent is threatening to escape his last man and enter into a winning race, you often have to take extra risks to contain him.

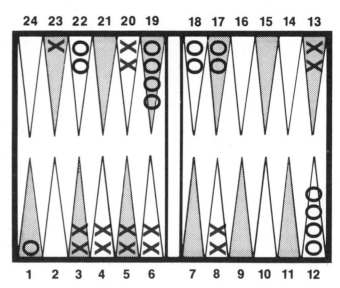

Position 1
X to Play 3–1

In Position 1, you should play 8/7, 23/20. Although slotting on your bar point won't prevent him from escaping with a 6 (on this roll nothing will), if he misses you can cover the bar point and make it very hard for him to escape later. The added impetus to slot on the bar point when your opponent has only one man back was discussed in detail in Chapter 17.

In Section I we observed that the five point is more valuable than the bar point. Even when your opponent has only one man back, it is still *usually* correct to make the five point, rather than the bar point. The only exceptions to this principle do occur when your opponent has only one man back. Here is one such exception:

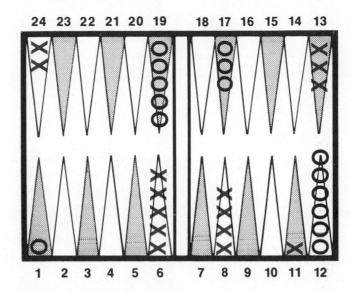

Position 2
X to Play 6–1

In Position 2, you would have to give up a builder on the eleven point to make the five point. This builder deters O from escaping into your outer board. For this reason, the preferred play is to make your bar point 13/7, 8/7, keeping the extra builder on the eleven point.

Moving into Your Opponent's Outer Board

Another method of containing your opponent's last checker is to place a man in your opponent's outer board.

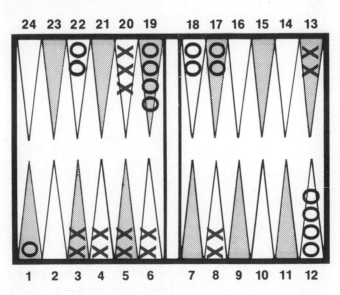

Position 3
X to Play 4–1

In Position 3, the correct play is 20/15. This involves less risk than slotting on the bar point 8/7, which is somewhat awkward because of the 4 left to play. Bringing a back man out leaves your opponent with few clear-cut winning shots, whereas slotting gives him a winning number: 6. By bringing an extra man into O's outfield, you exert extra control over *your* whole outfield. Even if O rolls a 6 (other than 6–5), you get a large double direct shot at him. Since you have an advanced anchor in his 2-point board, you need not worry much about being hit.

Hitting Inside and Slotting

A third method of preventing your opponent's escape is illustrated in Position 4.

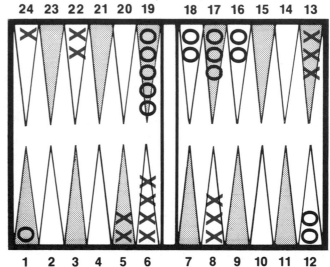

Position 4
X to Play 5–1

O again threatens to escape with a 6. A simple slot on your bar point 13/7 is possible, but there is a stronger play: 8/7, 6/1*. By simultaneously hitting O on the one point and slotting, you make it difficult for him to escape on his next roll. This play also has the advantage of "stealing" the bar point. Whether you are hit on the one point or not, you have excellent prospects for making the bar point on the next roll. For this reason (i.e., to get the bar

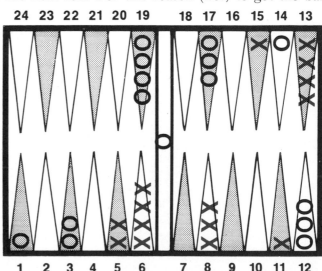

Position 5
X to Play 5–4

point), hitting inside and slotting on the bar is often used in other positions where your opponent doesn't necessarily have one man back.

For example, in Position 5 the correct play is 11/7, 6/1*. By putting a second man on the bar, you are practically assured of making your bar point. In both Positions 4 and 5, the idea behind hitting on the one point is *not* to make the one point, but to gain a tempo in which to make the bar point.

Creating Diversions

Still another method for at least temporarily forestalling your opponent's escape is to create a diversion elsewhere which he must take care of.

Position 6
X to Play 2–1

Position 7
X to Play 6

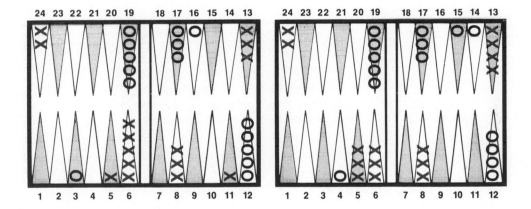

In Position 6, the correct play is 6/5, 24/22. By challenging O's man on the sixteen point, you force O to take action in his outer board and thus prevent his immediate escape from your inner board. This is another example of a **tempo move** — that is, the move itself may not have much significance except in that it forces O to waste part or all of his roll. You put yourself under somewhat more pressure by moving up to the twenty-two point; however, even if O points on you, he still has only a 2-point board (with the twenty-two point too deep to be immediately dangerous).

Similarly, in Position 7 the correct play is 24/18. Before O can successfully escape, he must hit this man. Thus, you prevent O from escaping from your inner board — at least for *this* roll. This play is very similar to the action play (see Position 2 in Chapter 18). In addition to preventing O's escape, you also hinder him from consolidating his position and create opportunities for a return shot.

Playing Aggressively and Forcing Exchange of Hits

Hit, If Possible

Position 7 illustrates your other important objective when your opponent has only one man back: You try to send a second man back. For this reason, when faced with the choice of hitting or making a key point, preference is usually given to sending back a second man. If you are unable to hit a new man, you may at least take advantage of your opponent's reluctance to be hit to secure good points and be otherwise provocative.

In fact, you may take extra chances that you ordinarily would not take. Chapter 17 warned against slotting while being split, and in Chapter 22 we warn against **coming under the gun** (i.e., splitting to your opponent's four or five point when he has extra builders bearing on these points). Both these injunctions apply when your opponent has one man back, but with less force and more exceptions. Similarly, plays involving splitting to your opponent's bar point in the hope of return shots occur more frequently when your opponent has one man back.

Position 8
(X 6–3 24/18, 13/10)

In Position 8, O opens with 6–5, taking a man to his midpoint 1/12. If you then roll 6–3 (or 6–2 or 6–4), this is a particularly good time to move up to O's bar point 24/18, 13/10. You welcome an exchange of hits (nullifying the value of his 6–5), which may result if O hits the checker on his bar point. If O doesn't hit, you exert control over all sectors of the board.

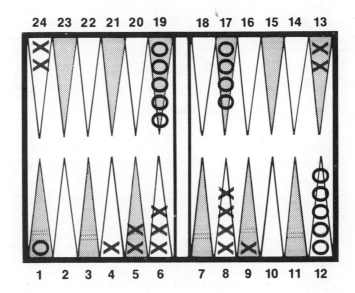

Position 9
X to Play 6–4

Similarly, in Position 9 the correct play is 24/18, 8/4.

Splitting to Your Opponent's Four or Five Point

In the preceding examples, you slot a man on your opponent's bar point when he has only one man back. It is also often advisable to come up to his four or five point (the twenty-one and twenty points, here) when possible.

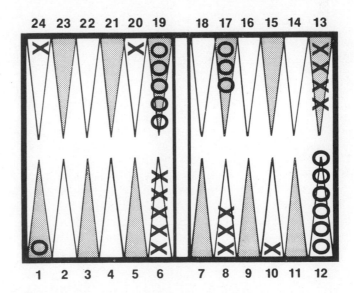

Position 10
(X 4–3 24/20, 13/10)

Suppose that O rolls 6–5 and plays 1/12 as shown in Position 10. X rolls 4–3 and plays 24/20, 13/10. This is the best play to make — it is a good time to go up to O's five point before he has any builders in his outer board to make it too dangerous. Because O has so few playable numbers, he will probably be forced to attack you on the twenty point and enter a blot-hitting contest. Usually, O would be glad to do this. Since he has fewer men back than you, however, an exchange of hits will be in your favor.

Response to Opening Rolls

Many of the plays on the opening rolls are optional — there is not one play which is clearly superior. If your opponent escapes a back runner at this point, however, the response is no longer optional. You *must* make the more provocative play.

For example, if your opponent begins with 6–5 (or runs with 6–3 or 6–4 and you fail to hit), you should try to split your back runners and *force* contact. Thus, when your opponent has only one man back, the following opening-roll responses become superior to any other: 3–2 (24/21, 13/11); 4–3 (24/20, 13/10); 6–3 (24/18, 13/10); 5–4 (13/8, 24/20); 6–2 (24/18, 13/11); 6–4 (24/18, 13/9).

CHAPTER 20.
GOLDEN POINT

A BACKGAMMON PLAYER is constantly exposed to unexpected pitfalls and accidents. Backgammon is often a game of sudden reverses: A player who is in a winning position may get hit by a freak shot, or stay out a crucial roll against a 2- or 3-point board. You can never completely prevent a sequence of fluke rolls and unexpected disasters. Indeed, it is precisely this aspect of the game that makes it so fascinating, even if occasionally frustrating.

You can gain a large measure of security throughout the game, however, by making a single point. This is *your opponent's five point*, called the **golden point**. It is the most important point for you to establish in the game.

The first part of this chapter will examine *why* the golden point is so valuable — not only in terms of what it prevents your opponent from doing, but also what it enables you to do. In the second part we examine the question of how and when to make this point, and when to leave it. In the last part we discuss holding other points in your opponent's inner board.

Value of the Golden Point

Ruining Your Opponent's Game Plan

Two main dangers that you face during the course of a game — which are your opponent's objectives — are (1) being closed out, and (2) being primed. Holding your opponent's five point offers a good degree of protection against both these possibilities.

First, it is impossible to be closed out if you maintain an anchor in your opponent's home board. If you hold the golden point, you can be almost sure of eventual re-entry and survival in case of an all-out attack.

Secondly, it is usually hard for your opponent to form a prime and blockade against his own five point. It is difficult to form a prime in one's outer board, and, when formed, it often proves awkward and unwieldy.

Thus, holding your opponent's five point gives you security and thwarts two of his main game plans: the attacking game and the priming game. This point will even often frustrate another important game plan for your opponent — the running game.

Assume that your opponent escapes his back men and is far ahead in the race. You can still make it hard for him to clear his midpoint and come safely home by holding his five point. The golden point always bears directly on his outer board, making it hard for him to bring builders down safely into this crucial region. For this reason, the golden point is the key to a successful holding game, which is one of the most frequently played types of games among advanced players.

The best holding games combine owning the golden point with at least one other point. For example, we have seen that merely owning the golden point and your midpoint makes it very difficult for your opponent to successfully clear *his* midpoint. Another type of holding position involves owning the golden point and the twenty-four point (your opponent's one point). Holding these two points also makes it difficult for him to bring all his men home safely.

Furthering Your Own Game Plan

The security which the opposing five point affords gives you much greater freedom of action in other areas of the board. You can usually take greater risks and withstand an adverse sequence of rolls far better than a player with an otherwise similar position who does not hold this point.

When you want to determine if you should take chances or leave a shot, we saw in Chapter 16 that the most important tactical criteria is: Do you have an advanced anchor? And in particular: Do you have the golden point? One of the most basic and effective methods for winning at backgammon is simply to establish this point and then go about your business of priming or attacking your opponent's back men. Even if you get hit once or twice in the process, you may still be successful.

Owning the golden point is a particularly strong incentive to attack your opponent. In the commonly occurring situation where you try to **blitz** him, holding his five point enables you to double him even if your chances for a successful blitz are not that great. Even if the blitz fails, you will have a sound game. Without the safety of the golden point, however, you usually need much better prospects for a successful blitz before doubling.

Because your opponent's five point offers you equity almost until the end of the game, and because it is difficult to be gammoned while holding this point, you can often accept doubles that you would not otherwise consider. Conversely, you must wait longer to double your opponent if he owns *your* five point.

When to Hold the Golden Point

Safe Play vs. Bold Play

We have stressed the importance of making and holding the golden point. Certainly one of the most important shortcomings of the average player is failing to realize the value of this point and consequently missing an opportunity to make it, or relinquishing it prematurely. Most players give up the point far too early without sufficient cause.

When should you make the golden point? This is a decision you must make whenever your opponent has taken his opening roll and you roll 2–2.

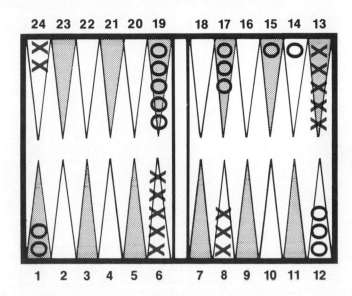

Position 1
X to Play 2–2
(O 3–2 12/15, 12/14)

In Position 1, O has rolled 3–2 bringing two active builders from his midpoint, 12/15, 12/14. The best play for X is 24/20(2), seizing the golden point. If you feel that your back men are becoming trapped, it is advisable to make the twenty point immediately.

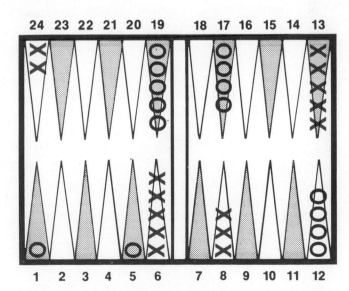

Position 2
X to Play 2–2
(O 5–4 12/17, 1/5)

In Position 2, on the other hand, O has no builders in his outer board, and therefore X does not feel threatened. The best play here is 6/4(2), 13/11(2). This play puts immediate pressure on O. X will probably have a good chance to split safely in O's inner board later in order to try to establish an advanced anchor.

We can see that the criteria in Chapter 16 apply: When the position is dangerous for you, try to make the golden point for security. When you don't feel threatened, you may consider another strong play elsewhere.

Position 3
X to Play 4–3

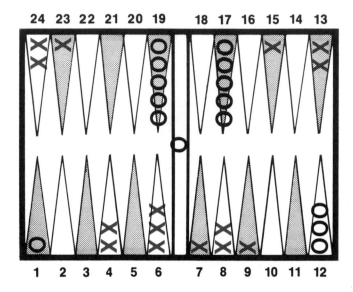

In Position 3, X does not feel trapped. X has more points closed in his inner board than O. O is on the bar. Therefore, X makes the more aggressive play, 9/5, 8/5, rather than making the golden point, 24/20, 23/20.

Giving Up the Golden Point to Hit

One reason you may wish to give up the golden point is to hit your opponent. We shall first consider the general question of the value of hitting. In Chapter 16, we examined the circumstances in which you are willing to risk being hit (usually by a direct shot). Here we will consider the *inverse* proposition — that is, how strong is your motivation to hit your opponent? We shall see that your desire to hit may be determined by your opponent's reluctance to be hit as determined in Chapter 16.

Hitting and Declining to Hit

When you hit, your opponent loses pips and his standing in the race deteriorates. By hitting, you can also make him lose a whole turn, or even several turns if he fails to re-enter. You might want to hit to keep your opponent from making a key point, to strip him of builders, and to protect yourself. You may also hit as a tempo move to deprive him of half a roll, and for various other advanced technical reasons.

Since you always advance your standing in the race by hitting, the question remains: Why *not* hit? You may refuse to hit because of the danger of return shots. Even if there is no immediate danger, you may be reluctant to relinquish a key point in order to hit. Also, the roll may be better used by making a key point. Advanced considerations sometimes come into play in backgames and holding games where you want your opponent to move and strip himself, and so you avoid hitting him.

When contemplating a hit, consider the criteria of Chapter 16 in reverse. If your opponent were to decide that a bold play is called for, then you probably gain little by hitting; if he studies *Safe Play vs. Bold Play* and decides that a safe play is called for, then you probably want to hit.

Tactical Criteria for Hitting

We began Chapter 16 with four tactical criteria. Obviously, you want to hit if the hit is dangerous for your opponent. The better your inner board, the more dangerous a hit is, while the presence of an advanced anchor in *your* inner board reduces the danger for him.

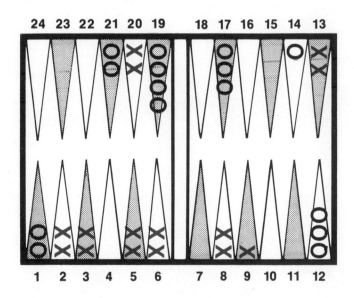

Position 4
X to Play 4–2

In Position 4, X should play 20/14* hitting O. You hope to get home and close additional points while O struggles to get in on your 4-point board.

Position 5
X to Play 4–2

In Position 5, however, you should not hit and relinquish the golden point since O's control of *your* five point and your weak inner board pose no strong threat to him.

You must also consider how dangerous your opponent will be to you should you hit him. First, look at the possibility of return shots. If you have an exposed blot in your inner board, you are less anxious to hit. Secondly, if you expose yourself to return shots when your opponent has a strong inner board and you do not, you are less willing to hit.

Instead of hitting simply play 8/2.

Strategic Criteria for Hitting

How do the strategic ideas from Chapter 16 apply to hitting from the golden point? First, consider the number of men your opponent has back. If

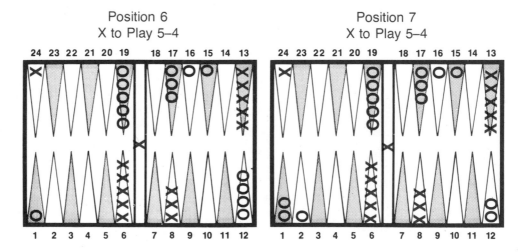

Position 6
X to Play 5–4

Position 7
X to Play 5–4

he has no men back, you are very strongly compelled to hit him so that you can try to trap at least one man. Chapter 18 was completely devoted to the problem of how to secure a hit in such a situation.

Furthermore, when your opponent has only one man back, you are also usually compelled to hit in order to (1) prevent him from winning the game by merely escaping his last back man (see Chapter 19 on how to prevent this escape), and (2) to equalize the race.

In Position 6, it is correct to play bar/16*, even though you have an opportunity to make the twenty point, bar/20, 24/20.

In Position 7, however, O already has three men back. You should make the golden point, bar/20, 24/20. Whenever O has *three or more* men back, you generally have less to gain by hitting.

Position 8
X to Play 3–1

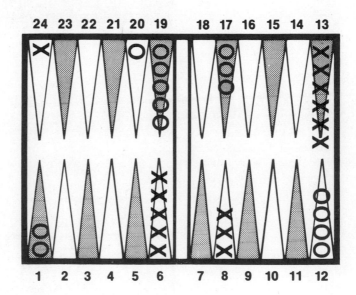

In Position 8, you have an extremely weak inner board so you have nothing much to gain by hitting. O has two men back to your one. If you hit him, 24/20*, he will re-enter easily and perhaps make an advanced anchor, or hit you back.

A much more constructive play is to make your own five point, 8/5, 6/5. Note that just because O has three or four men back you don't necessarily want to avoid hitting (excepting backgames); however, you may no longer have a strong inclination to do so.

The other important strategic criteria is the number of men *you* have back. If you have few men back — and/or less than your opponent — you are not anxious to get into a blot-hitting contest.

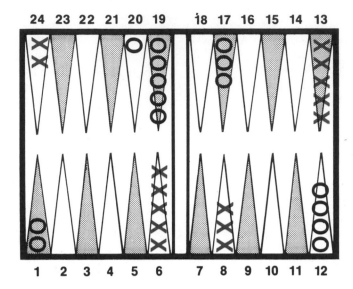

Position 9
X to Play 3–1

In Position 9, X again has the choice of hitting O, 24/20*, or making the five point, 8/5, 6/5. Both plays are good, but the slightly superior play is to hit. Since both sides have two men back and the race is about even, by hitting, you establish superiority in both these areas. In addition, you may have an opportunity to make the twenty point later. If you don't hit but make the five point, you give O the opportunity to make the twenty point, which would leave an almost equal position.

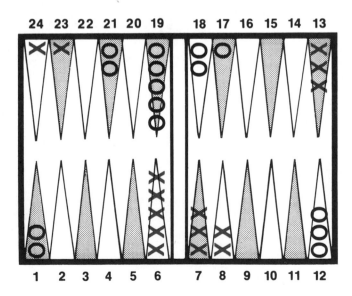

Position 10
X to Play 4–3

Position 10 is another case which is not clear-cut. Should you hit, 24/17*, or make the golden point, 24/20, 23/20? *When in doubt, make the golden* *point*. An experienced player will refuse to hit a blot in his opponent's outer board when he can make the golden point, unless hitting the blot is crucial to the overall development of the game.

Giving up the golden point to hit or for any other reason is a decision that should not be taken lightly. When giving up this point, you must consider not only the immediate danger of return shots, but also the danger in the next few rolls and the long-term loss of security. In fact, an expert player will often try to lure his opponent off the golden point by leaving blots in his outer board, if he can afford to be hit.

Giving Up the Golden Point to Run

Many players give up the golden point prematurely because they fear that if they stay too long they will end up at a disadvantage in the race. In practice, this fear is usually unfounded.

If your opponent still has men back, it is often better to work on attacking him or priming him, rather than running. If he has no men back, you should hold the golden point to prevent him from getting home easily. The extra trouble that you give him in coming home balances any time you may waste by staying on the point too long.

If your opponent doubles you in what is essentially a racing position — except that you hold the golden point — you should treat the position as if it were a straight race, accepting or declining accordingly.

Position 11
X Doubles

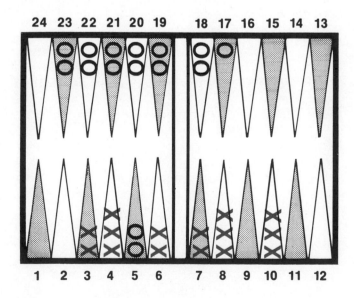

X doubles in Position 11, O is 10 pips behind in a **long race** (see Chapter 10). O accepts the double. The fact that X has O temporarily primed is not a major consideration. A large double would move O past the outside prime and put him ahead in the race. Section V will discuss this sort of holding position in more detail.

Leaving the Golden Point When Your Opponent Has Inner-Board Blots

You must be wary of leaving the golden point just because your opponent has a blot or blots in his inner board. Players are often lured off this point prematurely because they think their opponent will be unable to hit them safely, or unwilling to hit them at all.

Position 12
X to Play 6–3

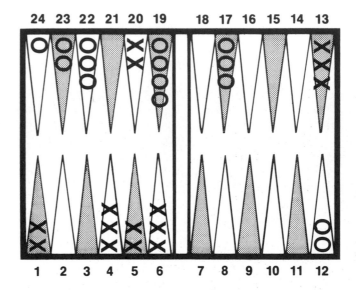

In Position 12, many players may think that this is a good opportunity to run since O will have a hard time hitting on the twenty point and covering all his blots. This reasoning is correct as far as it goes. There are only 6 combinations (4–3, 4–1, 1–1, 4–4) which hit and cover both blots. However, of the 20 direct shots that O has at the exposed man on the twenty point, 16 numbers allow O to hit and cover at least one of the blots. If X runs, he may then face the possibility of being on the bar against a 4½-point board (four points made and a blot on the fifth point). In this situation, X may come in and hit O, or miss and be doubled out of the game — do or die. Even if the return hit from the bar is a winner, X is taking an extreme risk by running; if O has an advanced anchor, the run is suicidal.

Position 13 is, in many ways, more deceptive than Position 12. Here, most players feel secure in running with one back man since if O hits on the twenty point he will also have to worry about safetying the three blots on the twenty-four, twenty-one, and twenty points.

However, of the 27 direct shots that O has, 20 of them hit *and* safety two blots! In other words, Position 13 is really *more* dangerous than Position 12. There are 20 numbers in Position 13 which force X to face a 4½-point board if he runs, and only 16 in Position 12. Although X is certain to get at least one direct shot if O hits, this may be his last shot. If X fails to re-enter and hit in both positions, he will be lost. O will probably make a 5-point board on his

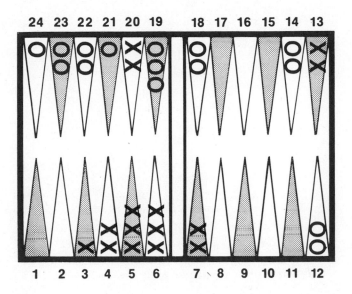

Position 13
X to Play 6–3

next roll and will certainly double if he hasn't done so already. Thus, the conclusion to be drawn is that even if you have a good inner board, be careful about running when your opponent has blots in *his* inner board. The blots may give you a false sense of security.

Finally we note that in both Positions 12 and 13, X is behind in the race. Why run at all? It would be better for him to try to hold O and wait for a shot instead of bolting now.

Holding Other Points in Your Opponent's Board

Although we have been specifically discussing your opponent's five point, his four point (your twenty-one point) basically serves the same functions. It provides a secure anchor for re-entry and it also is hard to prime. The four point is not *quite* as strong as the five point, but it is an excellent substitute. Your opponent's three point (your twenty-two point) and his bar point (your eighteen point) also may have merit.

Since your opponent's three point is deep in his inner board, it is more easily subject to being blockaded. Your eventual escape from his three point will also be more difficult. However, if your opponent already holds his four or five point, or if they are too difficult to make or too dangerous, his three point may still be quite valuable.

Your opponent's bar point is valuable to own since it keeps you from being primed, enables you to extricate men from his inner board, and makes it hard for him to come home safely. In fact, his bar point would be more valuable than his five point except for the important fact that it is not an anchor in his inner board. If you are hit, you do not have the security that your opponent's five point affords.

CHAPTER 21.
SPLITTING

SPLITTING IS SEPARATING two men that are together on the same point and leaving them as blots. In Chapter 12 we discussed some special cases where it is correct to split in your own outer board — when your opponent has two men on the bar, for example, and sometimes when he has a blot or blots in his inner board.

This chapter examines the question of when and how to split your back men, primarily in the early stages of the game. In splitting your back men off your opponent's one point (the twenty-four point), we distinguish between the **minor split** up to his two (twenty-three) or three (twenty-two) point, and the **major split** up to his four (twenty-one) or five (twenty) point. Before considering these splits in detail, let's examine the general reasons for wanting to split.

Why You Want to Split

As we have seen in Section I, a key part of your initial game plan is to extricate your back men. By splitting your runners, you move a little closer to home. More importantly, splitting diversifies your men, giving you more numbers to accomplish several possible objectives. By splitting, you have more numbers to run safely to your midpoint or, failing that, to run into your opponent's outer board. Splitting also increases your chances of making an advanced anchor (his four or five point), or his bar point. In order to diversify, it is particularly important to consider splitting if you have three men together on your opponent's one point.

In the previous chapter we saw the importance of making your opponent's five point (golden point). Often the best way to do this is to split a man directly to your opponent's five point, and then cover on the next roll. The second part of this chapter discusses in more detail when it is right and wrong to come up to your opponent's four or five point.

Splitting also hinders your opponent from building his inner board. He is unlikely to slot since he is reluctant to expose himself to a double direct shot. By moving up to his four or five point, you also exert direct pressure on his outer board, making it more dangerous for him to bring builders there. Even by splitting to his two or three point, you greatly increase the number of combination shots you will have at any loose builders in his outer board. Splitting may also "freeze" opposing men on already established points and prevent them from becoming active builders.

Liabilities in Splitting

One minor drawback to splitting is that doubles no longer play as well for you since your men can't move together. It is also inadvisable to slot in your inner board when split (see Chapter 17).

Let's look at the danger involved in splitting. On a basic level, you can afford to split your back runners because you stand to lose few pips if you are hit; if you are hit and then hit your opponent back, you gain a large number of pips in the race. However, there is also the possibility that your opponent may make a point directly on you. He may also hit two men. Finally, your opponent may hit with a blot where you run the risk of failing to re-hit him, or worse, staying out completely. When you are hit you also lose a tempo: half a roll even if you come in, a whole roll if you stay out.

In evaluating the danger of splitting, you must be aware of the number of active builders you expose yourself to. When your opponent has several active builders, a major split to his four or five point is usually inadvisable.

You must also take into account the points that your opponent has made in his inner and outer boards. This factor, however, often presents somewhat of a paradox: On one hand, the more points he has, the more dangerous is his position should you split and be hit; on the other hand, the stronger his position, the more you are trapped, and therefore your desire to split and escape is greater.

Relation to Overall Position

In evaluating your reasons for splitting, you must take into account your overall game plan. We have mentioned that a basic objective in splitting is to extricate your back runners. However, other goals include trying to prime your opponent and to attack him. In some important cases, it is impractical to work on all these aims simultaneously. For example, it may be better to go for an all-out attack which, if successful, will allow you to escape at your leisure, rather than attempt to escape directly. In such a case, splitting would be folly. Such advanced strategic considerations are discussed later in Section V.

Making a major split or splitting to your opponent's bar point are by their nature usually provocative plays. Since they exert direct control on your opponent's outfield, a man on an advanced point or on the bar point makes it very hard for your opponent to move his men around safely. For this reason, your opponent will often have no choice but to attack you. Your desire to be provocative, to engage in an exchange of hits, and your willingness to expose yourself to extra danger are fundamental considerations which depend directly on the criteria discussed in Chapter 16. Therefore, a thorough understanding of these principles is basic to any evaluation of the dangers and potential gains involved in splitting.

Major Split

The major split (splitting to your opponent's four or five point) has two basic functions: It exerts direct control on his outfield, and it gives you the possibility of establishing an advanced anchor. Unfortunately, this play is often dangerous since your opponent is likely to hit you or point on you. If you are hit, you not only lose ground in the race and lose time to develop, but if you fail to hit your opponent upon re-entering, he may establish his important four or five point. A key criteria for deciding when to make a major split is the number of opposing builders bearing on the point you want to split to. This is the criteria we shall examine next.

Coming Under the Gun

Let's look at an important case where a major split is usually wrong. Whenever your opponent has an extra builder (three altogether, including the original two on the six and eight points) or worse, more than one extra builder, we shall call such a split **coming under the gun**.

As a general rule, it is unnecessarily dangerous to come under the gun. You give your opponent an excellent opportunity to either point on your head or else hit two men. The risk of getting quickly into a losing game is not worth your possible gain.

Coming under the gun unnecessarily — especially when there is an acceptable alternate play — is one of the most common faults of the average player.

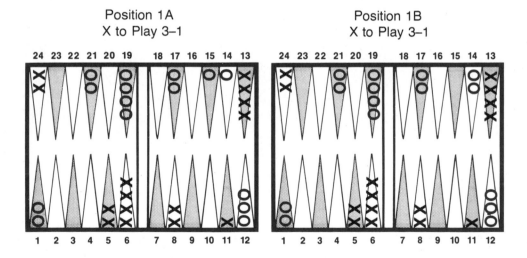

Position 1A
X to Play 3–1

Position 1B
X to Play 3–1

In Position 1A, O has a 2-point board and four builders (on the nineteen, seventeen, fifteen, and fourteen points) bearing on his five point (the twenty point). Playing 24/20 and coming under the gun would be extremely dangerous. In Position 1B, O has three builders bearing on his five point. Splitting, 24/20, would still be a serious error for X.

The correct play in both positions is 13/10, 6/5. You create an extra builder on the five point by moving off the "fat" six point and bring a second new builder into your outer board, giving you good prospects for making new points.

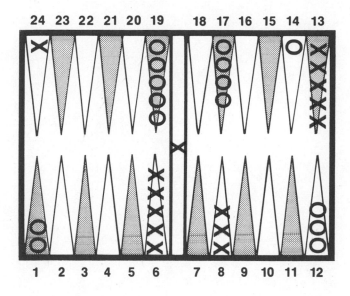

Position 2
X to Play 3–1

In Position 2, the correct play is bar/24, 13/10. Moving bar/21 comes under the gun unnecessarily. Another alternate move, bar/22, 6/5, does not constitute coming under the gun for two reasons: First, because we define coming under the gun as a major split to the opponent's four or five point, and more importantly, because the man on the twenty-two point is *not* exposed to extra builders. This latter play is nevertheless wrong because of the injunction not to slot while split as stated in Chapter 17. (Bar/24, 8/5 is also an improper slot — do you remember why?)

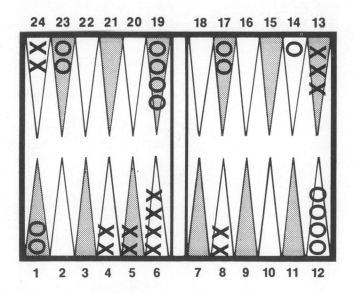

Position 3
X to Play 3–1

In Position 3, playing 24/20 again violates the rule not to come under the gun unnecessarily. The correct play is 24/21, 6/5 — which is not considered coming under the gun because the builder on the fourteen point is not bearing on X.

Although many games are lost by coming under the gun unnecessarily, there are several exceptions to the rule. Ironically, in the exceptional cases where coming under the gun is mandatory, many players are afraid to make the play.

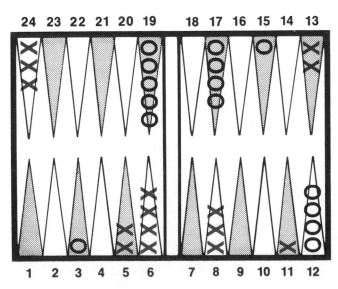

Position 4
X to Play 4–1

Exception 1. Position 4 is an action-play situation. O has escaped his back men while X has two men back. It is imperative to split immediately even at the risk of coming under the gun.

The **action play** (see Position 4, Chapter 18) is an extreme case of one of the basic criteria in Chapter 16 — namely, the less men your opponent has back, the more provocatively and/or dangerously you can afford to play. If most of

Position 5
X to Play 4

the basic criteria in *Safe Play vs. Bold Play* seem to be a bold play, it may be worthwhile to take the risk of coming under the gun.

For example, in Position 5 the correct play is 24/20. Here, O has not yet begun building his inner board. X's inner board is stronger and X has three men back (with an anchor) to O's one. All these are basic criteria in *Safe Play vs. Bold Play* and suggest a bold play. Further incentives are (1) the fact that O has only one extra builder bearing on the five point, and (2) the desirability to split your back men when you have three (or more) piled up on the same point.

Exception 2. If your opponent has a 5-point prime (or sometimes a 4-point prime), it is often correct to move up into a position where you can escape on the next roll even if he has a good chance of pointing on you. Whether or not the risk is justified is often an extremely complex and difficult decision, depending on the exact shapes of your primes and the timing of the game.

Position 6
X to Play 3

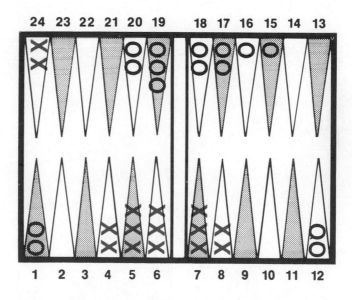

In Position 6, the correct play is 24/21. O is about to make a 5-point prime and has men on the midpoint to move. If you do not begin to move your back men, you will have to move the men holding vital points. Such decisions are discussed in more detail in Section V (particularly the third part of Chapter 28 which deals with **battle of primes**). We include this example even though it does not take place in the formative stages of the game.

Exception 3. If your opponent has a man on the bar, it is often right to seize this opportunity to advance in his inner board.

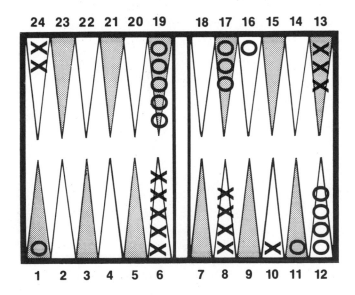

Position 7
X to Play 4–3

In Position 7, the correct play is 24/20, 16/13. The main reason you fear coming under the gun is because of the possibility that your opponent will be able to point on you. If he is on the bar, he cannot re-enter *and* point on you unless he rolls doubles (which you shouldn't worry about). At worst, O will be able to re-enter and hit you on the twenty point with a blot which would give you a double return shot at him (5's and 4's).

Position 8
X to Play 4–2

Similarly, in Position 8 the correct play is 24/20, 13/11*.

It is extremely important to take the opportunity to split when your opponent is on the bar. Advanced players often create such opportunities by hitting for the express purpose of splitting.

Hitting and Splitting

Position 9
X to Play 5–4

```
 24 23 22 21 20 19   18 17 16 15 14 13
```

(backgammon board diagram)

```
  1  2  3  4  5  6    7  8  9 10 11 12
```

X is already in trouble in Position 9. In the next few rolls, O has excellent prospects of making key points (his four, five, and bar points) and rapidly trapping X's back men. If X waits back passively on O's one point (13/8, 13/9, for example) he will probably drift quickly into a lost position. On the other hand, we know that as much as X would like to establish O's five point, a play such as 24/20, 13/8 is much too dangerous — in fact, a clear-cut violation of the coming-under-the-gun principles. The solution is 24/20, 6/1*, hitting a checker. We now have the same type of position as in *Exception 3*.

Hitting O on the one point, 6/1*, prohibits O from pointing on you on the twenty point since half his roll must be used to re-enter. If O hits the blot on the one point, you then have a double shot at covering the twenty point. Only 7 numbers allow him to re-enter and hit on the one point *and* hit on the twenty point, and in this case he still leaves a direct return shot for you on the twenty point.

You have little to lose by making the indicated play and a lot to gain. Even if a third man is hit, you may get your opponent's five point in the exchange. Owning the five point would nullify O's lead and give you security and time to build your own board and catch up in development.

This discussion indicates a new and important reason for hitting: as a tempo move. By automatically depriving your opponent of half a roll, you can make a play which would otherwise be too dangerous. In Position 9, you create a diversion by hitting on the one point, which enables you to move elsewhere.

We should emphasize that you do not hit with any prospect of keeping your opponent out, and, more importantly, you do *not* intend to make the one point. Should O miss you on the one point, you should not cover the one point, taking two men permanently out of play; resign yourself to the blot or even hope that it eventually will be hit and recirculated around the board.

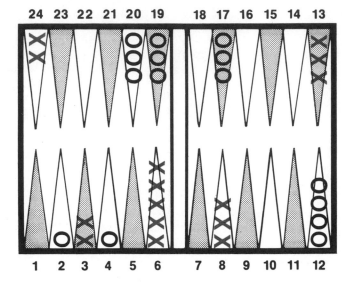

Position 10
X to Play 3–2

You can hit and split in Position 10 by playing 24/21, 6/4*. Here the hit on your four point has a two-fold purpose: you hope to establish the four point, and, as a tempo move, your split to the twenty-one point is protected. Even if O re-enters and hits in your inner board, you still may establish an advanced anchor on the twenty-one point. The hit-and-split play is a powerful tool. It represents one of the most effective ways for a player to seize an advanced anchor in his opponent's inner board.

A word of caution: don't confuse the approved hit-and-split play, which we recommend, with the inadvisable play of simultaneously slotting and splitting.

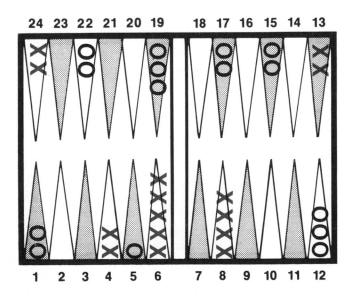

Position 11A
X to Play 4–1

In Position 11A, it is correct to play 24/20, 6/5*, hitting and splitting. It is wrong to slot and split, 24/20, 6/5, in Position 11B. A better play is 8/4, 24/23.

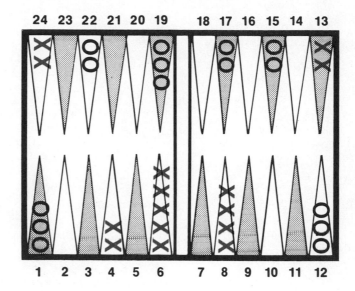

Position 11B
X to Play 4–1

Minor Split

The **minor split** to the two or three point is less dangerous than the major split since you are usually exposed to fewer enemy builders. Furthermore, your opponent is (or should be) reluctant to make a point as "deep" as his one or two point. Even his three point is not always good for him if he doesn't already have his four or five point.

As the minor split is less dangerous, so you also gain less since you exert less pressure on his outer board and you are not threatening to directly make an advanced anchor. In fact, if you split to the two point, you almost never want to make it. Only an inexperienced player consistently makes his opponent's two point. This point has almost no value — in fact, if your opponent holds his eight point (usually the case), then it is easier to escape from the one point than the two point. If you should make the two point early in the game, try to break off it at your earliest opportunity.

Splitting to your opponent's three point is a play whose merits are argued in expert circles. Unless your opponent has made it impossible for you to get his four or five point, the three point is too deep in his board to have the value of the four or five. However, the three point is closer to home and does exert a little extra pressure on him. One drawback — which is sometimes overemphasized — of a "1–3 split" (having a checker on his one and a checker on his three point) is the possibility of being wiped out by 5–5. You should not play to avoid specific doubles, especially in the formative stages of the game.

The main value of the minor split is that it diversifies your back runners and sets them moving. As compared with staying buttoned-up on your opponent's one point, the minor split gives you many more opportunities to run out to your opponent's outer board or to your midpoint, his bar point, or an advanced anchor.

The minor split also hinders your opponent in two less obvious ways: It discourages him from slotting because he would be exposed to a double shot; it may also freeze his men and turn them from active to inactive builders.

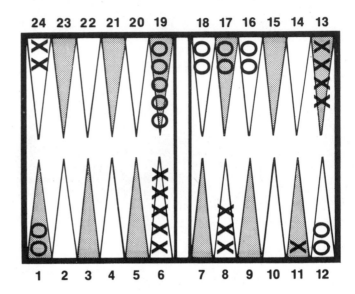

Position 12
X to Play 2

In Position 12, O has an **outside prime** — a prime beginning at the nineteen point and going into his outer board. Such primes are usually weak and ineffectual, so O might want to use the men on the nineteen and sixteen points to build key inside points. By playing 24/22, X bears on the nineteen and sixteen points; the extra men become inactive as builders unless O wants to leave a direct shot.

There are many positions where you may have the choice of using a 1 to split your back runners off your opponent's one point or else move constructively elsewhere. If the plays seem to have approximately equal merit, check how many men your opponent has on his eight point. If he has only two men, the split may be indicated because this inhibits him from giving up the eight point to make a more valuable inside point.

CHAPTER 22.
DOUBLING THEORY

DOUBLING IS ONE of the most important aspects of backgammon; correct doubling decisions alone will give a player an enormous advantage over his opponent. The doubling cube holds the key to being a winner or a loser. Good checker play will never compensate for serious errors of judgment in doubling.

Unfortunately, there are no easy rules to guide you in all doubling decisions. As you learn to play the checkers better, you will also achieve a better understanding of the dynamics of the game. This in turn will enable you to better judge the overall potentialities of a position and evaluate your chances. Thus, there is no shortcut to doubling strategy — it can only be improved as your understanding of the play and strategy improves.

With this in mind, we shall present a theoretical framework and some general rules for doubling. Their proper application relies heavily upon your understanding of the dynamics of the game and your ability to draw upon past experience. Two main decisions have to be made: when to double, and when to accept a double. Let's first look at the question of when to accept doubles.

Accepting Doubles

The 3-to-1 Principle

In Chapter 7 we mentioned that a commonly followed guideline is to accept a double if you have better than a 25% chance of winning and reject it if you have less. Using the language of odds, this is referred to as the **3-to-1 principle:** *If your opponent doubles when he is better than a 3-to-1 favorite — if he is going to win the game in question more than 75% of the time — you should pass. When his edge is less than 3 to 1, you should accept.*

To understand why, imagine your opponent is exactly a 3-to-1 favorite. This is a borderline case and, theoretically, you are indifferent about accepting or refusing. If you were to play the same position four times, passing each time the cube were turned to 2, you would lose a total of 4 points. On the other hand, if you decided to take each time, you'd lose on the average three times out of four at double the stakes for a loss of 6 units, and win one time for a gain of 2. So if you were to accept, the result would be a net loss of 4 points. You won't end up a winner, but in the long run you won't lose any more than you would have if you had passed each time.

Bear-off positions can sometimes be precisely calculated with this principle in mind.

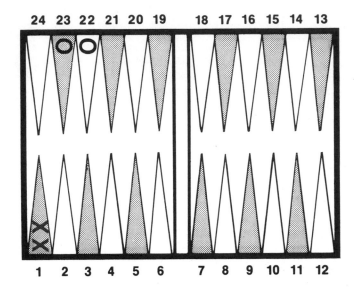

Position 1
O on Roll; O Doubles

For example, in Position 1, O's turn will win the game for him unless he rolls a 1. Therefore, 25 out of 36 possible combinations of the dice will take both his men off. The other 11 won't. This makes him a 25-to-11, or 2.2-to-1 favorite. Since this is less than 3 to 1, his double should be accepted. Remember that this doesn't mean you are a favorite to win — merely that you stand to lose less on the average by taking than by passing.

It is important to note that this rule applies to the person who has been doubled, not to the one who is making the offer. The doubler needn't have the odds so heavily in his favor; he can turn the cube when his possibilities are considerably less than 3 to 1. (In fact, occasionally it is correct for a person to double when he is actually an underdog.)

This 3-to-1 principle has some important exceptions: First, it fails to take into account the equity involved in actually owning the cube — in other

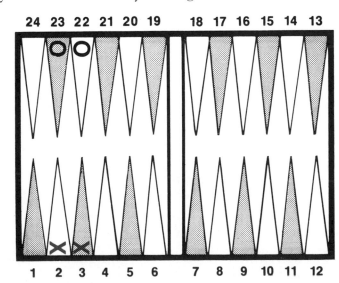

Position 2
O on Roll; O Doubles

words, the power of the cube and the ability to re-double at a favorable opportunity. Again we shall go to the bear-off for a concrete illustration.

In Position 2 with O on roll, it may be calculated that O is better than a 3-to-1 favorite. In other words, X has less than a 25% chance to win: O must first roll a 1 and then X must not roll a 1. However, it is correct for X to accept the double because if O *does* roll a 1, X has the privilege of re-doubling (which O should accept). Whenever X wins in such positions, he will receive enough extra to justify the gamble.

In practice, the main drawback to the 3-to-1 principle is that it is usually impossible to determine exactly what the true odds of winning are. The bear-off examples just given were cases where it was possible to figure out the exact odds (although we wouldn't recommend trying it in your head in Position 2). In table 7 at the end of the book, we give the exact odds for bearing the last two men off. In Section IV, we shall discuss the exact chances in many other endgame situations. Let us examine some comparatively simple positions which are not pure races or bear-offs and see how we may evaluate the chances.

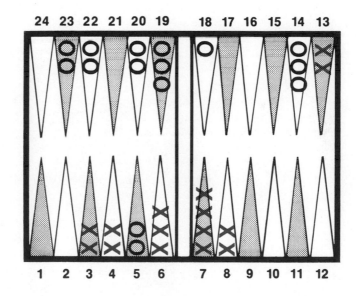

Position 3
X on Roll; X Doubles

In Position 3, X doubles. In order to determine his chances, O must realize that he has two distinct winning possibilities: He may win the race, or he may be able to hit X as he comes home. Neither possibility looks very appealing. O is 16 pips behind in the race, which is slightly higher than a permissible take (he could take with 13) in a pure race. O's chances of hitting X are also poor — they depend mainly on being able to throw a combination 8 (5/36) when and if X clears his midpoint, leaving a blot. Roughly, then, X will be hit about 10% of the time. If O had to count on either method alone (race or hit), he would pass. However, since the race is not too far from being a take, O, by adding on the extra 10% for the chance of hitting, has enough combined chances to take.

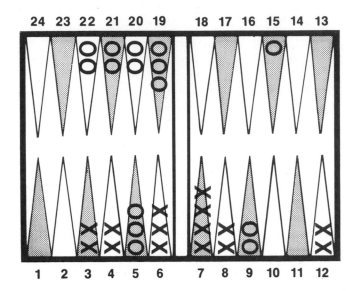

Position 4
X on Roll; X Doubles

In Position 4, O is 44 pips behind. Since X is on roll, O has virtually no chance in the race. O must therefore pin all his hopes on getting a shot and hitting X. It looks as if X is quite likely to give O a direct shot, which would give O better than a 25% chance to win and justify his take. However, to properly estimate O's chances, we must realize that in order to win, O needs three specific occurrences to happen: (1) X must leave the shot, (2) O must hit it, (3) O must win the game after hitting. We shall let P_1 stand for the probability (percentage of the time) that the first event occurs, P_2 for the second event, and P_3 for the third. Mathematically, the probability of all three occurrences happening can be shown to be the product of each one occurring independently, i.e., $P_1 \times P_2 \times P_3 = P$, the probability O wins.

Now, we may assume that occurrence (3) is close to a certainty, that is, $P_3 = 1$, since if X is hit O will almost certainly win since O will be able to double X out of the game. P_2 is O's chance of hitting X (assuming that X leaves a shot). If X leaves a shot on the twelve point, O will have $^{18}/_{36} = \frac{1}{2}$ to hit; we therefore assume $P_2 = \frac{1}{2}$. At first glance, P_1, the chance of O getting a shot, appears fairly high since there are only a few numbers (6–6, 6–4, 6–5, 5–5, 4–4, 5–4, 2–2, and perhaps 1–1) that allow X to move his men off the twelve point safely. However, X will probably have three or four rolls to get one of the numbers, so the odds are that X will probably have to leave a direct shot only about 1 time in 3. In other words, $P_1 = \frac{1}{3}$. Returning to our formula, then, $P = \frac{1}{3} \times \frac{1}{2} \times 1 = \frac{1}{6}$. O's actual probability of winning is less than 25%, so O should pass.

These last two positions were comparatively simple. In more complicated backgammon positions, any such calculations would be impossible. Basically, then, the 3-to-1 principle can be a helpful guideline, but mathematical odds can only help in a very limited number of cases and will never be a substitute for good general judgment.

Gammons

Another major exception to the 3-to-1 principle is that it only applies to situations in which there is no gammon involved. When you run a serious risk of being gammoned, you generally need much more than a 25% chance of winning in order to accept. In fact, in positions where *you* are certain to be gammoned if you lose but where your opponent is in no such danger, you need almost 50% rather than a 25% chance to win the game in order to accept a double. When you accept a gammon-prone double, you are risking three extra units, or four times the original stake.

A good part of the skill in accepting or refusing doubles lies in being able to recognize which positions are gammon-prone and which are not. In any position where you are under attack and have no anchor in your opponent's board, you risk being closed out and gammoned. Many seemingly inferior positions can be taken when you have an anchor so that you can play the game out until the very end and hope for a lucky shot without any chance of being gammoned. An anchor makes gammons harder, but by no means impossible.

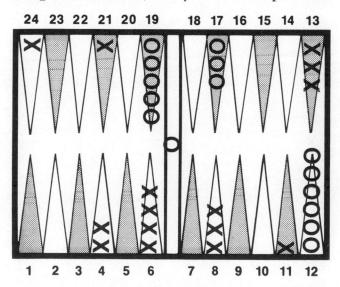

Position 5
X on Roll; X Doubles

Position 5 is a position where some people take a double. They argue that O is unlikely to be gammoned because even if O is closed out immediately, he will have only one man closed out. This is faulty logic for two reasons: First, O may have a second man picked up since he will probably be forced to leave other men exposed when he comes in; second, O may not be able to move any significant distance with his other men before he is closed out and will probably be gammoned. O should drop in this position not because X's game is so strong, but because his own game is so weak.

A word of advice: Never be afraid to decline a double. Paradoxically, the two words, "I pass," are your single most powerful weapon despite the tradition of fighting until the end and never saying "uncle." Both the ability to recognize bad doubles and the discipline to give up a particular game lead to winning backgammon.

There are many rationales and motivations for accepting bad doubles. Many players lose unnecessarily because they are unable to resist the temptation to see how the game comes out. Particularly in situations where you began a favorite and then suffered an incredible stroke of ill-luck, you may be tempted to see if you can turn the tables on your opponent. It is better to pass and begin the next game rather than compound the tragedy. Situations where you would normally accept a double but must pass because of the possibility of being gammoned are especially difficult to resist. If you consistently pass when you should do so, however, you may lose more games but will certainly win more points.

Each game must be considered on its own merits; you must try to avoid letting what happened during the last game cloud your judgment. There is no surer way to lose many points than to double prematurely and accept bad doubles to try to recoup past losses. From a theoretical viewpoint, the question of accepting doubles (and offering them also) should be considered independently of the level of the cube. In other words, it is never theoretically correct to accept a double at the 8 level which you would pass at the 2 level or vice versa. Some players lose their perspective when a game has been doubled and re-doubled several times; they have the dangerous habit of accepting doubles they would ordinarily pass. Other players lean to the opposite extreme and pass doubles they are clearly justified in taking because they become intimidated by the possibility of losing a big game. Of course, from a practical viewpoint there may be a limit to the amount you are willing to lose in the game; nevertheless, there is only one correct theoretical decision. An important exception to this rule, as well as many others, occurs in tournament and match play where you play to reach a specific number of points.

Offering Doubles

Advantages

Let us first examine the advantages of doubling. First, your opponent may pass, thus conceding the game and giving you a definite win. By forcing your opponent to pass, you eliminate whatever chance he has of winning.

The benefit of doubling is in simply increasing the stakes in a position which is favorable to you. You want to extract the maximum number of possible points for each game you win. You must make your opponent pay extra for the privilege of trying to continue to win a game at which he is at a disadvantage.

Disadvantages

The disadvantage in doubling is that you may not then double next. Let us examine why mere possession of the cube is itself often a considerable asset. By owning the cube, you have control over the stakes for which the game is being played. If the game goes badly, you can hang on to the cube and play the game out until the end without fear of ever being re-doubled. During these games, seemingly hopeless positions may come to life. If the game goes well, you can increase your equity in the game without changing the checker position, merely by doubling. Having the sole determination of when and whether to double is therefore an important consideration. If the position of the checkers gives either player about equal opportunity to win, the player holding the cube will be at a considerable advantage.

To illustrate the importance of the cube, consider the following proposition. You allow your opponent to begin the game with 1–1, and in return you get possession of the cube. Despite the fact that 1–1 is an extremely strong opening roll, it has been found that merely shifting the cube from the middle to your side virtually compensates for this opening role.

Because ownership of the cube is important, you must avoid doubling when you have only a small advantage because you do not want to give away the cube. For this reason, when considering whether to double, it makes a difference if the cube is in the middle or if you own it. When making the first double, you do not own the cube, whereas by re-doubling you are giving away what is already yours. You should be slightly freer about doubling if the cube is in the middle and slightly more conservative if you already own the cube. The reason for this lies in the power of your opponent to re-double. If you already own the cube and the game takes a turn for the worse, you will be able to play the game out until the end. If the cube is in the middle, you cannot prevent your opponent from doubling in a superior position.

Section IV
Endgame

This section analyzes the final stages of the game where one player has begun or is about to begin the bear-off. Chapter 23 examines pure racing positions in which no further contact is possible. The techniques for bearing in and off as quickly and efficiently as possible are considered. Chapter 24 examines how to bear in and bear off safely when your opponent still remains in your inner board. Chapter 25 examines what happens after a player is hit and the bear-off is interrupted.

CHAPTER 23.
NO POSSIBLE CONTACT

THE FIRST PART of Chapter 23 deals with bearing your men into your inner board without opposition. It is important to distinguish between wanting to save the gammon or win a race in bearing in; therefore we discuss these two subjects separately.

The second part of this chapter describes the bearing off process, again without opposition from your opponent.

Note that the relative standings of the players in the pure race itself have already been discussed in Chapter 10. In addition, both Chapters 10 and 22 advise how to double in many racing positions.

Bearing In

Saving the Gammon

Saving the gammon is the simplest case of bearing in since you try to bring your men in as quickly and efficiently as possible. You should not waste any pips in your inner board, but move them all in the outer boards. You should also try to maximize the number of **cross-overs**, i.e., checker moves from one quadrant to another. Each cross-over should be made as efficiently as possible, in other words, move 1 or 2 pips into the next quadrant, not 6.

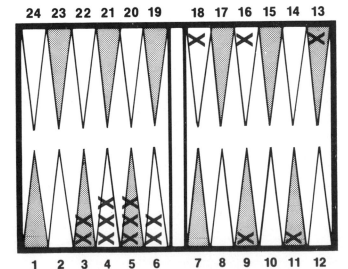

Position 1
X to Play 5–4

In Position 1, X plays 11/6, 16/12. By playing 11/6, you bring a man into your inner board without any wastage. When trying to save the gammon, you want to bring your men precisely into the six point — no deeper. For this reason, it would be a mistake to play 9/5 with the 4; this move wastes a pip in your inner board, and the single pip wasted here could cost you the gammon! 18/14 is not correct since it fails to make a cross-over, while playing 13/9 crosses over but does so too deeply into your outer board.

Exception 1: Last Roll. When you will have only one roll left after you complete your present move, it is not necessarily correct to play every pip outside. To figure out the proper play, it may be necessary to count the exact number of combinations that get you off the gammon. A common situation is shown in Position 2.

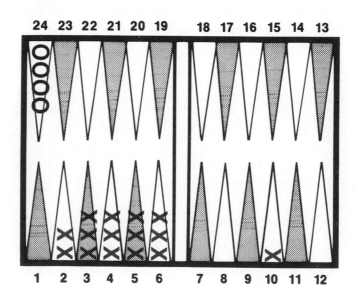

Position 2
X to Play 1

If X plays 10/9, any 1 will miss for a total of 11 numbers. By playing 2/1, however, any 4, 5, 6, and 2–2 and 3–3 will get X off the gammon for a total of 29 good numbers and only 7 bad numbers.

Analyze Positions 3, 4, 5, and 6 yourself. In each case, the correct play involves leaving a man outside, and in each case, by playing the number properly, you can guarantee getting off the gammon with the next roll.

Position 3
X to Play 2–1

Position 4
X to Play 6–2

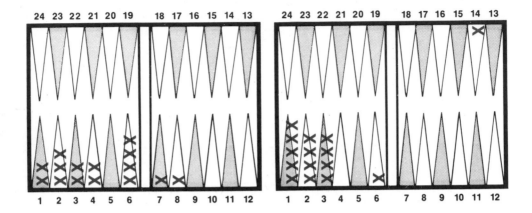

Position 5
X to Play 5–1

Position 6
X to Play 4–4

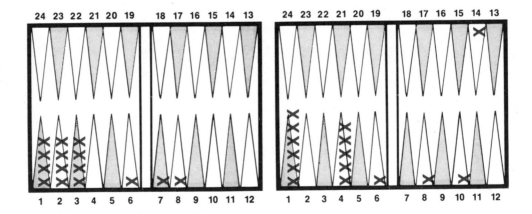

Answers: Position 3, 8/5; Position 4, 14/8, 6/4; Position 5, 8/3, 6/5; Position 6, 14/2, 10/6. 5–5 is now the only number that misses.

In another situation which commonly occurs, you have one roll left and little chance to save the game. By playing properly, you may be able to arrange the position so that as many big doubles as possible bear a man off.

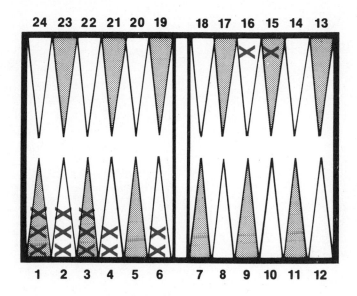

Position 7
X to Play 4–1
X to Play 5–2

In Position 7A only 15/10 will allow X to come off with 5–5 and 6–6. In 7B, only 16/14, 15/10 gets X off the gammon with 4–4, 5–5, and 6–6.

Position 8A
X to Play 4–3

Position 8B
X to Play 4–3

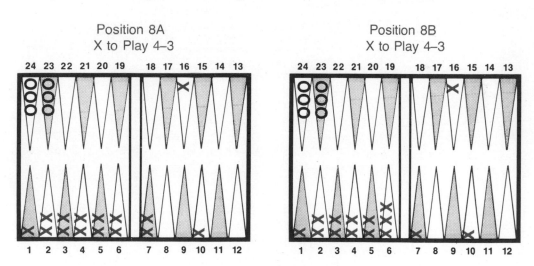

Exception 2: Two Rolls Left. In Position 8A, X must bear his remaining men in and take a man off in two more rolls. Therefore, he is forced to play 16/12, 7/4 to get two cross-overs. Any other play will force him to rely on doubles.

In Position 8B, X again has two rolls left. Here it is a mistake to waste 2 pips by playing 7/4, so the correct play is 16/9.

Race

In a race, it is unwise to pile all your men on the six point although you are trying to bring them in as quickly as possible to begin bearing off. You still want to maximize the number of cross-overs and to cross over as efficiently as possible. When bearing in, however, it is better to waste a few pips in order to insure that the four and five points will not be stripped. Do not worry about being void on the one, two, or three point, and don't waste pips which could be used outside by moving to these points.

Position 9
X to Play 5–2

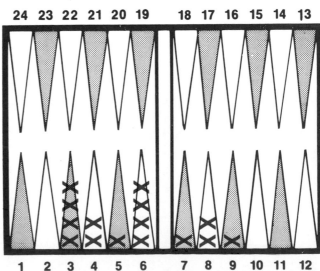

If X were playing to save a gammon in Position 9, the correct play would be 11/6, 10/8. However, in order to race, X wishes to avoid bearing in so that he has too many men on the six point and is stripped down on the four and five points. The correct play in a race, then, is 10/5, 6/4 to give a better distribution for the bear-off.

Position 10
X to Play 1

In Position 10, the correct play is 6/5 to avoid being stripped on the five point. 3/2 is unnecessary since being stripped on the two point does not matter at this time. 7/6 brings a man in but may prove costly later.

Let's see why positions with equal numbers of pips and men are not necessarily equal. You want to bear off as efficiently as possible without wasting any pips and avoid having to use a large number to bear a man off a lower point. You do not want to pile too many men on your one and two points where big numbers will later be used to bear them off.

It is important to have men on the four and five points; when the five point is stripped, you will have to use a 5 to move a man off the six point to the one point. By playing 6/1, you do *not* get 5 pips worth of value since a larger number than necessary will subsequently be used to bear this man off the one point. In other words, you have wasted pips. Similarly, if the four point is empty, you will eventually waste the full value of a four on the dice by playing 5/1 or 6/2.

For this reason, it is better to have an adequate number of men on the four and five points, even if distributing them in this way forces you to lose a few pips outside. Even if you lose a roll bearing your first man off, you will get your last man off quicker this way.

For the skeptic who thinks "you can't get 'em off 'til you get 'em in," we suggest the following exercise.

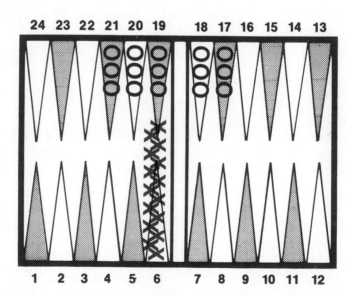

Position 11

Set up the pieces as shown in Position 11. Using the **symmetry method** to count pips, we see that each side has the same number of pips (90). Now roll the dice and play the same numbers for each side *simultaneously*. Of course, X begins bearing off first, but you will almost invariably find that at the end, either both X and O bear the last man off simultaneously, or else O wins.

The reason will also be apparent; X will waste 4's and 5's, while O will waste few pips. The reason it is *not* necessary to worry about being stripped down on the one, two, or three point is that if you roll these numbers you can take them from the higher points without piling them up on the one and two points; you can get the full value of the roll. The one exception occurs in Position 12.

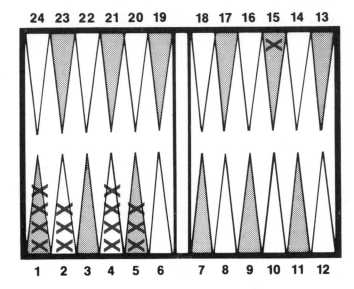

Position 12
X to Play 4–1

Here you are stripped on both your three and six points. The correct play is 15/11, 4/3. Ordinarily, 3's play constructively off the six point, so you need not worry about the gap on the three point; however, if the six point is also void, 3's are wasteful. In bearing in, you should take measures to prevent such a distribution.

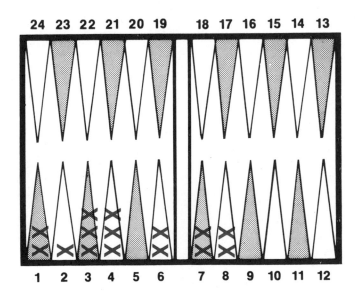

Position 13
X to Play 2–1
X to Play 6–4

If X has 2–1 to play in Position 13, the correct move is 7/5, 7/6, wasting a pip but covering the gap on the five point. If X rolls 6–4 in the same position, the correct play is 8/2, 7/3. This move leaves your remaining two men in the outfield spread out and gives you better opportunities to fill the gap on the five point. As a general rule, when you have two possible plays in bearing in, each having equal merit, choose the play which gives you the most diversification.

Bearing Off

When there is no possible further contact, you want to bear off your men as quickly as you can. Therefore, on each roll your highest priority is to take off as many men as possible.

Position 14
Xto Play 4–1

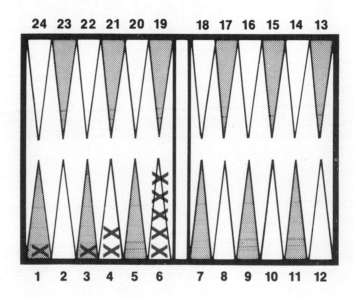

In Position 14, you should play 4/off, 1/off, taking two men off. Although you may be tempted to slot either the four point or the two point, a higher priority is to take off as many men as you can. The gap on the five point is unfortunate, but it is still better to bear a man off rather than to fill the gap now. The best time to worry about such a gap is when you are bearing in. For all practical purposes, remember that the prime consideration is to remove the maximum number of men on each roll; only if you can bear off the same number of men in more than one way need you consider the resulting positions. (In some rare cases it may be correct to bear off less than the maximum number of men. The nature of these positions — which occur very infrequently in practical play — are discussed in the technical note at the end of this chapter.)

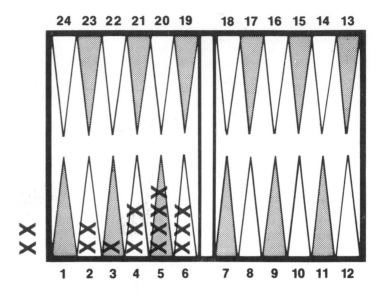

Position 15
X to Play 5–5
X to Play 2–2
X to Play 4–4

If X rolls 5–5 in Position 15, he automatically takes four men off. With 2–2, he uses the entire roll to take off the maximum number of men, 2/off(2), 4/off. If X rolls 4–4 in the same position, the most he can do is take off three men. After taking three men off the four point, he has a choice as to how to play his last 4. The correct play is 5/1, filling the gap on the one point. When you are unable to play a man off, play to fill up gaps so that you will be able to take off as many men as possible on succeeding rolls.

There are certain positions where a move which appears to be forced leaves a gap, although transposing the order in which you play the number avoids the gap.

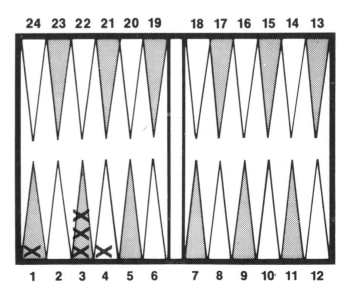

Position 16
X to Play 6–2

In Position 16, many players move 4/off, 3/1 without considering or realizing that there is an alternative. The correct play is 4/2, 3/off, avoiding the gap on the two point. Although you give up a pip, you will save an entire roll should you roll a 2 next.

Position 17
X to Play 5–3

Position 18
X to Play 6–4

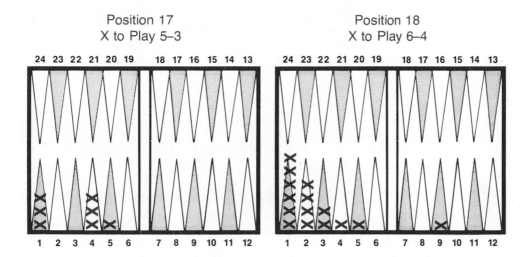

Similarly, in Position 17, the correct play is 5/2, 4/off, and in Position 18 the proper play is 9/5/off.

In addition to filling gaps, you must also try to smooth out the resulting distribution so as to avoid having too many or too few men on any one point. This will decrease the chance for gaps later on.

Position 19
X to Play 4

Position 20
X to Play 4

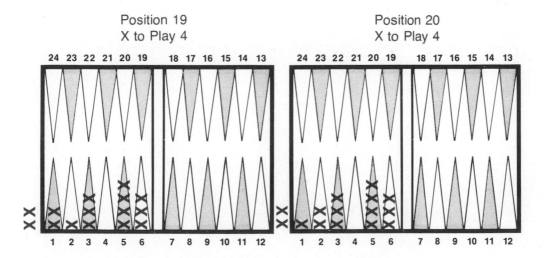

In Position 19, X is stripped down on the two point, so the correct play is 6/2, whereas in Position 20, X is in more danger of missing because of 1's, so he plays 5/1.

It is worse to be stripped or to have gaps on the four or five point than on the lower points, especially when there are several men left on the six point, or several men left on the five point when the four point is open.

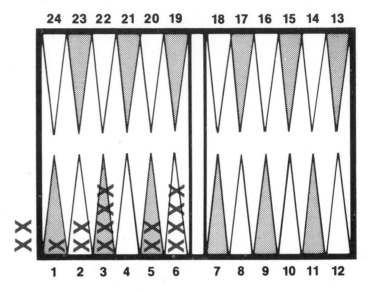

Position 21
X to Play 4

In Position 21, the correct play is 6/2 since having only one man on the five point is worse than having only one on the one point.

Sometimes having a better distribution without being stripped on the four or five point is better than filling a gap.

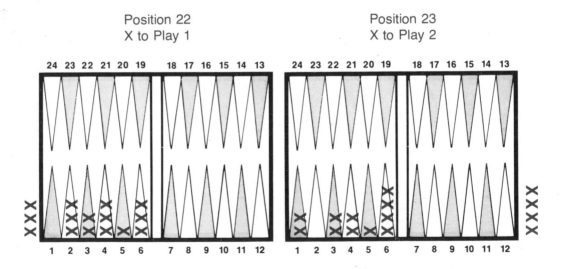

Position 22
X to Play 1

Position 23
X to Play 2

In Position 22, the correct play is 6/5 to avoid having too few men on the five point, and in Position 23 the correct play is 6/4 to avoid being stripped on the four point. Note that if X had a 1 to play in Position 23, it would not be correct to play 6/5 to avoid a possible future gap on the five point; the correct play is 1/off. Taking a man off directly *always* has precedence over both filling gaps and smoothing the distribution.

It is dangerous to be stripped down on the four point when you have several men on the five or six point. In Position 24 (similar to Position 23), X should fill the gap on the two point, 4/2. Since there are only two men altogether on the five and six points, it is not dangerous to have only one man on the four point.

Position 24
X to Play 2

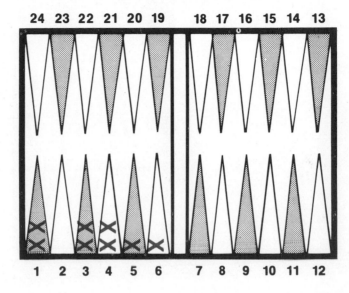

Position 25
X to Play 6–4

Position 26
X to Play 6–4

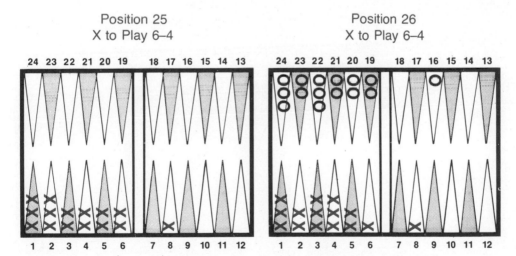

In Position 25, a good distribution is reached by playing 8/4, 6/off.

In Position 26, there is more danger in being stripped on the two point so the correct play is 8/2, 4/off. Notice that playing 8/4, 6/off is dangerous because you may be stripped on the two point, and you also leave yourself without any men on the six point. Although having too many men on the six point is often a problem, not having *any* would be wasteful. If you roll a 6, you take a man off the five point, thus wasting 1 pip, in effect.

So far we have been discussing bear-off positions without reference to your opponent's position. In most positions, you follow the procedure outlined above, which will minimize the number of rolls you need to come off. In certain positions where there are only two or three rolls left, it may be necessary to modify your play to take advantage of specific doubles.

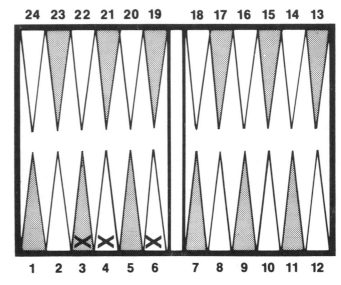

Position 27
X to Play 1

In Position 27, the correct play is 6/5; this is slightly superior to 3/2 if X wishes to bear off in two more rolls. However, suppose that O has only four men on his one point. After he takes two men off, you will have only one roll left to bear off your remaining men, so the correct play would be 4/3. This would allow you to get off with a 3–3 in addition to 4–4, 5–5, and 6–6.

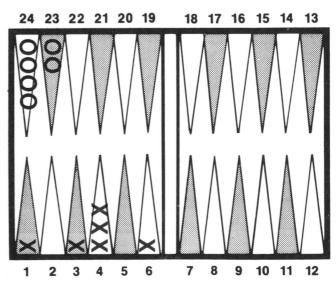

Position 28
X to Play 2

In Position 28, you will have at most two turns left after O plays. Since you must count on bearing off four men on one roll, the correct play is 6/4. Now 4–4, 5–5, and 6–6 will bear four men off. If O had an additional seventh man, you would play the more natural play of 4/2 in order to increase your chances of coming off in three rolls.

Technical Note. We mentioned that there are some bear-off positions where taking the maximum number of men off is *not* correct. One such case is shown in Position 29.

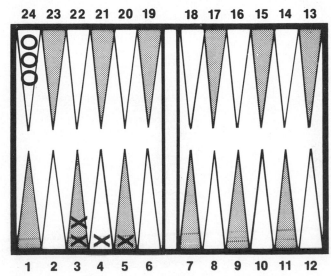

Position 29
X to Play 2–1

X must play 4/3, 5/3, in hopes of rolling 3–3. If X bears a man off (3/off), 3–3 no longer wins. In this example, X cannot bear a man off directly (i.e., with a single number on one die), but must use the combination of both dice to bear a man off.

Occasionally, when it is impossible to bear any men off directly, it may be correct to use both parts of the number to improve the distribution rather than bear a single man off.

In Position 30, X cannot bear any men off directly, so, rather than play 5/off, it is slightly better to play 6/4, 6/3. Thus, we may reformulate our basic

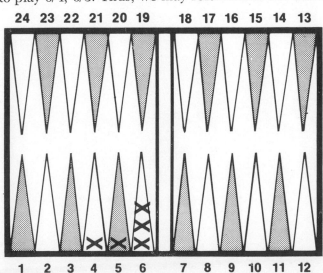

Position 30
X to Play 3–2

rule to always bear off as many men as possible. When no men may be borne off *directly* (with one number on one die), it may, in rare cases, be correct to improve the distribution rather than bear a single man off *indirectly*. In other words, in practical play whenever a man can be taken off directly, you should always do so. In fact, it may be proved that no possible position can exist when it is wrong to use a 1 to bear a man off the one point. There are, however, certain theoretical positions (which I have never seen arise in actual play) where it is correct *not* to bear off a man directly from the two or three point.

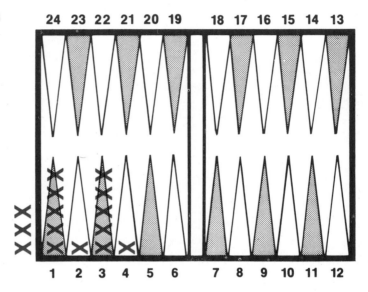

Position 31
X to Play 2

In Position 31, for example, the correct play is 4/2, not 2/off. This play protects against missing twice more if you roll two numbers with 2's.

CHAPTER 24.

AVOIDING CONTACT

THIS CHAPTER DISCUSSES bearing off against opposition; that is, when your opponent still has a man or men in your inner board or on the bar. In Chapter 6 we mentioned some of the basic principles for bearing off safely; these principles and others will be elaborated here. While the last chapter emphasized bearing off as *quickly* as possible, the first part of this chapter will discuss bearing off as *safely* as possible. The second part will deal with how and when to take risks in relation to gammoning your opponent.

Safety Principles

Immediate Safety

Your first concern should be for your immediate safety. When forced to leave shots, leave as few as possible. If you can play your roll safely, leave yourself in a position where there are the fewest possible numbers on the next roll that force you to leave a direct shot.

Note on the diagrams in this section that since we are not considering gammons but are only concerned with bearing off safely, we have shown only those men belonging to O which directly affect X's bear-off. Imagine that O has and is able to maintain a closed inner board or a prime with his remaining men.

Position 1
X to Play 2

Position 2
X to Play 1

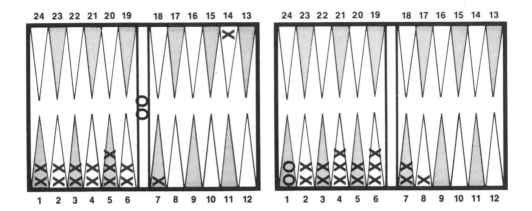

In Position 1, you appear to be absolutely safe. The 2, however, must still be played carefully. The correct play is 7/5, allowing you to play 6–6 safely next time. (Any other 2 will force you to leave a man exposed after 6–6.)

In positions where the game appears to be completely won, you should take the trouble to protect yourself against these exceptional numbers; it costs you nothing, and may save you from going home with another tale of misfortune. Even when you can play 6–6 safely, you must be alert to the danger of 5–5 as well — especially when your opponent has your one point.

In Position 2, playing 6/5 allows you to play 5–5 safely on the next roll.

Everything else being equal, leave yourself with the position that allows the fewest shots on the next roll.

Position 3
X to Play 6–3

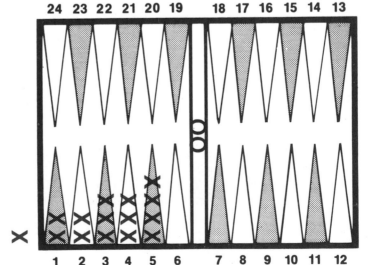

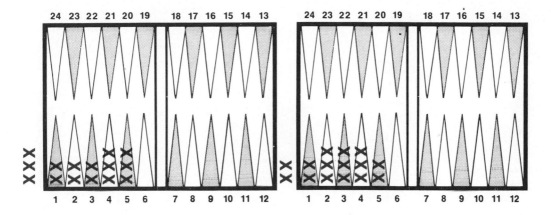

Position 3A
(X 6–3 5/off, 3/off)

Position 3B
(X 6–3 5/off, 5/2)

For example, if X plays 5/off, 3/off (Position 3A), only 6–5 (2 combinations) leaves a shot. However, by playing 5/off, 5/2 (Position 3B), 6–6, 5–5, and 4–4 (3 combinations) leave shots. On the basis of the safety factor, Position 3A, 5/off, 3/off, is preferred.

Position 4
X to Play 6–4

Position 5
X to Play 5–2

Position 4 is an example of a situation where the rules of the game are sometimes misinterpreted. The rules require you to play your full roll "if possible," meaning you must play both numbers of the roll.

In Position 4, many players do not realize that they have an alternate play and move 9/3, 4/off, leaving a blot on the four point. The correct play is 9/5, 5/off, leaving no blots. The standard, official, and universally accepted ruling is that this play is legal because using a 6 to remove a man from the five point is considered as using a full 6. Similarly, in Position 5, X can play 5/off, 4/2; however, a play leaving far fewer shots on the next roll is 5/3, 4/off.

Taking Chances

So far, bearing off sounds like a mechanical process; you should minimize the number of immediate return shots or minimize the number of ways of leaving shots on the next roll. But this is a serious underestimation of the complexity of bearing off against opposition. Many times the number of shots or the number of possible combinations that force a direct exposure will be equal; in those cases, you need some other criteria for deciding your play. Much more important, there are other considerations that often have priority. Remember, we said to choose the play with the best immediate safety, "everything else being equal." Since this is rarely the case, we will examine more closely the overall dynamics of bearing off safely.

When forced to leave a shot, you must consider your ability to play safely on the next roll if you are missed on this roll. Pay particular attention to safetying your blots.

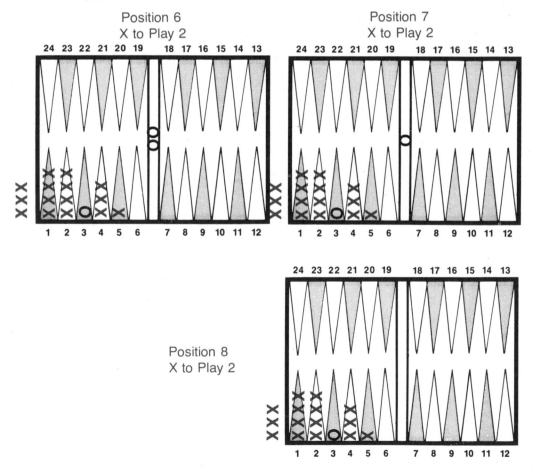

In Position 6, O has two men on the bar. O will have the same number of immediate return shots whether or not X hits the blot on the three point. If X does hit 5/3*, and O misses the shot, X may still not be able to safety the blot. In fact, if X rolls two large numbers (4's, 5's, and 6's), then X will be exposed to a double shot. By correctly playing 2/off, X leaves himself in a position where no number will force him to leave a shot on the subsequent roll.

You must hit in Position 7 to reduce the number of immediate return shots from 15 to 11. (By not hitting, you allow 3–2 and 6–2 to hit.)

In Position 8, the number of immediate return shots is the same whether you hit or not. This is a very important reason for hitting. If you fail to hit, there is the possibility of getting into trouble later when you are clearing your four point. By hitting, you hope to solve all your problems at once if O comes in on the five or six point.

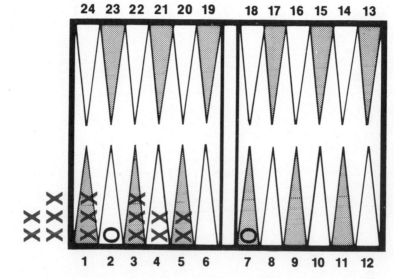

Position 9
X to Play 5–3

In Position 9, the correct play is 5/off, 5/2*, where you hope to get rid of O permanently.

In bearing in, your long-term interests and overall safety may also best be served by having extra builders rather than by minimizing the immediate number of return shots.

Playing 9/4 in Position 10 leaves only a 3–5 return shot, while playing 11/6 gives your opponent 3–5 and 3–6. Because of the enormously increased

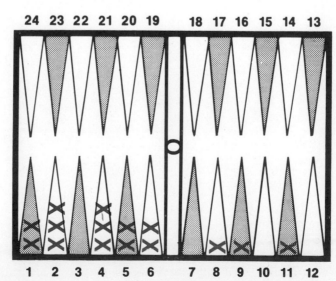

Position 10
X to Play 5

chances of making the three point and filling the potentially dangerous gap, the latter is the better play.

While it is extremely rare to purposely leave a direct shot in the actual bear-off, in certain bear-in positions, where you have a strong prime, it may be correct to leave a direct shot.

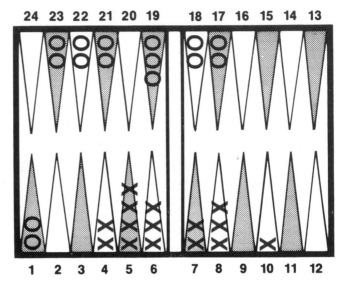

Position 11
X to Play 5

In Position 11, X can play safely 10/5, awkwardly piling his men on the five point. Because X's builders are not well distributed, there is a good possibility that X will be forced later to leave a shot when he no longer has his prime. A better play is to take the chance now, 8/3, while the 5-point prime is still intact. If O misses, X can cover the three point, thus greatly increasing his chances of bearing in smoothly. If O hits, X will still be a strong favorite in the game because O still has two men trapped behind X's prime.

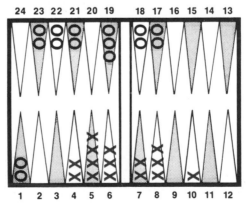

Position 12
X to Play 4–4

Clear Points in Order, Avoiding Gaps

Since we are concerned here with playing as safely as possible, the object is to *clear* points — not to restrain your opponent by holding on to them.

In Position 12, for example, X could hold on to his prime by playing 10/2, 6/2, 8/4. But the better play would be to clear the bar point immediately by playing 7/3(2), 10/6, 8/4.

There is, however, one overriding principle to remember in clearing your points safely: You must clear your points *in order* starting with those furthest from home.

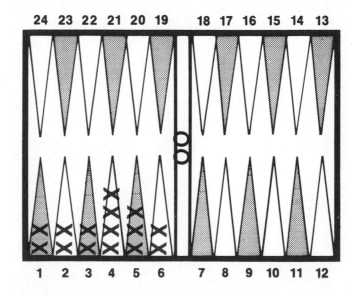

Position 13
X to Play 5–1

In Position 13, there is nothing particularly dangerous about 5/off, 4/3, but clearing the six point is safer for one reason: By clearing your points in order, you hope to have your opponent's men come in *behind* you and therefore eliminate any problems.

In Position 14, X clears his six point 6/4, 6/2, in preference to taking two men off. Remember, your main object is to get your men off as safely (not as

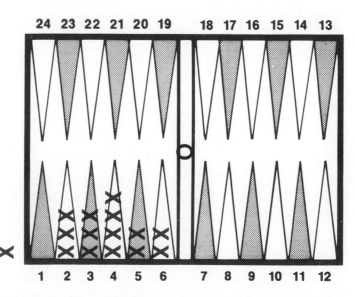

Position 14
X to Play 4–2

quickly) as possible. Even if you can afford to be hit, it is still better, as a general rule, to bear off safely (although more slowly).

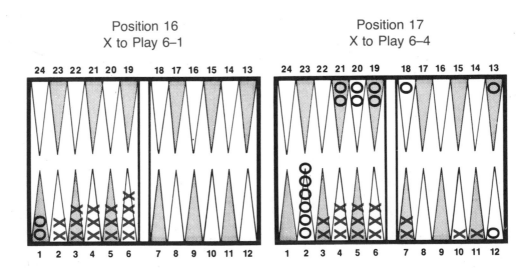

Position 15
X to Play 6–2

In Position 15, it is wrong to unthinkingly grab extra men. In the actual game where this position occurred, X was so disgusted at being forced to leave a shot that he carelessly played 6/off, 2/off, bearing the man off the two point instead of the correct play, 6/off, 3/1. This proved to be a costly mistake. O hit X, and X subsequently lost the game because of the blot on his two point.

Position 16
X to Play 6–1

Position 17
X to Play 6–4

Remember that you should always plan to clear your highest *remaining* point. Avoid having more men on this point than on the points below it.

In Position 16, X should simply play 6/off, 6/5. By playing 6/5, X prepares to clear his six point next.

In Position 17, the correct play is 10/6, 11/5. Although 11/7, 10/4 may appear equally good, it does not prepare you to clear the bar point immediately and is therefore slightly inferior.

Position 18
X to Play 2

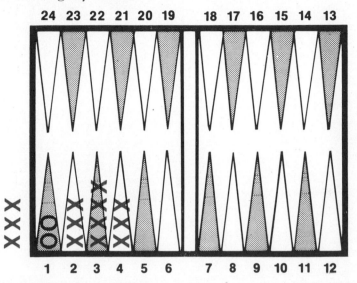

In Position 18, there is the same number of combinations (6) on the next roll whether you take a man off (2/off) or play 4/2. Since the immediate risks of both plays are equal, many players, understandably, wish to remove the extra man.

The correct play is 4/2, preparing to clear the four point. By taking a man off, not only do you expose yourself to the 6 combinations of numbers that force you to leave a shot now, but you will also eventually (barring a double) come down to the position with two men on the four point, where there are 6 more numbers that leave shots.

A more subtle version of the reasoning employed in Position 18 is shown in Position 19.

By playing 6/off, you have 4 bad numbers (6–1, 5–1); however, by playing

Position 19
X to Play 4–2

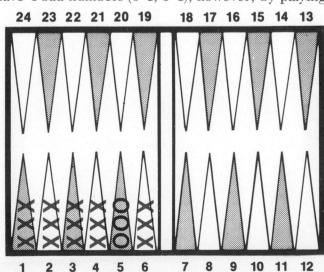

4/off, 2/off, you have only 2 bad combinations: 6–5. Most players, experts included, play the seemingly safer play by removing two men. However, this play is only safer on the *next* roll. If we analyze the position carefully, we see that it is actually safer to prepare to clear the six point immediately. This play leaves 4 bad numbers right away, but if successful, clears the six point and solves all your problems.

If you play 4/off, 2/off, you have 2 immediate bad numbers; and unless you roll a double, you may be in the position of having two men on your six point — still risking 4 bad numbers as well. Thus, basically, you are postponing reaching this position and leaving extra shots by taking off two men.

The main reason you should to clear your points in order is to avoid leaving gaps.

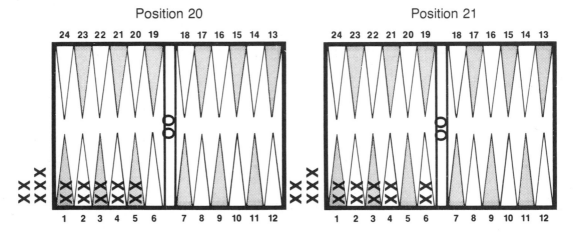

Position 20   Position 21

In Position 20, you can be assured of at least clearing the five point safely because the men on the five point can always use the lower points as safe landing spaces.

In Position 21, you have a gap on the five point; this means that if you roll a 1 (except 1–1), you will not be able to clear the six point safely. The lower a gap is in your board, the more dangerous it is.

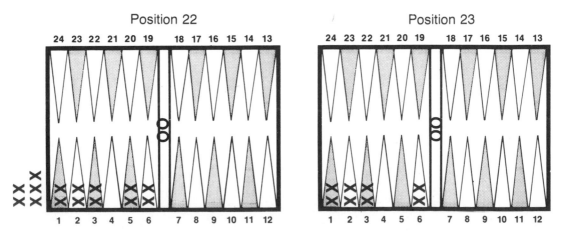

Position 22   Position 23

Position 22 is worse than 21 because you have two points (the five and the six point) to clear where the gap may cause trouble. The larger the gap, the more dangerous. Position 22 may lead to Position 23.

In Position 23, the larger gap makes it even more difficult to clear the six point safely.

It is rarely correct to leave gaps for the sole purpose of bearing off an extra man or two. Although leaving gaps cannot always be avoided, sometimes there are opportunities to fill pre-existing gaps or to move them higher in your inner board, thus reducing the danger.

Position 24
X to Play 4–2

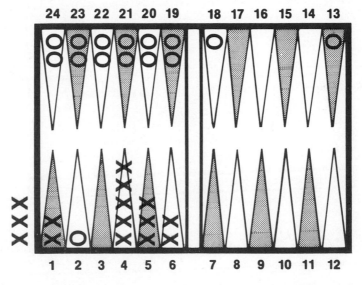

In Position 24, the correct play is 6/2*, 4/2, which makes the two point and destroys the dangerous double gap. Furthermore, it clears the six point and forces your opponent forward. Remember, if your opponent has only one man back, try to force him forward or, better yet, past you completely.

In Positions 25 and 26, gaps can be avoided at no extra cost by switching points. Play 8/3, 6/3 in Position 25, and 6/1*(3), 10/5 in Position 26.

Position 25
X to Play 5–3

Position 26
X to Play 5–5

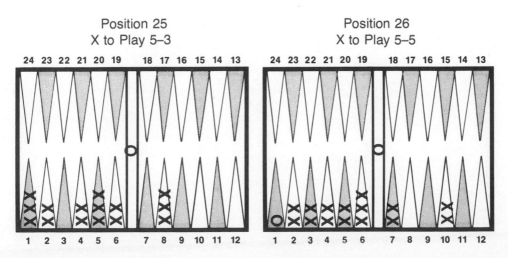

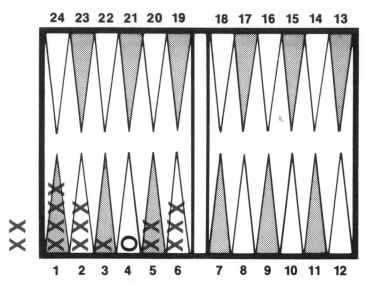

Position 27
X to Play 6–5

In Position 27, you should clear your six point: 6/off, 6/1. The alternate play 6/off, 5/off leaves an unnecessary gap on the five point and makes it more difficult to bear off on subsequent rolls.

There are some exceptions where leaving a gap may not be more dangerous because of the resulting distribution of men.

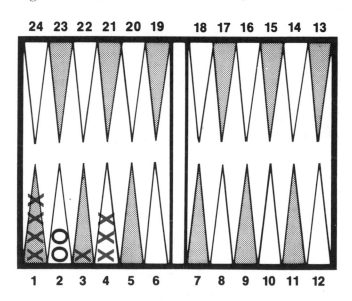

Position 28
X to Play 4–1

Position 28 is very misleading; most players instinctively play 4/off, 4/3 to narrow the gap. A careful analysis shows that 4/off, 1/off is exactly as safe since in either case you will be forced to leave another shot if and only if you don't roll a 1. This position is, therefore, the exceptional case where you might as well bear off an extra man since all other considerations are equal.

Note: If this position is modified so that O has only one man on the two point, the clearly superior play is 4/off, 3/2* to get O out of the way.

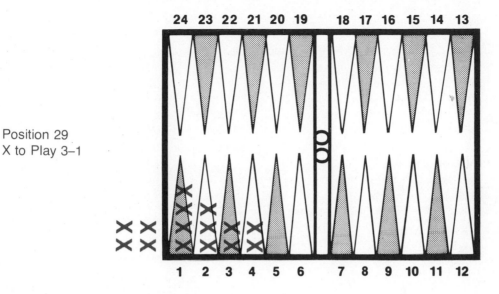

Position 29
X to Play 3–1

Position 29A
(X 3–1 4/3, 4/1)

Position 29B
(X 3–1 3/off, 3/2)

In Position 29, by clearing your points in order 4/3, 4/1 (see Position 29A), you leave three men on the three point. Now, if O stays out with at least one man, there are 12 combinations (6–5, 6–4, 6–3, 5–4, 5–3, 4–3) that will leave X exposed on his next roll. By playing 3/2, 3/off (see Position 29B), you leave only 8 bad combinations (6–1, 5–1, 4–1, 3–1). Clearing your three point, then, is actually the safer play.

The subtleties of the bear-off are illustrated by the fact that in Position 29, if O had only one man on the bar, the correct play would be 4/3, 4/1. In this case, the increased chance of getting rid of O more than compensates for the slightly greater number of bad shots should O manage to stay around.

For the mathematically inclined reader, we shall show how to get these results. Let's first consider the case where there is only one man on the bar. If you play as indicated in Position 29A, then in order to leave a direct shot, two separate events must happen: O must stay out (a probability of ¼), and X must leave a blot (a probability of ⅓). The probability of *both* these independent events occurring is the product of their two probabilities: ¼ × ⅓ = $1/12$ (about .0833). (Two events are said to be independent if neither one affects the occurrence of the other.) If you play 3–1, as shown in Position 29B, the chances of O's being in a position to hit (i.e., staying out or coming in on the three point) are $20/36$. Then our probability of leaving a shot is $20/36$ × $8/36$ = $160/1296$, or about .123, which is considerably greater. Therefore, Position 29A is preferred when there is only one man on the bar.

Similarly, we can calculate the original problem precisely when O has two men on the bar. In Position 29A, O will stay out with at least one man ¾ of the time. X's overall chance of being exposed to a single direct shot is therefore ¾ × ⅓ = ¼ or .25. In Position 29B, the corresponding chances are $32/36$ × $8/36$ = $256/1296$, or about .20, which is less, so this play is preferred. We shall now look at some other examples where the exact number of men on the bar and the distribution of builders determine the order in which you should break your points.

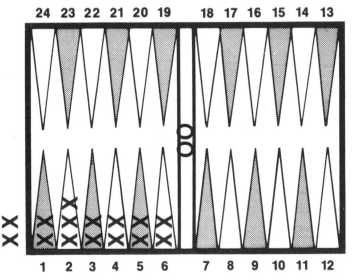

Position 30
X to Play 5–1

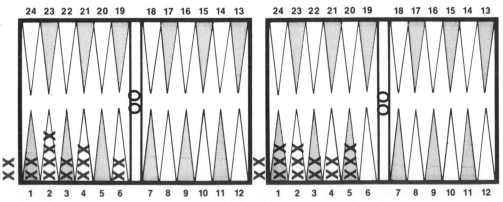

Position 30A
(X 5–1 5/off, 5/4)

Position 30B
(X 5–1 6/1, 6/5)

In Position 30, we can choose between leaving a gap by clearing the five point (as seen in Position 30A), or by clearing the six point (Position 30B). The correct play is to leave a gap by playing 5/off, 5/4 (Position 30A).

A very important principle guides this decision: The most dangerous positions are those in which you have a single isolated or spare man on the points furthest from home; such a position is far more dangerous than leaving one simple gap and must be avoided.

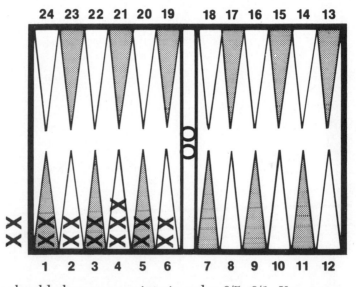

Position 31
X to Play 5–1

In Position 31, you should clear your points in order 6/5, 6/1. You are no longer in danger because the third man on the five point has a companion on the four point. You no longer have a single spare checker but two spare checkers, which together can be used to handle every number (except 6–5).

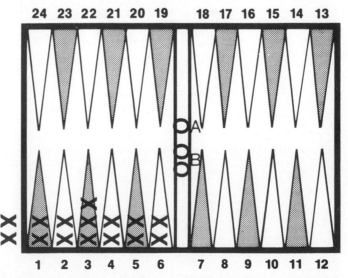

Position 32
X to Play 5–1

Position 32 illustrates an intermediate case where clearing the six point 6/1, 6/5 will leave a single spare checker on the five point. This checker is not completely isolated because of the man on the three point.

The correct play here depends on whether O has one or two men on the bar. With one man on the bar, the possibility of O's coming in on the six point makes clearing the six point correct. With two men on the bar, clearing the five point is slightly preferable (the computations are similar to those for Position 29).

Diversify

In order to avoid awkward numbers, you must have spare men to play with. One time-honored rule is to have an even number of men on the point furthest away from home. It is even better to have an even number of men on both your furthermost points *combined;* to do so insures that even large doubles can be handled successfully.

The principle of having an even number of men on the furthermost points is often overemphasized. In Position 31, for example, X has an odd number of men on his five point after he clears his six point, but is in a comparatively favorable position.

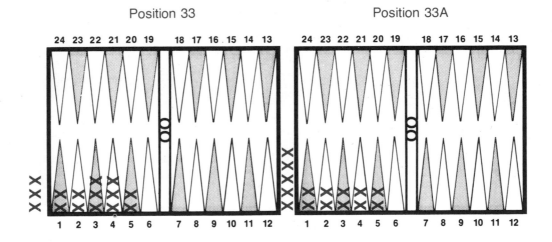

Position 33   Position 33A

Similarly, in comparing Positions 33 and 33A, many players believe that 33A is the safer since X is even everywhere and has a "smooth" position. However, despite the fact that there is no immediate danger in 33A and that X has an odd total of five men on his two furthermost points in 33 and is vulnerable to large doubles, 33 is actually a safer position. The reasoning behind this statement is that X has more flexibility when he can arrange his spare men according to the rolls. Even though X is even in Position 33A, all his moves will be forced. If X rolls a high number (4,5,6) and a 1, he will be forced to leave a single spare man on his furthermost point. If you roll out these two positions several times, you will see that in 33 the two spare men on the three and four points enable X to safely handle most sequences, while it is very possible to arrive at a dangerous position in 33A.

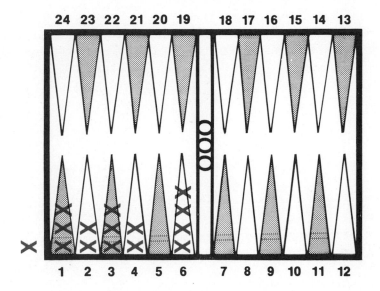

Position 34
X to Play 2

Similarly, in Position 34, the correct play to give you a flexible position is 6/4. The fact that this play leaves you odd on the six point is not at all important.

Although you should try to clear your points in order, you must also play to have spare men to handle the succeeding numbers.

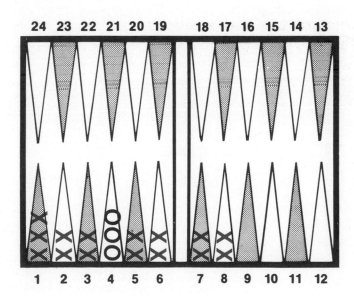

Position 35
X to Play 6–1

In Position 35, you should clear your bar point 7/1, 7/6 because the alternative, 8/7, 8/2, leaves you in a very dangerous inflexible position with a single spare man on the seven point.

To keep your position flexible it is important to avoid taking men out of play — just as putting men on the one point during the middle game seriously reduces your overall flexibility.

Position 36
X to Play 4

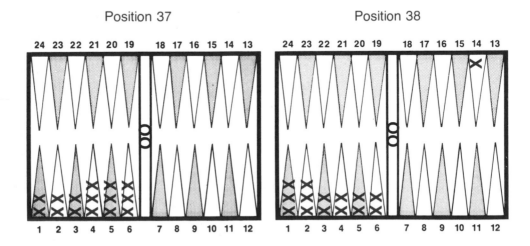

In Position 36, for example, the correct play is 10/6 rather than making the one point, 5/1.

Making the one point is a common error in bearing off against a two-point game (one in which your opponent holds only your two point). Similarly, when your opponent is closed out, you should avoid bearing in deep to your one, two, or three point and instead bear in to the points furthest from home. The ideal bear-in position to reach is shown in Position 37, where your spare men are on the four, five, and six points.

Position 37   Position 38

You should try to avoid having two extra men deep in your inner board, as in Position 38. Because these two men are effectively out of play, you have less freedom of choice in how to play your rolls and thus more chance to leave a shot.

Position 39 is another example of a bad bear-in position:

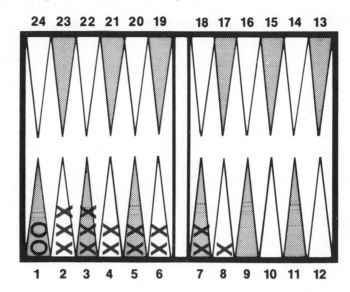

Position 39
X on Roll

Here almost all 6's will force X to leave a shot immediately. If X is lucky enough to roll 3–2, the correct play is to give up the bar point immediately rather than to play 8/3, which would again leave an inflexible and dangerous position.

You can often arrive at a sound position by clearing a point early, which is well worth the risk of a small number of indirect shots. Particularly when your opponent still has a man on the bar, you may use this opportunity to clear points which later may become problems.

In Position 40, X can play safely 8/6, 5/1, but this play is weak for several reasons: Since your opponent is on the bar, you should risk playing 9/3 and

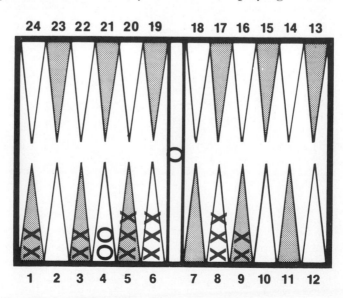

Position 40
X to Play 4–2

clearing the nine point as soon as possible, which would leave the rest of your men well distributed. On the other hand, playing 8/6, 5/1, leaves you without spare men since you have killed one more man on the one point, and you have piled up your only two other spare men on the same point.

Remember that an important principle in keeping your men active is to spread them out. Avoid stacking them on the same point.

The next three positions occur frequently and are almost always misplayed. In each of these positions, it is possible to bring two men in directly, which would leave a safe position. However, an even safer position can be reached by not allowing two men to end up on the same point.

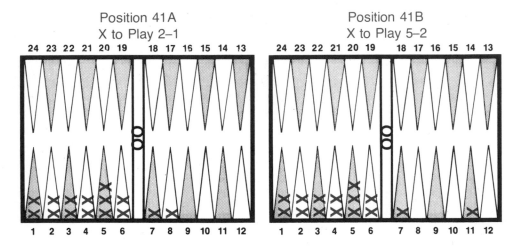

Position 41A
X to Play 2–1

Position 41B
X to Play 5–2

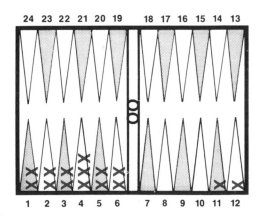

Position 41C
X to Play 6–5

The correct plays in 41A, B, and C are, respectively, 7/4, 11/4, and 11/5, 12/7. In each case, the added diversity of having the three men spread out will enable you to withstand almost any sequence of rolls.

The advantage of the recommended plays may be seen immediately if you compare the positions after X rolls 6–6.

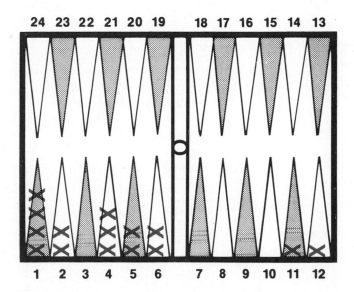

Position 42
X to Play 6–5

Position 42 is similar to Position 41C. The best play is 11/5, 12/7, despite the 17-to-1 shot (3–4) it leaves. The more obvious play, 12/6, 11/6, is immediately safe, but ultimately more dangerous. Because X's two men are together on the six point instead of being diversified, it is possible for X to run into trouble — particularly if he rolls several 3's.

A final example of diversification is shown in Position 43.

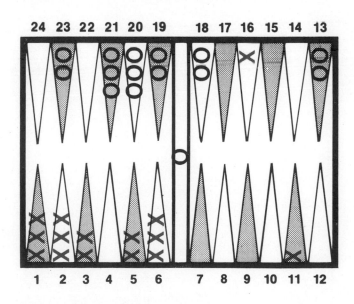

Position 43
X to Play 6–1

At first glance, there seems to be no reason for not playing safe and making the ten point. However, even if your opponent stays out, you will have to break the ten point on the next roll, leaving O a 17-to-1 shot: 6–4. Since you will have to leave a 17-to-1 shot anyway, it is better to do it immediately by playing 16/9 and leaving your men spread out. Now if O comes in, there are far fewer numbers (such as 6–5, 6–4, 5–3) which force you to leave a direct shot.

Note that playing 11/5, 16/15 is slightly inferior because X may not be able to bring the man on the fifteen point home safely in one roll after O re-enters.

Gammon Considerations

In the first part of this chapter, we discussed how to bear off as *safely* as possible. The possibility of a gammon in the endgame is another factor which may affect the play.

Your Opponent Is Closed Out

Assume that your opponent is closed out: he has a man on the bar against your closed board. Clearly, the more men you have closed out, the greater your chances for a gammon. The more men you have closed out, however, the more dangerous it is for you in bearing off — you may leave a man exposed before your opponent re-enters all his men. Each additional man you hit will increase the amount of time your opponent lurks on the bar waiting for a shot. For this reason, it is unwise to hit any more men than you need to insure a gammon. Closing out three men will make you a very strong favorite to gammon; more than three on the bar are superfluous and potentially dangerous.

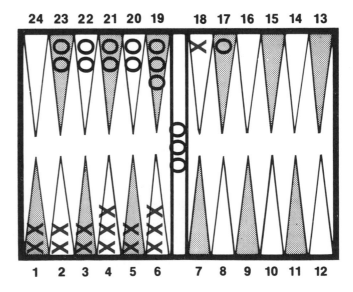

Position 44
X to Play 2–1

In Position 44, X should not hit. The correct play is 18/16, 6/5 (remembering to protect against 6–6). If you greedily hit the fourth man, you might lose in a situation such as the following: although you successfully clear the six, five, and four points, O re-enters only three of his men. Now you may have unavoidably reached a position with an uneven number of men on the three point. You are then forced to leave a shot which could still be hit by the last man on the bar.

When O has exactly two men closed out, with no other men in the outfield, he is a slight favorite to save the gammon. In this case, your chances of gammoning him are a little better than 40% — depending upon how many chances you take when you bear off. Thus, when your opponent has no men in the outfield, you generally try to hit a third man for a gammon. With only one opposing man closed out, you definitely try to hit a second man since there is virtually no chance to gammon O if his remaining men are in his inner board.

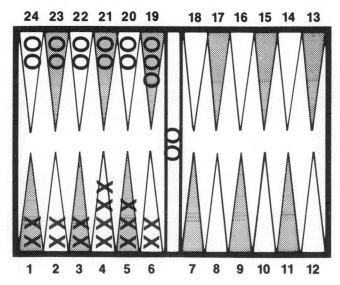

Position 45
(A) X to Play 5–1
(B) X to Play 3–1

With two opposing men on the bar, X is justified in taking moderate chances to get a gammon. The correct play with 5–1 is 5/off, 4/3; and with 3–1, 4/off. Note that clearing the six point would be the *safest* play (6/5, 6/1 in case (A); 6/5, 6/3 in case (B), but the risk involved in the indicated plays is minimal, and the small danger is more than outweighed by your increased chances of getting a gammon.

If O had either three men or one man on the bar, X would make the safest possible play. It is wrong to take risks with one man on the bar because you have such a small chance to gammon O. With three men on the bar, you are such a favorite to gammon O that additional risks are unnecessary.

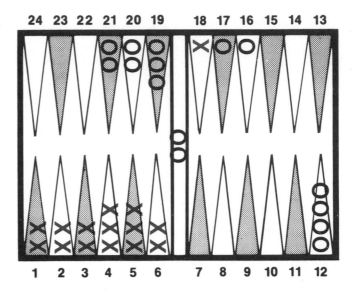

Position 46
X to Play 3–2

In Position 46, the correct play is 18/15/13. O has two men on the bar and six other men in the outfield which must be brought home to save the gammon. Since O will probably be gammoned, X wisely refrains from hitting (18/16*/ 13); even with only *one* man on the bar, it might be hard for O to save the gammon. In such a case, X would hit because the small extra danger involved would be more than outweighed by the increased chance of a gammon.

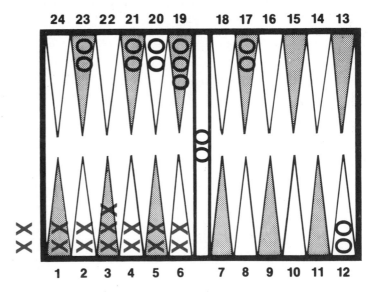

Position 47
X to Play 2–1

In Position 47, X can be relatively confident of a gammon because O has four extra men in the outfield. The correct and safest play is 6/5, 6/4, clearing the six point. The alternate play, 3/off, may appear safer because you distribute your men evenly, but will ultimately be more dangerous because of the absence of spare men to play with.

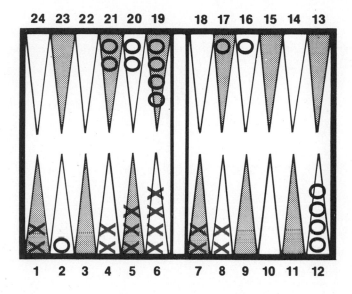

Position 48
O to Play 6–5

In Position 48, O has no men on the bar. There is a possibility that X can point on his head, close him out and gammon him. The correct play is 12/18, 12/17, bringing the outer men closer to home. This is not the time to waste pips by playing 16/22, 17/22.

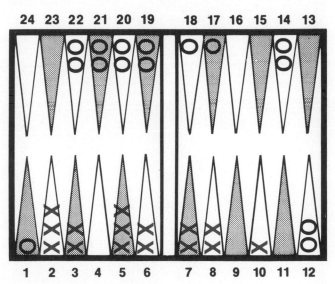

Position 49
X to Play 6–4

In Position 49, O has six men in the outfield. X may gammon O if he can stop him from moving immediately. The correct play is 7/1*, 5/1, with X hoping to make the four point later and close O out. If X fails to close O out immediately, O will gain a critical roll or two to bring his outfield men closer to home, thus effectively eliminating gammon chances.

Position 49 is also interesting in another respect: The indicated play may seem dangerous because of the immediate return shots (4–3, 4–6), but it is actually safer than playing 10/4, 8/4 and making a full 6-point prime. Ordinarily, trapping your opponent behind a full 6-point prime when you are not yourself trapped means a practically certain win. However, after making the 6-point prime, X may be fored to hit O with a blot on the one point. If O hits back, he will win despite X's prime because O will be able to form a prime which will last longer.

Your Opponent Is Not Closed Out

The chance of gammoning your opponent is considerably diminished if you are unable to close him out. If he establishes a point in your inner board — even your one point — you may have difficulty winning a gammon.

If we compare your gammon chances when your opponent owns an inner-board point, with those when he is closed out on the bar, we can see the radical difference in the gammon possibilities.

- When he has two men on your one point, you have practically no chance for a gammon. With two men closed out, the gammon will be a close issue.
- With three men on your one point, your opponent is a definite favorite to save the gammon. With three men closed out, he is almost certain to be gammoned.
- With four men on your one point, he still has a fair chance to save the gammon.
- With four men closed out, only a miracle will save the gammon (unless he is fortunate enough to hit you in the bear-off).

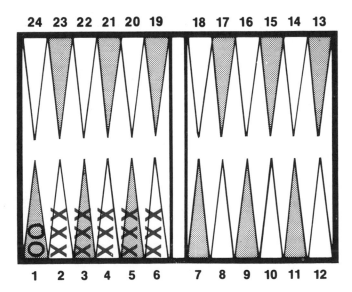

Position 50

If your opponent has established a point in your inner board, especially your one point, your chances of gammoning him are diminished for another reason — you are much more likely to be hit during the bear-off no matter how safely you try to play. When your opponent is closed out, if you play carefully you will bear off safely most of the time. However, the inherent danger of bearing off against a 1-point game is illustrated by the surprising fact that even starting in Position 50, you will be forced to leave a shot 90% of the time! Of course this statistic is somewhat misleading because you will be hit a much lower percentage of the time, and even if you are hit, you may have enough men off to win the game although you lose the gammon. Because it is more dangerous to bear off when your opponent holds an inner-board point, expert players often go for a complete close-out early in the game. They prefer taking extra risks — even after the game is seemingly won — rather than allowing their opponent to establish an inner-board point.

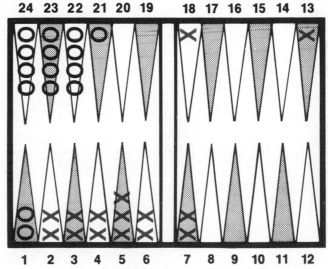

Position 51
X to Play 4–1

Occasionally, when your opponent has exactly two men back, you may be able to force him off his anchor and then close him out by means of the **trap play.** For example, in Position 51, the correct play is 7/6, 7/3. In the trap play, you purposely release your opponent from behind a 6-point prime in hopes of closing him out when he escapes with one checker. Because this play risks losing a winning position (if he comes out with a double, for example), you should use it only under the following conditions:

1. Your opponent has *exactly* two men on a point in your inner board. The rest of his men should be in his inner board so that he has no choice about coming out if he rolls the number that releases him. This play must not be attempted until your opponent has broken his inner board and holds four points at the most — preferably, only three.

2. You have adequate builders to attack the man remaining in your inner board after one man is released.

3. You have a man or men far enough back so that you will have the opportunity to pick up the released man after closing out the blot which remained in your inner board. This is a sometimes neglected, but absolutely essential, condition for attempting the trap play.

The idea behind this play is to enable you to close out *both* of your opponent's back men. You should not attempt the play if you don't have men sufficiently far back in the outfield, so that one of his checkers can't get past you immediately. In fact, it is usually best to try the play only when you have the prospect of keeping one of your checkers back at least one extra roll, since your opponent may not roll the releasing number immediately.

We have seen that when your opponent is closed out, the danger in bearing off is increased by hitting additional men. For this reason, you should usually abstain from hitting more men than necessary to ensure a gammon. When your opponent is not closed out, however, the danger involved in hitting additional men is *not* significantly increased. (We are excluding from this discussion backgame considerations where your opponent has two points closed in your inner board, and matters of timing are paramount.) For this reason if your opponent has a single point closed in your board, you should usually hit as many men as possible. Remember, hitting additional men is often necessary to ensure a gammon when your opponent has a point in your board. Since there is little additional risk involved in continuing to hit, there is even the possibility that you will get a backgammon. (In Chapter 25, methods of forcing your opponent to leave additional men exposed are discussed. Using these methods, you may often be able to send additional men back and gammon your opponent.)

There is, however, one situation where it is wrong to continue hitting—when there is a definite prospect that your opponent will have to break his board if you *don't* hit.

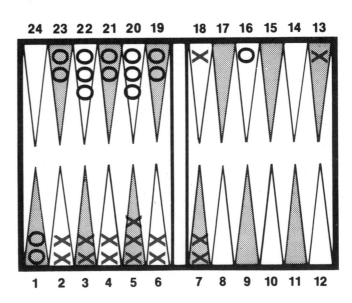

Position 52
X to Play 5–2

For example, in Position 52, the correct play is 18/13/11, not hitting. With this play, O will be forced to bust his board, which will give you added insurance against losing the game.

In the actual bear-off, you always have to weigh the danger of being hit as well as the most efficient means to gammon. In the next two positions, the chances of being hit are identical, so the sole consideration must be the best way to gammon.

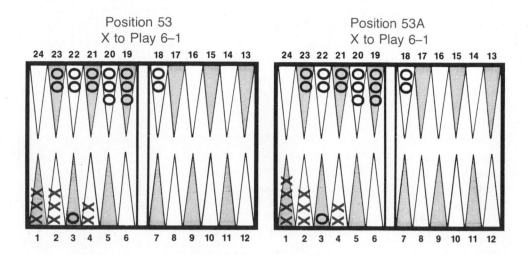

In Position 53, the correct play is 4/off, 1/off. If your opponent misses, you are left with an even number of men so you can bear off in three rolls. Although playing 4/3*, 4/off is no more dangerous, by failing to bear a man off you leave yourself with an extra odd man which will cost you an entire roll. In Position 53A, however, taking off two men instead of one will not get you off quicker, so you should hit 4/off, 4/3*. This will cost your opponent 3 pips in his race to save the gammon, at no extra cost to yourself.

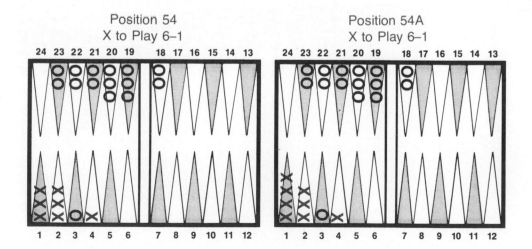

The same reasoning shows that in Position 54, the correct play is 4/3*/off; but in Position 54A, 4/off, 1/off.

In these last two positions, no extra risks are taken to increase the possibility of gammoning O. One consideration in taking extra risks is the strength of O's board. If he has all his remaining men piled up on his one, two, or three point, you may be justified in taking risks you would normally not take because you still expect to win the game even though you are hit. On the other hand, if O has a closed board or a prime, being hit may be fatal so extra care must be taken. More important than the strength of O's position is the question of whether you *need* to take extra risks. Extra risks are often taken gratuitously in these two extreme but common cases: There is little or no chance for a gammon, or the gammon is an actual certainty. In both these cases, playing as safely as possible is correct. Only when the gammon is still undecided are extra risks justified.

Before taking any extra risks, it is important to assess your chances. You can do this by using the gammon count. The gammon count is similar to the pip count, except that instead of counting the total number of pips needed to bear each man off, you count the total number of pips needed to bring all men that are outside the home board in.

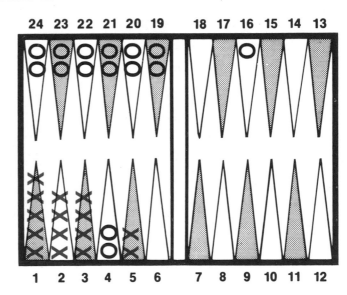

Position 55
X to Play 3–2

For example, in Position 55, how are O's chances of being gammoned evaluated? You simply count the total number of pips he needs for all his men to reach the nineteen point: The man that is now on the sixteen point has 3 pips to go, and the two men on the four point have 15 each; this is a total of 33 pips. Now you must convert this count, the gammon count, into the number of rolls needed to begin bearing off. The best way to do this simply is to divide the gammon count by eight (although the average roll is slightly more than eight). In this case, $33/8 = 4\frac{1}{8}$ or slightly more than 4. The most realistic assessment, therefore, of the total number of rolls O needs to take his first man off is five rolls, since allowances must be made both for wastage (overshooting) coming into the home board, and for the actual number needed to bear off the first man.

You can see in Position 55 that even if X takes two men off, he cannot hope to gammon O since he will probably require seven more rolls to complete his bear-off. Therefore, the proper play is 5/3, 5/2 to insure winning the game.

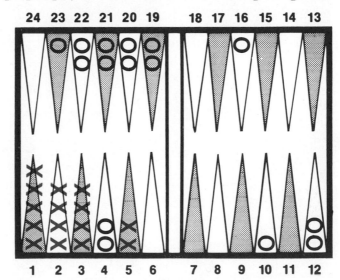

Position 56
X to Play 3–2

However, in Position 56, the gammon count is 56, which means that O will probably complete bearing off in seven or eight rolls. It is then likely to be a close decision as to whether O can prevent the gammon, so X should take the slight risk of leaving a blot on his five point on the next roll and bear off two men. If the position is rearranged so that O's gammon count is 80, X could then reasonably be assured of the gammon no matter what he did and so would return to the conservative play of clearing the five point.

The gammon count may also be profitably employed by the player who seeks to save the gammon. Suppose, for example, in Position 57, X has a roll of 3 to play. The gammon count is 61. This means that he will probably not be

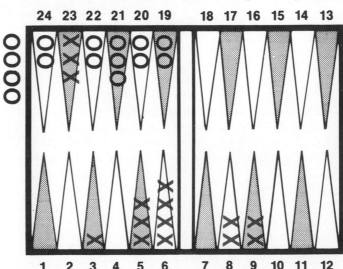

Position 57
X to Play 3

able to take a man off for eight more rolls. Since it is highly unlikely that O will need more than eight rolls to bear off, X should resign himself to being gammoned unless he can luckily hit O during O's bear-off. Thus X should prepare himself for the eventuality of a hit by covering his three point, 6/3.

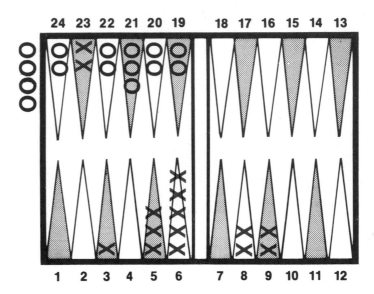

Position 58
X to Play 3

In Position 58, the gammon count shows once again that the gammon is uncertain. Many experienced players go wrong here in deciding whether to build their board or to use every possible pip to save the gammon. When the issue is so close, the general rule is: Always use every possible pip to bring your men home. Thus, in Position 58, the correct play is 9/6. Covering the three point is incorrect because the chance of O's leaving a blot and X's hitting it are small. Further, assuming that you have not covered the three point by the time you hit the blot, it is still unlikely that the three point's being open or closed will affect the final outcome of the game. In only an extremely small percentage of the times this position is reached will the three point decide the game; the 3 pips gained by bringing a man into the inner board will be a significant factor much more often. Therefore, the overall principle involved in such positions is that if the gammon is at all close, usually you should not waste pips in building your board. Only when you have no chance whatsoever to save the gammon, or when you have the gammon saved with at least a roll to spare, should you consider the luxury of building your board at the expense of bringing your men home.

CHAPTER 25.
AFTER CONTACT

Containing the Opposing Checker

After you hit a man in the bear-off, your first objective is to make sure he does not escape. In trying to contain one last man, there are two basic principles which insure the maximum number of return shots as your opponent tries to escape: (1) Stay far back so that he cannot go past you, but instead must come into full range of your shots; (2) Keep your men split up so as to insure the maximum number of return shots.

Position 1
X to Play 3

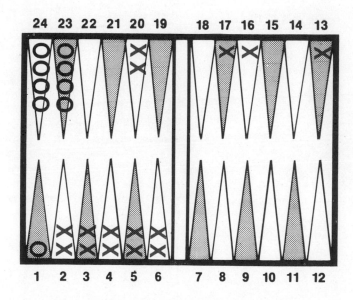

Position 1 is a typical case which illustrates both these principles. The correct play is 17/14. By keeping your men spread out, you insure at least a double shot should O run with a 6. Although you may be tempted to button up to block 6–6 by playing 16/13, this would be a serious mistake. In positions where you are trying to catch one last man, it is much more important to be diversified to insure getting the maximum number of return shots, rather than to try to avoid being hit at all costs. By playing 16/13, you may only get a single direct shot at O if he runs with a 6 on his next roll.

Notice that after correctly playing 17/14 your men will be 12, 13, and 15 pips away from O. Although at first glance, these may appear to be too far away, they are actually ideal distances. Remember: *The object is to let your opponent come into range of you,* and not vice versa. Generally speaking, by staying this far away, you will get the maximum return shots should your opponent roll an average number such as 7, 8, or 9.

Coming closer has three obvious disadvantages: first, you increase the chance he will hit you; second, you increase the chance he will leap over you; third, even if he lands within direct range (1 to 6 pips) of you, the *closer* he is, the *less likely* you are to hit.

When your opponent threatens to escape one man and win in a middle game situation, the same two basic principles of staying back and keeping your men diversified apply.

Position 2
X to Play 2

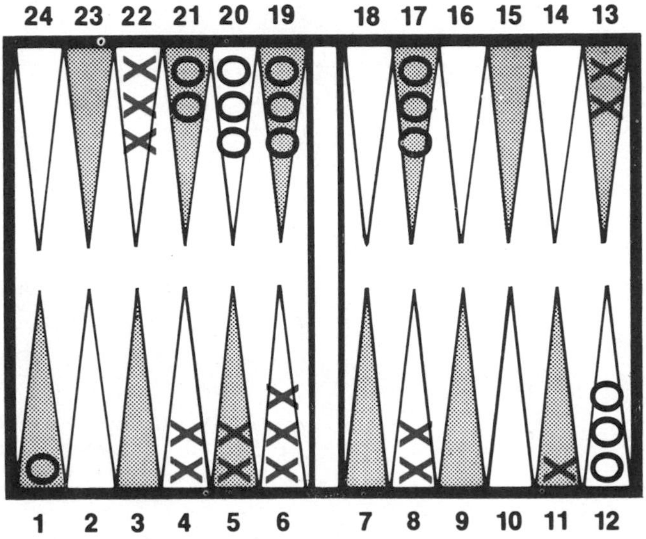

Position 3
X to Play 2

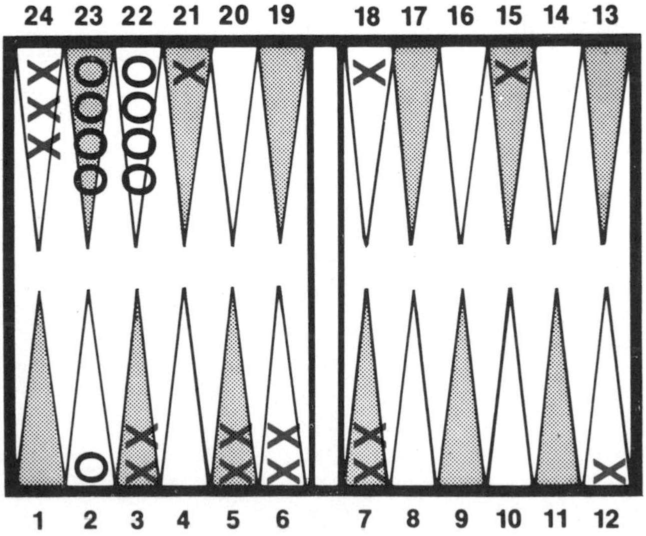

In Position 2, the correct play is 6/4 in order to help contain the man on the one point. Playing 11/9 is wrong despite the extra builder it creates for the three point (it would be correct if X had two men on your one point), because if O ran into your outer board, you would have only a single shot instead of a double shot.

In Position 3, the correct play is 18/16; this gives you better coverage of your outer board than 15/13. Since O has no option but to come out all the way, this play gives you a better reception committee (i.e., more return shots) if he comes out to your nine, ten, eleven, twelve, or thirteen point. Moving 12/10 would be a poor play despite the fact that a checker on the ten point is a builder for your four point.

Position 4
X to Play 4

Position 5
X to Play 4

In Position 4, the correct play is 18/14 in order to insure maximum coverage and give the possibility of a double shot when your opponent runs.

Although Position 5 seems similar to Position 4, the correct play is 16/12. If O rolled a 6 (except 6–1) in Position 4, he would have no option but to come out into direct range of your men on the fourteen and sixteen points. In Position 5, however, O can come out with the 6 *and* play the other half of his roll in his inner board if he chooses. It is necessary, therefore, to bring at least one man into range of his escape square (your bar point) in order to insure a direct shot.

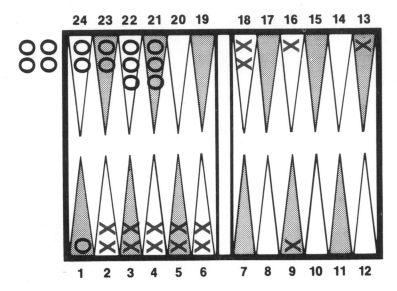

Position 6
X to Play 5

In Position 6, the correct play is 9/4. Your object is not only to get return shots but also to prevent O's escape by hitting him and eventually closing him out. It is usually a better plan to move into your inner board to hit and close your opponent out, rather than to expose men repeatedly in your own outfield in an attempt to make your bar point.

Playing 18/13 to block 6–6 is a luxury you cannot afford. Perhaps the most important reason that 9/4 is correct is that the man on the nine point has practically no defensive value whatsoever in containing O. If O rolls any number that comes out besides 6–1, he will either hit the man on the nine point or go past it.

Playing 13/8 and leaving a man 7 pips away from O is worse yet, since this move doesn't contain anything at all. It is bad to be 7, 8, or 9 pips away from your opponent since such checkers have little chance of containing him. In

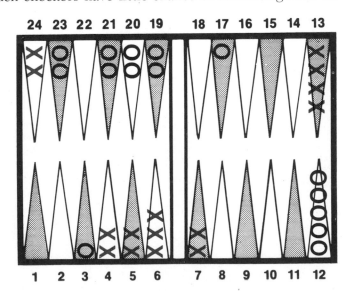

Position 7
X to Play 6–2

general, you should either bring men into direct range (1 to 6 pips) to attack your opponent, or stay 11 to 15 pips away.

Position 7 from the middle game is another illustration of these concepts. Here X wants to prevent O's man on the three point from escaping. Many players move 13/7, 13/11, putting another man in the outfield to hinder O's escape. This is wrong; the value of this man on the eleven point (only 8 pips away) is largely an illusion (unfortunately, an illusion which misleads many players). Since you are only 8 away, you will gain extra shots on only a few numbers (note that you will also lose on 6–2 and 5–3). Playing 13/5 is much more constructive since you are bringing a third builder to bear on O.

Diversify your men even if this slightly increases your chances of being hit. Be cautious, however, if your opponent has a 5- or 6-point board. Even if he doesn't have a strong board, it is still inadvisable to leave direct shots since only a few closed opposing points may greatly reduce the number of your return shots if you are hit.

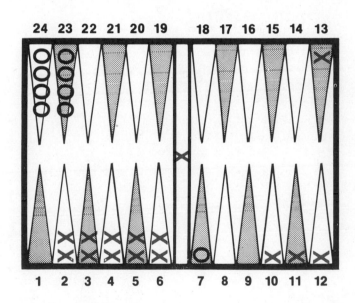

Position 8
X on Roll

Position 8 is somewhat deceiving; X is on the bar and is quite certain (8 to 1) to re-enter. It may appear that X has virtually a quadruple shot and is therefore also a strong favorite to hit O. A closer inspection, however, reveals that far from being a strong favorite to hit O, X is actually a favorite to miss altogether. In fact, because of the unfortunate duplication (X needs the same numbers to come in and to hit), any 1 or 2 — 20 numbers altogether — will miss.

In general, it is more important to keep your men diversified than to worry about blocking specific large doubles. However, if you have such excellent coverage that your opponent's main hope lies in throwing a large double, or if it will cost you nothing, then it may be correct to figure out how to block certain doubles.

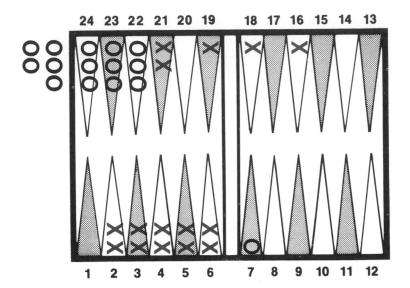

Position 9
X to Play 2

In Position 9, for example, the correct play is 21/19. In this case, you block 3–3, 4–4, 6–6 with a number that can't help you elsewhere anyway.

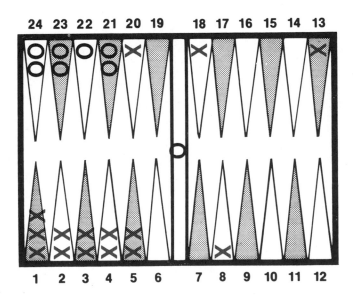

Position 10
X to Play 1

Even if X could make a point to block 6–6 in this position, he would not wish to tie up his men to do so. Since he can't block 6–6, he might reason that 18/17 at least avoids being hit by 6–6. This reasoning is wrong on several counts. First of all, even if O does roll 6–6, X wants to be hit so he will have a return shot at O's twenty-two-point blot. Secondly, even if there are no return shots, O will win the game if he rolls 6–6 whether he hits X or not, so it is senseless to worry about it. Thirdly, the correct play is 13/12, bringing a builder to bear on the six point. If O fails to re-enter, it is important for X to slot a man on the six point immediately — this would be true even if O didn't have an exposed man. (To see why slotting is necessary here, see Chapter 17.) Finally, note that X has a man on the eight point. Since O is on the bar, this man may be considered to be 8 pips in front of O — an undesirable position. This is a common and serious error in this type of position where your six point is open: Never try to contain an opposing man on the bar by bringing your men *too* close (putting them on the seven, eight, or nine point).

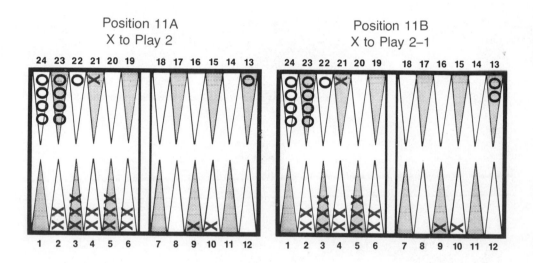

In Position 11A, X follows the basic principle of staying as far back as possible in order to increase the chance of getting a shot and hitting O. The correct play is 9/7, bringing another man to bear on the one point.

Position 11B is an unusual exception to this principle. Beause O has two men left to bring home and has no flexibility, the correct play is 21/19 to bring a man into direct range. This play virtually assures a good direct shot because even if O moves one man safely, the other will still be exposed.

For doubling purposes, it is sometimes important to form an idea of what the chance of escaping a last man is. Whenever there is one man trying to get around one man, the side trying to escape should double. Whether the double is taken depends on how far back the restraining man is.

X should double in Position 12. Being 9 pips away gives O just barely a 25% chance of hitting X and winning, so O has a marginal take. Were X any closer (8 pips or less away), O should definitely pass. Here X has practically no spare numbers to play (except 1's and 2's) and therefore, will probably be forced to come into range of O. If X had more numbers that would allow him to stall, even 9 pips away would be a pass. Other contingencies — such as X already having several men off, or if there is a possibility of gammoning — may likewise affect the odds.

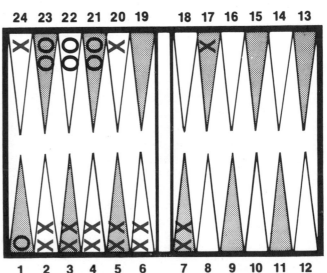

Position 12
X Doubles

Hitting Additional Men

In many endgame situations, you may hit your opponent, even after he has borne off as many as thirteen men, and *still* be a favorite to win the game. This is because, with proper play, it is often possible to force him to expose *additional* men, which may also be hit. Hitting a second man will generally win the game for you, regardless of the number of men your opponent has already borne off.

If you want to force your opponent to leave *extra* blots, you must not close him out too soon, for this would stop him from moving his checkers. Instead of closing him out, allow him to come in behind a prime, so he will have to take his moves in his home board. In other words, give him enough rope to hang himself!

Position 13
X to Play 3–3

In Position 13, it would be a tragic mistake to make the one point 7/1(2). Although owning the cube still allows you to retain some equity in the game, you will be an almost certain winner by going after a second man. Leave O alone and play 17/5. Now whenever O rolls a 1, 2, or 3, he will probably be forced to expose a new man (a 3 may leave a double shot with two men exposed). If you hit a second man, you become an overwhelming favorite to win the game — so much so that you can double out your opponent.

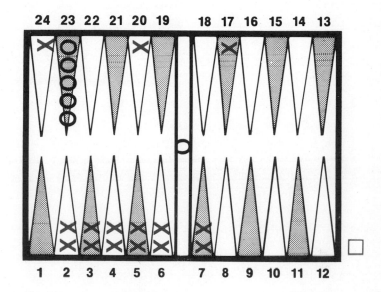

Position 14
X to Play 3–3

Similarly, in Position 14, it would be wrong to close the board 7/1(2). Although there are no bad numbers for O to roll now, you must patiently wait until he re-enters on your one point. Then you must wait until he rolls another 1, which would force him to hit you and leave a blot on the twenty-four point. Even if O fails to come in and/or fails to roll a second 1 before you are forced to close him out, you have lost nothing by trying to get a second man. A large percentage of games are won by proper use of this technique.

Let's examine Position 14 further and see why our strategy may fail. It may fail if O does not roll enough 1's before we are forced to close him out. Given sufficient time, of course, O will eventually come in and blot on the twenty-four point, but our spare men may have come around the board before then. What we need is time. We may be able to create time artificially by blotting on the one point and forcing O to hit, thus gaining 24 extra pips of time.

If X has 4–4 to play in Position 14 (instead of 3–3), the correct move is 17/1. X does *not* do this with the intention of covering the one point. When O re-enters he will have to put X on the bar, giving him extra time to wait until O rolls the second, and possibly fatal, 1.

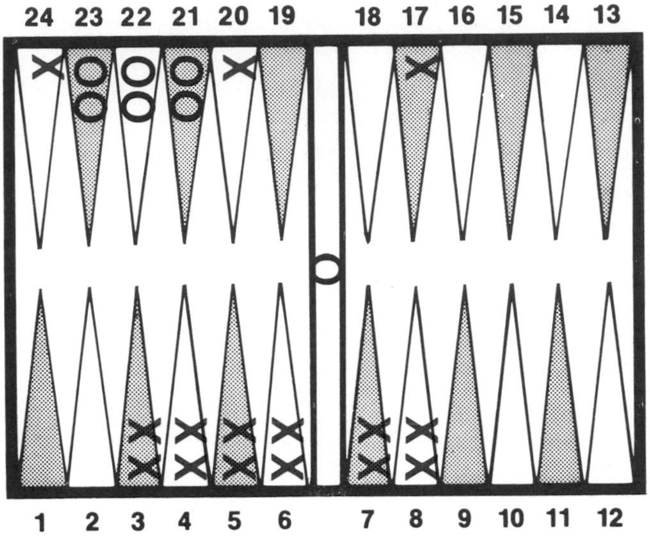

Position 15
X to Play 3–3

In Position 15, it would be counterproductive for X to move his prime further into the inner board by making his two point. X wants O to come in *behind* his prime and bust his board. As long as you have a full, secure prime, you want to give your opponent every possible opportunity to re-enter behind it. The correct play is 20/8 so that you may blot on the two point with a 6.

You may have to plan ahead to hit a second man even before the first man is hit.

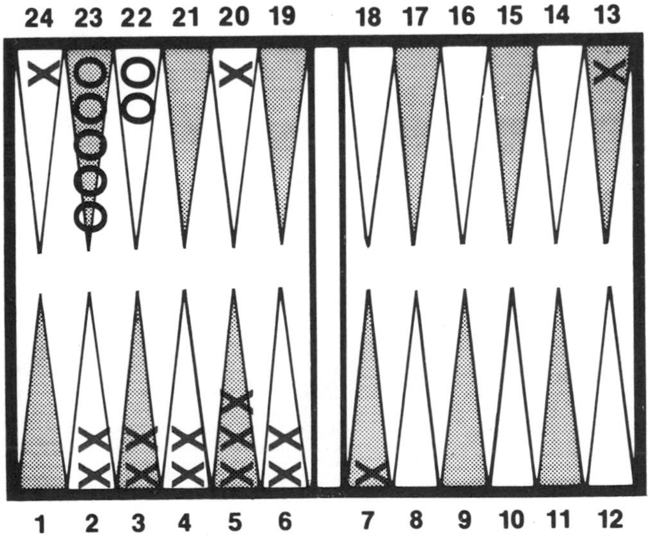

Position 16
X to Play 6–4

In Position 16, making the one point 7/1, 5/1 would be a mistake since it would eliminate any possibility of getting a second man even if you are fortunate enough to get a shot and hit the first man. The correct play is 13/7 to complete the prime, and 5/1 to gain additional time later if you hit a man.

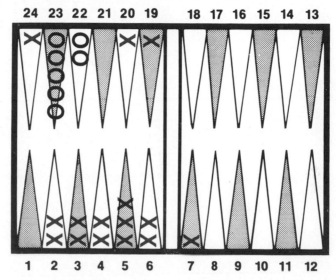

Position 17
X to Play 6–4

Even where it is impossible to make the prime immediately, as in Position 17, it would still be a serious mistake to make the one point and eliminate the possibility of hitting a second man. The correct play is 19/13, 5/1, preparing to make the bar point.

Let us now examine the winning technique of circling back to hit a second man in more detail: Assume that in Position 17 you are fortunate enough to hit O and make your prime, reaching Position 18.

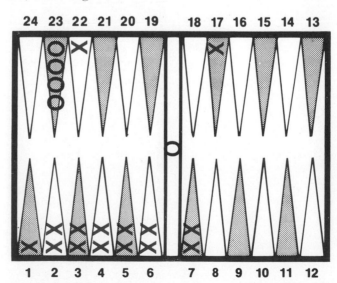

Position 18

Now, waiting for O to re-enter with a 1, move your *closest* spare man (in this case, the man on the seventeen point) nearer to your inner board.

Assume now that O has re-entered and simultaneously hits your blot on the one point, reaching Position 19.

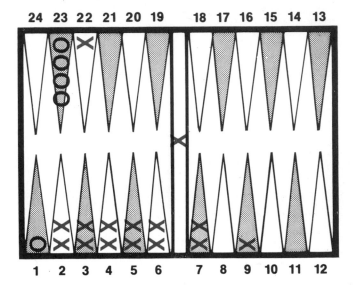

Position 19
X to Play 4–1

In Position 19, you must re-enter on the twenty-four point and play your nearest spare man into your inner board (bar/24, 9/5). Notice that the essential idea is to keep a man back on the twenty-four point as long as possible so that when O rolls another 1 he will be forced to hit you with a direct return shot.

A few rolls later we may arrive at Position 20.

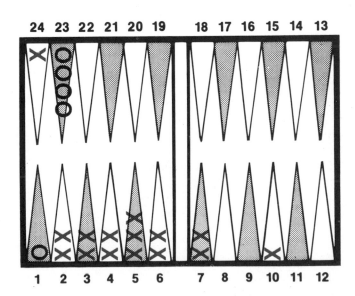

Position 20
X to Play 4–1

Here we keep a man back on the twenty-four point and play 10/6, 5/4. Hitting on the one point is wrong because we want O to be forced to use the 1 he rolls to blot on the twenty-four point.

Let us now assume that O does roll a number with a 1 (they are all the same except 1–1), reaching Position 21.

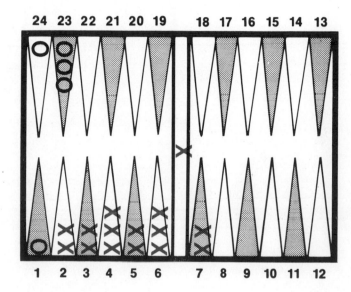

Position 21
X to Play 5–4

If you roll a 1, you will hit the second man, accomplishing your basic objective, but let's assume you miss your 1-shot. Does this mean that all this effort has been in vain, that at most you can hope for one *single* direct shot?

No, you still have an excellent chance of winning the game. However, you must not allow O to cover the blot on the twenty-four point.

In Position 21, you play bar/21, 6/1*. This prevents him from covering with a 1 since he must use a 1 to re-enter. If O now rolls a 1 (except 1–1), he will be forced to re-enter and hit you, giving you a second chance to hit his blot.

In order to get more shots, it is imperative to hit O before he can cover the twenty-four point. If you had rolled a 6–4 in Position 21, the correct play would have been bar/21, 7/1*. It is far better to give up the prime, which may be recovered later, than to risk having O cover. Even if O rolls a 6–1, you will at least get another chance to hit the blot on the twenty-four point.

As long as you prevent O from covering by hitting him every time he re-enters, he will give you a new chance to hit the second man. Thus you create a perpetual-motion situation until you successfully hit a second man, or are forced to close the one point, or until he covers the twenty-four point. This strategy is effective because you will probably have several chances to hit the second man.

Position 22
X to Play 5–3

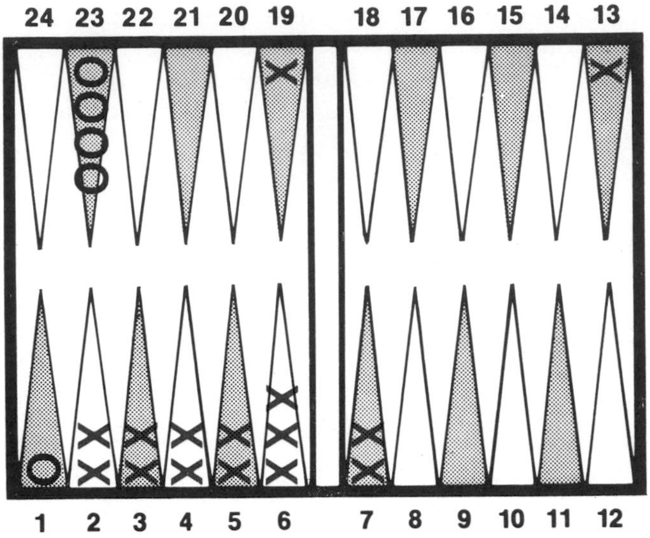

In Position 22, X would rather have a man back on the twenty-four point than on the nineteen point. As we have seen, it is desirable but not essential to have a man back on the twenty-four point. You may fail to have a man there for several reasons: (a) as in the illustrated example, you were hit off the one point; (b) you had a man on the one point but were forced to leave; (c) you were never on the one point. Whatever the reason, you may find yourself in Position 22.

In this position, it is a serious mistake to hit; you want O to be able to roll a 1 and blot on the twenty-four point, and *then* hit for the return shot. The correct play is 13/5. Bringing the closest spare man home, 13/5, is superior to 19/11 because it is essential to be able to hit or slot the one point at the right time.

Position 23
X to Play 5–3

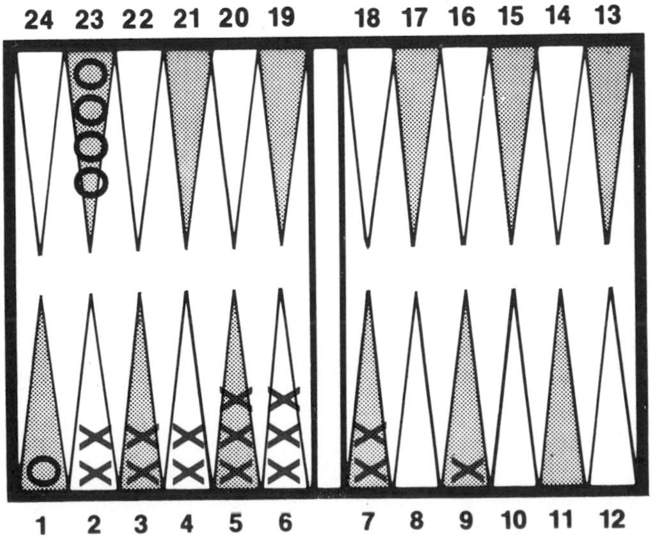

Position 23 is an exception. You want to wait until *after* O rolls a 1 to hit, but, unfortunately, you are running out of time and will soon be forced to close O out. Therefore, the correct play here is 9/1*. Now if O rolls a 1, you will gain extra time bringing the hit man around and may be able to avoid closing O out.

Section V

Advanced Positional Play

CHAPTER 26.
PRIMING AND BLOCKING

BACKGAMMON STRATEGY IS subtle and complex because backgammon is not only a running game — it is also a blocking game. This chapter examines where and how to make points to block your opponent's men. Although we consider the location of the opposing men, we will postpone, for the most part, the question of whether playing a blocking game is the best overall strategy. Discussions of alternate game plans and their relation to blocking and priming will be found in Chapters 28 and 29. The discussion of topics in this chapter cannot be considered complete without reference to these later chapters.

Types of Primes

The main way to block your opponent's back men is to build a **prime**, a series of points in a row. Ideally, you would like to make a full **6-point prime**.

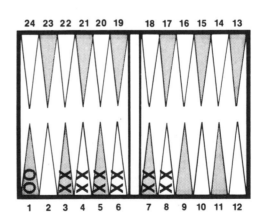

Position 1
6-Point Prime

As you can see in Position 1, there are no possible numbers which permit any of your opponent's back men to escape when behind a 6-point prime. (You may wish to review Chapter 8 to appreciate the power of the full prime.)

A **5-point prime** is also extremely hard to bypass. You begin the game with your six and eight points. You should mentally plan to construct a 5-point prime from your four point to your eight point.

Then try to extend it to the ideal 6-point prime (three to eight points) shown in Position 1. When your opponent is behind a 5-point prime, he must first get to the single point directly in front of the prime (the edge of the prime), and then roll a specific 6 to escape.

Position 2
5-Point Prime

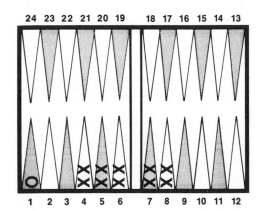

In Position 2, O needs a specific 2 and then a specific 6 to escape his back man. Even without interference from X, this will require several rolls — 5.70 rolls on the average.

Position 3   Position 4

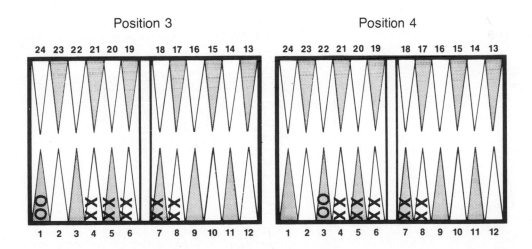

With *two* men back, as in Position 3, it is even harder to escape — it requires 9.50 rolls on the average.

If you have built a solid 5-point prime, there is only one point which your opponent can escape from: the point *directly* in front of the prime. In Position 4, this is the three point. Even if the back men are at the edge of the prime, as in Position 4, it will still take 6.20 rolls on the average to escape. (These figures are not important and need not be memorized.)

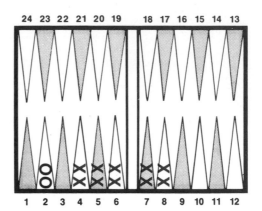

Position 5

Having both back men on the two point seems to bring O closer to escaping. However, it is actually harder to reach the three point — the edge of the prime — from the two point (11 numbers), than from the one point (12 numbers). It will take O a whole roll longer, on the average, to escape in Position 5 than in Position 3.

Let's look at the effectiveness of a 4-point prime.

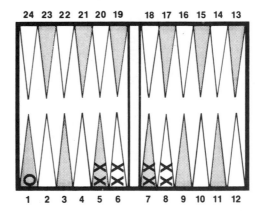

Position 6

If O is allowed to move without interference, as in Position 6, it is much easier for him to escape than from behind a 5-point prime. Here O has two points of departure: the three and four points. Furthermore, O has 2 numbers that leap over the prime from the four point. Therefore, O will be a favorite to clear a 4-point prime with one man on one roll *if* he is at the edge of the prime. In actual play, however, O may not be able to move freely up to the edge of the prime (or even to the three point) because X may have spare builders which can hit or point on O. If it is dangerous for O to approach the edge of the prime, then 4 points in a row will often form a very effective blockade.

So far, we have been discussing **solid primes**, i.e., an unbroken series of points. If you have a series of points in a row with an uncovered point in their midst, this is referred to as a **broken prime**. Sometimes a broken prime can be an effective blockade.

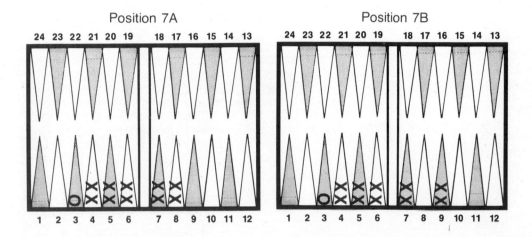

Position 7A   Position 7B

The broken prime in Position 7B is just as hard to escape from as the solid prime in Position 7A, since O needs 1 particular number in each case: a 6 in 7A, a 5 in 7B. However, if O has a single man on the one point (instead of the three point), the value of a solid prime over a broken one becomes apparent. Behind a broken prime, O has 2 numbers (1, 2) which bring him to a position where he can escape; behind a solid prime, O needs a specific 2, or 1 number.

Order of Points

We indicated that at the beginning of the game you should think of making a 5-point prime ideally from the four point to the eight point. For this reason, the five and bar points are important. Since you open with the six and eight points, the bar point is clearly going to be part of any prime you may wish to construct. Why, then, are the four and five points so important? Couldn't you form a prime just as well from the six point to the eleven point?

Owning the four and five points serves two functions: these points are part of the prime, and by owning them you also close two key inner board points. The figures we quoted on the number of rolls O needs to escape were based on the assumption that there was no opposition from X. If X however, owns the four or five point (or both), O may not be able to come up to the three point for fear of being hit. Owning the four or five point also serves to prevent your opponent from seizing these valuable points himself and establishing an advanced anchor.

What about the three point? Why do we not recommend making it with an opening 5–3? The three point does not fit into the prime as naturally as do the four or five point. Basically, you should try to make your points in order and in a row. If you make the three point on the opening roll, you leave a double gap on the four and five points. The three point, thus, has greatly reduced blocking power. It also allows your opponent the chance to make the four or five point himself.

If you use an opening 5–3 to bring two men down, 13/8, 13/10, you create a builder for the more vital four, five, and seven points. However, assume that both players start with 4–2 (Position 8), and X has a 5–3 to play.

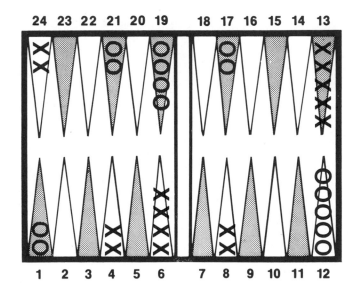

Position 8
X to Play 5–3

In this position, we recommend making the three point despite the blot on the eight point. Since we already own the four point (or if we already own the five point), the three point fits in much more naturally as part of the prime. By making it in this position, we do not create a double gap in the prime—
— only a single gap.

What about making the two point? Making this point very early in the game is almost always a mistake. The men on the two point are effectively out of play and have very little blocking potential. They only serve as part of a prime if your opponent has men on the one point. If you own three of the other four inside points, the two point is more valuable, and you do not create large gaps in making it. You have established a significant number of points in your inner board and your opponent is wary of being hit.

The main idea to remember is that you want to make your points in a row and to avoid gaps. Making the two or three point as the game develops is a reasonable play if you already have established most of the intervening points. Leaving large gaps — especially by owning only the six and two points, or, much worse, the six and one points — is seldom correct.

Another reason making the two point is often conceptually incorrect may be seen in Position 9.

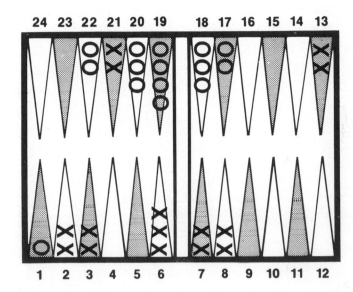

Position 9

Here you waste men because you own the two point and the eight point. Both points cannot be part of the same 6-point prime. Since the eight point has no real blocking power you should give up the eight point without hesitation so the men on it can be put to better use. Similarly, once the one point has been made, the bar point loses most of its value, and holding both the nine and three points implies some wastage of men.

Relation to Your Opponent's Points

So far we have been examining making a prime and blocking without considering exactly where your opponent is. To choose the points which most effectively block O, you must take O's position into account. In Section I, you learned that if your opponent has a point in your inner board, *the most effective blocking point is the one 6 pips away* (5 away is also excellent).

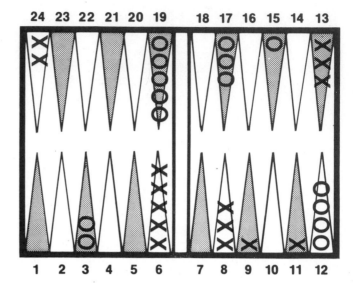

Position 10
X to Play 4–2

In Position 10, the correct play is 13/9, 11/9, blocking the men on the three point. Moving 11/9 does *not* take away an active builder since you always want to maintain the nine point. Note that playing 11/9 and splitting 24/20 brings you under the gun unnecessarily.

In this position, the nine point is a more valuable blocking point than the bar point. If O owned the five point, the value of the bar point would be even more diminished. If you already own the ten or eleven point to block your opponent, the bar point is not as valuable since building a solid prime in the outfield is an unrealistic goal. It is better to hold two or three points in front of your opponent and deploy your other men elsewhere.

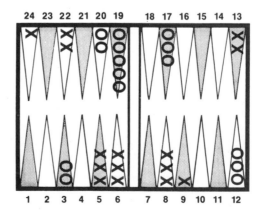

Position 11A
X to Play 5–4

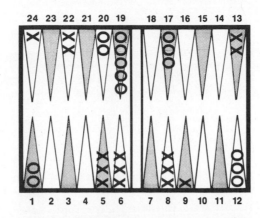

Position 11B
X to Play 5–4

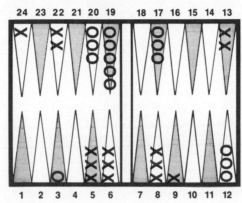

Position 11C
X to Play 5–4

The same principle also applies in Position 11A, where the correct play is 13/9, 13/8. By making the nine point along with the eight point you very effectively block O's men on the three point. In Position 11B, making the four point, 9/4, 8/4, is a much stronger play.

The rule about blocking O by making a point 5 or 6 pips in front of him applies primarily to blocking a point which O holds. When O has only *one* man back, the rule loses much of its force. This is illustrated in Position 11C, where it is better to make the four point, 9/4, 8/4, than the nine point, 13/8, 13/9, despite the fact that the nine point is 6 pips away from the opposing man on the three point. The man on the three point is not likely to stand still — O will either try to run away or you will have to move in and attack him. The value of the nine point in this position will be temporary. Rather than giving up the midpoint (discussed in Chapter 27), you should make the four point and put more pressure on O. In Position 11A, however, O cannot easily or safely leave the three point, so the nine point has more lasting value.

When you are trapped behind a solid or broken prime, you must take into account which points your opponent holds before making any opposing inner board points yourself.

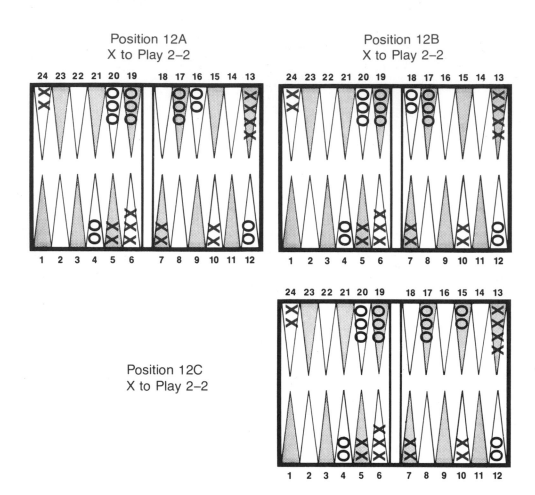

Position 12A
X to Play 2–2

Position 12B
X to Play 2–2

Position 12C
X to Play 2–2

In Position 12A X would be foolish to use part of his roll to make the twenty-two point, 24/22(2), since O holds the sixteen point, 6 pips away. If X later leaves the twenty-two point, the man left behind will be exposed to several builders. The correct play is 13/9(2), creating your own broken 5-point prime.

In Position 12B, however, it is very important to move up to the twenty-two point, 24/22(2), 13/11(2). If you remain on the twenty-four point, O will soon have you trapped behind a 5- or even a 6-point prime. By making the twenty-two point, you have a guaranteed exit since it will be difficult for O to ever make the sixteen point. The twenty-two point (or O's three point) thus becomes a valuable advanced anchor.

In Position 12C, the twenty-two point is again a valuable point to make. In this case, it is even more valuable than the twenty-one point (or O's four point) since O owns the fifteen point.

When and How to Make Primes

Before deciding how to make points and block your opponent, you should determine whether you want to block him or hold him back at all. Let's look at Position 13, where X is well ahead in the race.

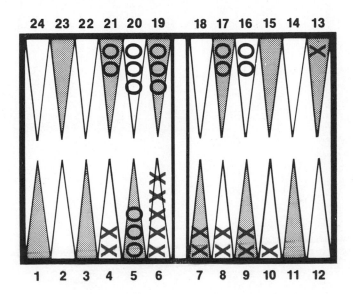

Position 13
X to Play 4–3

In this position, you do not want to hold your opponent back — you merely want to get past him and come home safely. You should avoid the problem of clearing the ten point later by simply never making it and playing 13/9, 10/7. (This particular type of position, where you must decide whether or not to hold your opponent, was discussed in Chapter 10. Other important game plans where holding or blocking your opponent is *not* your objective will be considered in the remaining chapters of Section V.)

We now turn our attention to *how* to create an effective prime or blockade. The main technique is to create builders and see that your men are in an effective and fluid position. As we saw in Chapter 12, making points rapidly and efficiently is not just a matter of luck but also depends on having your men in the right place at the right time. In order to use your men effectively to block your opponent, you must be careful not to waste men by making the deep inner board points or by stacking your men on a few points. You must also consider which of your inner points your opponent holds. To block him you must make points *in front of him*. Therefore, you must avoid making points or taking builders *behind* points he already holds. You have a limited number of men at your disposal, and every man you bring behind your opponent is one less you can use to make points in front of him.

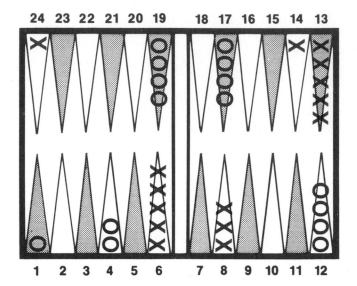

Position 14
X to Play 5–5

For example, in Position 14, it is a mistake to make the one point with part of your roll, 6/1*(2). Even hitting on the one point is meaningless since you have no need for a tempo play. The correct play is 13/3, 8/3, 14/9. This play allows you to make a point in your inner board, and more importantly, you threaten to make the nine point in front of the four point held by O. If O hits you, he must abandon the four point to do so.

If O has made the five point, you want to make the ten or eleven point to block him. If you cannot make the point directly, it is best to slot a man on either of these points (assuming you can withstand a hit) and then cover later. Remember that O must give up a valuable anchor in order to hit your slotted man.

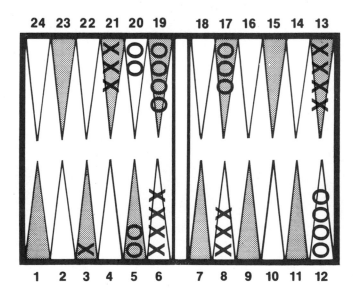

Position 15
X to Play 3–2

In Position 15, the correct play is 6/3, 13/11. Slotting on an outside block-ing point is a very effective strategy because O is generally very reluctant to give up the five point unless the hit is of prime importance. (Chapter 20 detailed many examples of when and when not to hit from the opponent's five point.) Many games may be won against a less experienced player by drawing him off a vital advanced anchor in just such a fashion. If your opponent wisely refrains from hitting, you may be able to partially block him by covering the slotted point.

Sometimes you can increase the effectiveness of a prime without lengthen-ing it. If your opponent is trapped in your inner board, you want your prime to extend as far into your board as possible, provided you are not giving him a direct exit. When you move an already established prime forward (usually by moving off the back point and making a new point on the forward edge), it is called **advancing the prime.**

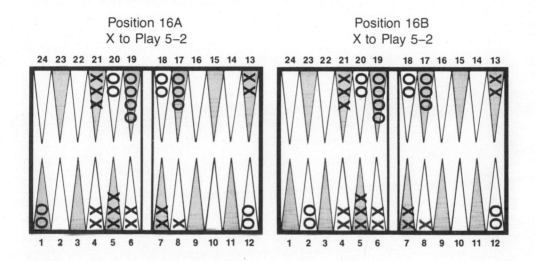

In Position 16A, X should play 8/3, 5/3, moving the prime deeper into his inner board and retaining the point 6 pips away from the point O holds. Advancing the prime to the three point restricts O more than making the eight point.

In Position 16B, X should play 13/8, 13/11. Since O owns the two point, it is essential for X to hold the eight point to block direct 6's.

Another important technique to use in building a prime is to make it in reverse. We usually want to lengthen a prime by adding additional points to the front, but in some cases it is much easier and quicker to add on points in back.

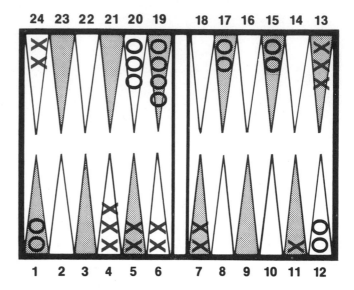

Position 17
X to Play 5–1

In Position 17, X rolled 1–1 early in the game and has a solid 4-point prime. It is a mistake to bring the builder on the eleven point into the six point, 11/6, to try to make the three point. There is no reason to risk slotting the three point, and without slotting, it will be difficult to make it naturally. Even with a third active builder on top of your prime, it may take many rolls until you get the number to make the three point exactly.

A much easier way to lengthen your prime is to play 13/8, 11/10. Unless O rolls a lucky combination shot, the eight point will be there for the taking. In fact, you might even cover the eight point and start the nine point. How much easier it is to make a prime by adding to the back where your opponent can't easily interfere! A general rule: When you have a partial prime, if your opponent is not bearing directly on the back of the prime, consider using your builders to make rear rather than forward points.

Let's look at Position 17 again: Note that X plays 13/8, 11/10 instead of splitting the back runners 13/8, 24/23. Although we have a strong game, we want to make at least a 5-point prime (and cover the eight point blot) before exposing our back men. If X splits now, O might attack and in the ensuing scuffle X may never close the fifth point of the prime.

Whenever a player has his opponent trapped behind a partial prime, both players usually struggle for the point directly in front of the prime. The trapped player wants to make this point so he can escape; the priming player to prevent his opponent's escape and to lengthen the prime. Thus, there is often violent action on this point since neither player can readily afford to concede it.

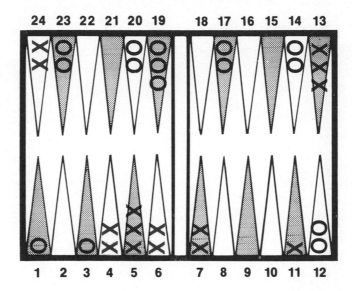

Position 18
X to Play 3–2

In Position 18, O has correctly split to X's three point. Even though the danger is great, O had to move up to the edge of X's prime before X could lengthen it or bring down additional builders to make such a split even more dangerous. When your opponent has a solid prime, the principle of not coming under the gun ceases to apply.

X has 3–2 to play. He could handle it safely (11/6, for example), but the correct play is 11/8, 5/3*, hitting O on the three point and slotting a man on the eight point. Unless O gets an immediate return hit, X will be in a position to form a deadly 5-point prime. Even if X is hit, O still has the problem of escaping. It is better to take a chance now than to allow O to make the three point freely. Attacking on the edge of a prime is a standard motif in advanced play.

CHAPTER 27.
CONTROL OF
THE OUTSIDE

Value of the Outfield

Control of the two outer boards is a very important positional consideration. Your outer board and your opponent's outer board are together called
the **outfield,** or **outside.** To understand the value of controlling the outer
boards, let's look at the basic flow of men in Position 1.

Position 1
U-Shaped
Direction of Movement

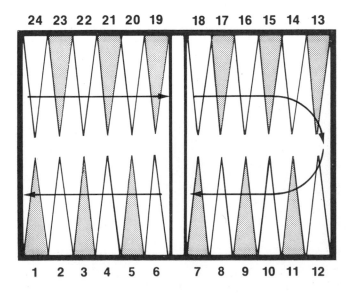

Your men move around a U from your opponent's inner board to his outer board, around to your outer board, and into your inner board. The middle of the journey is the outer boards, or the **outfield.** When you control the outfield, therefore, you control the center of the board. To see this more clearly, try the following mental experiment:

Position 2

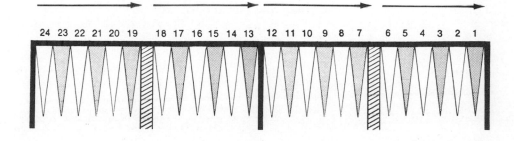

Rearrange the board, as shown, so that the 24 points are in a row, and the movement is straight from one end to the other. The game is exactly the same as in Position 1, but the importance of the outfield becomes clearer. The outfield controls the entire flow of men from one end of the board to the other.

If, for instance, you have all your men in the inner boards, your army is cut in half. Your men don't "communicate" with each other, and thus any men in your opponent's inner board may be stranded. In order to extricate your back men (the stragglers of your army), it is necessary to bring them through the outfield. If your opponent controls the entire outfield, escaping becomes difficult or impossible because of the length of hostile territory to be traversed. Conversely, if you control the outfield, you have a double advantage: any men trapped in your opponent's inner board have a shorter way to go to reach friendly territory, and your opponent's back men are cut off. Thus, by having a strong presence in the outer boards, you can control the flow of traffic. Your army is linked up, and you are free to move the men you wish, when you wish. Your opponent often finds his movement awkward, while you control the flow of the game.

Let's look at a concrete example of what we've been discussing.

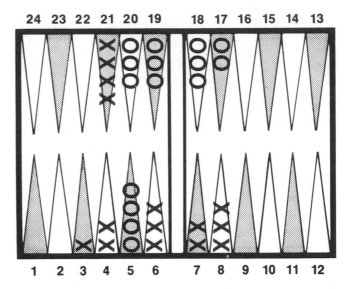

Position 3
O on Roll

In Position 3, the outfield (sixteen to nine points) is a no-man's-land; neither player controls it. The first player to have even a single checker in this critical area will be at an advantage.

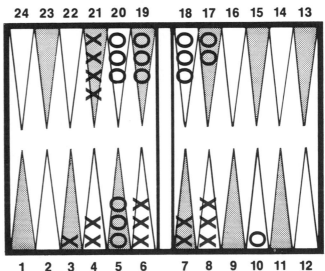

Position 4
X to Play 5–3
(O 4–1 5/10)

In Position 4, O has established the first outside foothold. If X does not contest this outpost, O may gain complete control of the outfield. If O controls the entire outfield, he has only to move 4 pips from the five point to reach friendly territory. X, however, would have to run through 13 pips of hostile territory to land safely. For this reason, X contests control of the outfield before O can get a second man there by playing 21/16, 6/3. It is better to fight for control than to play passively.

Typically, what happens in this sort of position if X passively allows O to control the outfield is that X will run out of useful moves and be squeezed; he will be forced to strip down the points in his board and eventually will have to leave the twenty-one point, whatever the danger. Even if by making the correct play X is hit, the hit will remove the man now guarding the outfield and give X a chance to get out and exert control. Thus, you should try to increase your number of men and points in the outfield while driving or luring your opponent away.

Holding Your Midpoint

Even when you cannot totally control the outfield (this is impossible when your opponent has a point there), you should try to keep some sort of presence there. Fortunately, you always open the game with one key point in the outfield — your midpoint or thirteen point. When the game begins, you have three extra men on your midpoint, as does your opponent.

As long as you have men back in your opponent's inner board, you should not give the midpoint up — unless you have established some other outfield point. Giving up the midpoint prematurely is a common error. A common stratagem, in fact, is to lure your opponent off his midpoint, after which you take control of the outfield and eventually strangle him. Therefore, you should not only try to retain your midpoint as long as possible, but also take every opportunity to bring men into the outer boards (particularly your opponent's outer board). Experts will repeatedly come into the outfield, often leaving single or even multiple direct shots, in order to establish their own presence and lure away their opponent's men.

In many games, a good player will establish an advanced anchor in his opponent's inner board and then repeatedly move spare men from his opponent's inner board into the outfield — seemingly risking being hit for no apparent reason. After hitting him several times, his opponent will run out of men and allow the good player to establish control of the outside. This will eventually lead to a win.

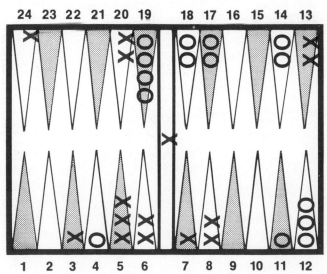

Position 5
X to Play 6–3

In Position 5, all the basic criteria in Chapter 16: *Safe Play vs. Bold Play* call for a bold play since X has little to lose by being hit. Even though making the bar point, bar/22, 13/7 may appear very tempting, this is definitely incorrect. By moving 13/7, you give up your last foothold in the outfield, and you are left with one man on your midpoint which will, in all likelihood, be hit or forced to move. Thus you will be yielding total control of the outfield.

The correct play is bar/16. Now you have three men in your opponent's outfield and you retain your midpoint. Although you are extremely likely to be hit (even though O will not hit with a 2), you do not mind. In fact, by making this play several times, you may force O to relinquish the fourteen or twelve point.

Position 6
X to Play 6

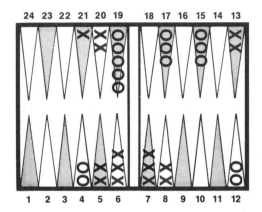

In Position 6, you should not play 13/7. The reason this play is incorrect is not because of the danger of leaving a 1-shot (*Safe Play vs. Bold Play* criteria say you have little to lose), but rather because you should be very reluctant to give up the outfield without a fight. There is no convenient way to play the 6, but the lesser evil is to put a man on the one point, even though this effectively takes him out of play.

If instead X has a 5 to play in the same position, the correct play is 21/16. This type of play is second nature for expert players, but often overlooked by others. You hope to either contribute another soldier to the fight for the center, or else to lure your opponent off his midpoint.

Moving into the Outfield

Let's look at several reasons you might move into the outfield with a blot. Position 6 illustrated the two basic reasons for slotting in the outfield: to increase your presence there and to lure your opponent off key points. As a matter of fact, if O now rolls a 4 without a 1 in Position 6, he should not hit — he has little to gain — but should preserve his midpoint and build up his inner board. This also illustrates another reason why going into the outfield in the face of multiple shots is often much less dangerous than it first appears: Often your opponent cannot hit you with several of the numbers at his disposal, either because of the enormous return shots or because he will have to give up too valuable a point. Therefore, seemingly dangerous plays may be comparatively safe because your opponent cannot hit you conveniently.

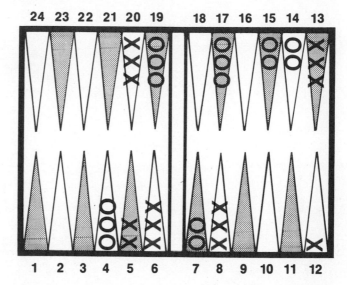

Position 7
X to Play 4

In Position 7, for example, X should play 20/16. O has little to gain by hitting since he has only a 1-point board, and X has the golden point. More importantly, O cannot hit without giving up a valuable point. The blot on the sixteen point — which appears to be exposed to a double shot — is, for practical purposes, not exposed at all since O wants to maintain the fourteen and fifteen points.

At other times you may leave a man exposed in front of a point which is frozen because of the danger of return shots.

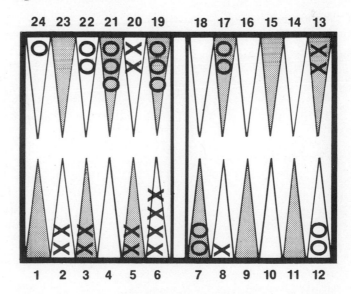

Position 8
X to Play 3

In Position 8, X should play 6/3 (instead of 8/5) so he will not be forced to take a 6 awkwardly next roll. This entails virtually no risk, since O cannot afford to hit and risk being hit back. This type of position occurs often and is also illustrated in Position 9.

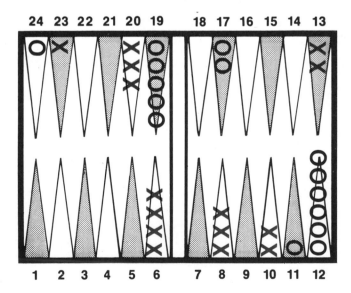

Position 9
X to Play 6–4

The correct play is 8/2, 6/2, rather than the obvious 13/3. This move strengthens your inner board and gives you a more flexible position than playing 13/3 and stripping the midpoint. Since you hold an anchor in O's inner board — which is weaker than your own — a hit would not be fatal for you. The strong inner board you create will be important later if you decide to risk splitting your back men.

Position 10
X to Play 4–3

In Position 10, X should play 20/16, 8/5, instead of the "safe" 20/13. Since O has no men back, you want to provoke an exchange of hits. By planting a checker squarely in O's outer board, you get in his way and make it harder for him to move his men safely.

Still another reason you may want to come out is to avoid getting hit, or pointed on, in your opponent's inner board.

Position 11
X to Play 5–4

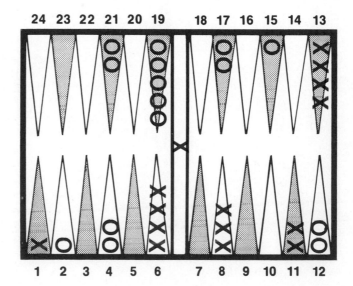

In Position 11, the correct play is bar/16. The basic criteria mentioned in Chapter 16 all point to an aggressive play by O. Therefore, you have no desire to stay on the twenty point (bar/20, 13/9). This move would encourage O to hit on the twenty point, even with a blot. Any return shots you would get would have little value compared to the danger of O's quickly building a powerful board. By coming out bar/16, you prevent O from hitting and simultaneously establishing a key inner point. You may also force O off his midpoint if he hits with a 4.

You may have noticed that the suggested alternate play, bar/20, 13/9, would duplicate 5's. O would need 5's to hit the blots on either the ten or the twenty point. This consideration, however, has practically no relevance to the position. X would achieve the duplication at the expense of creating a new blot. In other words, when forced to leave blots in different places on the board, you may wish to look for duplications; however, don't expose yourself unnecessarily in order to duplicate numbers. Duplication is very often *not* the most important consideration in the play.

You may also want to come out to your opponent's outer board in order to bear on your own outer board and make it more difficult for him to escape his back men. This is particularly important in cases like Position 12 where O has only one man back (see also Chapter 19).

Position 12
X to Play 6–3

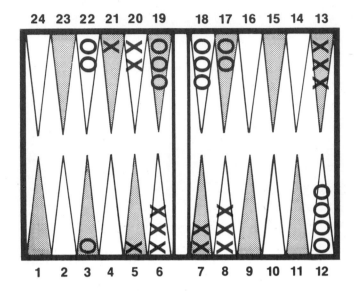

The correct play is 8/5, 21/15. Should O get past your blockade on this roll, you will have a double shot at him. Since you have three men back to his one, a stronger inner board, and an advanced anchor, contact would be in your favor.

Concept of Control

Although it is obviously important to control key sectors of the board to allow your men to move freely and to hinder your opponent's movement, the concept of control bears more careful examination. One way to control a point is simply to make the point. A more dynamic — and often more effective — way is to have a man or men bearing directly (i.e., 6 pips or less away) upon a point.

In the game of chess, a piece doesn't threaten the square it is on but the squares it may move to. Similarly, in backgammon, it is the 6 points directly in front of the checker which come under the checker's "sphere of influence." Each checker that is not tied down to a static position can be thought of as radiating a force field — a strong field of influence extending 6 pips in front of it. Every blot which moves into this sphere of influence naturally runs the danger of being hit.

In these terms, the value of the golden point (your opponent's five point) is that it bears directly upon your opponent's outer board. Similarly, part of the value of bringing men into your opponent's outer board is that they then bear upon *your* outer board. If you think in terms of spheres of influence, you will see that sometimes it is possible to exert control over the entire board, making it impossible for your opponent to play safely.

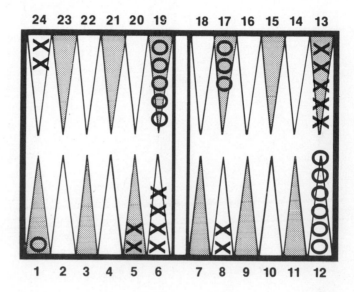

Position 13
X to Play 6–2

In Position 13, the correct play is 24/18, 13/11. Now each quadrant of the board is under at least one man's control. The man on the twenty-four point controls O's inner board. The man on the eighteen point controls O's outer board. The men on the thirteen and eleven points control X's outer board, and the builders on the eight and six points control X's inner board. Note that the men on the five point don't exert control since they are in a fixed position.

By making the correct play, you exert some control over all the open points and make it very difficult for O to move safely. O will probably be forced to attack you in order to contest your control; in doing so, he will leave himself exposed. Since O has only one man back, this is what you want.

You can often restrict your opponent's good numbers by making sure you control the key areas to which he wishes to move. In the case where your opponent has escaped his back men early in the game, it is particularly important to split to his five point or bar point (see Chapter 18) to exert control on his outer board and to prevent him from moving freely.

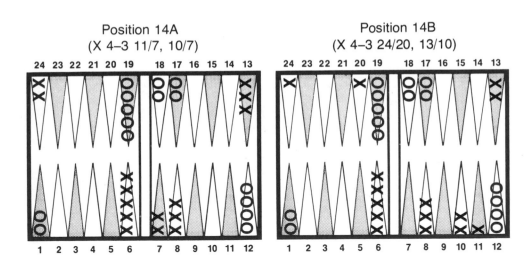

Position 14
X to Play 4–3

Position 14A
(X 4–3 11/7, 10/7)

Position 14B
(X 4–3 24/20, 13/10)

We mentioned earlier that owning a point is *not* always the best way to get control. This is most clearly illustrated in Position 14, where most players routinely make their bar point 11/7, 10/7 (Position 14A). This move establishes an excellent point but leaves you with a static position, which also exerts little control over O's movement. With this play, you have no direct influence on O's outer board. One man bears on your own outer board and two active builders on the six and eight points bear on your inner board.

Compare this play with 24/20, 13/10 in Position 14B. This is a much stronger and more aggressive move, leaving your men dynamically placed. Your outer board is stronger because you have a new point (the ten point) and a builder back on the eleven point. If we compare the plays with respect to the inner boards, we also see a striking difference. You now have four active builders bearing on the five point and three on the four point. Therefore, you exert much more influence and inhibit O's advance more effectively *without* the bar point, rather than with it.

In Position 14B, it is very dangerous for your opponent to attempt a major split and come under the gun; if you had made the bar point (Position 14A), it would be an ideal time for him to split to the four or five point. Usually, when a player makes his bar point early in the game, it is a good time for his opponent to try a major split before extra builders can be brought down.

By playing 24/20 we split to O's five point (the twenty point) and exert pressure on his outer board — pressure which we wouldn't be able to do had we made our bar point. Our checkers are now actively placed and have many ways to make all the key points (the twenty, five, four, and bar points). In the comparatively static Position 14A, there is little prospect of establishing new points immediately.

You should study the difference between Positions 14A and 14B carefully to increase your positional understanding of the game.

CHAPTER 28.
TIMING

We shall now look at the game from a more dynamic point of view. Although we have examined individual isolated positions, it should be borne in mind that the position as a whole is always changing. The game is never completely static; it progresses and takes new shape every roll. As the position changes, so may your objectives and overall game plan. In any case, both you and your opponent may need time, which in backgammon means rolls, to accomplish your objectives. In other games, such as chess, a tempo refers to a unit of time.

Even setting your opponent back half a roll may upset his plans. First, we shall consider plays simply designed to rob your opponent of a crucial roll or half a roll. Such plays are called **tempo plays**. Later on we shall examine longer-range aspects of timing.

Tempo Moves

Tempo moves are needed when your opponent threatens to do something on the next roll which you can't tolerate. If you can't stop him directly, you may be able to create a diversion to forestall him. This type of situation frequently occurs when you have a man exposed and vulnerable which you can't safety.

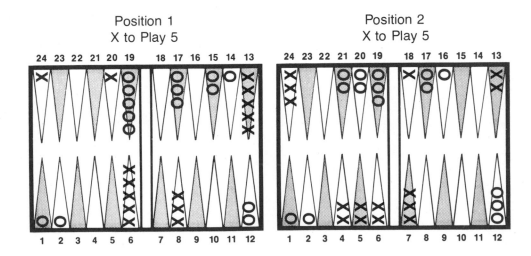

Position 1
X to Play 5

Position 2
X to Play 5

In Position 1, X's man on the twenty point is in grave danger of being pointed on since he's under the gun. X can neither cover it with a second man nor move it away. Therefore, X plays 6/1*. X makes O waste half a move— — one tempo — to come in. Barring doubles, O will not be able to both come in *and* point on X.

In Position 2, X's man on the eighteen point is exposed to a triple shot. X can safety the man 18/13, but this leaves him with three men stranded on the one point. A more daring play is 7/2*. This temporarily protects X's man on the bar point since there are few numbers that re-enter and hit this man (note that the 1's and 2's duplicate). We are taking a chance, but if we succeed in making the opposing bar point, we will have an excellent game since all our men now *communicate*.

In this second position, we also have the possibility of gaining more than a tempo — we might gain a whole roll if O stays out. Therefore, Position 2 is partly an attacking move, whereas Position 1 is a pure tempo move.

Another minor difference between Positions 1 and 2 is that in Position 1 we have no wish to make the one point, whereas in Position 2 the two point may be useful if we can cover. In either case, however, the basic idea remains the same: We have a man under fire which we protect indirectly by hitting and distracting our opponent elsewhere. Not only does this tempo move protect a man already threatened, it also may enable you to put a checker in a position that normally would be far too dangerous.

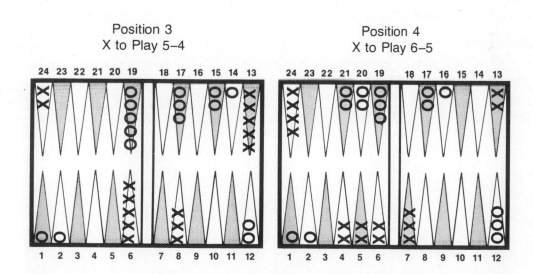

Position 3
X to Play 5–4

Position 4
X to Play 6–5

Positions 3 and 4 are identical to Positions 1 and 2, respectively, but with the whole roll to be played. These two positions are basic examples of the hit and split play discussed in Chapter 21. The correct plays are respectively 24/20, 6/1* and 24/18, 7/2*.

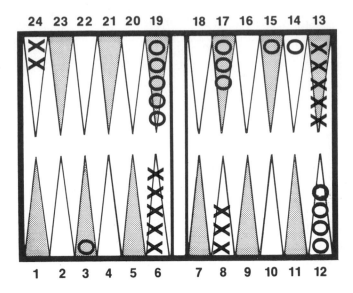

Position 5
X to Play 5–3

A tempo move may also be called for when your opponent is threatening to make a good point and consolidate his position. With an opening 5–3, we recommend taking two men down, 13/8, 13/10. In Position 5, however, the three point should be made.

This move probably prevents O from escaping immediately; more importantly, it deprives him of half a roll. You gain a tempo and prevent him from making a good point.

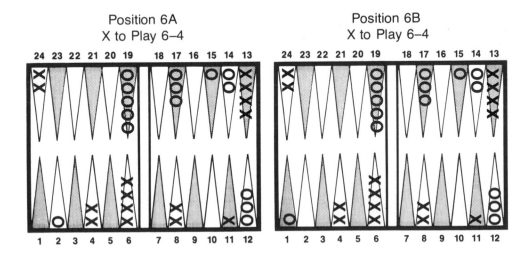

Position 6A
X to Play 6–4

Position 6B
X to Play 6–4

Similarly, in Position 6A we make the two point in preference to the bar point because we hit simultaneously and prevent O from making a key point. In Position 6B, however, we do not gain a tempo by making the two point, so the bar point, 13/7, 11/7, is more valuable.

When your opponent has slotted, you may be able to prevent him from covering, even if you can't hit the slotted man directly.

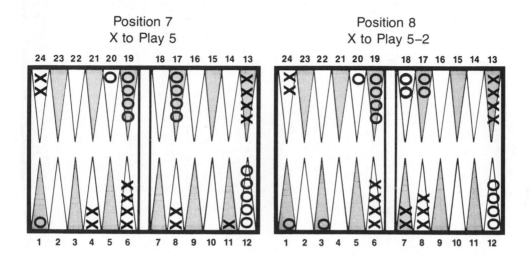

Position 7
X to Play 5

Position 8
X to Play 5–2

In Position 7, the correct play is 6/1* this more than cuts O's ways of covering the slotted man in half (from 24 to 11 — notice the duplication of numbers to come in and to cover: 1 and 3). Thus, we may get a second crack at hitting this man before O covers. Notice also that we do not want to make the one point; we only want to stop O from making his five point. Therefore, if O doesn't hit the blot on the one point, we will not rush to cover it. In this position, we welcome an exchange of hits for several of the basic reasons in Chapter 16: O has only one man back, we have more men back; we have a better inner board, he has a blot in his inner board.

In Position 8, O has just slotted on his five point. We can hit two men 8/3*/1* — an ideal tempo move — since O's whole succeeding roll must be used to come in. Except for doubles, we completely eliminate O's chance of covering his man on the twenty point.

In both Positions 7 and 8, O had unwisely slotted on the previous roll. As we discussed earlier in Chapter 17, O violated the principle of not slotting while his back men were split or exposed. These examples show why slotting and splitting is wrong. After taking the risk of slotting, you expect to be able to reap the benefit of making the point should your opponent miss. However, if you are split or exposed, you may be hit once or even twice, and while you are occupied coming in, you may miss the opportunity to cover the slotted man.

Taking Risks

When deciding whether to take large risks, you must examine not only the immediate dangers and gains, but also the possibility of having to take the same chance after waiting several rolls. Such positions frequently occur when you are well ahead in the race and your opponent is playing a holding game. Here your only concern is to get home safely.

In Chapter 14, we considered the most advantageous way to expose yourself if you are forced to do so. Here we consider the possibility of voluntarily leaving a shot immediately instead of leaving a more dangerous shot later.

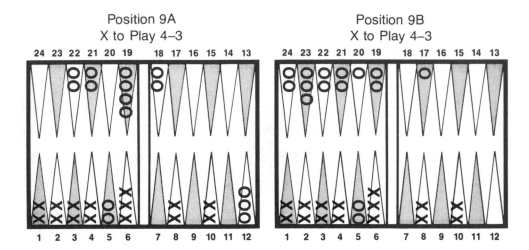

Position 9A
X to Play 4–3

Position 9B
X to Play 4–3

In Position 9A, the correct play is 10/6, 10/7, leaving an immediate direct 2-shot. Of course, you can play safely 6/2, 4/1 and hope to avoid leaving any shot at all, but the indicated play has two advantages. The minor advantage is that you are giving your opponent only 11 combinations to hit with, whereas later, if you are forced to break and leave a man exposed on your ten point, you will be leaving 15 combinations. The major advantage is that even if you are hit in the present position, you may still win because you are ahead in the race and retain a 5-point board, while O's twenty point is still open.

Let us see what happens if we delay leaving a shot. Over the next few rolls your opponent's position will improve, since he will bring builders down to make his five point. In addition, in these next few rolls you will have broken your 5-point inner board and weakened your position. Thus the timing is said to be unfavorable or against you, since every extra roll where you can't clear your ten point improves O's position while yours deteriorates. Should you be hit later, you would have virtually no chance to win.

In Position 9B, you have the same situation, but your opponent is much further advanced. The correct play here is *not* to leave a shot but to stall by playing 6/2, 4/1. Rather than improving, his position will deteriorate. He has run out of time to make constructive moves and is faced with the unpleasant prospect of either breaking up his inner board and killing checkers, or relinquishing your five point.

The general rule may be summarized as follows: *You must strongly consider taking immediate additional risks to come home safely if your opponent's position is improving with each roll and your position is deteriorating and a shot later on seems likely anyway.* However you should consider waiting and playing safe if

(a) your opponent's position is deteriorating or about to deteriorate,

(b) your position is either improving, or at least deteriorating at a less critical rate than your opponent's,

(c) there are good prospects of getting home safely without ever leaving any shots.

Positions such as 9A and 9B are very common in actual play. Although in some cases the rules summarized above will not give you an unambiguous answer, it is still vital to look ahead and see how the position will develop before making your decision.

These same principles also apply in another important type of position — the two-way holding position. This position occurs when both players have an advanced point in their opponent's board.

Position 10

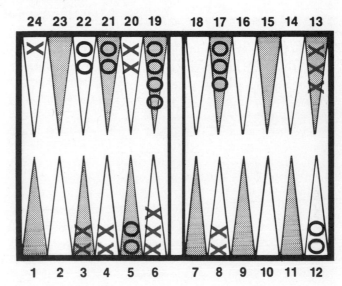

Positions 10 and 11 are typical positions in which each player has the other's five point. As we have seen in Chapter 20, this gives each player a large measure of tactical security and it is longer-term development and planning that will determine the eventual outcome. In this type of position, the first person to give up his anchor in his opponent's inner board is usually exposed and vulnerable and thus at a distinct disadvantage. In order to be able to hold onto your anchor, you must have time to play your other men without ruining your position.

In Position 10, O is clearly ahead in the race. However, because of his lead, he is in trouble. O will soon run out of constructive plays and then be forced to give up the five point, which is very risky. X does not have this problem precisely because he is behind in the race and has the time to wait until O must move. X's third man back on the twenty-four point is actually a benefit in disguise. This man is in no real danger. Further, X will be able to move him out and around the board, thus gaining the extra rolls which O lacks.

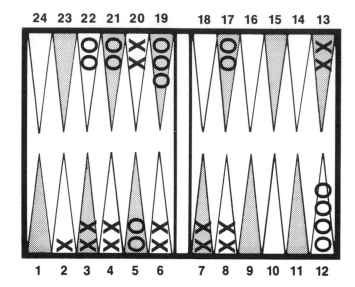

Position 11
(A) X to Play 5–2
(B) O to Play 5–2

Position 11 is similar except that now X is ahead in the race. O can safely play his next few rolls constructively since he has two extra men on the twelve point, but X is almost out of constructive moves. He will soon be faced with the unpleasant choice of breaking his inner board, giving up the five point, or giving up the midpoint. The timing, therefore, is clearly in O's favor. X realizes the inferiority of his position and the fact that he will eventually be forced to give up the twenty point. Rather than wait until his position deteriorates as O's improves, X correctly plays 20/13. Although in Chapter 20 we emphasized the importance of keeping the Golden Point, X reluctantly decides to give it up now when he can conveniently play to the midpoint.

Now let us analyze the same position, but with O instead of X to play 5–2. By the same reasoning that X used, O realizes he is a favorite and that the timing is on his side. He should, therefore, play a waiting game; to abandon the five point now, 5/12, would be a critical mistake. The correct play is simply 12/19, waiting for X's next play.

Let us briefly consider two other possible errors O could make. Ordinarily, O might consider playing 12/17, 12/14 to lure X off the twenty point. However, in this position, as we have seen, X is actually looking for an excuse to get off the twenty point before his position deteriorates. Therefore, he would welcome the opportunity to run and hit simultaneously because the hit would leave his remaining man on the five point in less danger. Furthermore, if X doesn't hit with a 6, O will not have gained since he has no adequate way to cover the blot on the fourteen point. If O rolls a 2, he doesn't gain by covering since this would give up the midpoint, releasing X's two men on the midpoint. Finally, it is also an error to play 12/17, 19/21. Although it may appear that O gains time by doing this, he actually gains nothing at all. The recommended play, 12/19, gives a better distribution of O's builders and gives him a double instead of a single shot, should X run from the five point with one man.

The more experienced a player becomes, the more he learns to anticipate the future course of the game. If the game appears to be leading to a favorable type of position, keep it along its present path. If, however, you anticipate slowly drifting into a lost position.it may be wise to take corrective action immediately, even if it involves risk.

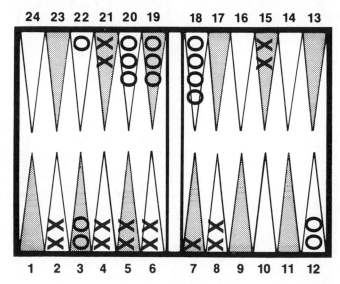

Position 12
X to Play 6–1

Position 12 is another simple case where merely looking a little ahead will make the correct play obvious. Here, if X stays back on the twenty-one point and plays 8/2, 8/7, he will be squeezed almost immediately. Furthermore, each roll X waits to come out will make his position more dangerous, since O will be building his board. O has enough spare men on the eighteen, nineteen, and twenty points to strengthen his position and wait. X, therefore, must play 21/15 and 7/6. Now if O attacks with only two points closed and a blot in his inner board, it will be much less dangerous than if he had attacked when his board was stronger. Understanding the next section in this chapter depends critically on your grasp of the concept of timing and your ability to view a given position not as an isolated entity but as a part of a whole chain of events.

Battle of Primes

One of your basic objectives in backgammon is to form a prime in front of your opponent, preferably a full 6-point prime. Similarly, you try to avoid being primed by him. If you find yourself trapped behind a prime — even a full prime — the game need not be lost, but the only way to win in such a position is to force your opponent to break his prime. Attacking him and closing him out will clearly not accomplish your objective; rather you must try to form a prime yourself in front of his back men hoping to force him to break his position first. This section is concerned with those positions in which both sides have primes — a **battle of primes**.

When a battle of primes forms, several factors, such as the number of men trapped and the length of the primes, may shape the final outcome, but one factor is usually decisive: timing.

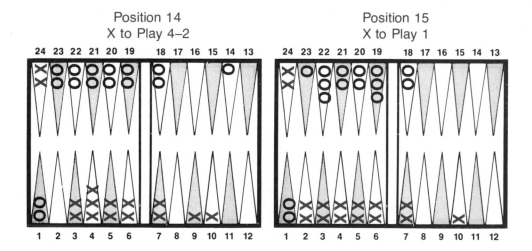

Position 13
X on Roll

In Position 13, O has a full prime, but X is nevertheless the favorite. The reason is that if neither side escapes, which is likely, one side will be forced to break up his own prime. Because X is behind in the pip count 14 pips, he has more time than O to hold his prime. If O breaks his prime first, X may escape his back men without ever having to break his position until the bear-in.

In some cases, it may be a close decision as to who will break first. Then you naturally wish to roll small numbers so your opponent will run out of time before you. Careful play, however, may enable you to maintain your prime a key extra roll.

Position 14
X to Play 4–2

Position 15
X to Play 1

In Position 14, it is vital that you play 9/7, 10/6. Now you are in a position where you cannot legally play 6's. In other words, if you roll a 6, you don't have to play it at all, and thus you slow yourself down. Although in some elementary holding positions you wish to save a number to avoid breaking a point and exposing yourself, you also must be aware of those positions where you can slow yourself down by depriving yourself of a number altogether.

To force your opponent to break first, you wish to move forward as slowly as possible, while hoping your opponent moves forward too quickly. Therefore, you must be careful not to slow your opponent down.

For example, in Position 15 the correct play is 10/9, *not* hitting. O is a favorite to break his bar point on the next roll, thus potentially releasing your back runners. While he is on the bar, you run a considerable risk of having to break your prime first. By hitting him, you may keep him out for several rolls.

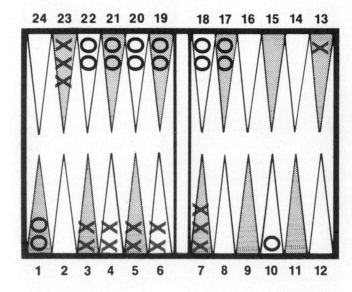

Position 16
X to Play 3–4

In other cases, however, hitting O may speed him up! For example, in Position 16, O's main source of time is his one loose man on the ten point. By hitting this man, you leave him stripped down without any spare men to play with on his side of the board. Now most of the numbers that re-enter will also force him to break his prime. The correct play is 13/10*/6. Remember: you deprive yourself of playable 6's by bringing this man into your home board.

When deciding whether to hit a spare man, you must not only weigh the number of useful pips you are taking away from your opponent, you must also consider the length of time and the number of pips O may save by staying out. Also, you should look out for positions where by hitting his last spare man, you may be able to force him to come in and at the same time break his position, leaving a shot.

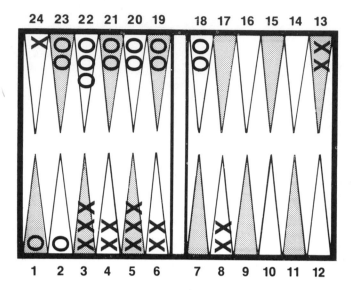

Position 17
X to Play 6

Position 17 is a more difficult example; here you have to make the worst of a bad situation. Since O has almost no time left on his side of the board, you may immediately think to leave him alone by playing 13/7, gambling that he doesn't roll a 5 or a 6 next time. However, even if O doesn't roll a 5 or a 6 he is likely to roll a 2 and hit you, forcing you to roll an immediate 1 in return. There are, in fact, only 6 numbers (1–3, 1–4, and 3–4) which leave you in an advantageous position. (Even with these, your opponent may well salvage the game if he breaks a point in his inner board to make a desperation hit.)

Let us now examine the alternate play, 8/2*. This may appear wrong at first because you want O to be able to move so he can break his prime. Notice; however, that there are 6 numbers (1–3, 1–4, 1–5) that force O to come in *without* hitting you back and which also break his prime. In other words, you have the same number of shots here that leave you with an immediate advantage. Furthermore — and this is the main point — you are happy if he stays out altogether. Although you want him to come in and break, there is no need for him to do so immediately. You still have three men outside — two of which are way back on the thirteen point — therefore, you can afford to wait many rolls for O to re-enter. In fact, you will be pleased to make the two point and wait for him to come in on the one point and break his board. You may even be able to make your bar point if he stays out for several rolls.

Position 18 is a simpler position where you clearly want O to be able to move and break immediately. Unfortunately, you have no choice but to hit him on the two point. You must *not* cover, but instead play 8/2*, 8/7. You want to expose the man on the two point so that O may be forced to hit you. Being hit and possibly staying out on O's 5-point board will slow you down. This play also deprives you of 6's and allows O to re-enter immediately so that he can break.

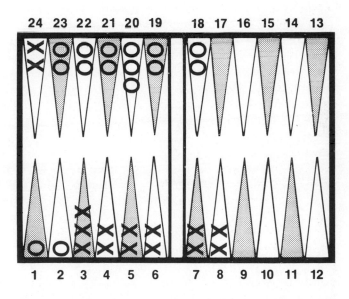

Position 18
X to Play 6–1

Position 19
X to Play 6–2

In Position 19, the same reasoning applies: You try to gain time by forcing O to hit you. The correct play is 8/2*, 3/1*, leaving two men exposed.

Battle of primes positions are made more complicated by the fact that if your opponent doesn't have a full prime, you may be able to win by simply escaping. Sometimes your best chances lie in attacking and possibly closing him out, and then escaping even a 5-point prime.

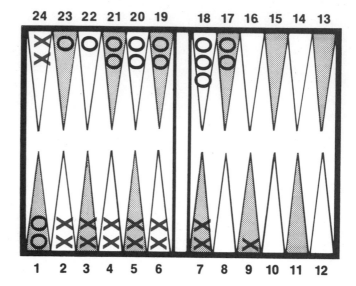

Position 20
X to Play 1–1

For example, in Position 20, X clearly has much worse timing than O and will almost certainly have to break first if he plays 9/5. The correct play is 24/23*/22*(2). Now, if X rolls a 6 in the next two rolls (he is a favorite to do so), he will probably win since the first man released will give him additional time to wait for the second 6. Furthermore, X may well have additional time to roll a 6 even after he gives up his bar point since it may take a long time for O to re-enter both his men.

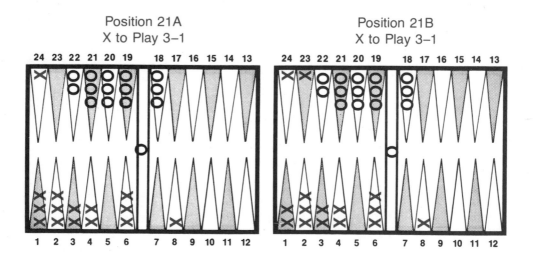

Position 21A
X to Play 3–1

Position 21B
X to Play 3–1

In Position 21A X would like to complete the close-out, 8/5, 6/5, but unless he rolls a 1–6 immediately, he will have to break his board on the next roll. The correct play is 24/23, 6/3. Although you will never be able to close O out, in order to have any real winning chances it is absolutely essential to move up to the edge of his 5-point prime.

In Position 21B, you have the problem of escaping two men from behind O's 5-point prime. The correct play here is 8/5, 6/5. You already have one 6 to play out. Playing 24/23 is important but not as essential as in Position 21A, since if you escape the first man, you will have a few rolls to get a second 1 to move up against the edge of the prime.

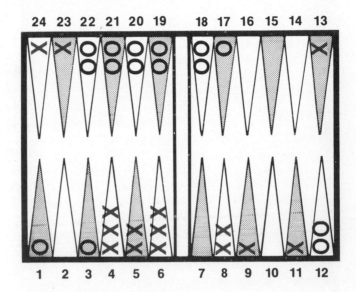

Position 22
X to Play 2–2

In Position 22, you are behind a powerful prime, but you can form one yourself by playing 13/7, 9/7. However, if you examine the resulting battle of primes position, you see that O actually has much more time than you and even threatens to make a 6-point prime with a 5. Even if O rolls a 6 to escape with one man, or a 2 to make your three point, you will be at a definite disadvantage. Because you are not pleased with these prospects, you may examine the position for another game plan: Attack with 9/3*/1*! Of course, if O hits you back with a 1, you will probably lose. However, if he doesn't, there are good prospects of being able to continue the attack and close him out altogether. Furthermore, his blot on the seventeen point now becomes a liability since you are likely to be able to pick it up in the ensuing struggle before he can safety it. If you are able to close him out, there is a good chance that you will be able to escape his prime before you break up and allow him to re-enter.

The battle of primes positions illustrated in this section are just a small sample of the types of positions that can arise in actual play. With the delicate interplay between immediate tactics and timing, these positions are some of the most fascinating, but also most difficult and treacherous, in backgammon.

CHAPTER 29.
HOLDING GAME
AND BACKGAME

Holding Game

In a holding game, you hold one or two opposing points (either in your opponent's inner board or his bar point). You hope to hit your opponent as he is coming home. Sometimes a holding game may be your only chance when your opponent is ahead in the race and manages to escape his back men. Frequently, however, a holding game may be played not just as a last resort, but as an overall game plan with excellent prospects.

In many of the most successful holding games, you have two points in your opponent's inner board: one that is deep, and another that serves as an advanced anchor. These two points are often the opposing one point and five point. By holding these two points, you make it extremely difficult for your opponent to clear his midpoint and other outfield points and to safely make additional inner board points. The two points you hold exert control over all the points on his side of the board: the five point prevents him from safely leaving blots anywhere in his outer board, while the one point prevents him from safely dropping blots behind the five point. Once you have a strong holding game, you merely wait for the anticipated shot while building up your inner board so that you will be a winner when you do hit.

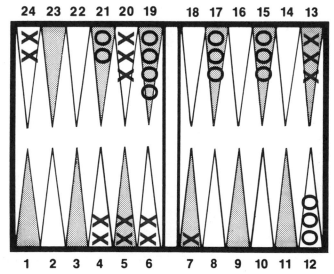

Position 1
X to Play 4

Position 1 is a good example of a one-five point holding game. Even though O has established two new good points — the twenty-one point and the fifteen point — he will have a difficult time coming home safely. X's main concern in this position is his timing. X wants to make sure he can preserve all the key points he has now while he waits for a shot. He has only two spare men which he is completely free to play with — the men on the twenty point and on the midpoint.

The correct play in this position is 20/16, leaving a shot. X hopes to be hit and thus readjust his timing. Although many men may be back in a holding game, the same ideas apply even with much fewer men back.

Position 2
X to Play 4-4

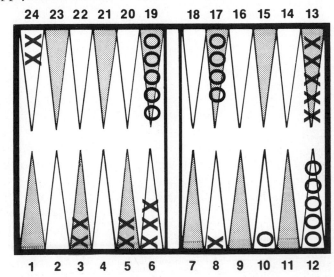

In Position 2, X can set up a one-five point holding game with only two men by playing 24/20, 13/5, 13/9.

A very common situation in a holding game is to have three men in O's inner board: two hold an advanced point, and the third man is as far back as possible to prevent him from moving safely in his inner board. Position 3 is such a case.

Position 3
X to Play 4-3

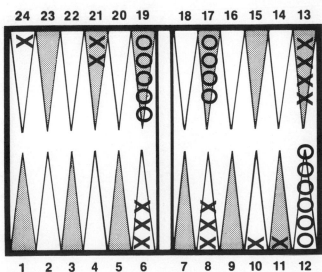

The correct play is 13/9, 8/5, building your inner board as quickly as possible. It would be a very serious mistake to play 24/21 — this would allow O to play his awkward numbers behind you.

Keeping a man back to force O to leave a shot is a key element in the holding game strategy. A similar position in a middle game situation would be played differently if O still had men trapped in your inner board. In such a case, you might bring the single back man up to your anchor so you would either have a spare man to move or to hit with in O's outfield.

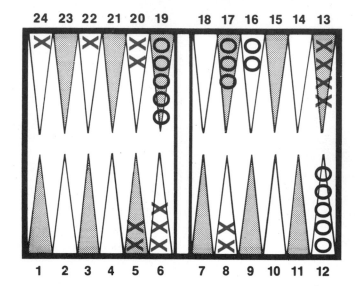

Position 4
X to Play 2

It is for these reasons that you bring the extra man up 22/20 in Position 4. Playing 24/22 would be a mistake since this would enable O to play behind you to his one or two point. You cannot play a three-five point holding game and expect to hold on to both points in this position because you do not have enough time to wait for a hit before your board collapses.

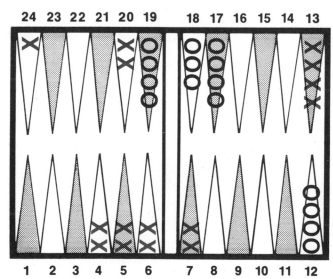

Position 5
O to Play 6–5, then
X to Play 5–2

Let's look at Position 5 from O's point of view: We see that the man on the twenty-four point keeps O from moving safely within his inner board. There-fore, the correct play is 19/24*, 18/24, which makes the twenty-four point and forces you forward. This type of position is an exception to the general rule in the middle game which says: Don't make your one point, especially when you haven't made any other points in your inner board or when your opponent already has an anchor.

X now rolls 5–2. It is essential that you re-enter on the twenty-three point, bar/23, 13/8.

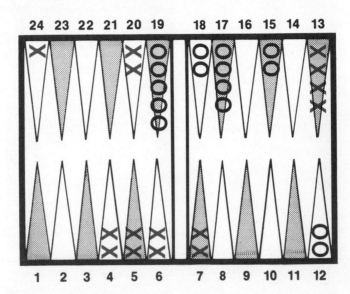

Position 6
O to Play 6–1

In Position 6, O cannot play safely, so the correct play is 17/24*, again with the hope of forcing you to re-enter further forward.

So far, we have considered playing a holding game by having two points, or at least one point and a blot, within O's inner board. In many holding positions, however, you have only *one* key holding point.

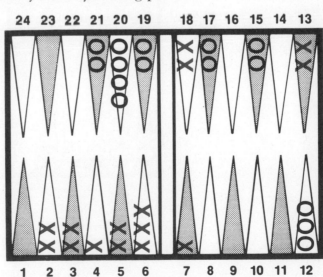

Position 7
X to Play 6–4

In Position 7, for example, you hold O's bar point. You want to prevent O from clearing his midpoint and coming home.

The correct play here is 13/7, 13/9, breaking your midpoint. It is a mistake to try to hold on to the midpoint for two reasons: first, you do not want to weaken your inner board position — especially since you will probably have to give up your midpoint next roll anyway; second, your midpoint has very little holding value. The only number you really block is 1–1.

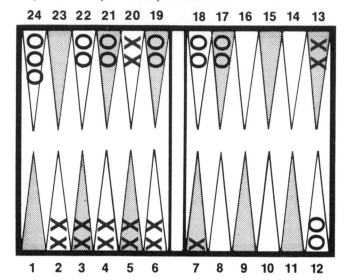

Position 8
X to Play 6–2

In Position 8, you hold the twenty point. Again you want to prevent O from clearing his midpoint safely. However, in this position, it is vital that you

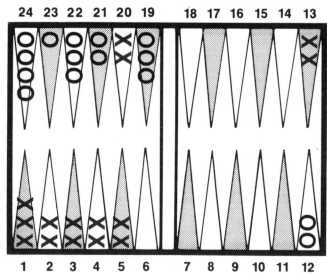

Position 9
X to Play 5–3

keep your midpoint. Here the twenty point alone will *not* prevent O from coming down safely — as opposed to the situation in Position 7.

Although your midpoint appears to block very little, let's compare what happens with and without it. If you mistakenly play 13/7, 13/11, O will bring one man down from the midpoint. Now, if you fail to hit an indirect 8-shot ($5/36$ probability), he will bring the other men down safely on his next roll. In other words, giving up the midpoint allows him to clear his midpoint one man at a time.

The proper play is 7/1, 3/1, which maintains your midpoint as long as possible. As long as you hold both your midpoint and the twenty point, O must roll 6–5 or doubles to clear his midpoint.

Position 8 might lead to Position 9. Here it appears that you have no choice but to give up your midpoint. The correct play, however, is to move only one midpoint man, 13/5! To give up the midpoint entirely would allow O to come home easily in a race in which he is way ahead. Of course, there is some danger in leaving a direct shot, but this is your best chance of winning. Even if O hits you with a 1, you will probably get a direct return shot at the blot on the twenty-three point. If O doesn't roll a 1, you will be holding him on the midpoint, or you might force him to leave an immediate direct shot if he rolls a 6 (except 6–6) or 5–4. If you were holding the eighteen point instead of the twenty point in Position 9, the midpoint would no longer be vital to you. You would simply play 13/8, 13/10.

The Backgame

Object of the Backgame

The backgame is perhaps the most fascinating area of backgammon. It is certainly one of the most difficult. If played properly, it may enable you to become a strong favorite in what otherwise would be a hopelessly lost position. Let's look at the overall strategy of the backgame first.

The fundamental prerequisite for a backgame is to establish at least two points in your opponent's inner board. (In rare and usually favorable cases, you may be able to establish more than two points.) It is usually necessary to hold two points which are close together and deep in your opponent's inner board. In the section comparing the holding game and the backgame, we shall discuss which points are best and the vital distinction between the two games.

The second part of the basic game plan is to allow O to bring his men around the board and to begin the bear-in process. As he bears in, he will, necessarily, have to abandon whatever prime he may have. He may have to give up key points in his inner board and pile up his remaining men awkwardly on his remaining points. After he weakens his position in this way, you hope to reach the third stage.

In the third stage, you expect your opponent to be forced to repeatedly leave shots until you hit him. We have already noted that it is hard to bear off safely even against a 1-point game; bearing off safely without ever having to leave a shot against two deep inner board points is almost impossible. Since each shot that is left will probably be a double shot, you can reasonably expect to carry out stage three successfully.

The fourth stage is to win the game by containing the man you have hit (and possibly hitting another man). Because your opponent in the second stage presumably has already broken his prime, taken men out of play, and sometimes even broken points in his inner board, he will be unable to fight back successfully.

It is critical not to take any men out of play while waiting for the opportunity to hit. You must avoid piling them on the one and two points at all costs, since all your men are needed to win the game after hitting. Remember, the key to a successful backgame is to give yourself enough time to play your remaining men (without killing any) while waiting for shots. It is around this issue — timing — that all the vital maneuvering and strategy takes place. The issue of timing can be extraordinarily complicated. Unfortunately, an in-depth analysis cannot be attempted in this volume. For now, let's look at the stages through which a typical backgame goes.

Illustrative Game

Position 10
X to Play 6–2

Position 11
X to Play 5–2

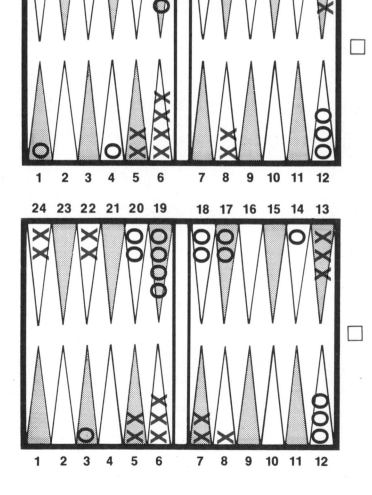

In Position 10, X has fallen behind and begins to consider the possibility of playing a backgame. He has not committed himself to a backgame yet; he lacks a second point in O's inner board, without which a backgame is impossible. The correct play is 13/7, 6/4*, attacking and making one last attempt to win the game by going forward.

The attack fails; O has hit X and escaped one of his back runners. X has established a second point and is ready to go into a full backgame. Indeed, in this position, it would be a mistake to try to win the game otherwise.

In Position 11, the correct play is 8/3*, 6/4. X no longer hopes to successfully attack or contain O — in fact, he hopes to be hit. By being hit, he may be able to bring a man back into O's inner board and then around the entire circuit. In this way, X will give himself more *time*. By continually recirculating his men in this manner, X avoids running out of time and having either to relinquish one of the two key points or kill men. Because X wishes to be hit and sent back, the overall strategic plan has been called "retreat to victory."

At this point, O unwisely doubles, and X accepts. O is forced to hit X twice before getting out of X's inner board. A few moves later, Position 12 is reached.

Position 12
X to Play 5–1

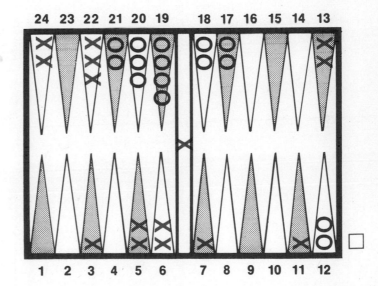

X stayed out on the previous roll. Ordinarily, this is bad, but when playing a backgame, it is favorable since you gain time by not moving. The correct move in Position 12 is bar/24, 13/8. You purposely leave an additional blot as bait for O. O should avoid hitting you if possible. He hopes to roll small numbers and come home slowly. *The key to defeating a backgame is to spoil your opponent's timing.*

A few rolls later, Position 13 is reached:

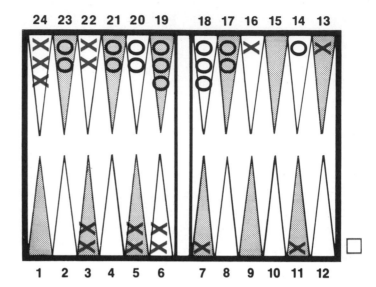

Position 13
X to Play 5–2

O is closer to home and appears to have X hopelessly trapped. X, however, is actually a favorite in this position; he plays 24/22, 13/8. It is crucial that X not hit O now. Remember, the object at this time is *not* to prevent O from getting home safely. In fact, X wants O to come home quickly and break up his prime. Only after O breaks his prime can X consider trying to win the game while going forward. To hit and try to contain the hit man, *and* also escape all five of his back men from behind a 5-point prime, is a near-impossibility.

Position 14
O to Play 5–4, then
X to Play 4–3

In Position 13, it is important that X play his 2 up to the twenty-two point. The object of having extra men sent back is to enable him to gain time by bringing them around the board. In order to ensure being able to escape and bring them back around, it is mandatory for X to bring the spare men up to his most advanced point in O's inner board.

Soon Position 14 is reached: O has awkwardly stacked men on his two and four points, while X has begun building a strong position on his side of the board. In order to win, X must not only make a strong position, but, more importantly, he must also be able to hold it. The vital time gained by having two extra men hit enabled X to reach the present position now instead of many rolls earlier. The spare man on the sixteen point is crucial since X may still have to wait a few more rolls until O gives him a shot.

We now assume O rolls 5–4. He is forced to play 18/23, 19/23, leaving a man on his bar point exposed to a double shot. Since O's prime is gone, X is prepared to hit. Even if X misses the double shot, he will almost certainly get more shots later. Fortunately, he rolls 4–3 and plays 22/18*, 16/13, preparing to make his bar point. O stays out. X doubles, and O must pass.

Comparison of the Holding Game and Backgame

The backgame and the holding game have many similarities: both involve holding key points to prevent your opponent from bearing in and off safely. (In this sense, it may be argued that the backgame is really a special type of holding game.) Both may involve waiting with many men back in your opponent's board. Timing is often the key consideration in both types of positions; you may purposely allow yourself to be hit in order to slow yourself up enough to maintain your key points. Because of these similarities, the two types of positions are often confused. However, the underlying strategy and the specific tactics employed are fundamentally different. You cannot play a holding game as if it were a backgame, or vice versa, without disastrous results.

The difference between a holding game and a backgame lies in the *time* at which you wish to hit your opponent. In a holding game, you are always looking for the chance to hit your opponent so you can go forward. You hope to prevent him from clearing his midpoint and other points in the outfield, and also to prevent him from making additional points in his inner board— — in other words, you try to hit him as he comes home. In a true backgame, you have given up all hope of going forward at an early stage; you must wait until O comes home and breaks up his position. Only *after* he has weakened his position can you seriously consider going forward. Indeed, hitting prematurely is often a fatal mistake.

Because of this difference in strategy, the same two points may form a good holding game but a bad backgame, or vice versa.

Position 15A   Position 15B

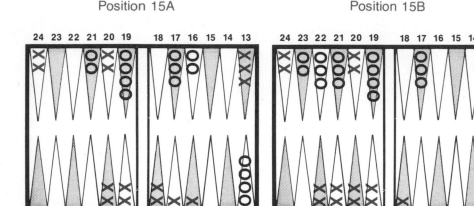

In Position 15A, the twenty-four and twenty points give X an excellent holding game. However, should O succeed in coming home safely and reaching Position 15B these same two points would form a poor backgame. Here, O may well be able to clear the nineteen and seventeen points, at which time X's backgame would become a mere 1-point game. The best backgame requires you to hold two points deep within your opponent's inner board. Because the points are deep, your opponent will have more trouble clearing all the points in front of your two points.

In the best backgames, you hold your opponent's two and three points. Next best is to hold his one and three points. The one–two-point backgame — which is considered the best by many players — actually tends to work out quite poorly in practice. The reason is that a key to a successful backgame — adequate time to hold these points and keeping your own inner board intact — is difficult to achieve with the one–two-point backgame. This is because it may be hard to recirculate your extra men if you are holding these two deep points. The one–four and the two–four-point backgames may also be excellent positions, although the one–four suffers somewhat because your two points should not be so far apart. Other combinations are generally inferior backgames although they can form excellent holding positions.

Position 16A
X to Play 6–2

Position 16B
X to Play 6–2

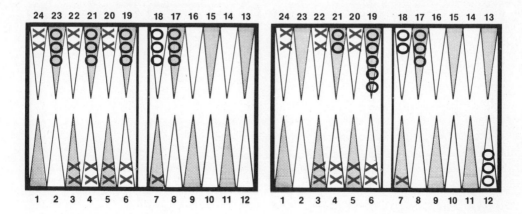

In Positions 16A and 16B, you are fortunate enough to have three points in your opponent's inner board, although you must give up one. In 16A, O has already cleared his outfield points and is well on his way home. In this case, your best strategy is to play a backgame and keep the one and three points by playing 20/12. In Position 16B, however, you still hope to keep O from coming home safely, and so you enter a holding game by playing 22/20, 22/16.

Let's compare your attitude toward being hit and staying out. With a holding game, you often want to be hit a few times so that you can readjust your timing. You must, however, be careful about staying out too long or allowing too many men to be picked up at one time. While you are on the bar, there is the danger that your opponent may make more points in his inner board and, more importantly, clear difficult points in the outfield and sneak home. In a backgame, however, you generally welcome staying out as long as possible while your opponent comes home.

In a holding game, you generally build a strong inner board as quickly as possible and maintain it, so you are ready to hit at the first good opportunity. With a backgame, however, you do not even begin to try to build a strong inner board until you are ready to hit. This does not happen until very late in the game. In fact, building a strong board earlier often proves to be a fatal mistake when playing a backgame.

Despite all we have said in this chapter, we have barely touched upon the intricacies of the backgame. All aspects of backgammon, in fact, contain surprises and mysteries enough for a lifetime of study, play, and of course, enjoyment.

Glossary

Accept a Double: See **take.**

Ace Point (guff): A player's one point.

Acey-deucey: A variant of backgammon popularized in the Navy.

Across: See **movement of checkers.**

Action Play: A specific type of play to provoke contact used when opponent has escaped his back runners.

Active Builder: See **builder.**

Advanced Anchor: An anchor on the opponent's four or five point. See also **golden point.**

Airball: (From basketball) a complete miss; an unexpectedly nonconstructive roll.

Anchor: A point held by player in his opponent's home board.

Around the Corner: See **movement of checkers.**

Attacking Game: A position where you hit and attempt to close out your opponent, usually hitting in your inner board.

Automatic Doubles: If each player rolls the same number on the first roll of the game, the doubling cube remains in the middle but may be turned to 2. Players usually agree to limit the number of automatic doubles to one per game.

Backgame: A game where you hold two or more points in your opponent's inner board and you hope to hit him in the latter stages of the game as he attempts to bear his men in and off.

Backgammon: (1) The game of backgammon; (2) **triple game** or **backgammon** occurs when the winner bears off all his checkers before his opponent bears off any, and does so while his opponent has one or more checkers in the winner's home board. In this event, the winner receives triple the points shown on the doubling cube. Outside the U.S., a backgammon is only scored as a double game.

Back Man (back runner): A player's checker in his opponent's inner board.

Bar: The strip in the middle of the board which separates the inner and outer boards. When a checker is hit, it is placed **on the bar:** Checkers on the bar must re-enter the game in the opponent's home board. If a player has a checker on the bar, he cannot move any other checkers until all his checkers on the bar have been re-entered.

Bar Point: A player's seven point.

Battle of Primes: A type of position in which both players have their opponent's men trapped behind primes.

Bear (as in **bear on a point, bear on opposing checker**): A checker 6 or less pips away from a given point is said to bear on that point.

Bear In: To bring your checkers into your inner board in preparation for the bear-off.

Bear Off (**take off**): To remove a man from the board by playing him off your inner board according to the rolls of the dice.

Bear-Off: The final stage of the game where you remove your men from your inner board.

Beaver (**binache**): A special convention by agreement in advance whereby a player, when doubled, may at this point re-double the stakes again but retain possession of the cube.

Big Play (**strong play**): A bold or aggressive play when a safer but less constructive play is available.

Binache: See **beaver.**

Blitz: To attack in one's own inner board with the intention of closing the opponent out. See also **close out.**

Block: To form points in front of your opponent, hindering his progress.

Blockade: A contiguous series of points established in front of your opponent to hinder his progress. See also **prime.**

Blot: An exposed or single checker on a point.

Blot-Hitting Contest: A position in which there is a rapid exchange of hits.

Board: (1) The entire backgammon table. (2) One of the four quadrants of the backgammon table. (3) **1-, 2-, 3-, 4-, 5-, 6- point board:** The number of points closed in the inner board. A 6-point board is called a **closed board.**

Book a Checker: Safety a man by making a point.

Box (**in the box, man in the box**): The player in a chouette who plays alone against all the others.

The Boys: A roll of double 6's (6–6) on the dice.

Break the Board: To give up points you have established in your inner board.

Break a Point: To relinquish a point already owned.

Break Up: See **break the board.**

Bring Men Out, Up, Down, In, Off: See **movement of checkers.**

Broken Prime: See **prime.**

Build a Board: Construct points in your inner board.

Builder: A spare checker bearing on a point or blot. **Active Builder:** A checker you are completely free to use as a builder. **Inactive Builder:** A checker that appears to be a builder but should not actually be moved because it serves another function where it is. **Semi-Active Builder:** A checker that may or may not be used freely as a builder, depending on the exact roll and position.

Bullet-Proof: Adjective describing an opponent who miraculously avoids being hit time after time.

Bump: See **hit.**

Bump and Pass: See **hit and pass.**

Button Up: To safety a checker by bringing it together with another checker.

Candlesticks (as in **to make candlesticks**): To pile all your checkers on a few already established points.

Captain: In chouette play, the leader of the team playing against the man in the box. The captain moves the checkers and makes final decisions for his team.

Checker (**counter, man**): A playing piece, or man.

Chouette: A form of playing backgammon allowing more than two players to participate at one time. Rules are given on page 14.

Clean (as in clean play): A move completed legally.

Clear a Point: See **point**.

Closed Board: See **board**.

Close a Point, Closed Point: See **point**.

Close Out (**shut out**): When you make all 6 points of your inner board while your opponent is on the bar.

Cocked Dice: Any die (dice) which lands illegally. Dice which have landed on a checker, off the board, or in any manner other than flush and flat on the half of the board on the player's right.

Coffeehouse: Misleading talk to confuse the opponent. For example, in a chouette, when a team player advises the captain not to double knowing full well that the captain will double, he tempts the box to unwisely accept (ethically — borderline, at best).

Combinations of the Dice: The number of possible rolls out of the possible 36 to accomplish a specific objective.

Combination Shot: See **shot**.

Come In (**come on, enter, re-enter**): Re-enter opponent's home board after having been hit.

Come Under the Gun: Move your back men forward in your opponent's inner board so that he has at least three builders bearing directly on them.

Communicate: To keep checkers within 6 pips of each other for mutual support.

Consolation Flight: Players eliminated early in the main tournament are eligible to compete in the consolation tournament or flight.

Contact: To hit your opponent's men and/or be hit.

Contact Game: Game where opposing checkers have *not* gone past each other and still may hit each other.

Control of Outside: Having points in, or having men bearing on the outer boards.

Control a Point: See **point**.

Count: See **pip count**.

Counter: See **checker**.

Cover: (verb) To place a second checker on an exposed blot of the same color, thus making a point.

Crawford Rule: In match play, when a player is within one point of winning a match, no doubling is allowed for one game.

Cross-over: A move from one quadrant to another.

Cube (**doubling cube, doubling block**): A three-dimensional cube or block with the numbers 2, 4, 8, 16, 32, and 64 on it. It is used for raising the stakes and for indicating the amount of points being played. **Own, Control the Cube:** A player owns the cube after he has accepted a double from another player, until he re-doubles. The player who owns the cube alone has the right to re-double if he chooses. **Cube in the Middle:** Indicates the game has been doubled by neither player. Either player may offer the first double.

Cup (dice cup): Cup used to shake up and roll the dice.

Dead Checker: A checker buried deep within a player's board which no longer can serve a useful function.

Deep (as in deep in your inner board): Usually refers to the one or two point, occasionally to the three point.

Deprive Yourself of Numbers: To move your checkers in such a way as to make certain of your numbers legally unplayable.

Dice (singular: die): Small cubes marked with 1 to 6 spots on each face, used to determine the moves.

Dilly Builder: A builder which only bears upon points deep in your inner board.

Direct Shot: See **shot.**

Diversify: Spread your men out so as to increase your chance of a favorable roll.

Double (give a little present to, turn the crank, twist): Increase the stakes of the game to twice their previous size.

Double Ducks (quacks): The roll of double 2's (2–2) on the dice.

Double Dummy (play results): Speculating or discussing what would have been the correct move in light of what has been rolled, usually used by disgruntled players in chouettes to prove their sagacity.

Double Game: See **gammon.**

Double Hit: To hit two opposing blots in the course of a single move.

Doubles (doublet): When both dice come up with the same number. Four units of that number are then taken by player.

Double Shot: See **shot.**

Doubling Cube, Doubling Block: See **cube.**

Doubling on the Come: Doubling in the expectation of a good roll.

Down: See **movement of checkers.**

Drop: (1.) **Drop a double:** to pass; (2.) **Drop a man:** to slot a man.

Ducks: See **double ducks.**

Duplicate (as in duplicate your opponent's good numbers): Leave your opponent identical numbers that are good or necessary for him at different places of the board thus reducing his chance for a favorable roll.

Edge of a Prime: The open point directly in front of a prime.

Endgame: Positions where one or both players have begun the bear-off.

Enter: See **come in.**

Exposed Man: See **blot.**

Fan: To fail to re-enter opponent's home board after having been hit.

Field Goal: When the opponent has two men exposed 2 pips apart, a number which fails to hit either one but lands in between.

Five-Point Board: See **board.**

Fly Shot: An indirect shot with few combinations.

Forced Move: When there is only one legal way to take a roll.

Forward Game: See **running game.**

Four-Point Board: See **board.**

Freeze (Opponent's) Builder: To bring a checker to bear upon a point held with only two men by your opponent, thus restricting these men from being active builders.

Gammon (double game): When the winner of a game bears all his checkers off the board before his opponent bears off any, he wins a gammon, or twice the value on the cube.

Save the Gammon: To avoid being gammoned where the possibility of being gammoned exists.

Gammon Count: A method of assessing a player's chances of being gammoned.

Gap: The space(s) between established points.

The Girls: A roll of double 5's (5–5) on the dice.

Give a Little Present to: See **double.**

Golden Point: The opponent's five point.

Go Out (as in **match play**): To achieve the total number of points necessary to win the match.

Guff (ace point): A player's one point.

Half a Roll: One number of the two on the dice.

Heavy Point: Point with more than three checkers on it.

Hit (bump, knock off, send back): Move one or more of your men to a point occupied by a blot of your opponent.

Hit and Pass (bump and pass, pick and pass): To hit an opposing checker and continue your checker on to safety.

Hit and Split: To split your back runners while simultaneously hitting elsewhere on the board.

Holding Game: A type of game where you hold a point or points in your opponent's inner or outer board in order to prevent him from safely coming home.

Holland Rule: In a match play, after one player has reached match point, and after the Crawford Rule game has been played, for the next two games neither player may double until two full rolls on each side have been completed.

Home (as in **coming home, bringing men home**): Bringing all your remaining men into your inner board.

Home Board (inner board): See **board.**

In (as in **to bring a man in**): See **movement of checkers.**

Inactive Builder: See **builder.**

Indirect Shot: See **shot**.
Inside: Refers to the inner boards.

Jacoby Rule: Players can agree before the game begins that gammons and backgammons will count only as 1 point if the cube has *not* been doubled by a player during the course of the game.
Juice: See **vig**.

Kill a Man: See **dead checker**.
Knock Off: See **hit**.

Leave a Shot: To leave checker exposed within range of an opposing checker.
Loose Checker: A blot.
Lovers' Leap: Moving 24/13 with a 6–5 on the opening roll.

Make a Point: See **point**.
Man: See **checker**.
Match Play: A method of play usually used in tournaments whereby the first player to reach an accumulated total of a predetermined fixed number of points is declared the winner.
Match Point: One point less than the number of points needed to win the match.
Match Point Game: Any game where one player is at match point.
Material: See **builder**.
Middle Game: The main body of the game after the opening moves and before either player begins to bear off.
Midpoint: A player's *thirteen* point (equals opponent's *twelve* point) where five men are initially stationed.
Mix Up (Mix It Up): See **blot-hitting contest**.
Movement of Checkers (down, in, off, out, up, around the corner, across): (1) **In** — from the bar to opponent's home board (not to be confused with [5]. (2) **Up** — moving forward within opponent's home board. (3) **Out** — moving from opponent's home board to opponent's outer board. (4) **Down or Around the Corner** — moving from opponent's outer board to player's outer board. (5) **In** — moving from a player's outer board to his home board (not to be confused with [1]. (6) **Off** — moving from player's home board off the board permanently in the bear-off. (7) **Across** — moving from any of the four quadrants to any other quadrants.

Naturally (as in **make a point naturally**): See **point**.
No-Brainer: A running game where no further contact is possible and the outcome depends only on the roll of the dice.
No-Contact Game: Game in which no further contact is possible.
Number of Shots: See **shot**.

Off: (1) As in **bear off, take off:** See **movement of checkers**. (2) As in **off the board:** See **bar**. (3) As in **stay off:** fail to come in from the bar.
1-Point Board: See **board**.

One-Point Game (**ace-point game**): Game where a player is reduced to merely holding his opponent's one point and hoping for a shot in the bear-off.

On Roll: The player whose turn it is said to be **on roll.**

On the Bar: See **bar.**

Open Point: A point that is not closed or a point that is *owned* (by either player).

Out: (1) As in **come out:** See **movement of checkers.** (2) As in **stay out** (**stay off**): fail to enter from the bar.

Outer Board (**Outer Table**): See **board.**

Outfield: The outer boards.

Outside: Refers to the outer boards.

Own a Point: See **point.**

Own the Cube (**Control the Cube**): See **cube.**

Pass: To refuse to accept the cube when doubled by the opponent, thus giving up the game and losing the value indicated on the cube before the double.

Pick and Pass: See **hit and pass.**

Pick Up: See **hit.**

Pip: (1) The number of dots on the face of a die. (2) The units of movement; e.g., 3 pips forward means 3 units or points on the board forward.

Pip Count: A method of determining the relative standing in a race.

Play Results: See **double dummy.**

Point: (1) Any one of the 24 triangles labeled 1 through 24 on the backgammon board. **Clear a Point:** To give up an already established point. **Control, Own a Point:** To have two or more men together on a given triangle. **Make, Establish, Close a Point:** To bring two or more men together on a given triangle. **Point On:** To make a point on top of an opposing blot. **Make a Point Naturally:** To create a point without slotting. See also **heavy point.** (2) As in **scoring:** The units of scoring are referred to as points. Each game is initially worth one point (or unit of value). For example, a 4-point game is one where the winner has won 4 units of value.

Prime: (1) 6 closed points in a row. (2) Also (loosely) any number of points in a row — e.g., a 4-point prime means four points in a row. **Break a Prime:** To open points in the prime. **Broken Prime:** A prime with a gap in it. **To Prime:** To form a prime. **Priming Game:** A type of game in which the chief objective is to trap some of the opponent's men behind a prime. **Rolling Prime:** A special technique for advancing a prime around the board.

Proposition Position: The same prearranged position to be played over many times.

Quacks (**double ducks**): A roll of double 2's (2–2) on the dice.

Quadrant: One of the four divisions of the backgammon table. Each quadrant contains six points.

Rail: See **bar.**

Railroad Tracks: See **candlesticks.**

Re-double: After accepting the cube and thus doubling the stakes of the game, a player can then re-double his opponent, again doubling the stakes.

Re-enter: See **come in.**

Refuse a Double: See **pass.**

Return Shot: The shot your opponent will have back at you after you have hit him.

Rim: See **bar.**

Roll: To throw the dice (verb); the numbers thrown (noun).

Rolling Prime: See **prime.**

Roof: See **bar.**

Runner: See **back man.**

Running Game (**forward game**): A type of game in which the chief objective is to enter as rapidly and efficiently as possible into a race.

Safe: A play where you are not exposed to being hit, e.g., playing safe.

Safe Play: See **safe.**

Safety a Checker: Move it out of danger of being hit.

Safety Play (not to be confused with a **safe play**): A play which, while not in the long run the safest or strongest, does leave the least possible good numbers for the opponent on his next immediate roll. This technical play is used when you own the cube or when the cube is in the middle in preparation for doubling.

Save Gammon: See **gammon.**

Save Numbers: To leave certain numbers available to play so you are not forced to take them elsewhere.

Semi-Active Builder: See **builder.**

Send Back: See **hit.**

Settlement: A payment of points made by one player to another based upon the fair value of the position.

17-to-1 Shot: See **shot.**

Shot: An opportunity to hit a blot when the blot is in range of an opposing checker. **Direct Shot:** When a blot is 6 or less pips away from an opposing checker. **Combination or Indirect Shot:** When a blot is 7 or more pips away from an opposing checker — hence, a combination of both numbers on the dice is needed to hit it. **Single Direct Shot:** When only one number is available to hit directly. **Double Direct Shot:** When only two numbers are available to hit directly. **Triple Direct Shot:** When only three numbers are available to hit directly. **Number of Shots:** The number of rolls out of a possible 36 that hit (*not* the number of blots). **17-to-1 Shot:** A shot where the odds against hitting are 17 to 1, i.e., where there are two ways out of 36 of hitting. **35-to-1 Shot:** A shot where the odds against hitting are 35 to 1, i.e., where there is one way out of 36 of hitting.

Sheshbesh: A Middle Eastern variant of backgammon.

Shut Out: See **close out.**

Slot: To leave a checker exposed on a point you wish to make, hoping to cover it on the next roll.

Slot and Split: A play, usually undesirable, where one slots a checker in his own board while his back runners are split.

Small Play: A safe, but usually timid, play when a stronger, more aggressive play is available.

Split: To separate two men which are together on a point. **Minor Split:** Splitting one of the back runners to the opponent's two or three point. **Major Split:** Splitting one of the back runners to the opponent's four or five point.

Stay Back: Remain in opponent's inner board.

Stay Off, Stay Out: Fail to come in from the bar.

Steam: To lose control and be prone to doubling recklessly and accepting doubles in hopeless positions. **Steamer:** One who steams.

Stripped: A position barren of spare men or builders, thus one prone to awkward numbers. **Stripped Point:** A point lacking in extra builders.

Strong Play: See **big play.**

Switch Points: To give up one point in order to simultaneously make another.

Table: See **board.**

Take (accept a double): To agree to receive the cube when doubled by the opponent and continue the game for double the previous stakes.

Take Off: See **bear off.**

Tempo: A unit of time in backgammon, or half a roll. **Tempo Move:** A move designed to deprive the opponent of a tempo.

35-to-1 Shot: See **shot.**

Three-Point Board: See **board.**

Timing: The position viewed in terms of the general future development of the game.

Tric-Trac: A Middle Eastern variant of backgammon.

The T.P.: A player's two point.

Triple Game: See **backgammon.**

Triple Shot: See **shot.**

Turn, Turn the Crank: To double the game.

Twist: To double the game.

Under the Gun: See **come under the gun.**

Up (as in **bring a man up**): See **movement of checkers.**

Vig, Vigorish: The small extra possibilities that affect the odds in a given situation.

Wash: To switch points and hit an opposing checker.

Ways: See **combinations.**

Tables

Table 1.
Probability of Hitting a Single Shot

Number of Pips or Distance to Blot	Probability of Hitting
1	$^{11}/_{36}$
2	$^{12}/_{36}$
3	$^{14}/_{36}$
4	$^{15}/_{36}$
5	$^{15}/_{36}$
6	$^{17}/_{36}$
7	$^{6}/_{36}$
8	$^{6}/_{36}$
9	$^{5}/_{36}$
10	$^{3}/_{36}$
11	$^{2}/_{36}$
12	$^{3}/_{36}$
15	$^{1}/_{36}$
16	$^{1}/_{36}$
18	$^{1}/_{36}$
20	$^{1}/_{36}$
24	$^{3}/_{36}$

Table 2.
Probability of Hitting a Double Shot

Numbers Which Hit	Probability of Hitting
6, 1	$^{24}/_{36}$
6, 2	$^{24}/_{36}$
6, 3	$^{28}/_{36}$
6, 4	$^{27}/_{36}$
6, 5	$^{28}/_{36}$
5, 1	$^{22}/_{36}$
5, 2	$^{23}/_{36}$
5, 3	$^{25}/_{36}$
5, 4	$^{28}/_{36}$
4, 1	$^{21}/_{36}$
4, 2	$^{23}/_{36}$
4, 3	$^{24}/_{36}$
3, 2	$^{21}/_{36}$
3, 1	$^{20}/_{36}$
2, 1	$^{20}/_{36}$

Table 3.
Probability of Coming in from the Bar with One Man

Number of Closed Opposing Inner Board Points	Probability of Coming In
1	$^{35}/_{36}$
2	$^{32}/_{36}$
3	$^{27}/_{36}$
4	$^{20}/_{36}$
5	$^{11}/_{36}$

Table 4.
Probability of Coming in from the Bar with Two Men Out

Number of Closed Opposing Inner Board Points	Total Probability of Coming in with: both men	one man	neither man
1	$^{25}/_{36}$	$^{10}/_{36}$	$^{1}/_{36}$
2	$^{16}/_{36}$	$^{16}/_{36}$	$^{4}/_{36}$
3	$^{9}/_{36}$	$^{18}/_{36}$	$^{9}/_{36}$
4	$^{4}/_{36}$	$^{16}/_{36}$	$^{16}/_{36}$
5	$^{1}/_{36}$	$^{10}/_{36}$	$^{25}/_{36}$

Table 5.
Probability of Re-entering from the Bar with One Man

Number of Points Closed	In No More Than:				
	One Roll	Two Rolls	Three Rolls	Four Rolls	Five Rolls
3	.750	.937	.984	.996	.999
4	.556	.802	.912	.961	.983
5	.306	.518	.665	.767	.838

These figures may also be interpreted as the probability of escaping within a given number of rolls from directly behind a prime of a corresponding length with the number of points closed.

Table 6.
Number of Ways to Make a Point

Number of Builders	With Doubles	Without Doubles
1	1	0
2	4	2
3	9	6
4	16	12
5	25	20
6	36	30

Table 7. Probability of Bearing Last Two Men Off

Number of Point(s) Men Are On	Probability They Get Off	Probability They Fail to Get Off
1, 3	$34/36$	$2/36$
1, 4	$29/36$	$7/36$
1, 5	$23/36$	$13/36$
1, 6	$15/36$	$21/36$
2, 2	$26/36$	$10/36$
2, 3	$25/36$	$11/36$
2, 4	$23/36$	$13/36$
2, 5	$19/36$	$17/36$
2, 6	$13/36$	$26/36$
3, 3	$17/36$	$19/36$
3, 4	$17/36$	$19/36$
3, 5	$14/36$	$22/36$
3, 6	$10/36$	$26/36$
4, 4	$11/36$	$25/36$
4, 5	$10/36$	$26/36$
4, 6	$8/36$	$28/36$
5, 5	$6/36$	$30/36$
5, 6	$6/36$	$30/36$
6, 6	$4/36$	$32/36$